GENERAL HOFFMANN AT BREST-LITOVSK
WITH COUNT CZERNIN, TALAAT PASHA AND DR. VON KÜHLMANN

MAJOR-GENERAL MAX HOFFMANN

WAR DIARIES

AND OTHER PAPERS

VOLUME TWO

TRANSLATED FROM THE GERMAN BY
ERIC SUTTON

The Naval & Military Press Ltd

Reproduced by kind permission of the Central Library,
Royal Military Academy, Sandhurst

Published by

The Naval & Military Press Ltd

Unit 10, Ridgewood Industrial Park,

Uckfield, East Sussex,

TN22 5QE England

Tel: +44 (0) 1825 749494

Fax: +44 (0) 1825 765701

www.naval-military-press.com

© The Naval & Military Press Ltd 2004

*In reprinting in facsimile from the original, any imperfections are inevitably reproduced
and the quality may fall short of modern type and cartographic standards.*

Printed and bound by Antony Rowe Ltd, Eastbourne

CONTENTS OF SECOND VOLUME

THE WAR OF LOST OPPORTUNITIES

THE TRUTH ABOUT TANNENBERG

THE
WAR OF LOST OPPORTUNITIES

The translation of *The War of Lost Opportunities* is by Mr A. E. Chamot, and is included by arrangement with Messrs Kegan Paul, Trench, Trübner & Co. Ltd.

CHAPTER I

RUSSO-JAPANESE REFLECTIONS

THE order for mobilization found me at Mülhausen, in Alsace, where, for a year, I had been the commander of a battalion in Prince Wilhelm's Baden Infantry Regiment. For the last two years my mobilization orders had been "First General Staff Officer" to the Commander-in-Chief of the detachments appointed for the Eastern Theatre of War. This employment was familiar to me : I had served as lieutenant and commander of a company, and I had likewise had various other appointments on the General Staff in East Prussia and Posen. Having been stationed in East Prussia for seven years, it had become like a second home to me.

I knew the Russian Army both theoretically and practically. In the winter of 1898-1899, after I had passed my examinations at the Staff College and as Russian interpreter, I had been sent for six months to Russia, and afterwards, for five years, I had been attached to the Russian department of the Great General Staff. Besides this I had also gone through the Russo-Japanese War as military attaché on the Japanese side. I had been with the 2nd Japanese Division at the Mo-tien-ling Pass near Liauyang, at Shaho and Mukden, and I had seen the Russians fight.

I wish to remark here that the Russians had unquestionably learned very much in the Japanese War. If, in the campaign against us, they had acted with the same want of decision, if they had attacked in the same defective way, and if they had reacted in the same nervous manner to every threatened attack from the flank — if they had thrown away uselessly as many of their Reserves as they did in the Manchurian campaign, the struggle would have been much easier for us.

Kuropatkin, the Russian Commander-in-Chief, in every battle in the Manchurian campaign had victory in his hand; he only wanted the firm decision to close his hand in order to grasp the victory, but he never had the energy to take this resolve.

The battle of Liauyang was a typical example of his method. The Japanese frontal attack on Liauyang from the south had miscarried. General Kuroki decided to make the bold attempt of withdrawing the mass of his 1st Army across the Taitse-Ho and to bring about a decision by attacking the heights east of Liauyang. Between the Taitse-Ho and the division of the Guards that was fighting in connection with the 4th Japanese Army—a distance of about five English miles—he left only six companies, which were distributed in small groups on the summits of the hills to deceive the Russians into the belief that they were strongly held. The Russians had only to attack these points for the fate of the Japanese Army to have been sealed. The Guards Division would then have been encircled, the 1st and 2nd Japanese Armies would have been forced to the south-west, and Kuroki would have been driven into the hills. I myself passed forty-eight hours with one of these Japanese Groups : we had the Russians, at a distance of 2500-3000 metres, in thickly lined trenches in front of us; they did not move. When Kuroki's troops made themselves felt on the north bank of the Taitse-Ho, and the 15th Brigade attacked the height that the Japanese call Manju-Yama, and the Russians Suikwantum, Kuropatkin's whole attention and care were concentrated upon this one point. His entire Reserves were massed in this one menaced spot and exhausted in hopeless counter-attacks on the height that the 15th Brigade had taken. The Southern Front, where an easy success was beckoning to him, was neglected; and when it became clear that they could not retake the little height Suikwantum, a retirement was ordered, without any reason. Thus it was at Liauyang, and likewise at Shaho and Mukden.

This was not the method of war the Russians adopted against us. The mistakes they had made when opposed to the Japanese they did not repeat in the campaign against us.

One of my last tasks while I was in the Russian department of the Great General Staff was to construct the plan of a Russian attack on Germany from the information we possessed. Our Intelligence Service had not worked very well during the years of peace. The chief cause of this was that the large sums of money which are necessary to enlist agents and spies abroad were not at its disposal.

As far as I can remember it was only once, in the year 1902, that we succeeded in buying the whole Russian plan of attack from a colonel on the General Staff. From that time we only knew that the plan had been changed, but in what way remained doubtful for many long years. In the year 1910—if I am not mistaken—the Intelligence Officer, Captain Nicolai, of the General Staff of the I. Army Corps in Königsberg, was able to obtain a copy of orders for the defence of the frontier by a detachment of the 26th Russian Division that was then stationed at Kovno. From this it appeared that of the troops which would at first be at their disposal, the Russians would advance two armies against us: the so-called Vilna Army and the Warsaw Army. They were both to attack East Prussia, the one from the north and the other from the south of the Masurian Lakes. The two armies were to advance their inner wings in the direction of Gerdauen and attempt a junction behind the chain of the Masurian Lakes. The orders we had in our hands gave no instructions about the formation of the two armies. At first the troops belonging to the military district of Warsaw and those belonging to the military district of Vilna were naturally to form part of the force. The troops that were stationed in the southern portion of the Warsaw district and those stationed in the military districts of Kiev and Odessa were destined for the advance on Austria-Hungary. On the other hand, we knew nothing about the probable employment of the troops in the military districts of Petersburg, Finland, Moscow, Kasan, the Caucasus and all the Asiatic troops. With regard to the last-named, our General Staff took it for granted, at least as long as I was in the Russian department (autumn, 1911), that the Russians would not be in a position to throw them all into Europe, as they supposed that our diplomacy would succeed in keeping Japan from joining the alliance of our enemies. If our Foreign Office succeeded in this, which according to ordinary human understanding seemed no very difficult task, the Russians would be obliged to keep at least part of their East Siberian troops in the Far East.

It is true I personally could not allay certain apprehensions that I had concerning our relations with Japan. I remember a remark made in the spring of 1904 by Terauchi, who was then Minister of War. Report said that Terauchi was not very favourably disposed towards us Germans. At a dinner-party the conversation turned upon this point. Terauchi admitted that his opinion was formed not so much on account of the German military measures as of German politics, and that Germany, moreover, was to blame for Japan making war on Russia.

"In 1897 we took Port Arthur from the Chinese," Terauchi said, "and we were in possession of it. The Ultimatum of Germany, France and Russia forced us to surrender Port Arthur to the Chinese. That Russia sent us the Ultimatum was comprehensible. They wanted Port Arthur and the ice-free port of Dalny. That France supported her was natural, as she was allied with France. But what had you to do with the whole matter?"

I asked myself the same question, more especially when I heard that the Ambassador we had at the time in Tokio had allowed himself, and, as far as I know, without any instructions from the Wilhelm-strasse, and in no very skilful manner, to be pushed forward by his abler colleagues from Paris and Petersburg at the presentation of the Ultimatum.

I remember, when in the winter of 1905 I was standing with my wife in Shimonoseki before the tea-house where the Peace was signed, having given expression to this fear: "Let us hope that some day we shall not have to pay for this stupidity."

Unfortunately my fears were realized, and the Japanese Ultimatum, which caused such an unwarranted storm of indignation among us Germans, was nothing more than a literal translation of the Ultimatum of the year 1897, only in place of the words "Port Arthur" the word "Tsingtau" had been inserted.

I have just mentioned General Terauchi. In the first campaign he had gone through as a young man, during the Civil War of 1888, he had been wounded in the arm by an arrow. In consequence of this wound his arm remained stiff. He always appeared to me as a symbol of the rapid development of the Japanese Army. In the short space of thirty years it had advanced from being armed with bows and arrows to machine guns and modern breech-loading fire-arms, and the man who in his youth had fought with bows and arrows was in his old age the Minister of War of a modern army in a modern war. For the principles on which the development of the Japanese Army was carried out they had at first to study the European armies, and two opposite opinions prevailed : one party swore by France, and the other by Germany. At the time that the well-known General Meckel was acting as instructor in the Japanese Military Academy the last opinion carried the day. At the beginning of the war the instruction of the troops was conducted quite on German principles — they had simply translated the German Service Regulations into Japanese, and in the same way they had endeavoured to model the General Staff on German principles.

In this way our German principles for the command and the instruction of the army were tested in the war, and we can be satisfied with the results. By their success the Japanese were " justified in the trust they had placed in our military system."

After the war, when I presented my order of recall, I met General Fuji, the Chief of the General Staff of the 1st Army, and told him I was anxious to know what changes in the Japanese Regulations would be introduced owing to their experiences in the war; he answered : " So am I. We will wait to see what new Regulations for the Service Germany will issue on the basis of the reports that the officers who have been sent here will make, and we will translate these Regulations as we did the former ones."

I cannot close the chapter of my Japanese reminiscences without mentioning some of the foreign military attachés with whom chance had brought me in contact in the 1st Army of General Kuroki. They were destined to play special parts in the World War. Besides the well-known English General, Sir Ian Hamilton, and Major Caviglia, who afterwards became the Italian Minister of War, there were three Americans: Colonel Crowder and Captains Payton March and Pershing. They all three became celebrated in the new American Army that took part in the World War: Colonel Crowder in the Organization Department, Payton March as Chief of the General Staff, and, lastly, Pershing as Commander-in-Chief. I was specially intimate with Captain March, who gave me English lessons, and who was exceedingly sympathetic to me owing to his intelligent military views and his straightforward and outspoken opinions.

As I have already said, the Russians learned much from the Manchurian campaign. It is characteristic, however, of Russian conditions that these lessons were learned more owing to the initiative of a single person than to the instructions given by the Central Department. General Rennenkampf, who had not distinguished himself very greatly as leader in the Manchurian campaign, wrote a scheme of new Regulations for the infantry, based on his experiences in that campaign, which he first introduced in the III. Army Corps, and afterwards, when he became the Commander of the Military District of Vilna, he adopted it for the troops of that district. His scheme was then accepted, provisionally, for the whole army, but it never was properly drawn up in the form of Regulations.

When we considered in what way the Russian leaders were likely to make use of the bulk of their troops, the correct and most natural method appeared to be, in our military judgment, to begin by throwing the greater number of troops against Germany. We were the strongest adversary; if they had succeeded in defeating us, the campaign against Austria would have been mere child's play. I therefore believe that if the German General Staff had had the disposition of the Russian armies, only those of the Kiev and Odessa districts would have been employed as a defensive force, all the others would have been sent against Germany. If the Russian High Command had arrived at this correct decision, many weeks would have had to elapse before the advance on the German frontier could have been undertaken—that is to say, before all the troops, including the Siberian Divisions, could have arrived. We were as ignorant of the intended employment of the chief Russian forces as we were of the formations of the millions of trained soldiers who were at the disposal of the Russian High Command. Until the Japanese War the Russians differed from the German and French opinion, holding that even in times of peace a certain number of skeleton formations were necessary, as cadres for the Reserves. With the low standard of intelligence of the Russian soldier and the want of officers of the Reserve and non-commissioned officers they could draw upon, such a standpoint was quite justified. For this purpose they had a number of Reserve Brigades. In the event of a mobilization, by doubling them they could be formed into Reserve Divisions "of the first order," and by quadrupling them Reserve Divisions "of the second order."

Apparently Reserve Divisions formed in this way had not proved satisfactory in the Japanese campaign. I call to mind the check that Orlov's Reserve Division suffered at the Yentai coal-mines. The Division came suddenly upon a Brigade of the 12th Japanese Division in the thick "giauliang" fields, which, with their long stems 2 or 3 metres high, hid everything from sight. The Japanese made a bayonet charge and repulsed the Orlov Division without their offering the slightest resistance. Consequently after the war the Reserve Brigades were disbanded and Reserve Divisions according to the French system and under French guidance were organized. We did not know how many of such Reserve Divisions had been organized, how long the organization had taken, or if they were included in the Reserve Corps.

CHAPTER II

THE RECALL OF GENERAL VON PRITTWITZ

ON the evening of the first day of the mobilization I arrived in Posen, the mobilization station of the "Army High Command 8." This Army [1] was under the command of Colonel-General von Prittwitz. The Woyrsch Corps had also to assist the extreme left wing of the Austrians in their offensive movement.

For this task it was quite insufficiently equipped; above all there was a want of heavy artillery, and what can even be called a crime was the want of proper medical equipment. The influence of the High Command of the 8th Army over the Corps was but small. The telephone communications were bad, and became entirely

---

[1] It was composed of the
  I. A.C. (General von François).
  XVII. A.C. (General von Mackensen).
  XX. A.C. (General von Scholtz).
  I. Reserve Corps (General Otto von Below).
  3rd Reserve Division (General von Morgen).
  1st Cavalry Division (General Brecht).
  2nd Landwehr Brigade.
  6th Landwehr Brigade.
  70th Landwehr Brigade.
Under the command of this Army were also included the Military Areas of the I., II., V., VI., XVII. and XX. A.C., and the Eastern fortresses, and, further, the Woyrsch Corps, composed of the Posen and Silesian Landwehr, XX. and I. A.C., that were stationed to defend the frontier.
  These troops had the following areas for their advance:
  XVII. A.C., the district of Deutsch-Eylau.
  I. Reserve Corps, the district of Nordenburg.
  3rd Reserve Division, the district of Hohensalza.
  1st Cavalry Division, the district of Gumbinnen.
  2nd Landwehr Brigade, the district of Tilsit.
  70th Landwehr Brigade, the district of Goslershausen.

disconnected as the Corps advanced, owing to the want of material. I succeeded only twice, at the beginning, in getting into touch with the Corps —a very agreeable surprise! One of our most gifted and clever officers of the General Staff, Lieutenant-Colonel Kundt, who was my best friend, answered to my call. I had supposed he was in South America. Before the war he had gone on leave, with several other officers, to Bolivia, and just before the outbreak of the war he had obtained a furlough to go home, and had arrived safely in Germany. Now I was glad to know that we had one of our most capable officers among our fellow-combatants.

Our army had orders to defend East and West Prussia against a Russian attack. At the same time it was to take care not to allow itself to be overpowered by superior forces or to be driven into the fortress of Königsberg. In the event of the advance of greatly superior Russian forces the instructions were to give up West Prussia east of the Vistula and take up positions behind that river.

The last portion of these Orders certainly contained great psychological dangers for weak characters.

However, the instructions, as well as the strength of the forces that had been destined for the Eastern Front, were no surprise to us, as they corresponded approximately with our suppositions.

As is now generally known, according to the plan of campaign which Count Schlieffen, the former Chief of the General Staff, had worked out for a war on two fronts, the greater part of the German forces with a strong right wing was to advance on the Western frontier, make a surprise dash through Belgium, envelop the northern wing of the French Army and roll it up. By these means the decisive action in the West was to be brought about quickly. The East during this time had to look after itself, and only when the decisive battle had been fought in the West could it expect support from thence. This plan was quite familiar to us officers of the General Staff of Schlieffen's school; we had played it out dozens of times in the war game and in staff rides.

The Commander-in-Chief of the Army, General von Prittwitz, was well known to me as a clever though somewhat harsh superior. I also knew very well the Chief of his General Staff, Major-General von Waldersee. Waldersee was generally considered a highly trained and able officer of the General Staff. At the beginning of the mobilization he was Quartermaster-General, and belonged therefore to the élite of the Chiefs of Staff. Unfortunately at the time his physical powers were not equal to his mental, as he had but recently undergone a serious operation, and his nerves were still suffering from its effects.

The first considerations that occupied the attention of the Chief of the General Staff and myself concerning the task that awaited our army were as follows.

We had no fear of the great Russian cavalry invasion which was so much talked about; our frontier guards would deal with that: on the contrary it was to be desired that the Russians should effect such an invasion, and meet with a failure at once. We had first of all to reckon with the advance of the armies, probably consisting of the troops from the military districts of Vilna and Warsaw (without the XVII. Army Corps which was stationed on the Austro-Hungarian frontier). We could take for granted that their mobilization would be concluded by August 15th, so that we could expect the advance of both armies between August 15th and 20th, as the deployment would be made from the garrisons that lay near the German frontier and would not take long. It was doubtful if they would be strengthened by part of the troops from the Petersburg and Moscow military districts. Taking into consideration Russian military logic, it was possible to conclude that troops would be advanced somewhere in the neighbourhood of Grodno, as Reserves and line-of-communication troops for both armies. But it was probable there could be no Reserves yet in their appointed places, as their mobilization would require a considerable time.

On entering German territory the Russian advance would be divided by the obstacle of the Masurian Lakes. The Russians could only advance by sending one army to the north and the other to the south of this chain of lakes. Our army had therefore to be prepared to attack one of these armies while they were disunited by the Masurian Lakes and defeat it. Which of the two would offer us the better opportunity could not be foreseen. It could, however, be taken for granted that the army from Vilna would appear somewhat sooner on the theatre of war than the army from Warsaw, which would have to make its way through a district near our frontier that was both boggy and deficient in roads.

Events proved the general correctness of our views. During the next few days the Russians made small cavalry attacks, which were repulsed with ease. The Vilna Army advanced in larger detachments with great energy on our eastern frontier, while the southern frontier of both East Prussia as well as West Prussia remained comparatively quiet.

Reconnoitring against the Warsaw Army was

extremely difficult. The agents—Polish Jews—who during the first days had brought in news, failed us as the Russian occupation of the frontier districts became denser. The army had only one detachment of airmen at its disposal, which was obliged to restrict itself to flying over the communications that connected us with the frontier twice a day. Nevertheless we should not have been so taken by surprise by the sudden appearance of the Warsaw Army if the Russians had not been so cautious, marching only at night and keeping the troops under cover during the daytime.

The mobilization and the deployment of our army was accomplished in accordance with our arrangements. The Army Headquarters moved on August 8th to Marienburg, and from that day assumed the supreme command.

Before their arrival in Marienburg the Army Headquarters had trouble with the Commander-in-Chief of the I. Army Corps, General von François. As the Commander-in-Chief of the East Prussian Army Corps, General von François felt himself specially called upon to protect the province. It was quite natural that, from his point of view, he should make sure that no Russian should set foot on the soil of East Prussia and that no East Prussian village should experience the horrors of war. He was of the opinion that the task of the frontier defence was therefore to act offensively, and wanted, by attacking the Russian frontier troops, to keep them off the frontier. He failed to see that by such tactics the I. Army Corps would be removed from its contact with the rest of the army; and if the Army Headquarters had agreed to his plan it might easily have happened that the army would have been obliged to support the I. Army Corps on the frontier, or possibly east of the Russian frontier, and consequently the army would lose cohesion and eventually might be obliged to fight on the other side of the Masurian Lakes, and thus forgo the geographical advantages they offered. General von François made the mistake of omitting to inform Army Headquarters of his intentions; so that Army Headquarters believed that the chief part of the I. Army Corps was stationed on the Angerapp, while in fact it had been advanced much farther eastwards.

Up to August 14th the information we were able to obtain about the enemy was that our opponent was advancing with strong forces to the north and the south of the Rominten forest. He was developing especially energetic activity to the south of the forest. Headquarters concluded, as they had already supposed, that the Vilna Army had advanced somewhat sooner than the Warsaw Army, more especially as the airmen's reports still continued to show that no movement of troops could be observed on the roads coming from the south. The Chief Command decided to prepare the mass of the army for the attack on the Vilna Army.[1]

And in anticipation of the expected battle they moved, in the evening, from Marienburg to Bartenstein.

[1] XX. A.C. was concentrated with its chief forces near Ortelsburg and held the frontier against advances from the south; on the right it was supported by the
Frontier Defence Detachment of Dantzic at Neidenburg.
Frontier Defence Detachment of Graudenz at Lautenburg.
Frontier Defence Detachment of Thorn at Strassburg.
Also the 70th Landwehr Brigade at Mlawa—Soldau.
On the Lake line, Nikolaiken—Lötzen, were stationed:
3rd Reserve Division with 6th Landwehr Brigade.
I. Reserve Corps on the Angerapp, with its right wing on the Mauer Lake.
XVII. A.C. was sent by train to Darkehmen.
I. A.C. was ordered to remain at Gumbinnen-Insterburg.
The chief Reserves from Königsberg were dispatched to Insterburg.
1st Cavalry Division remained in advance of the left wing.
2nd Landwehr Brigade held the Memel line at Tilsit.

To his great astonishment Major-General Count Waldersee received on August 17th, from the Chief of Staff of the I. Army Corps, a dispatch from which it appeared that General von François had not executed the orders that had been given him, but had marched forward with the bulk of his troops and had brought on an action near Stallupönen. Both by telegraph and telephone the army was ordered to break off the action instantly. The Quartermaster-General, Major-General Grünert, was sent in a car to General von François to transmit to him the order personally. One cannot help comparing this high-handed action of General von François with the occurrences that took place in the Austro-Hungarian Army in the battle of Lemberg. There General Brudermann had also received an order to advance and to stop, and only to attack when he received an order to do so from G.H.Q. Contrary to this positive order General Brudermann attacked, and by so doing contributed greatly to the loss of the battle of Lemberg. Whether, if the High Command could have taken a strong line and stopped him, it would have been possible to support him in his position, I am unable to judge. In the case of General von François it was possible to recall the Corps in time.

The battle of Stallupönen that was broken off in this manner was still quite a success for the I. Army Corps. Superior Russian forces were repulsed and the Corps took many thousand prisoners. But all the same, having regard to the general position, it was a mistake. The I. Army Corps, although the victor, also had losses, both in men and material, and chiefly in attacking power, which ought to have been husbanded for the great battle. Besides, we had no interest in delaying the advance of the Vilna Army; on the contrary, the quicker it advanced the easier it would be to defeat it, before the Warsaw Army was able to make itself felt in the south.

In the meantime the deployment of the army on the Angerapp line was carried out as ordered.

The Commander-in-Chief of the Army went early on the 19th to have a consultation with General von Mackensen in Darkehmen, and then removed to Nordenburg.

In the afternoon of the 19th the High Command had the impression that the Russian troops that were advancing to the north of the Rominten forest had come near enough, and they gave the order to attack.[1]

In accordance with this order the 8th Army made the attack early on the 20th. Late in the afternoon the engagement presented the following picture:

Our right wing, under General Otto von Below, had defeated the enemy that was opposed to it; the right wing, under General von François, was also victoriously advancing. On the other hand the centre, under General von Mackensen, as they advanced, driving the Russian vanguards before them, had come upon a well-constructed Russian field position to the east of the River Rominten. Without waiting for an adequate artillery preparation Mackensen's troops attacked it, suffered severe losses and were held up. The Corps Command announced, about 3 P.M., that the Corps was defeated and that the position was serious.

The 3rd Reserve Division, under General von

---

[1] The attack was to be made by the
    I. Reserve Corps.
    XVII. A.C.
    I. A.C.
    The chief Reserves at Königsberg.
    1st Cavalry Division.
    The I. A.C. was to outflank the north wing of the enemy, while the 3rd Reserve Division with the 6th Landwehr Brigade was to be ready in Lötzen to make an outflanking attack on the enemy's left wing.

Morgen, had been ordered by the Commander-in-Chief to leave Lötzen about midday of the 20th, as the position south of the Rominten forest appeared not to be clear. Thus their assistance could be counted on only early on the 21st.

Notwithstanding the check that Mackensen's Corps had received, the position of the battle was favourable for the 8th Army. It could be reckoned that by continuing the attack, owing to the outflanking of both the enemy's wings, a complete success would be attained.

About half-past six in the evening I was standing with Major-General Grünert before the office in Nordenburg. We had just been discussing the favourable prospects for the battle on the following day, when a message arrived from the General of the Artillery, von Scholtz, reporting that " the Russian Army from Warsaw with a strength of four to five Army Corps had begun to cross the German frontier opposite the front Soldau—Ortelsburg."

I remarked to General Grünert: " I am afraid the nerves of the Commander-in-Chief and the other chiefs are not strong enough to receive this message. I would be best pleased if we could suppress it. To-morrow we would end the battle here and then turn on our Warsaw opponent."

General Grünert answered: " You surely would not keep back such important information from the Chief!" He knew very well that I was not in earnest.

At that moment the Commander-in-Chief and the Chief of the General Staff came out of their quarters next to the office, and I saw by their faces that they had already received the message.

General von Prittwitz asked us to come into the office with them.

" Gentlemen," he said, " I see you have also received the message, and you know that the Russian Army from Warsaw will advance on our rear if we continue the battle, and cut us off from the Vistula. The army will therefore break off the fight and retire behind the Vistula."

General Grünert tried to explain his and my different standpoint—"that the battle near Gumbinnen was in a favourable position; that in two to three days we would be able to make an end of the Russian Army from Vilna; and that it would then be time enough to turn on the enemy from Warsaw. Until then General von Scholtz and his Corps would have to shift for themselves."

General von Prittwitz cut short General Grünert's discourse abruptly, and said that he had decided to retire beyond the Vistula; for the tactical decisions of the Command only he and the Chief of the General Staff were responsible, and not the First General Staff Officer nor the Quartermaster-General. This was followed by orders given to me by Count Waldersee to make the necessary dispositions for the retreat of the army beyond the Vistula. I explained that I considered it would be impossible for the army to retire beyond the Vistula, and I therefore requested to be instructed how the Commander-in-Chief wished the retreat to be effected.

Then the question of how the retreat was to be carried out was discussed. General Grünert and I showed, with the compasses, that a simple retreat beyond the Vistula would be impossible, as, in order to retire in that way, we should have to deal with the left wing of the Russian Warsaw Army, which was nearer to the Vistula than we were. That therefore it would be necessary to stop the advance of the Warsaw Army, and the easiest way would be by an offensive thrust at the left wing of that army.

General von Prittwitz, who as well as General Count Waldersee had for the moment lost control of his nerves, saw the necessity of the measures we proposed. However, he stuck to his opinion that it was necessary to break off the battle against Rennenkampf, but he gave up the intention of retiring beyond the Vistula, and agreed with our opinion, that it was necessary to take up the offensive against the left wing of the Warsaw Army. According to these changed opinions, orders were given on the evening of the 20th which were the preliminaries of, and led directly to, the battle of Tannenberg.

Orders were as follows:

> The XX. Army Corps to be concentrated behind its right wing in the neighbourhood of Hohenstein.
>
> I. Army Corps and 3rd Reserve Division to be sent by train, the first from Insterburg, the last from Angerburg, to the right wing of the XX. Army Corps.
>
> Chief Reserves from Königsberg to cover the entraining of the I. Army Corps and then proceed to the fortified line Pregel—Deime.
>
> I. Reserve Corps and XVII. Army Corps to move straight back in a westerly direction.

On the arrival of the I. Army Corps and the 3rd Reserve Divisions at the right wing of the XX. Army Corps the advance of the Warsaw Army was to be checked by an offensive thrust of these three units against its left wing and flank. If, however, the I. Reserve Corps and the XVII. Army Corps were successfully disengaged from the enemy, without the latter pursuing them very energetically, the High Command had in view a general reunion of the whole 8th Army in the neighbourhood of Osterode, with the intention of giving battle to both the

Russian armies east of the Vistula. Whether it would be possible, and how it could take place—whether the action would be offensive against the Warsaw Army and defensive against Rennenkampf, or defensive against both—could not be said at that time, as it principally depended on Rennenkampf's attitude.

I have lingered somewhat long over these details, as I consider it my duty to the memory of the dead General von Prittwitz to lay stress on the fact that the fundamental instructions for the battle of Tannenberg were given by him, because public opinion still only thinks of him as having wanted to lead the army beyond the Vistula. He also had the intention of calling up the I. Reserve Corps and the XVII. Army Corps. That the possibility of the employment of these two Army Corps in the south could not have been reckoned with at that moment must be quite clear to every soldier, and even to every man without military knowledge: nobody could suppose that when, early in the morning of the 21st, Rennenkampf received the report of the German retreat he would remain inactive; it was natural to suppose that he would have pursued energetically with all his forces.

G.H.Q. was informed, through a telephone conversation between General von Prittwitz and General von Moltke, of the first intention of drawing the army back beyond the Vistula, but not of the change in his decisions. G.H.Q. were not satisfied with this decision and recalled General von Prittwitz and the Chief of his General Staff, Major-General von Waldersee.

They were replaced by the Infantry General von Benneckendorff und Hindenburg, and Major-General Ludendorff.

CHAPTER III

THE BATTLE OF TANNENBERG

IT is idle to ask the question : " Would there have been a victory at Tannenberg if the Commanders had not been changed ? " I think : Yes, — though perhaps not to so complete a victory, for the original Commanders, as former experiences had shown, did not possess the necessary energy. There were at once difficulties with General von François, and I do not know if the old Commander-in-Chief would have been able to get over them as easily as General Ludendorff did, and if he would have been able to support the strain that was put on his nerves during the next days by the question: " Will Rennenkampf advance or not ? "

The form of their recall was uncommonly harsh. The subordinate Generals-in-Command heard of it sooner than the Commander-in-Chief. Orders were sent by G.H.Q. to the Generals-in-Command without the Commander-in-Chief being informed. For example, the I. Reserve Corps and the XVII. Army Corps were ordered to take a day's rest, the necessity for which order is at least open to doubt.

Headquarters had moved on the morning of the 21st to Bartenstein and on the 22nd to Mühlhausen, in East Prussia. The reports that came in showed that the retirement of the troops before the Vilna Army had been surprisingly successful.

Colonel Hell, the Chief of the General Staff of the XX. Army Corps, reported that the Corps had been successfully concentrated in the neighbourhood of

Hohenstein, and he received the order to draw up the Corps on the line Gilgenburg—Lahne. He expressed his doubts about the left flank of the Corps, as it would take days to transport by rail the troops that were still on frontier duty, and therefore requested that the 3rd Reserve Division should not be sent to the right wing of the XX. Army Corps, as G.H.Q. had ordered, but to have it sent to the left wing in the neighbourhood of Hohenstein. This was approved by G.H.Q.

It was only in the afternoon of the 22nd that we heard of the change in the High Command, when a telegram sent to the O.C. Field Railways announced the arrival of a special train with the new Commander-in-Chief and Chief of the General Staff. It was only a few hours later that His Majesty's order arrived which placed General von Prittwitz and General Count Waldersee on the unattached list. General von Prittwitz bore this stroke of fate extremely well, and he took leave of us without a single word of complaint.

On the evening of the 22nd a telegram from Ludendorff announced his arrival in Marienburg on the following day with the new Commander-in-Chief, who expected to find the chief Commanders there. When he sent this order, General Ludendorff supposed that the Army Headquarters was already west of the Vistula, and wanted it transferred forward to Marienburg, but Prittwitz's proposed retreat had not been carried out; he was, in fact, shifting us back.

Hindenburg and Ludendorff arrived in the evening of the 23rd. General von Hindenburg, who afterwards became the idol of the German people, was up to that time but little known beyond the district of his old Corps. I had never seen him. Ludendorff, on the contrary, was a well-known and often-mentioned personage in General Staff circles. His efforts to strengthen the army, which were only partially carried out in the great defensive plans, and also his endeavours to persuade the Ministry of War to keep larger supplies of munitions, in the event of a mobilization, which met with the same fate, were much discussed. There could be no question that the first success of the war, the important capture of Liège, was entirely owing to him, and it was generally thought so in the army. At the beginning of the war he was Quartermaster-General of the 2nd Army under Bülow, and had joined one of the columns — the 17th Infantry Brigade—that was appointed for the capture of Liège.

When the Commander of this Brigade, General von Wussow, fell, he succeeded to the command, and it was owing to his energy and activity that the fortress was taken; while all the other columns were more or less unsuccessful.

I knew Ludendorff very well; we were General Staff officers at Posen at the same time, and from 1909 till 1913 had lived in the same house in Berlin.

General Ludendorff heard my report of the position, and approved of the measures that had been taken till then by the High Command.

Our reports as to Russian movements were to the effect that at least five Army Corps and three Cavalry Divisions were advancing from the front Soldau—Ortelsburg. Between Rennenkampf's army and our retreating troops there was a distance of about fifty kilometres, and Rennenkampf had made no efforts at pursuit up till then.

In the afternoon of the 23rd, and in the early morning of the 24th, strong forces of the Warsaw Army attacked the left wing of Scholtz's Corps, the 37th Infantry Division; after furious fighting they were repulsed with severe losses.

In connection with this fight a small incident occurred—in itself of but small consequence, but which was of vital importance for the success of the battle. It turned out that the position of the victorious 37th Division had not been happily chosen and that a better position lay farther back. The High Command had gone early on the 24th to Tannenberg for a consultation with General von Scholtz. The General asked for permission to withdraw the 37th Division, after repulsing the attack, to the better position. The High Command agreed to this.

The voluntary retreat of the 37th Infantry Division proved to be a happy manœuvre: it aroused in the Russians the belief in a general retreat of the German Army.

The enemy Commander, General Samsonoff, issued an order to the army to pursue. The order was sent by wireless from the Russian station, not in cipher, and we intercepted it. This was the first of numberless orders that in the beginning the Russians sent, with quite incomprehensible carelessness, unciphered; afterwards they were in cipher. This carelessness greatly facilitated the control of the operations in the East, and in many cases even made the initiative possible for us. The cipher orders caused us no difficulties either; we had two men on the Staff who proved themselves quite geniuses in deciphering, and in a very short time they found out the key to the new Russian code.

It appeared from Samsonoff's order that in the advance of the Russian Army the I. Army Corps, which formed the left wing marching on Soldau, was to be deeply echeloned to the left and undertake the duty of covering Thorn. A similar order for covering Lötzen was given to the VI. Army Corps, which formed the right wing and was to advance through Ortelsburg—Mensguth.

In the meantime General Rennenkampf's army remained stationary for some unaccountable reason. Only its cavalry advanced slowly; the infantry did not move. In consequence of this the High Command turned the I. Reserve Corps and the XVII. Army Corps to the south, in order to bring about a decisive action against Samsonoff.

The High Command ordered the decisive attack to be made on the 26th. Here again there were differences with General von François. General von François wanted to postpone the attack for one day, as some of his columns had not arrived, and he also wanted the attack to be more far-reaching— that is to say, that it should extend in the direction of Mlava. In the opinion of the Army Command, time did not allow of this. Every day we lost might see Rennenkampf begin his advance, and an out-flanking of Samsonoff's left wing near Mlava would lead only to a disunion of the 8th Army, which was already very weak.

Orders were therefore given to break through at Usdau—in my opinion the decisive point of the whole battle of Tannenberg.

On the 26th the I. Army Corps, with the assist-ance of Mühlmann's Force (troops from the Vistula fortresses of about the strength of a mixed Brigade), had succeeded only in taking the heights of Seeben.

The right wing of the XX. Army Corps, the 41st Infantry Division, had on the same day driven the enemy back south of Mühlen. South of Lautern, on our left wing, the I. Reserve Corps and the 6th Landwehr Brigade had come upon the VI. Russian Army Corps, which was advancing northwards via Ortelsburg, and defeated it.

On August 27th the I. Army Corps, together with Schmettau's section of the XX. Army Corps, stormed Usdau, and drove the I. Russian Army Corps southwards beyond Soldau.

The XX. Army Corps had to defend itself from very strong Russian attacks.

The I. Reserve Corps and the XVI. Army Corps pursued the retreating Russians southwards beyond Ortelsburg.

On the same day the Russians, not meeting any opposition, reached Allenstein.

I would like again to mention a little episode which shows what demands are made on the nerves of the leaders even during successful fighting.

The Staff had been standing till midday on a small hill south of Gilgenburg, whence it had watched the storming of Usdau, and in the afternoon it had returned to Headquarters at Löbau. The reports that came in from all sides were favourable and the I. Army Corps was advancing victoriously.

In Löbau we came upon columns and transport trains of the I. Army Corps which, to our surprise, were going the other way, and had turned their horses' heads northwards.

When in my astonishment I questioned the leader, Cavalry Captain von Schneider, that officer explained that an order had come to make everything ready for a retreat to the north.

When I got to my office I was called to the telephone: the Commander of the ammunition column and transport train of the I. Army Corps reported himself from Montovo station and gave me the following information:

" The second battalion of the Grenadier Regiment has just reached Montovo, quite disorganized. The Commander of the Battalion reports that the

I. Army Corps has been completely defeated and it, as well as the XX. Army Corps, is retiring. He has been able to save himself and his battalion from the general disaster only by making a rapid retreat. For all eventualities he has given orders to the column to turn round with the horses' heads to the north."

I did not doubt that this must be one of the numerous panics that so often occur—but it was just possible that after we had left the field of battle the I. Army Corps had had to sustain a counter-attack.

I next ordered the Commander of the Battalion to come to the telephone, and I was very peremptory. I ordered him to turn his battalion round and to continue to march until he came upon the enemy. Then the Second Aide-de-Camp on the Staff, Captain Caemmerer, who afterwards became so well known as the personal aide-de-camp of Field-Marshal Hindenburg, was sent in a car with the order to drive on until he came upon either German or Russian forces.

Nevertheless, the next hour, while awaiting Caemmerer's return with his report, was a very trying one. This incident was soon explained. The Commander of the battalion that had been sent to serve as a connection between the I. Army Corps and the Mühlmann detachment had received reports that were partly false and partly exaggerated, and believing there was an advance of strong Russian forces against his flank, he had lost his nerve.

On August 28th the I. Army Corps with the 1st Division and Mühlmann's Force drove the enemy back beyond Soldau, while the 2nd Division and Schmettau's detachment were already advancing on Neidenburg to envelop the Russians.

In the middle of the battle the High Command

had ordered an encircling attack to be made on Hohenstein.[1]

Some difficulty was caused by the fact that the attack of the 41st Infantry Division at Waplitz had been repulsed by the Russian XXIII. Corps. However, the advance of the 2nd Infantry Division on Neidenburg soon eased the situation. The 3rd Reserve Division (General von Morgen), supported by the von der Goltz Division, stormed Hohenstein. The XV. Russian Army Corps called by wireless to its assistance the XIII. Army Corps, which was already advancing along the highway Allenstein—Grieslinen. Although by its attack von der Goltz's Landwehr Division was brought for a time into difficulties, it was soon relieved by the XIII. Army Corps being attacked in the rear by the I. Reserve Corps.

The XVII. Army Corps blocked the forest and lake districts in the east; General von François, who judged the position rightly, had advanced his 1st Division on Neidenburg and had sent the Schmettau detachment as far as Willenburg, and so completed the encircling movement from the south.

The fate of Samsonoff's army was sealed. At least that was the opinion of the High Command in the afternoon of the 29th, and they ordered certain units, which seemed to be no longer needed for the last struggles, to be ready to march away on August 30th, to prepare for the imminent battle against Rennenkampf, when an incident occurred that might easily have had very unpleasant consequences.

On the morning of the 30th an airman's report reached the Army Command, as well as General von François, that the reinforced I. Russian Army

---

[1] XX. A.C. and 1st Reserve Division from the west; the Landwehr Division that had been transported from Schleswig by train and detrained in Biessellen from the north; I. Reserve Corps from the west.

Corps was marching from Mlava on Neidenburg, and that its vanguard, at the time the message was sent, was only about six kilometres distant from the troops of General von François that were stationed at Neidenburg.

The Commander of the Russian I. Army Corps, General Artamonov, had rightly decided that by an attack on Neidenburg he might be able to break through the forces that surrounded them.

The Chief Command sent all the troops they could dispose of against this threat to Neidenburg.[1]

But at first the I. Army Corps was without any support, and had to see how it could help itself in the difficult position. The energetic General von François was the right man to do so. He sent Mühlmann's Force against the flank of the Russian advancing Corps, and made a frontal attack on the enemy at Neidenburg with all the troops he could scrape together, without abandoning the encircling movement from the north.

The attack was repulsed after a comparatively easy fight. It is impossible now to decide if the enemy leader, after the heavy losses he had sustained in the fights round Usdau, had no longer the will for victory, or whether he feared an attack in the flank from the direction of Saberau, where the four heavy batteries of Mühlmann's Force had been firing very effectively.

The enemy commander Samsonoff shot himself when he realized the complete defeat of his army.

It is natural to ask, what were Rennenkampf's reasons for not coming to his assistance in spite of all the requests Samsonoff had sent him by wireless?

---

[1] The Landwehr Division von der Goltz; the 3rd Reserve Division; a detachment under General von Unger; and a Division from both the XVII. and XX. A.C.'s.

The explanation that his inactivity was caused by the very severe losses his army had sustained in the battle of Gumbinnen, where some units had lost fifty per cent. or more of their effectives; that the information he received spoke only of a retreat of the German 8th Army to Königsberg, and that therefore an advance of his army in a south-westerly direction would expose it to a flank attack from the fortress of Königsberg, are not sufficient to satisfy our military notions. Any advance by Rennenkampf would have prevented the disaster of Tannenberg. I must therefore mention the rumour, which cannot be quite ignored, that Rennenkampf did not go to Samsonoff's assistance from motives of personal enmity. We must naturally conclude that he did not realize what importance the effects of his decision nor what the extent of Samsonoff's defeat would be. I know that a personal enmity existed between the two men, dating from the battle of Liauyang, where Samsonoff with the Siberian Cossack Division was defending the Yentai coal-mines, but in spite of the conspicuous bravery of his Cossacks he was obliged to evacuate them, as Rennenkampf, who was on the left flank of the Russians with his detachment, remained inactive in the face of repeated orders. Witnesses told me that after the battle there had been a very venomous interview between the two leaders on Mukden station.

I remember that during the Tannenberg days I spoke to General Ludendorff about the feud between the two enemy leaders, and of my suspicions of the possible psychological influence it might have.

On one of the last days of the battle of Tannenberg General Ludendorff summoned me to his telephone. He had been called up by Colonel Tappen, the Chief of the Operations Department of G.H.Q.

Ludendorff said to me: " Take the second receiver, so that you can hear what Colonel Tappen wants, and my answer."

Colonel Tappen informed him that three Army Corps and one Cavalry Division from the Western Army had been ordered to reinforce the 8th Army, and asked in what direction these troops were to be dispatched. General Ludendorff gave the necessary instructions, but explained clearly at the same time that we were not positively in need of these reinforcements; if the Western Front found any difficulty in sending them the Corps might remain there. Colonel Tappen explained that the troops could be spared from the West.

The following day the same thing happened. Again Colonel Tappen called us up—I had the second receiver of the field telephone — and he informed us that only the XI. and Reserve Guard Corps and also the 8th Cavalry Division would come, but that the V. Army Corps which he had mentioned on the previous day was wanted in the West. General Ludendorff assured him once more that the Corps would arrive too late for the battle then in progress, and that we were able, if necessary, to manage alone, and therefore if the Corps was needed in the West, to bring about a quicker decision, G.H.Q. need not have any consideration for the East.

I wish to lay special stress on these two conversations because it has often been asserted that G.H.Q. had decided on the "fatal" dispatch of these two Army Corps only in consequence of urgent demands for help from the East.

CHAPTER IV

AT THE MASURIAN LAKES

SAMSONOFF's army had been practically destroyed. Of his five Corps three and a half were either dead or prisoners, the remaining, about one and a half, Corps had to be sent back into the neighbourhood of Warsaw for re-formation. Our hands were free to act against Rennenkampf.

On September 5th the deployment [1] against Rennenkampf was concluded. His army had advanced by that time, and its right wing (about two Divisions) had been brought up to our positions on the Deime; about three Army Corps were stationed from that point along a line, Gerdauen—Drengfurth, as far as Lake Mauer, the weaker forces of its left wing stretched eastwards past Lötzen, with detachments at Arys and Johannisburg.

The Russian Army had taken advantage of the delay to construct well-fortified field positions.

With Rennenkampf's army were also four Divisions of Reserves, but I knew nothing about their individual formation. Moreover, the Finnish Army Corps also appeared on its southern flank.

---

[1] The forces were stationed as follows:

3rd Reserve Division (von Morgen) at Friedrichshof.

I. A.C. (von François) east of Ortelsburg on the roads to Johannisburg and Nikolaiken.

XVII. A.C. (von Mackensen) at Mensguth.

XX. A.C. (von Scholtz) at Wartenburg.

XI. A.C. (von Plüskow) at Seeburg.

I. Reserve Corps (von Below) with the 6th Landwehr Brigade at Heilsburg.

Guards Reserve Corps (von Gallwitz) at Preussisch—Eylau.

A.O.C. in Allenstein.

Goltz's Landwehr Division and the 70th Landwehr Brigade covered the right flank at Mlava and Myszyniec.

From papers captured at Tannenberg the High Command learned of the so-called "Grodno Reserve." Besides the Finnish XXII. Army Corps, the III. Siberian Corps ought to have formed part of it, but at that time they could not be reckoned on, as the troop trains from East Siberia could not have arrived as yet.

The Army Command had decided to make an attack on the whole Front.

Three Corps (Scholtz, Plüskow and Gallwitz) were to make a frontal attack, while Morgen, François and Mackensen, advancing southwards, past the Masurian Lakes, were to bring about the decision by an outflanking attack.

The 1st and 8th Cavalry Divisions were to proceed through Lötzen to the right wing to be ready for the pursuit when the decisive moment had been reached.

The frontal attack did not progress, but the outflanking movement of General von François was decisive.

In a series of engagements, on the 7th at Johannisburg, on the 8th at Arys, on the 9th to the north of Widminnen, he forced the Russian detachments to retire, disengaged General von Mackensen's XVII. Army Corps from Lötzen, and by an enveloping pressure on Rennenkampf's right wing obliged him to retreat.

Already on the fourth day of the battle the report of an airman had come in, who said he had the impression that the principal Russian positions were only weakly occupied, or not occupied at all; and on the following morning the Staff received the positive news that Rennenkampf did not mean to resist the attack, but had apparently given the order for a general retreat already on the previous day. Though this information deprived us of the hope of completely defeating Rennenkampf, I would not deny that the news of his retreat was welcome.

The frontal attack on the admirably planned positions of the Russians would have been very difficult. It appears to me doubtful if we should have been successful. It would only have been necessary for Rennenkampf to defend himself from the enveloping attack on his left wing by the three Divisions of Generals von François and von Morgen. Rennenkampf had for this purpose at the very least the Finnish Army Corps and six Divisions of his Reserve. He could easily have turned this defensive into an offensive action. Even if our 8th Army had not suffered a defeat, it would not have been free for its next task—the support of the Austrians in South Poland.

On the receipt of the information that the Russian Army was retreating the Chief Command gave orders for its pursuit, to be carried out as follows:

I. Army Corps south-east of the Rominten forest towards Mariampol.

XVII. Army Corps north of the Rominten forest towards Wistyniec.

XX. Army Corps through Darkehmen, Walterkehmen towards Pillupönen.

XI. Army Corps north of Darkehmen past Gumbinnen towards Stallupönen.

I. Reserve Corps by Insterburg towards Pillkallen.

Guard Reserve Corps from Allenburg towards Gross-Aulowöhnen.

Königsberg Main Reserve, towards Tilsit.

1st and 8th Cavalry Divisions were to go in advance of the I. Army Corps and push forward to Wirballen—Kovno main road.

These orders were only partially carried out.

On the morning of the 11th a report reached the

High Command from the Command of the XI. Corps that it was being attacked by superior forces. We already knew of the attack from a Russian wireless. From this it appeared only to be an attack by three regiments of a Russian Reserve Division. Although this was pointed out to the Army Command, they insisted on the correctness of their report of the attack by superior forces.

It was quite possible that Rennenkampf might try, by a strong offensive attack, to break through and thus to prevent the pursuit of the 8th Army. The High Command allowed itself to be misled, and ordered the XVII. and I. Army Corps to go to the assistance of the XI. Army Corps. This caused a quite unnecessary stoppage in the pursuit, and, in spite of the utmost efforts of the Army Command, this loss of time could not be made up.

On September 17th there was a sharp rear-guard engagement at Wylkowyszki. Notwithstanding the skill the Russians displayed in the retreat, notwithstanding the recklessness with which they allowed the columns to march alongside each other on the sides of the roads, congestion occurred, more especially during the march through Stallupönen. The rear-guard was therefore sacrificed at Wylkowyszki in order to give the rest of the army time to escape. With this rear-guard engagement the battle of the Masurian Lakes was finished. The chief merit of this great success must be awarded to General von François' Corps, and especially to von Morgen's Reserve Division, which covered the right flank of François' offensive and defeated the Finnish Corps in many attacks.

Besides the liberation of East Prussia, this battle gave us the certainty that Rennenkampf's army was out of action for a long time. His losses in both men and material were very considerable, so that it would take weeks to reorganize while resting beyond the protective barrier of the Niemen and its fortresses. It is true Rennenkampf had not been completely defeated, and I do not think that it would have been possible for us to inflict such a defeat on him.

An envelopment of both wings was impossible with the forces we possessed, and in the country in which we had to operate. Of course it would have been possible to have been more economical with the forces employed in the frontal attack, but even if we had brought into action on the Deime the two newly arrived Army Corps, as General von François suggests in his book, two Army Corps would have been inadequate for attack on a front of fifty kilometres.

We were quite ignorant of the strength of the Russian Reserve Divisions or of the reinforcements brought up in the meantime, and, for all we knew, every offensive they made might have had the most fatal consequences. On the one hand, if the two Army Corps had made an offensive beyond the Deime sector they would have met with considerable difficulties. If the attack had succeeded, Rennenkampf would probably have begun his retreat a day sooner, which the attack of these two Corps would not have been able to hinder.

On the other hand, it is a disputed question whether it might not have been better to have employed another Army Corps to assist in the outflanking action on the right wing.

CHAPTER V

WHILE our army was fighting the battles of Tannenberg and of the Masurian Lakes the positions on the Western Front and of the allied Austrian Army had developed unfavourably.

After the victorious advance of the German Army in the West, on September 9th, General von Bülow had taken his fatal decision to retire. We heard of what was happening in the West only by rumours. We knew that a reaction had set in, and that the German advance had come to a standstill. Why and where this had happened we were not informed.

However, more exact intelligence reached us of Austrian reverses near Lemberg, and of their retreat beyond the San in the direction of Cracow. It was necessary to send our ally the assistance to which he was entitled according to arrangements that had been made before the war between the Chiefs of both General Staffs. G.H.Q. therefore ordered us to provide two Army Corps, and to dispatch them to Silesia. They were to serve there as the cadre for a new army under the command of General von Schubert, and General Ludendorff was Chief of the General Staff.

General Ludendorff went to Silesia, got into touch with the Austrian High Command, and was convinced that two Army Corps were insufficient, and that energetic action was necessary in order to assist our ally, who had been much more seriously damaged than at first had been supposed. He proposed to employ for this purpose the chief part of the 8th Army under Hindenburg's command.

General Ludendorff's suggestion was carried out. The 9th Army,[1] under the leadership of General Hindenburg, was formed, with General Ludendorff as Chief of the General Staff. Part of the Headquarters Staff of the 8th Army, including myself, was transferred to the Headquarters Staff of the 9th Army. General von Schubert undertook the command of the rest of the 8th Army,[2] which remained for the defence of East Prussia.

The task of the army that remained in East Prussia could naturally only be defensive. It was hoped that it would be able to hold the line Suwalki — Wylkowyszki, beyond the German frontier, that had been taken up after the battles near the Masurian Lakes. The last order given by the late Chief Command which I had taken to Wylkowyszki to General von François was at once to begin the construction of a fortified position beyond the German frontier.

General von François had at that time no great opinion of fortified positions. He believed that the task of keeping the Russians out of East Prussia would be better effected by a few offensive thrusts. The order to construct this position was not executed, and only the construction of the Angerapp position, which had been already begun, was continued.

---

[1] The Guard Reserve Corps.
  XI. A. C.
  XVII. A.C.
  XX. A.C. and the Main Reserves from Thorn and Posen, each with the strength of one Division.
[2] I. A.C.
  I. Reserve Corps.
  3rd Reserve Division.
  Goltz's Landwehr Division.
  Königsberg Main Reserve.
  1st Cavalry Division, as well as a few Landwehr Brigades.

There were several opinions about the way the
9th Army was to be employed. The High Command
had at first intended that it should make an offensive attack from East Prussia on Sielce, then that
the left wing should advance from Thorn along the
Vistula, towards Warsaw.

During the first weeks of the war an attack
through Sielce had been asked for several times by
Colonel-General Conrad von Hötzendorff. Such a
movement had played a considerable part in the
correspondence that General von Conrad had had
with General von Moltke before the war. Conrad
had alluded to it several times as the most effective
way of supporting the Austro-Hungarian offensive.
It was now too late. The condition of the Austrian
troops demanded immediate support. It was
necessary to fight with them shoulder to shoulder
at once.

Therefore the 9th Army received an order from
G.H.Q. to get as near to the north of Cracow as
they could.

The Headquarters of the Army went to Beuthen.

On September 18th General Ludendorff drove
to the Austrian Headquarters at Neu-Sandec in
order to consult with the Austrian Commander-
in-Chief, Archduke Friedrich, and the Chief of the
General Staff, Conrad von Hötzendorff, about the
operations that were to be executed. He received
a bad impression of the condition of the Allied
Army. Enormous Austrian losses in the battle of
Lemberg and on the subsequent retreat was the
only explanation he could find for the main body
of the Austrian Army, about seventy Divisions,
being crowded into the narrow space on the west
bank of the Visloka between the Carpathians and
the Vistula. A large number of the young officers
and of the not too numerous non-commissioned

officers had fallen—a loss that was irretrievable and from which the army never recovered during the whole war.

From Ludendorff's account of the interview I got the impression that they were of one mind about reassuming the offensive as soon as possible. For that purpose the 9th Army was to be reinforced by Woyrsch's Landwehr Corps and Dankl's 1st Austrian Army, which were already under its orders, as they would soon have to cross to the north bank of the Vistula. In Karl Friedrich Novak's book, *The Way to Disaster*, which is based upon communications and statements made by General von Conrad, this agreement is denied. General von Conrad's opinion was that at first they were to act on the defensive and together form a strong united front, and that an offensive movement could be gradually developed later. Although I greatly esteem General von Conrad's vast knowledge and eminent capacities as a leader I cannot share this opinion. The Russians had pursued the Austrians with all their forces as far as the San; only weaker forces had passed the San and surrounded Przemysl, but it was evident that this relief for the Austrians was only temporary and caused by the Russian difficulties in getting up reinforcements. It was essential to act quickly and to free the Austrian Army as soon as possible from being wedged in between the mountains and the Vistula. For this purpose the 9th Army had if possible to compel the Russians to draw off strong forces from the pursuing army and to bring them into action against the 9th Army. This was to be attained only by active measures—by an advance on the Vistula.

So far, there were in the Government of Warsaw —at least in that part of it where the operations of the 9th Army were likely to take place—only a few cavalry and Cossack regiments.

The High Command did not doubt for a moment that the 9th Army was strong enough to inflict a decisive defeat on the Russian Army opposed to the Austrians.

On September 27th the 9th Army was ready for operations.[1]

On September 29th the advance began on the line Opatov—Ostrowiec—Ilza—Radom—Tomaszov—Koliszki to the east of Lodz.

At first the enemy offered no resistance, small detachments of cavalry and Cossack sotnias retiring before our advance. For the time all the information of the bulk of the Russian Army that we had were some wireless messages we had intercepted, from which we learned that the Russian Chief Command had recalled three Army Corps. The messages were, however, so out of date that they could not be connected with our present advance; we supposed that these troops had been sent to support Rennenkampf's army when news had been received of the East Prussian disaster.

When the Russian Commander-in-Chief, the Grand Duke Nicolai Nicolaievich, saw that the 9th Army was advancing, he came to a bold decision: he recalled about fourteen Army Corps from the main body of the army that was fighting against the Austrians and had the troops sent partly by train and partly by road northwards across the Vistula. Then the smaller part of the army was to

---

[1] XI. A.C. close to Cracow on the north.
Guard Reserve Corps, XX. A.C., XVII. A.C., 35th Reserve Division (Thorn Main Reserve), between Kattowitz and Kreuzburg.
18th Landwehr Division (Posen Main Reserve) and 8th Cavalry Division between Kempen and Kalish.
35th Reserve Division, 18th Landwehr Division and 8th Cavalry Division united under the command of the Bavarian General, von Frommel, as Frommel's Corps.

cross the Vistula and attack the German Army in front, while the greater part of the army, reinforced by the Siberian Corps, that had been detrained about that time in and near Warsaw, was to make an outflanking attack on our army on the line Novogeorgievsk—Warsaw.

The idea was a good one. The Grand Duke had judged very rightly that it was necessary for him to get the 9th Army definitely out of action and then to settle with the Austrians. Of course, at that time, we did not know his plan; it was only by messages from the Russian wireless station, which continued to indicate to various Army Corps their positions, that we knew that considerable Russian forces were moving to the north of the Vistula.

The first effects of the Grand Duke's plan were very convenient for our allies; the Austrian troops were able to resume their march; they were able to advance satisfactorily, and on the 9th reached the San almost without any opposition and entered Przemysl.

Already on the 4th we had had a small engagement before Opatov with two Russian skirmishing Brigades that had been sent by the Russian Guard Corps across the Vistula as their advance-guard.

The Guard Reserve Corps, which by advancing farther east would have been in a position to cut off these two skirmishing Brigades, allowed itself to be misled into attacking the enemy's left wing too soon, which caused the skirmishing Brigade to make a rapid retreat.

Mackensen also had a small engagement with two Cossack Divisions near Radom.

In the meantime the High Command had realized that the Russians were withdrawing very large forces from the Austrian Front to bring them into action against the 9th Army. It was natural that at that time the whole extent of the operations that the Grand Duke Nicolai Nicolaievich intended was unknown to us. On the other hand it appeared, from the slight resistance that the Austrians had so far met with in their advance, that it might be possible by an energetic offensive to inflict a serious blow on the Russians, while the 9th Army would hold in check the Russian forces that opposed them on the Vistula by a containing action.

It was therefore of importance to find out what the position at Warsaw was, and at the same time to prevent the Russians from crossing the Vistula with large forces between Sandomir and Warsaw.

The 9th Army was to advance considerably more to the north, and to extend its line as well as the line of the 1st Austrian Army, which was under its command, so as to cover the whole front from the mouth of the San to Warsaw.

General von Mackensen, under whose command Frommel's Corps also was placed, received orders to march northwards straight from Radom on Warsaw.

As far as I can remember there were no reports at that time of the detraining of Siberian Army Corps at Warsaw, as General Ludendorff asserts in his *Reminiscences of the War*. On the contrary these very rumours said that Warsaw was full of sick and about 60,000 wounded from the battles in East Prussia.

On the right wing of the army the 38th Division of the XI. Army Corps was stationed at Annapol in support of Dankl's army and also in case of need to cross the Vistula later at Annapol—a good place for the purpose if the Austrian offensive succeeded in crossing the San and in advancing.

Another Russian advance-guard crossed the river at Novo-Alexandria and, being attacked by us, was forced to recross it.

A Brigade of the XX. Army Corps came upon enemy forces which had crossed the river north of Ivangorod at Koshenice. The Commander of the Brigade probably over-estimated the strength of the enemy that had already crossed the river and hesitated to attack, in consequence of which the Russians—Caucasian troops—succeeded in establishing themselves on the left bank of the Vistula and building a bridge. Notwithstanding all our efforts we were afterwards unable to drive the enemy, who fought with surprising bravery, from the left bank of the stream.

While marching on Warsaw, Mackensen's Corps, that had been reinforced, came upon the enemy —a party of Siberian skirmishers—at Grojec. After a sharp engagement they were defeated and forced to retire on Warsaw, pursued by Mackensen's Corps, which on the 12th took up a position close to Warsaw on the south.

After the battle of Grojec an Army Order and sketch was found on the body of a Russian officer which revealed to us the whole of the Russian plan.

Mackensen was then sharply attacked by the Siberian Corps from Warsaw. He repulsed these attacks.

The enemy again tried to cross the river at Kalvaria, south of Warsaw. He was forced to retire by the 37th Division of the XX. Army Corps. To the south of the 37th Division the other Division of the XX. Corps was stationed near the mouth of the Pilica. It was reinforced by an Austrian cavalry Division. In touch with them was the reinforced Guard Reserve Corps. It was stationed opposite Koshenice and Ivangorod and cut off the fortress.

However, we did not succeed, as has already been said, in forcing the III. Caucasian Corps to

recross the river at Koshenice. The weather was
horrible at that time. It rained unceasingly; it
was impossible to entrench in the saturated and
flooded ground of the Vistula lowlands. The trails
of the Russian gun-carriages were literally in the
Vistula, but the Caucasians had set foot on the left
bank and clung to it fast; moreover, they even
tried to gain more ground by constant attacks.
These attempts were not successful, as every attack
they made was driven back with great loss.

To the south of the Guard Reserve Corps
Woyrsch's Landwehr Corps was stationed opposite
the bridge-heads of Novo-Alexandria and Kasimierz.
At the last-named place the Russians also made an
attempt to cross the Vistula, but they were easily
prevented by the Landwehr Corps.

To the south of the Landwehr Corps stood the
main body of the XI. Army Corps.

Thus the Russians had been prevented from
crossing the Vistula, with the one exception of the
bridge-head of Koshenice; the Vistula was barricaded between the mouth of the San and Kalvaria
by the 9th Army, and the position on this portion
of the Front was in general secured.

It was now only a question of time for the Russians
to bring up more reinforcements, and by making an
enveloping attack on the Mackensen Group from
Novogeorgievsk and the south-west they could have
rolled up the whole front of the 9th Army—
which was indeed what the Grand Duke Nicolai
Nicolaievich had planned.

Mackensen had therefore to be reinforced, to
enable him to hold out until the Austrian Army
had been able to cross the San, and to achieve the
success that General von Conrad still hoped for.
The 1st Austro-Hungarian Army was at our disposal for that purpose. There were two possible

means of employing it: either the whole of the Austro-Hungarian 1st Army could be moved behind our front to the north and placed at the disposal of General von Mackensen, or it could be stationed on the Vistula, and thus release German troops, which could be shifted up to Mackensen.

This movement would naturally have required time, and as time pressed, the High Command was in favour of the first plan.

General von Dankl, who had gone with the Chief of his Operations Section, Lieutenant-Colonel von Waldstätten, to consult with the Army Command at Radom, declared, however, that he had received strict orders to allow his army to be employed only south of the Pilica. Nobody in the Army Command could understand the reason for this order. Telegrams were sent to the Austro-Hungarian High Command and also direct to the Emperor Franz Joseph, as well as through the intervention of the German Emperor, to beg him to annul that order, and to place the Dankl army unconditionally at the disposal of the Army Command. All our endeavours were, however, in vain; the Emperor Franz Joseph refused to intervene in the matter.

As an alternative, General von Dankl proposed that the High Command of the 9th Army should withdraw the German troops from Ivangorod, and he would advance his 1st Army to the south of Ivangorod, facing north. The Russians would then come out of Ivangorod and the Austro-Hungarian 1st Army would attack and defeat them. The High Command of the 9th Army would then be able first to dispatch the troops withdrawn from Ivangorod to Mackensen, and secondly, General von Dankl hoped that when he had beaten the Russians advancing from Ivangorod he would be able to obtain permission from his G.H.Q. to employ certain units of his Army to the north of the Pilica.

While General von Dankl was consulting with Field-Marshal von Hindenburg and General Ludendorff about these operations, Lieutenant-Colonel von Waldstätten and I were exchanging opinions on the same subject. I drew his attention to the two defects I found in the Austrian plan : first, it was not at all certain that the Russians would attack at once if we withdrew our troops from Ivangorod ; it might happen that the Austro-Hungarian Army would remain inactive, while Mackensen would be obliged to retreat owing to his left wing being outflanked. The second and more serious question was whether the Russians would not cross the Vistula with strong forces and that the 1st Austrian Army would not only not be successful but that, on the contrary, they would be defeated.

Unfortunately my fears proved to be correct.

In the meantime the danger that Mackensen's army would be attacked in flank increased. The troops of the 1st Austrian Army advanced but slowly ; the relief of the German troops on the Vistula took too much time, and the High Command found itself compelled to withdraw its left wing. This withdrawal was effected on the line Mrava—Skerniewice—Lowicz.

The Landwehr Corps was transferred to the line Novomjastov—Mrava.

It was then possible to assemble the XX., XI. and Guard Reserve Corps south of the Pilica. On the new front Mackensen's Group and the Landwehr Corps were to give battle to the pursuing Russian forces from Warsaw, while the above-named three Army Corps were to make a united thrust to the north. For the success of this action the conditions were that the position in the rear of these three

Corps should be secure: and, consequently, that the Austrian troops which had relieved the XI. Army Corps and the Landwehr Corps should maintain the defence of the Vistula, and that the main body of the Austro-Hungarian Army stationed south of Ivangorod should hold in check the Russians advancing from Ivangorod.

The danger for Mackensen's left wing had naturally not disappeared by this withdrawal; the Russians had strength enough to be able to envelop him by a simultaneous frontal attack. This danger had to be reckoned with as long as there was hope that the Austrian Army would defeat the Russians on the San.

Unfortunately this hope was not fulfilled. The Austrians did not succeed in crossing the San. On the contrary, in the night of the 17th to the 18th the Russians crossed the San and attacked the Austrian 7th Army.

In the night of the 18th to the 19th Mackensen began to retreat. He succeeded in reaching the above-mentioned position without any considerable loss of men or material.

On the 25th and 26th the 37th Infantry Division, the Landwehr Corps and the Mackensen Group on the line Novomjastov were attacked very vigorously. The attacks were repulsed, but Mackensen's left wing was forced back, and the Army Command found it necessary to recall to the south bank of the Pilica the 37th Infantry Division that was fighting at Novomjastov, as the position of the Division had become dangerous owing to the river being swollen by the rains and there being only one bridge behind them, which was exposed to the Russian artillery fire.

It was high time to act if the German troops that were stationed south of the Pilica were to

make their offensive thrust to the north, but the
first necessary condition, the safety of their rear,
had not been secured. The second alternative that
I had suggested to Lieutenant-Colonel von Waldstätten as possible had occurred. The Russians had
advanced with strong forces from Ivangorod and
their positions near Koshenice; the Austrians had
attacked and been defeated.

On the receipt of the first report that the advance
of the Austro-Hungarian Army had become difficult
and that the attack had failed, the Army Command
again ordered the Guard Reserve Corps to make an
attack in the direction of Koshenice, so as to
strengthen the left wing of the Austro-Hungarian
Army.

On the 27th, about 1 P.M., a lance-corporal of
our telephone section rang me up. During the
change of the Headquarters of our High Command
from Radom to Konskie he had remained with
a part of our telephone section in Radom. He
reported:

" I have just intercepted an Austrian Army
Order which I think will interest you. The 1st
Austrian Army is to begin a retirement at once,
but the German Guard Reserve Corps is not to be
informed of this until six o'clock this evening."

I was naturally furious. I rang up Lieutenant-
Colonel von Waldstätten, and gave him a bit of
my mind. My protestations succeeded at last in
obtaining the assurance that at least the left wing
Division of the 1st Army would remain in position until we were able, when it began to get
dark, to withdraw our Guard Reserve Corps, which
was now successfully advancing and about to
attack in support of the 1st Austro-Hungarian
Army.

In the meantime the XI. Corps was ordered to

move to the north of Lodz to strengthen Mackensen's left wing in that direction.

With the failure of the Austrian troops before Ivangorod the whole position had become untenable. It was probable that the retrograde movement would also affect the units of the Austro-Hungarian Army that were stationed farther south, and the 9th German Army would remain entirely unsupported. The 9th Army had also to retire, and to go back a considerable distance in order to attain the necessary power of action.

It has been asserted by Austrian writers, and by some German ones too, that the retreat of the Austro-Hungarian 1st Army was caused by the defeat of the German Army before Warsaw, which had therefore been obliged to commence a retreat. This is not correct, as I have shown above.

The cause of the failure of our attack on Warsaw was that the Austrian armies which were fighting south of the Vistula were unable to cross the San or to defeat the Russians, weakened as they were, owing to having been obliged to send certain units for the operations against the 9th Army.

Now the 9th Army had to endeavour to escape from the Russians without their being able to pursue them too soon. As has already been stated, the High Command was aware at the time of its advance that the 9th Army would not be strong enough to achieve decisive success if the Russians opposed us with considerably superior forces. Already during the advance preparations had been made for the destruction of railways and roads in the event of the 9th Army meeting with a reverse that might force it to retire.

The demolitions that had been arranged were now at the commencement of our retreat energetically carried into effect.

The retreat itself,[1] that had been ordered on the 27th, was carried out in perfect order and without any difficulties.

The Russians pursued us energetically along the whole Front. They also attacked East Prussia and our frontier defences near Mlava. The position was serious on the whole of the Eastern Front.

I quite agree with the opinion of our eminently capable Quartermaster-General, Privy Councillor Dr Keber, that the advance of a German Army must come to a standstill when it gets about a hundred kilometres from the railway. We calculated that by giving the Russians an additional twenty kilometres, in consequence, firstly, of their exceedingly modest requirements, and secondly, of their great want of consideration for their horses, and came to the conclusion that if we could succeed in destroying the railways so completely that it would require a long time to reconstruct them, we should be able to stop for a time the enemy advance, which was still on Russian soil, to the east of the German frontier. We reckoned on a halt of several days. This period the 9th Army would have at its disposal to begin new operations, and the time must be fully utilized.

Gradually the High Command came to the

---

[1] The following units retired:
   Guard Reserve Corps, XX. A.C., Landwehr Corps, to the district north of Cracow—north of Czestochova.
   XVII. A.C. and Frommel's Corps to Vielun.
   XI. A.C. south-west of Sieradz.
On the left wing were assembled:
   8th Cavalry Division.
   7th Austro-Hungarian Cavalry Troops Division that had been placed at our disposal, and also
   5th Cavalry Division that had been sent from the West.
General von Frommel took the command of these three Cavalry Divisions, and the command of the former Frommel Corps was given to the leader of the 18th Landwehr Division—General Count Bredow.
   The retreat of the Austro-Hungarian troops was carried out chiefly along both the banks of the Vistula towards Cracow. Weaker units retreated towards the Carpathians.

conclusion that such operations could only consist of a concentration of a large portion of the army in the district south of Thorn; the troops were to be transported by rail or to march there by road, and they were to be reinforced by troops sent from East Prussia or from the Western Front. They were to make an offensive thrust along the Vistula against the left wing and the left flank of the Russian Army that was in pursuit of the 9th Army in the direction of Silesia.

That this permanent destruction of the railways and roads was successful was largely owing to the energy and circumspection of a very able officer of the Bavarian General Staff, Captain Sperr, who from the first had been entrusted by General Ludendorff with the direction of these measures.

In the last days of October, General Ludendorff was summoned to Berlin for a consultation with General von Falkenhayn. And it was only there that the High Command became acquainted with the details of the events that had taken place in the Western seat of war.

CHAPTER VI

SCHLIEFFEN's original plan of operations was not carried out. He had intended that the left wing of the German attacking army should not advance, but, on the contrary, should retire to the line Metz —Strassburg and the fortifications of the Upper Rhine before a possible French attack.

I do not know if Count Schlieffen had afterwards changed his plan of advance in any way, or if the alterations had been made under the direction of his successor. On this point, only the two Chief Directors of Operations who succeeded him, the present Generals von Stein and Ludendorff, would be able to give any information. It is possible to suppose that the strengthening of the left wing of the German Army was resorted to for the following reasons. At the beginning of the advance any considerable accumulation of troops on the German right wing must have met with difficulties. It was awkward to move several armies one after the other without infringing the neutrality of Holland. It was only after the capture of Liège that there was room to move in Belgium and it was possible to send a second and third army to follow each other in echelon. If, at the beginning, a second and third army had been advanced in echelon on the right wing, it would have been quite possible during the first days of the campaign for these units to have been obliged to remain inactive on their place of deployment. It is therefore possible that the plan

64

was adopted (with a view also of making equal use of all the railway lines) of sending a part of the troops destined for the right wing first to the left wing. It was probable that in the first days of the campaign the French would attempt to re-capture Alsace and Lorraine by making an attack on those provinces. An early success in this direction would without doubt have greatly raised the spirits of France and the *morale* of the French Army. If this could have been prevented without interfering with the deployment of our own army, and our plans of attack, it would certainly have been a practical move. It was possible to do so if, as already mentioned, a part of the troops destined for the right wing had at first been sent to Alsace and Lorraine, where they would have repulsed the French advance; but then the troops would have at once had to be entrained and dispatched for their real destination, to take part in the offensive on the right wing. If these considerations were the causes of the weakening of the well-known Schlieffen plan, or if there were others, is, as I have already stated, unknown to me.

Judging by the conduct of German Great Headquarters, this seems not to have been the case, as the strong forces on the left wing were kept there permanently; they allowed the battle of Lorraine to be continued by an offensive action of the 6th and 7th Armies, and approved of the attempt to break through the French line of forti-fications on the Moselle. This was certainly a conscious alteration of Schlieffen's original plan. Schlieffen wanted the decision to be reached by a powerful attack on the right wing, which should outflank the French line of fortifications. If Count Schlieffen had considered that to break through the French line of defence on the Moselle was as easy as the Commander-in-Chief of the 6th Army, General Tappen, seems to imply in his work, *Until the Marne, 1914,* he would certainly have laid before the Kaiser another plan of operations, and would have avoided the breach of the neutrality of Belgium.

If Count Schlieffen's plan had been strictly followed, troops would have been taken from the left wing as soon as the Plan of Advance would have permitted it, and sent by railway or road to the right wing to follow it in echelon order. Only the right wing was in fact in any danger in the course of the operations; moreover, the right wing was to bring about the decision, and one of the chief principles of military science is that in a decisive action one can never be strong enough. Not only did the Highest Command not send reinforcements to the right wing, but on the contrary, during the further development of the operations, took away from the right wing the two Army Corps which they dispatched to the 8th Army in East Prussia without ever having been asked by it to do so.

When General Tappen writes that the reports received up to the 25th by Great Headquarters of the successes of all the armies had led them to suppose that the great decisive battle had already been fought in the West, and had resulted in the success of the German Army, this seems incomprehensible. Even if the armies had sent exaggerated reports of their successes—a general and natural occurrence in war—the small number of prisoners, the little booty that was taken, the condition of the railways and roads, the absence of any signs of the retreat of enemy forces, ought to have taught G.H.Q. a better lesson; and when the excuse is given that G.H.Q. was too far in the rear, and had to depend solely on the scanty reports from the armies, this certainly was their own fault; they ought to have moved in time to the rear of the right wing—or, if the whole apparatus was too large, at least the Operations Staff might have moved— and they ought to have been in constant touch, not only with the different Army Commands but, when necessary, with individual Corps Commands. This they could easily have done by means of liaison officers in motor-cars. They had plenty of officers and cars.

It is also incomprehensible that Lieutenant-Colonel Hentsch never received a written order for the mission on which he was sent, a mission that was of such vital importance for the fate of the whole German Army; surely Great Headquarters could have afforded to wait the ten minutes that a skilled officer of the General Staff would have needed to write such an order. However, the Hentsch mission has been sufficiently elucidated in the statement made by Lieutenant-Colonel Müller-Löbnitz. The question that Müller-Löbnitz raises in his statement remains of permanent interest : what would have happened if Field-Marshal von Kluck and General von Kuhl had refused to obey the order Lieutenant-Colonel Hentsch had brought them, and had insisted on the attack by the 1st Army which they considered right and meant to execute? If they had done so, perhaps they would have become the national heroes of the campaign.

The total of the above-mentioned errors and omissions of Great Headquarters led to the reverse of the Marne.

In place of Field-Marshal von Moltke, who had fallen ill, General von Falkenhayn was appointed Commander-in-Chief, and he had to decide how the operations of the German Army were to be carried on after the failure in the West.

He rightly decided that the first thing to be done was to stabilize the whole of the Front. But then he had to make a decision how the campaign was to be continued.

It is my opinion that there would still have been time to take up again the original Schlieffen plan. Ten Army Corps should have been transferred from the left wing to the right wing, and with these united forces an attack might again have been made. If in consequence of this transfer the position on the left wing had become for a time more difficult, if large portions of Alsace and Lorraine had passed temporarily into French hands, that must have been accepted as a necessary condition, and it might even have had a good influence on the sentiments of the populace.

In August 1916, when we were in Brest-Litovsk, General Ludendorff told me that General Gröner, who had been at that time in charge of the Field Railways, had suggested a similar idea to General von Falkenhayn, and he had even worked out a plan for the transfer by rail of six Army Corps from the left to the right wing. The suggestion was, however, rejected.

Great Headquarters had therefore definitely given up all idea of carrying out Schlieffen's plan.

Why was it, then, that Count Schlieffen arrived at the idea of moving the greater mass of the German troops to the West and seeking a decisive battle in that quarter? In the first place it was doubtless because here, at the very beginning of the war, he would come upon the newly deployed French Army, which would be obliged to accept battle and would not be able to escape him. During the first weeks of the war there would be no reason for a German attack on a large scale on the East Front. The mobilization and the deployment of the armies would take considerably longer, and the Russian troops that would first come into position could easily escape from a German attack by retiring into the endless depths of the Russian Empire, and without affecting the general position unfavourably by doing so.

It might have occurred to G.H.Q., if they felt themselves too weak to repeat an offensive on a large scale in the West, to try if it would not have been advisable to transfer the chief field of action to the East. The mobilization of the whole of the Russian Army was now complete. The question was only if in the near future the Russian Army would offer the possibilities for a great battle with the prospect of success for us.

Had it been decided to transfer the chief theatre of war to the East, it would have been necessary to release, as quickly as possible, troops in the West; and likewise to give up the useless fighting round Ypres and by strict orders to force the troops to construct positions. In this way, considerable forces would have been released, and it would have been possible to wait for an occasion that called for them on the Eastern seat of war. And the occasion appeared.

CHAPTER VII

THE SECOND CHANCE

I DO not know if General von Conrad offered the same advice and proposed that after the failure of the German offensive in the West the chief centre of the war should be transferred to the East, or if he asked General von Falkenhayn to send him local assistance only to aid the German and Austrian armies in extricating themselves from their difficult position in Poland. In any case the Chief of the Austrian General Staff had asked General von Falkenhayn to send strong forces to the East. General Ludendorff related on his return from Berlin that General von Falkenhayn had refused this request as he required these forces at Ypres.

In the meantime the position of the German Army on the Russian Front had become very serious. The 8th Army in East Prussia had fought with varying success against the Russian forces, and had till then been able to maintain its position on Russian soil. The High Command had sent in support of it the XXV. Army Corps, that had been formed according to plan, but which was subject to the same disability as the reinforcements sent to the West, being composed, on the one hand, of enthusiastically patriotic but quickly and insufficiently trained soldiers, and on the other, of old officers and non-commissioned officers who were physically no longer fit to support the fatigues of the campaign. Our Ministry of War also recognized

70

this organic defect, and later new units were formed on a different basis.

It was sad to see a part of our best youth sacrificed in this way, and a feeling of anger is aroused when one thinks how these young men, who were glowing with love for the Fatherland, went singing to a futile death at Ypres.

The 8th Army was also strengthened by new formations from the fortress of Königsberg. In the same manner Zastrow's Corps, about two Divisions strong, was formed in the neighbourhood of Soldau, out of the garrisons of the Vistula fortresses and the Landsturm.

With energetic vigour General Ludendorff drew from the Eastern fortresses all that could be extracted from them for the reinforcement of the 9th Army. From Posen, exclusive of the 18th Landwehr Division, which was already in the field, a whole Corps, under General von Koch, was obtained. That this was possible, and in so short a time, is thanks to the special services of Colonel Marquard, the Chief of the Staff at Posen, who, unfortunately, died too soon. The fortress of Thorn, whose Main Reserve, the 35th Reserve Division, was also already fighting in the open field, had to give up its 2nd Main Reserve, the so-called Westerhagen Brigade, that already, during the advance of the 9th Army on the Bshura, had been pushed forward, but during the retreat had been recalled to Thorn. Out of this Brigade the Dickhuth Corps was afterwards formed.

Like Posen, Breslau was also to provide a Corps, but here progress was very slow, and the requisite strength was never attained.

On the whole of the Eastern Front we had to expect fighting, as our retreat from Warsaw was naturally celebrated as a victory by the

Russians, and a great impulse was given to the whole of the Russian Army to make an energetic advance.

The Russians followed the 9th Army as quickly as the destroyed roads would allow. They attacked vigorously in East Prussia, and there was fighting also with Zastrow's Corps near Mlava.

General Ludendorff had not concealed from General von Falkenhayn the seriousness of the position, and had specially emphasized that, in his opinion, the Russians would now try to bring about the decisive battle of the campaign on the whole of their Front. It was urgently necessary, before all things, to have a single High Command on the Eastern Front in order to provide reinforcements for the weaker points, at least for the most important places. In consequence of his report the post of " Commander-in-Chief, Eastern Front," was created. On October 1st, H.M. the Kaiser appointed Field-Marshal von Hindenburg as Commander-in-Chief of all the fighting forces in the Eastern seat of war. General Ludendorff became Chief of the General Staff. As the senior officer on the General Staff I also went over to the newly formed Staff. General von Mackensen was appointed Commander-in-Chief of the 9th Army, and General Grünert became the Chief of his Staff. Lieutenant-Colonel Kundt was my successor.

In the meantime our calculations of how far the Russian Army would be able to follow us without a railway proved to be correct. At the distance of 120 kilometres from the railhead the Russian Corps wireless announced that they were unable to continue the pursuit.

The army had now a few days to reorganize before recommencing active operations.

In the meantime, after long consultations and deliberations, the plan for the new operations had gradually crystallized. It was decided that the left wing should advance from the direction of Thorn along the Vistula to encircle the right wing of the Russian Army that had followed us from Warsaw and to defeat it. The main body of the 9th Army was to be sent by rail and road towards the north, and to be strengthened as much as possible by forces sent from the 8th Army in East Prussia. In place of the 9th Army that had been transferred northwards other troops had to occupy their former front, otherwise the province of Silesia, with its mines, would be open to an invasion, if only a temporary one, by the Russians. Here Field-Marshal von Conrad came to our assistance.

This man of genius saw at once that an attack from Thorn was correct, and also the necessity of employing all the forces of the 9th Army in the undertaking. He declared he would assist with all the forces at his command. He transferred by railway the whole of the Böhm-Ermolli army from the Carpathians to replace the 9th Army in the neighbourhood north of Czestochova. If G.H.Q. had only shown a similar appreciation of the plans of operation formed by the Eastern Command it would most probably have been possible to strike a decisive blow at the Russian Army.

In the first place, it was very desirable that besides direct reinforcements for the advance from Thorn, Zastrow's Force, near Mlava, should be strengthened. If an offensive could be made from here at the same time as the attack from Thorn, even though with weaker forces, it would be possible to pin down at least the Russian troops stationed to the north of the Vistula and prevent them from taking part in the desired decisive battle south of the Vistula. Unfortunately the West placed only a few Cavalry Divisions at our disposal.[1]

The wish of the Commander-in-Chief to release all the units of the 9th Army could not be realized. The *morale* of the Austro-Hungarian Army was not over good, and General von Conrad was therefore of the opinion that it would be necessary to leave those German troops that were still in the neighbourhood of Czestochova if the Commander-in-Chief wished to have the co-operation of the Austro-Hungarian Army in the offensive north of the Vistula.

The Commander-in-Chief transferred his Headquarters to Posen on November 1st; the Command of the 9th Army took up its quarters in Hohensalza.

On November 10th the 9th Army was ready for operations.

In the meantime the Russians had continued their offensive in East Prussia and round Mlava.

[1] From the 8th Army the I. Reserve Corps, General von Morgen, and the XXV. Reserve Corps, Freiherr von Scheffer-Boyadel, were sent to Thorn. The last unit had unfortunately suffered very much in the previous fights in East Prussia, and came in a low condition and with an insufficient number of officers, so that it could not be looked upon as ready for action.

The XX. A.C. and Litzmann's 3rd Guard Division of the Guard Reserve Corps were sent by railway to the district south of Hohensalza, the XVII. A.C. to the district south of Gnesen.

In the same place were concentrated the Cavalry Corps of Richthofen, the 6th and 9th Cavalry Divisions.

The XI. A.C. advanced along the frontier in German territory in the neighbourhood of Wreschen.

South of this point, between the Prozna and the Warthe, Frommel's Cavalry Corps was stationed, in close touch with Novikov's Cavalry Corps.

Behind Frommel's Corps the Corps from Posen was advancing.

Farther south, Landsturm and the Breslau Corps, that was in process of formation, were stationed.

From Bielun up to south of Czestochova—Kamen stood the remaining part of the 9th Army under General von Woyrsch—viz.

35th Reserve Division.

Landwehr Division, Count Bredow.

The Landwehr Corps and the Guard Reserve Corps, except the 3rd Guards Division.

In the area north of Czestochova the army of Böhm-Ermolli was then squeezed in.

The 8th Army being weakened, by having had to give up two Corps, was unable to hold the German frontier. A change in the command had also taken place during this time. General von François, from personal reasons, had petitioned to be relieved from the command. General von Below, one of the most capable leaders of the war, succeeded him.

He led the army back to the fortified lines of the Masurian Lakes and the River Angerapp, and from thence repulsed every attack of the Russians. Zastrow's Corps was also obliged to retire to the positions on the line Soldau—Neidenburg. This line was retained.

The enemy had pursued us from Warsaw, and some part of his forces were stationed round Vloclavek, but his main body stretched from Sieradz through Novo-Radomsk to the area east of Cracow. He was unable to advance from that line owing to the disorganization of his communications, but we gathered from his wireless that he proposed to do so within the next few days. It was therefore high time for the 9th Army to begin operations.

At that time General Ludendorff applied again to G.H.Q., explained to them what good prospects of success the proposed operations presented, and requested General von Falkenhayn, by desisting from the attacks on Ypres, to put himself in a position to send reinforcements to the East. G.H.Q. promised reinforcements, but we only gradually received information as to the number of troops we could expect, or the time when they would be sent. Although it was very desirable to postpone the commencement of operations until these reinforcements arrived and then to deal a heavy blow with them, this proved impossible. As I have already mentioned, we had to expect a renewed Russian attack in a few days; the time that fate had given us to make preparations for the new operations had expired — we were obliged to act with the forces we had at our disposal.

The High Command ordered the advance for November 11th.[1]

The Russians were taken entirely by surprise. There was sharp fighting at Vloclavek, Kutno and Dombe, in which our troops remained victorious and drove the enemy back with heavy losses.

Then the left wing of the army was sent forward to make an enveloping attack on the Russian forces at Lodz. The Generals, Baron von Scheffer-Boyadel, Litzmann, von Scholtz and Baron von Richthofen, broke through the line Lodz—Lowicz and forced their way victoriously to the rear of the Russians in the district of Brzeziny, while Plüskow and Mackensen made a frontal attack and stormed Lodz. The left flank of the army was covered by General von Morgen with the I. Reserve Corps in the area north of Lowicz. At that place he had several engagements with the Russian forces which had advanced from the northern bank of the Vistula, they having crossed it at Novogeorgievsk and west of that town.

They advanced singly, and were defeated in turn by General von Morgen. However, in consequence of their attacks, General von Morgen was unable to reach Lowicz and the district south of it in time also to cover the outflanking movement against Warsaw.

---

[1] The following units were to advance:
  The Posen Corps on Sieradz—Lask.
  Frommel's Cavalry Corps north of Sieradz on Lodz.
  XI. A.C. via Kolo on Dombe.
  XVII. A.C. towards Lenczyca.
  XX. A.C. and 3rd Guard Division from the area south of Hohensalza towards Kutno.
  XXV. Reserve Corps and I. Reserve Corps via Vloclavek and south of Lowicz.
  The Breslau Corps was to join up to the south of the advancing army.

General Scheidemann, the Russian Commander at Lodz, sent constant reports by wireless of the desperate position he was in, but continued to defend himself furiously.

It was on the 18th — if my memory does not deceive me—that we intercepted a Russian wireless message that ordered the retreat of the Russian Army from Lodz. Instructions were at once given to the army to pursue; unfortunately it turned out otherwise : the Grand Duke Nicolai Nicolaievich annulled the order to retreat and ordered the army to remain where it was.

Plüskow's Corps, supposing that there was to be a pursuit, had advanced, and suddenly came upon advancing Russians and found itself in a very difficult position.

In the meantime the victorious outflanking wing of the army had reached the district south-west of Brzeziny, and turning westwards was preparing to advance in the rear of the enemy at Lodz. General Baron von Richthofen's cavalry had pushed forward almost as far as Piotrkov — Tomaszov. If the movement was not interrupted from the direction of Warsaw great things could be expected from it.

The Commander-in-Chief had warned the 9th Army very seriously of the danger that might be expected from Warsaw and had more than once advised that Litzmann's Guard Division should be left at Skiernewice. The High Command had probably hoped that General Morgen would have been able to push through to Lowicz sooner than he did and cover the attack on Warsaw. The enveloping wing also was instructed to secure itself against attacks from Warsaw at Skiernewice; apparently this order had been issued too late and it never reached the Commander of the enveloping troops. Headquarters was too far in the rear:

it had remained in Hohensalza instead of following the wing of its army that was to bring about a decision.

Thus at the moment we had hopes of a great success a serious reverse took place. Between the left wing of General von Scholtz's army and the forces that were advancing in the rear of the enemy, communications were suddenly broken; Russian troops had pushed in between them. At the same time the Russian leader succeeded in sending a new Division from Warsaw and through Skiernewice, which together with the troops that had remained there at the time of the German break-through now advanced on Brzeziny. Richthofen's Cavalry Corps, which was advancing from the south in support of Scheidemann's army, was driven back.

The XXV. Reserve Corps, the 3rd Guards Division and Richthofen's Cavalry Corps were cut off and surrounded by the Russians. The Russian wireless triumphantly announced the expected great success. The Russian Command was counting quite positively on the capture of these units. Orders were given by wireless for the preparation of some sixty empty trains for the transport of the hoped-for German prisoners, when in the night from the 24th to the 25th the German troops broke through victoriously to the north.

Every unbiased critic must unquestionably award the chief merit of this success to the Commander of the 3rd Guards Division, General Litzmann.

After having broken through the lines these troops took up positions in the front between von Scholtz's Corps and Morgen's Corps. The Commander-in-Chief had also the 1st Infantry Division of the 8th Army brought up from East Prussia. Notwithstanding the small number of his troops, General von Below gave them unhesitatingly. In this way a connected line was formed which the Russians vainly tried to break.

Although in this way greater misfortune was avoided, the great tactical success we had striven for was not attained.

Already in the middle of November the Austro-Hungarian Army, together with Woyrsch's Force, had begun an offensive to the south of our positions; in the beginning they progressed very well, but soon had to pause, and were brought to a standstill as soon as the Russians commenced a counter-attack.

From the beginning of December the promised reinforcements began to arrive from the West.[1]

These reinforcements did not arrive simultaneously but in detachments.

At the request of General von Conrad the 47th Reserve Division of Gerok's Corps was sent to the Austro-Hungarian Front, and took a prominent part in the splendid success at Limanova.

The arrival of these reinforcements gave the Front a new impulse to advance. Lodz was taken on December 6th, and the Russians were driven back beyond the sector of the Ravka and the Bshura.

I would like here to mention a small episode which I think is worth preserving in history, although it is not of a military nature. On the day Lodz was taken, the Chancellor of the Empire, von Bethmann-Hollweg, paid us a visit in Posen. After dinner the conversation turned on the question of

---

[1] III. Reserve Corps (General von Beseler) and XIII. A.C. (General von Fabeck) were brought into action on the left wing of the 9th Army.

II. A.C. (General von Linsingen) was stationed to the east of Sieradz.

XXIV. Reserve Corps (General von Gerok) reinforced the Breslau Corps.

peace, and especially how it could be attained.
Asked by the Chancellor for my opinion, I said that
in my belief the first condition, before peace could
even be talked of, would be for Germany to declare
publicly by the mouth of the Chancellor that we did
not want to keep a single square yard of Belgian
land, as England would never tolerate a German
Belgium and would fight to the bitter end to prevent
it. Besides, I thought an addition of Belgian subjects
to the Empire was not at all desirable for Germany.
The Chancellor replied: " You are the first soldier
from whom I have heard this opinion. I quite agree
with your point of view. But if I tried to express
it in Berlin, in the Reichstag, the storm of public
opinion would sweep me from my post." I felt
deeply affected by the thought that the Chancellor
of the German Empire could not dare to say something that he thought was right for the German
people from fear of being obliged to vacate his
Ministerial seat!

The Eastern Command has been blamed for
having sent to the Front the troops that came from
the West as they arrived; it is urged that it would
have been better to have brought them into action
all at the same time in order to attempt once more
the operation of outflanking the Russian Northern
wing. I do not think, after the moment of surprise
that had assisted us in our attack from Thorn was
passed, that we could have achieved much more,
while on the other hand, without the rapid reinforcement of the line as the troops arrived, many
points held by the 9th Army would have remained
in a somewhat critical position.

Naturally it would have been otherwise if G.H.Q.
had realized that the fortunes of war were offering them the possibility of giving the Russian

Army such an overpowering blow that it would never have been able to recover from it afterwards. If it had desisted at the proper time from the little fights round Ypres and had taken from thence, and from other points of the Front, troops for the East, and had decided to make a grand attack on that Front, there would have been a certain prospect of such a success.

Let us suppose that the arrival of reinforcements from the West had come in sufficient time, that they would have prevented the reaction at Brzeziny, and that the outflanking movement against Scheidmann's army had fully succeeded, the bulk of the Russian Army would have been squeezed together in the bend of the Vistula. The greatness of the Russian defeat could have been increased if, at the same time as the outflanking movement from Lodz was begun, an attack had been made towards Warsaw by several Army Corps from the direction of Mlava, on the other side of the Vistula. At that time the Russian Army Command would have sent all the stronger forces from the north bank of the Vistula to the south bank, to repulse the attack of the 9th Army. It had been possible for the Landsturm of Zastrow's Corps, strengthened only by the 2nd and 4th Cavalry Divisions, to penetrate as far as the line Ciechanow—Prasnysz. An advance of two or three strong Army Corps would have found it easy to reach Warsaw and the main Warsaw railway, which was the chief line of communication for the Russian Army. The results of such an operation are scarcely to be imagined. At that time the Chief of the Operations Staff, Colonel Tappen, while passing through, stopped at Posen, and I saw him in his railway compartment, where I implored him, almost on my knees, to persuade the Commander-in-Chief to put at our disposal, besides the promised reinforcements, at least two Army Corps more for such an attack from Mlava—Warsaw; but it was refused.

In my opinion the campaign in South Poland is the finest operation of the whole war; the dash from Cracow towards the Vistula to relieve our allies, the retreat on Czestochova, the throwing of the army from there to Thorn, and the renewed attack on the right wing of the fleeing Russians are, as operations, to be classed much higher than the plan for Tannenberg or any other of the victorious battles of the Eastern Front. It is lamentable that G.H.Q. lost the chance of allowing this fine operation for a decisive success to come to maturity.

Although the operations of the 9th Army and the Austro-Hungarian Army were not able to go as far as the Carpathians—that is, the decisive success was denied them which would perhaps have aroused in the Tsar the wish to approach the question of peace—still, they resulted in preventing the "Russian steam-roller" from entering Silesia and Posen, and eventually brought it to a standstill. The enemy was driven back into their well-known permanent positions, which they were never able to leave afterwards. Unfortunately parts of East Prussia had to be abandoned to the Russians.

General Boroevicz's attempts to come out of the passes of the Carpathians between Dunajec and San and press upon the Russians' Front soon had to stop, as the Russians again began to advance, and the chief point of their attack was directed against the left wing—*i.e.* against the passes of the Carpathians.

CHAPTER VIII

THE 9th Army in their permanent positions on the Ravka and the Bshura were continually engaged for several weeks, but in spite of this the Commander-in-Chief had a feeling of temporary quiet and relief.

The troops had an aversion to the construction of trenches and a war of position, and it required the whole of General Ludendorff's energy to get them under-ground; in any case the construction of fortified positions was sooner resorted to in the East than it was in the West.

After the construction of the positions it was possible to tak econsiderable forces from the Front of the 9th Army and to employ them in other ways. Some were used on the frontier of East Prussia, and others were sent to support our allies in the Carpathians.

Unpleasant news came at this time from Serbia. General Potiorek, deceived by his first successes, had allowed himself to be completely defeated by the Serbians.

The Russian High Command wished, by a great offensive against its two opponents, to bring the war to a decisive end in the spring of 1915. The number of its units that had now arrived at the theatre of war, and the enormous masses of thoroughly trained troops that it had at its disposal to fill up the gaps caused by losses, permitted it to attempt decisive battles at the same time in the north and in the south: in the south against the passes of the Carpathians, in the north against East and West Prussia.

General von Conrad had the intention of meeting the Russian attack by an offensive from his side, and at the same time to relieve the fortress of Przemysl that had again been surrounded after the Austrian retreat from the San; he brought up all the forces he could dispose of and formed a new army under General von Pflanzer-Baltin in the Bukovina, but at the same time he asked for German reinforcements. General Ludendorff was in favour of sending these reinforcements, even if they had to be sent by the Commander-in-Chief in the East. These reinforcements were formed of three new Divisions of the German Southern Army under General von Linsingen and dispatched into the neighbourhood of Munkacz, where four Austro-Hungarian Divisions also were placed under von Linsingen's orders.

General Ludendorff was sent to be the Chief of the General Staff of the new army for a time. The object of this measure was not very evident. The Southern Army already had a Chief of Staff in the person of General von Stoltzmann; General Ludendorff was placed above him as First Chief of the General Staff. The Army was too small for such a prodigality of Staff officers. It appeared to us on the Staff of the Commander-in-Chief that it was only done to separate General Ludendorff from General Hindenburg, who in the meantime had been appointed Field-Marshal, as these two personages had become as one in the mind of the populace. Field-Marshal von Hindenburg protested against being deprived of his Chief of Staff in a report he sent to H.M. the Kaiser, and succeeded in getting General Ludendorff back after a few weeks and before the beginning of the winter battles in the

Masurian district. During his absence I was entrusted with the business of Chief of the General Staff.

At first we naturally knew nothing of the Russian plans against the Germans; we only heard through various wireless messages and also by the reports of our agents of a " gigantic " plan for an offensive against East and West Prussia. It was not until later that the reports crystallized, and we learned that in the beginning of the year 1915 the Russians intended to make an outflanking attack from the north on East Prussia, while at the same time strong forces were to attack the weak German positions at Mlava and, entering from the south, penetrate into Prussia.

The Prussian Ministry of War was forming four new Army Corps within the country. The first new formations had taught it experience and these Corps were composed in a more practical manner. They were given a sufficiently strong parent unit of trained non-commissioned officers and men and an adequate staff of efficient officers. Unfortunately the number of such officers was already becoming scanty in the army. The first battles, especially in the West, had left enormous gaps in the effectives among lieutenants and captains, which could never be made good afterwards.

The Commander-in-Chief made it clear to G.H.Q. that he required the four new Corps to be placed at his disposal. On the one hand he was expecting the great Russian attack on East Prussia, and the forces he had would certainly be insufficient to meet it, and on the other hand East Prussia was demanding very justly to be released from the Russian occupation.

On the occasion of a short visit that the Minister of War and the Chief of the General Staff, von Falkenhayn, paid to Posen, I had the opportunity of repeating this pressing demand verbally and at the same time of explaining how the Commander-in-Chief proposed to employ these four Corps. It was planned that three of these Corps should be sent to the left wing of the 8th Army close to the south bank of the River Memel to envelop and roll up the free north wing of the Russian Army. At the same time the fourth Army Corps that was put at our disposal, reinforced by an Infantry Division from the 8th Army, was to break through the evidently weak left wing of the Russian Army south of the Masurian Lakes, or drive them back, and in this way outflank the Russian Army on both sides.

From our previous experience we could suppose that this offensive on our part would take the Russians quite by surprise, and it appeared certain that we would have a great success over the forces that were opposing the 8th Army, and the liberation of East Prussia would be the result. How the operations would afterwards develop I could naturally not foretell nor explain to the Chief of the General Staff. Even if the Russians were completely defeated, we were not strong enough to continue the operations against the fortified line Grodno—Kovno. On the other hand we might hope, after the Russians had been beaten by the envelopment of both their wings, that we should succeed in advancing southwards over the lines Grajevo—Augustovo, crossing the Bobr south of Augustovo and capturing the important fortress of Osoviec from the rear. The preliminary condition for the success of these operations was that we should hold the southern frontier of East Prussia, which till then was held only by the bulk of Zastrow's Corps and two Cavalry Divisions. Here the enemy had commenced the concentration of strong forces in preparation for his " gigantic " plan. In order to parry the expected attack we would have to send to the

Southern Army all the troops that the 9th Army could spare and bring them into action there.

I suggested to the Army Command that the newly formed army should be placed under the command of H.I.H. the Crown Prince. Unfortunately my suggestions were not adopted. On the contrary the Commander-in-Chief was told that three of the new Corps and the XXI. Army Corps that formed the 10th Army under the command of Field-Marshal von Eichhorn would be ready to be placed at his disposal in the first half of February for the operations that had been planned. One of the new Corps had been exchanged against the XXI. Corps, which was composed chiefly of Alsatian and Lorraine Reserves, as it was desired to transfer this Corps from the Western to the Eastern Front. I am unable to judge of the complaints that were raised in the West about the behaviour of the men of this Alsace-Lorraine Corps; in the East they fought as splendidly as our other Reserves.

General Ludendorff returned to Posen before the beginning of the battle and resumed his duties as Chief of the General Staff.

It was naturally important to conceal from the Russians the movement of the 9th Army towards the north [1] in order not to draw their attention on East Prussia too soon, and by so doing to render the surprise of the attack that was being prepared somewhat doubtful. The Commander-in-Chief was therefore glad to agree to a proposal made by G.H.Q. for the 9th Army to make an experiment with gas ammunition. G.H.Q. placed 18,000 shells at his disposal, a number that after the later experiences of the war would raise only

---

[1] XX. A.C. in the district south of Ortelsburg.
I. Reserve Corps and 6th Cavalry Division, near Willenberg.
3rd Infantry Division, near Neidenburg.
1st Guard Reserve Division, from Woyrsch's Force near Soldau.

a smile, but which at the time we considered very important. General Schabel arrived with this ammunition from G.H.Q. He was a great authority on artillery attacks on a large scale and in the use of gas shells.

The 9th Army proposed to make the attack at Bolymov, in order to improve the position at that place—that is to say, the Army Command cherished very extensive and optimistic hopes of the result, as General Schabel had represented the effects of the gas ammunition as very great indeed.

I arrived in Bolymov on the 31st, the day that had been chosen for the intended attack, and watched the fight from the belfry of the Bolymov church. I was a little disappointed; from what General Schabel had told me I had expected much greater results from the employment of this ammunition in—as we then imagined—such large quantities. That the chief effect of the gas was destroyed by great cold was not known at that time. The tactical success, with the exception of considerable losses that the Russians sustained in killed and wounded, was only a local improvement of our position; this affair, however, drew the attention of the Russian Front and Command to the 9th Army.

By the evening of February 6th the 8th and 10th Armies stood ready for the attack.[1] The

---

[1] From the 10th Army there were in the front line:

10th Landwehr Division, with its right wing north of Darkehmen: connected with them the Landwehr Division of Königsberg (formerly Main Reserve).

5th Guard Infantry Brigade, 1st Cavalry Division as far as the forests south of Memel. Behind them the XXXVIII. Reserve Corps, XXXIX. Reserve Corps, XXI. A.C., all three north of the highroad Insterburg—Gumbinnen.

South of the 10th was the 8th Army; XL. Reserve Corps and 2nd Infantry Division, between the frontier and the Spirding Lake; behind them the 4th Cavalry Division.

In the fortified positions of Lotzen, the 11th Landwehr Division and Landsturm.

On the Angerapp from Angerburg to Darkehmen, 1st Landwehr Division and 3rd Reserve Division.

Commander - in - Chief had removed his Headquarters to Insterburg.

The XX. Army Corps was still being detrained
at Ortelsburg; it was to defend the right flank of
the Reserve Corps, to march on Myscziniec and to
reconnoitre in the direction of the Narev. The
Commander-in-Chief also decided to carry on the
task of defending the flank by an offensive action.
The command of the forces that were stationed
between the Vistula and the Orzyc and the troops
that were still to be concentrated there was undertaken by the Commander of the Guard Reserve
Corps, General von Gallwitz.

On February 7th the Southern storm troops,
under General von Litzmann, commanding the
XL. Reserve Corps, began the attack on Johannisburg and the Pissa sector to the south of it; the
10th Army began only on the following day. The
front of the 10th Army had orders, as soon as any
signs of the enemy's retreat were observed, at once
to attack him, and keep close at his heels.

It was no easy matter to keep to these dispositions. For many days there had been a real East
Prussian snowstorm. Everywhere the snow lay
metre-high, and the cutting east wind drifted it
in places and formed high waves and walls; to
advance in close column was out of the question,
the artillery and the wagons remained sticking in
the snow.

The Russians did not notice what we were
planning. On the morning of the 7th, and also on
the 8th, the reports that came in were: " Position
of the enemy unchanged, everywhere he is seen
shovelling the snow out of the trenches."

Already, in the afternoon of the 7th, General
von Litzmann had crossed the Pissa to the south
of Johannisburg, on the 8th he took Johannisburg

and, having left troops to mask Osowiec, forced his way during the next few days as far as Raigorod. Here he met with strong Russian resistance, while at the same time the enemy made an attack from Osowiec.

Thanks to the bold but careful orders given by General von Litzmann, the enemy was defeated at Raigorod and the attack from Osowiec was driven back.

The advance of the 10th Army, that was begun early on the 8th, met with but slight resistance from the Russians. They were taken quite by surprise and, as always in the case of an outflanking movement, they sought safety in a rapid retreat. The retiring Russian right wing was soon joined by the centre. The 8th Army then took up the pursuit and followed close at the retreating Russians' heels. In those days the chief enemy of the 10th Army was not the Russians, but the weather; it was only with difficulty that the troops could work their way forwards. The columns of infantry were straggling, the bulk of the artillery and the vehicles remained sticking in the snow; only a few of the guns, to which twelve or eighteen horses were harnessed, and assisted by the infantry, were able to get on. Notwithstanding all these difficulties, in the night of the 10th-11th the columns of the 10th Army were able to reach the highroad to Kovno, not far from Wirballen and Stallupönen.

Besides a great number of prisoners—troops from the Russian Front that were retreating along the highroads and had been cut off—our troops captured large quantities of food, and all sorts of provisions, which were partly stored in depots and partly still unloaded and standing in railway trains. Only this enabled the units of the 10th Army to advance, as in the then state of the roads it would have been impossible to send supplies after the columns.

Although at the Front the commanders and the soldiers, to the last man, did all they could, the expected great success failed, owing to the physical impossibility of advancing quickly in such weather; large portions of the 10th Russian Army were able by retreating to get to a safe place before the circle could be closed around them.

On the 17th the pursuing 8th Army took Lyck, which was defended by the III. Siberian Corps. Unfortunately General von Litzmann was unable to advance quick enough, and the Corps escaped through Augustovo and took refuge beyond the Bobr, while Litzmann reached Augustovo only after hard fighting in the night of the 16th-17th.

The encircling columns of the 10th Army reached the approximate line Suvalki—Seiny on the 17th.

The Commander of the 10th Army still hoped, however, to be able to cut off considerable numbers of the enemy round Augustovo, and therefore issued orders for the further advance of the troops from the line Suvalki—Seiny.

In the meantime the weather had changed and the snow turned into impassable mud and floods.

The advance-guard of the XXI. Army Corps, which was advancing from Seiny in execution of the orders of the Commander of the 10th Army, who hoped to cut off the enemy near Augustovo, came upon strong Russian columns retreating along the highroad through the Augustovo forest. They were defeated and some prisoners taken.

The Commander of the 10th Army, then realizing that it had become impossible to overtake the enemy near Augustovo, came to the bold decision of sending strong units of his left wing along the outskirts of the Augustovo forest as far as the district north-west of Grodno, and to cut off the enemy when he issued from the forest, without paying any regard to the Grodno fortress.

The advance-guard of the 8th Army which reached Augustovo had already received reports of the concentration of strong Russian forces around Lomza.

Two Divisions were taken from the 8th Army, which had become congested as it advanced, and sent against Osowiec. One reason for this was that we wished to prevent enemy forces from issuing from Osowiec, and another was that an attempt should be made to take it, as the Commander-in-Chief still entertained hopes that the XL. Reserve Corps, during the further development of the operations, would succeed in crossing the Upper Bobr and in opening the outer fort from the rear.

The position of the troops of the 10th Army which were sent to cut off the Russian forces coming through the Augustovo forest, west of Grodno, was precarious, as on the one side the XX. Russian Army Corps, which found itself cut off in the forest, continued to make desperate efforts to break through, while from the other side the Russians in Grodno, where fresh troops had arrived, made constant sorties to assist their comrades who were shut in to find a way out. But all the attacks from the East and the West were repulsed, and at last the Russian troops that were shut up in the forest had to surrender.

However gratifying it was to have defeated the 10th Russian Army, to have captured more than 100,000 prisoners, to have taken more than 100 guns and quantities of provisions, we did not succeed in carrying out the operations to the desired end, nor in attaining the full strategic advantages we had looked for. General von Litzmann was not able to cross the Bobr. The country was very difficult to negotiate : the thaw, to which was now added constant rain, had turned the Bobr lowlands into a swamp; on the high banks the III. Siberian Corps was stationed in fortified positions—the troops said they were of "concrete." I did not believe in the "concrete," but my belief was not sufficient to discredit the soldiers' conviction, and we were therefore obliged to give up the attempt to cross the Bobr. A year later, on the occasion of a reconnaissance, I was able to satisfy myself that I had been right, and that there were no traces of concrete to be seen.

Notwithstanding the participation of heavy artillery, the frontal attack on Osowiec had no success.

Already on the day before, while the Commander-in-Chief had still hopes of the progress of the operations on the other side of the Bobr, General Ludendorff had ordered the construction of a position in the rear on the lines east of Augustovo, east of Suwalki—Niemen.

The 10th Army now received an order to withdraw its right wing into this position. The left wing was allowed free action. At the same time it received orders to release forces that were urgently needed farther west.

Although by the offensive of our 8th and 10th Armies we had destroyed the first half of the "gigantic" plan of the Russian High Command —the outflanking of the German Army to the north in East Prussia—the execution of the second half, the advance of strong forces against the southern frontier of East and West Prussia, began to make itself felt.

The 10th Army decided to withdraw its left wing only in the district of Seiny and north of that place, and to attack the Russians there if they attempted to pursue. The Army Command hoped to repeat the tactics of the winter battle on a smaller scale.

However, the Russians followed up only hesitatingly, and retired if we attempted to attack. The High Command therefore decided to give up the idea of attacking and withdraw the left wing to the line Kalvaria—Mariampol—Pilviszki. During March the Russians attacked these positions, but were repulsed with ease.

At the beginning of the attack of the XL. Reserve Corps, the XX. Army Corps and the 37th Infantry Division went by way of Myszeziniec, with the 41st Infantry Division by way of Kolno, towards Lomza, in order to cover the flank of General Litzmann's attack. The Corps came upon strong enemy forces, and its strength only sufficed to cover the flank eastwards as far as Staviszki.

In the space between Staviszki and the Bobr, the 3rd Reserve Division and the 5th Infantry Brigade were now brought into the line.

The above-mentioned units arrived just in time to meet an attack of the Russian Guards Corps and the V. Army Corps from Lomza. A desperate struggle ensued; the Russians attacked bravely, regardless of losses, and the 3rd Reserve Division was able to maintain its position only with the greatest difficulty. Not until the beginning of March was it possible to send the 1st Landwehr Division there, and thus to give to that Front the necessary strength and density.

Similar furious attacks were made on the line Ostrolenka—Novgorod against the 37th Infantry Division, which was holding the line south of Myszeziniec between the Orzic and the Pissa.

The Commander-in-Chief found himself obliged

to send more and more troops to its assistance,[1] the vast extent of forest and bogland unfortunately obliging him to do so.

Fighting continued here during the whole of March, but the German troops were able to hold out.

In the middle of February the Russians had received reinforcements to the west of the Orzic, opposite the Gallwitz sector, and they began to advance towards Mlava.

When the reinforcements from the 9th Army had arrived, General von der Gallwitz decided to anticipate the Russian attack, and to make a thrust into their main body.

The attack that was begun on February 22nd by the I. Reserve Corps, the 3rd Division Landwehr and Landsturm, under General von Morgen, progressed at first successfully. General von Förster's Division even succeeded in taking Prasznicz; but then the tide turned. One of the Landwehr Brigades failed us. Strong Russian forces pressed forward from the south on Prasznicz, and tried to outflank us from the Orzic.

With their flank menaced, the I. Reserve Corps and the 3rd Division had to give up Prasznicz and to retreat. Farther south, where the frontier positions were still being constructed, General von Ludendorff stopped the troops. In the first week of March the Russians made bitter attacks on our positions between Mlava and the Orzic, but they were all repulsed.

After the arrival of the reinforcements, General von der Gallwitz began an advance on March 8th,

---

[1] 2nd Infantry Division.
75th Reserve Division.
10th Landwehr Division.
4th Cavalry Division.
And later, 76th Reserve Division.

on both sides of the Orzic; by the 12th he had
succeeded in driving the enemy back to the north
of Prasznicz. Here again there were strong
Russian counter-attacks, which although they were
unsuccessful brought our advance to a standstill.

The fighting continued till the end of March,
and then grew gradually weaker.

By April the Russian attacks had been repulsed
along the whole of the Prussian Southern Front,
and thus the second part of the Grand Duke Nicolai
Nicolaievich's " gigantic " plan came to an end.

Our Austro-Hungarian ally did not succeed in
carrying out his plans so successfully. The offensive
for the relief of Przemysl had to be stopped as soon
as the Russians began a counter-attack. The fate
of Przemysl was sealed.

From the middle of February casual fighting began
in the corner of East Prussia north of the Memel.
The Russians had still frontier-guard detachments
on German territory north-east of Tilsit.

The Commander-in-Chief naturally desired to
clear this corner of German soil of the enemy.
General von Pappritz, the Governor of Königsberg,
was given the order to do so; his Chief of Staff
was Colonel Nehbel. He had at his disposal only
the Landsturm that served as frontier guards and a
little artillery from Königsberg. Nevertheless, the
offensive succeeded. By February the enemy was
driven across the frontier and Tauroggen was taken.

The satisfaction we felt at having freed the whole
of German territory from the enemy was of short
duration.

On March 17th Memel was attacked by a small
body of frontier guards and territorials, under the
command of General Potapov. The attack took
us by surprise; reports had been received of the

concentration of Russian troops opposite Tauroggen and Memel, but they were not considered of much importance; it must not be forgotten that alarming reports of concentrations of troops and some sort of enemy attack were received in dozens every day, and it was not necessary to give credence to every report that came in.

More accurate news of the entry of the Russians into Memel came from the telephone girl of the Memel post office, Fräulein Röstel. She displayed more energy than her male colleagues, and spoke with me until the post office was occupied by the Russians. Our conversation was closed on her side with the words: "They are just coming up the stairs."

At the same time that Memel was surprised the Russians also attacked Tauroggen, and General von Pappritz was forced to give it up, as he required all his weak forces against Memel and the enemy who was there. The Commander-in-Chief had no sort of Reserves at his disposal to send as reinforcements to General von Pappritz. The Command of the II. Army Corps in Stettin sent us two *Ersatz* battalions.

We had luck: the Russians themselves were not strong. They evacuated Memel when Pappritz approached the town, and we succeeded in recapturing 3000 prisoners they were carrying off. Pappritz then turned against the enemy at Tauroggen, drove him over the frontier, and retook Tauroggen on March 29th.

Something had to be done to prevent such a surprise being repeated. The 6th Cavalry Division, which for the time was not needed on Gallwitz's Front, was transferred to the district east of Memel.

In the middle of April the situation on the Eastern Front was pretty well quiet.

CHAPTER IX

In the meantime the situation had not developed in a very satisfactory manner in the southern theatre of war.

As has already been mentioned, the attack on the Carpathian Front that General von Conrad had decided to make had not been successful. At the very outset it met with a Russian counter-offensive and was stopped. The more the Russian High Command became convinced that their plans against East Prussia and the German Army would not succeed, the stronger their attacks became against the Austro-Hungarian troops. This spring they wanted to bring about a decisive battle, regardless of what it might cost them in men.

There were fierce and bloody battles between the Carpathian ridges in the midst of snow and ice, which, although they caused the Russians unheard-of losses, drove our allies slowly back. The position of the Austro-Hungarian Army became very critical. If the Russians succeeded in breaking through the line, and passing over the Carpathians into the plains of Hungary, the Dual Monarchy would be broken up. Germany was obliged to do something energetic to support her allies.

Captain von Fleischmann, the Austro-Hungarian liaison officer, told us every day in the office of the Headquarters Staff, when he made his report, that the situation was very grave, and each day he repeated it with more and more emphasis. The

Commander-in-Chief was of the same opinion, and he represented the matter to G.H.Q. From his own forces the Commander-in-Chief sent a Division acting as Reserve to the 9th Army. It reached the Carpathians in the middle of April, at a very critical moment, just when Boroevic's army was beginning to waver. G.H.Q. approved of the dispatch of this Division (25th Reserve Division) and they ordered two other Divisions to be sent as reinforcements to the Carpathian Front, and the Staff of the XXXVIII. Reserve Corps was also to proceed to that Front. General von der Marwitz was appointed commander of this newly formed Beskiden Corps by order of G.H.Q. The Commander-in-Chief gave up these four Divisions, and also a newly formed Division.

G.H.Q. had begun shortly before this time to take from each of the Divisions on the Western Front one infantry regiment, and to form new Divisions out of the regiments obtained in this way. They gained in this way a large number of tactical units. It was possible in a war of positions for each Division to give up three battalions, as new positions continued to be built. This inspired idea originated with General von Wrisberg, of the War Office. Later on, before the end of the war, a dispute arose between the different military authorities as to whether it was more practical to keep the Divisions at nine battalions or to raise them to twelve battalions as before. The smaller Divisions had the advantage of being easier to control, but the disadvantage for some purposes of being too weak in infantry. For Germany no decision could be arrived at on this disputed question, as by the fatal Decree of Versailles our fine army was doomed to dissolution, and all such controversial questions that arose out of the experiences of the war have now only an academic interest for us.

About this time we, in the East, began also to re-form our Divisions in this manner.

The German reinforcements that were sent to the Carpathians were unable to produce a sudden change; they were only able to hold the position. But it was not only in the Carpathians but on all the Fronts that the position of the Allied Monarchies became more and more serious.

The Serbian Army began to move, and the chief thing was that it became more certain every week that Italy would openly join the alliance against us. I leave it an open question whether it would have been possible, through sacrifices made by Austro-Hungary and adroit negotiations on the part of the Central Powers, to have persuaded Italy to maintain her neutrality; in any case, the Austrian High Command found themselves obliged to reinforce the garrisons along the Italian frontier if they did not wish to be taken quite by surprise, in a military sense, if Italy joined the war. They were obliged to take these reinforcements from the Russian Front, which was already weak.

If the German G.H.Q. had followed the suggestion of the Commander-in-Chief on the Eastern Front, and had sent to the East, in the late autumn of 1914, the reinforcements that were necessary in order to defeat decisively the main Russian forces then wedged in behind a bend of the Vistula, all these difficulties would have been avoided. Thus, lost opportunities are a phenomenon of this war that we shall often have to notice. The right thing is suggested at the right moment, when success can be achieved with but a comparatively small employment of force, but the suggestion is set aside; then enemy movements take place that oblige G.H.Q. to send more reinforcements than had previously been asked for: with only this difference, that the forces now no longer serve to gain a decisive victory but only to retrieve a reverse that has occurred in the meantime.

Some time previously, General von Conrad had already suggested to General von Falkenhayn, in a personal conversation, the idea of breaking through the Russian Front at Gorlice, and so rolling up the Russian forces standing before the Carpathian passes. The plan was the only one that then offered any hope of clearing the Carpathian Front in time; naturally it was desirable to make the thrust at one of the wings and to outflank the Russian Army in this way. The outflanking attack is always the most effective. It was, however, impossible to begin the operations against the Russian wing in the Bukovina. The Austro-Hungarian railways were so untrustworthy that it was quite out of the question to rely on them for moving large bodies of troops.

It was quite possible to attack the Russian northern wing by an outflanking movement, to take Kovno, and to make a strong thrust in the direction of Kovno—Vilna. The plan offered good prospects of success. This operation would, however, have taken a long time before its effects could have been felt on the Russian left wing in the Carpathians. Therefore to break through the Russian line at Gorlice was a much better idea. General von Falkenhayn had acknowledged this to General von Conrad at a consultation they had had together in the Hôtel Adlon, in Berlin, but had refused to place at his disposal the forces necessary for the execution of this plan.

Now, however, General von Falkenhayn realized that something had to be done to prevent a complete breakdown of the Austro-Hungarian Front in the Carpathians. The number of German troops that General von Conrad would have required for this defensive action was nearly as large as would have been required if the offensive solution of the position had been adopted. General von Falkenhayn reverted to General von Conrad's plan of breaking through at Gorlice.

In his book, General von Falkenhayn is silent about the originator of the idea.

During the campaign we often had occasion to complain of the deficiencies of the Austro-Hungarian Army; we ought therefore all the more to acknowledge the help that we received from our ally. The ideas of the Chief of the Austrian General Staff were good—at least as far as they became known to me—they were all good, and this cannot always be said of the ideas of our own Commander-in-Chief. The misfortune of that man of genius was that he had not the proper instrument by which he could transform his ideas into facts. The troops failed; while with us, on the contrary, whether they were well or badly led, they never failed—until the summer of 1918.

The decision of G.H.Q. at last to try to obtain a decisive result in the East must be acknowledged, as it was to be expected that this attack on the Russians would produce attacks in the West to relieve the pressure. The great French attack in Champagne in February and March had indeed been repulsed, but it had cost us dearly. It was necessary to be prepared to meet similar attempts to break through, possibly on a large scale.

The command of the 11th Army that was appointed to effect the break-through was given to General von Mackensen, and the Chief of his Staff was Colonel von Seekt; the place of General von Mackensen was taken by Field-Marshal Prince Leopold of Bavaria, who had been waiting impatiently at home for an appointment at the Front, and he willingly placed himself under Field-Marshal von Hindenburg, though Hindenburg was junior to him in the service.

In order to mask the preparations that were being made for the attack on Gorlice, and to draw the attention of the enemy off this point, the Commander-in-Chief was ordered to make demonstrations on his Front so as to attract as many enemy forces as possible and pin them down there.

In accordance with the instructions received from G.H.Q., the Commander-in-Chief decided to attack the enemy at three different points. A gas attack was to be made by the 9th Army; the 10th Army was to make a local attack at Suwalki, in order to improve its positions; and, lastly, we planned a greater invasion of Northern Lithuania and Kurland. While the first two attacks were of only local importance, we expected that the last one would have great results, as the Russians would be obliged to take measures on a large scale to repel it.

For the execution of the gas attack one of the newly formed Gas Battalions had been sent us some time before; by reconnoitring, a place in the neighbourhood of Skiernewice had been found that was favourable for such an attack, and the cylinders for the emission of the gas had been dug into the ground at that place. The preparations had all been made at that time, and the 9th Army was waiting only for a favourable wind.

I am not greatly in favour of gas warfare : there were but few places on the Front that were suitable for it; the digging in of the apparatus was very complicated, and at any moment there was the danger of the enemy noticing the work of digging in and by strong artillery fire destroying the apparatus, and the gas would then stream out in our own trenches. Besides this, the weather conditions of our theatre of war were very unfavourable for such gas attacks; in the East we required a west wind— in the West an east wind, but as on our Front the wind was mostly contrary, the employment of this invention was rendered still more difficult. The hope on the German side that our opponents would not be able to imitate this process was also not realized. Later on I was able to ask the clever inventor of our gas substance, Geheimrat Haber, how he had come to devise such an unlucky process. He explained to me that he had foreseen all these defects, and from the first he had considered it would have been better not to emit the gas, but to use it in the form of gas shells; but at the begin- ning he was not given space enough to make this ammunition. It was only for this reason that he had thought of emitting it from cylinders.

It is very much to be regretted that this idea of Geheimrat Haber was not carried out from the beginning. If his scheme had been properly taken up from the first, and a large quantity of ammuni- tion filled with gas substance had been secretly prepared; if at some great fight to break through the line in the West it had suddenly been employed —at a time when the enemy still knew nothing of the danger of gas attacks, and gas-masks had not been introduced—then it would have had a success beyond all description.

On May 2nd, the wind being favourable, the 9th Army made an attack with gas. We heard later that its success in the Russian positions was very great; unfortunately this was not realized by our troops. The soldiers believed that the enemy would be entirely destroyed after the gas cloud had passed over their positions; when our infantry advanced and were shot at from several places, it was thought that the gas attack had not succeeded, and the advance was given up. A later attempt with gas also made by the 9th Army was likewise not calculated to increase the confidence of the troops. This time gas had only just been emitted when the wind veered round and a part of the gas cloud was blown back into our own trenches and we had considerable losses. The troops in the East were not provided with gas-masks until much later than the Western Army, as was always the case with everything.

The attack made by the 10th Army had the desired tactical success—a slight improvement of the position. Further attempts of the 9th and 10th Armies succeeded in attracting the attention of the Russians to them : they did not succeed, however, in fulfilling the commission that G.H.Q. had given to the Commander-in-Chief in the East—of obliging the Russians to concentrate large forces on that Front. We were only able to secure this by attacks in North Lithuania and Kurland.

The direct impulse to this attack was given by G.H.Q. In the second half of March they inquired of the Commander-in-Chief if he considered a cavalry raid from his left wing, in the direction of Kovno perhaps, as possible. As he answered in the affirmative, G.H.Q. sent him two cavalry Divisions from the West for the execution of this raid. They arrived about the middle of April.

On April 26th we were ready for the undertaking.[1]

On April 27th, General von Lauenstein began to advance with these units from the line Jurborg—

---

[1] The troops employed were :
  Bavarian Cavalry Division and 3rd Cavalry Division south of Jurborg. Behind them, 36th Reserve Division.
  78th Reserve Division on the Tauroggen highroad.
  6th Cavalry Division and 3rd Reserve Division in the Memel area.

Memel, for the attack on Kurland.   He drove the weaker Russian forces back and reached Schaulen in a single dash.   The Russians sent reinforcements, and fighting began on the line from the River Dubissa—Schaulen—Mosheiki, that obliged us also to send reinforcements.   From them and Lauenstein's original group, the Niemen Army, under the command of General von Below, was formed later.   In place of General von Below, General von Scholtz undertook the command of the 8th Army.

In the severe fighting that took place in the months of May and June we were able to maintain our positions on the Dubissa, and our left wing was able to hold the Windau.   Owing to Russian superior forces we were obliged to give up Schaulen.

On our extreme left wing the small fortress of Libau was taken by a surprise attack on May 7th. The 3rd Cavalry Brigade, as well as a small party of Landsturm and artillery from Königsberg, took part in this lucky undertaking.   The attack was led by Colonel von der Schulenburg and a very capable officer of the General Staff, Captain von Willisen, who was afterwards often mentioned in dispatches.

On May 2nd the 11th German Army and the Austro-Hungarian Army, under the command of General von Mackensen, took Tarnov, the first Russian position near Gorlice.   In the following days Mackensen stormed the second and third lines and forced the whole of the Russian Front in the Carpathians to retire.

On May 15th the 11th Army reached the San.

In the beginning of June Przemysl was taken.

After a short pause on the San the attack was continued, and on June 22nd Lemberg fell.

Ravaruska was stormed and the Russians were driven back towards the Bug.

At each of these stages Falkenhayn wanted to stop the advance and break off the operation. Each time it was only thanks to Conrad's insistence that he was induced to allow the advance to be continued.

On our Front the Russian defeat made itself felt also, as everywhere the Russians were bringing up forces in order to dispatch them to the south.

The Commander-in Chief was not strong enough to prevent it; all he could do was to bring up forces too, and to hold them in readiness for a new operation. The question was only where they could best be employed.

Our discussions at Headquarters on this subject often became very lively. From the beginning I supported the opinion that we had now perhaps for the last time the possibility of dealing the Russian Army an overwhelming blow. General von Mackensen's offensive would gradually wear itself out, as he had always to make frontal attacks : the continuation of his advance could never result in an overwhelming blow for the Russian Army. The only enemy wing which was still open to our attacks on the whole of the Continent was the right Russian wing that lay opposite the army of the Commander-in-Chief. Against this wing a large outflanking operation ought to be made to the north or the north-east, so that the middle of the Russian line which was still before Warsaw on the Ravka and the Bshura would not be able to escape the blow by retiring, but would be cut off.

I therefore supported the opinion that all the forces that the Commander-in-Chief could spare from the area under his orders, as well as all the troops that could be obtained from G.H.Q., should be brought into action on the left wing of the 10th Army. Kovno should be taken in the shortest time

possible and the offensive carried through Vilna to
the rear of the chief Russian forces.

It is still my opinion that, if these operations had
been carried out, the results would have been most
satisfactory, and would have led to the complete
defeat of the Russian Army.

Major von Bockelberg, who enjoyed the special
confidence of General Ludendorff, from having
worked together with him for many years in the
Second Division of the Great General Staff, pleaded
—of course not in official reports, which he had no
right to make, but in private conversations—for an
offensive across the Bobr on both sides of Osowiec.
I considered an offensive across the swampy lowlands of the Bohr, where we would be quite unable
to assist the attacks of our infantry with the bulk of
our artillery, was wrong, and that such an attempt
would be doomed to failure from the very beginning.
His chief objection to my plan was that the capture
of Kovno would take too much time. Later events
proved that I was right; in August we took Kovno,
if not in opposition to the wishes of G.H.Q. at least
without much support from them, in ten days. If
the plan that I proposed had been carried out,
this time even might have been shortened by a
few days.

General Ludendorff was of my opinion.

We were all of the opinion that an offensive
against the sector of the Front west of Lomza would
be useless. By such an attack we would naturally
be able to force the Russians to give up their positions in the centre, and to evacuate Warsaw; but
it would never bring about a decisive defeat. If
we made the attack so far to the west the Russians
could easily draw in the outer curve of their
Front to form a straight line, and we would soon
be doing exactly what Mackensen was doing in

the south: making a frontal advance as the enemy retired.

The preparations for the advance on Kovno and beyond were begun. The orders, as far as concerned the replacement of troops in the area under the Commander-in-Chief on the Eastern Front, were already planned out, when Field-Marshal von Hindenburg and General Ludendorff were ordered by telegraph to make a report to H.M. the Kaiser in Posen on July 1st.

General Ludendorff and I did not doubt that His Majesty would approve of the plan to make an attack on Kovno; General Ludendorff arranged with me that immediately after the audience he would ring me up, and that then I was to send out the orders that were already prepared.

I waited in vain for the telephone call.

It was only in the afternoon that I received instructions to stop everything; it turned out otherwise than we had expected. His Majesty while in Posen had approved of General von Falkenhayn's plan, by which General von Gallwitz was to break through the Russian Front opposite his positions, and make an attack towards the Narev. By this move, in my opinion, the last possibility of making a destructive attack on the Russian Army was lost. This Gallwitz attack might be as successful as it could be, but it could only result in the Russians having to give up Warsaw and their salient positions in Poland.

The 12th Army[1]—the former Gallwitz Group

[1] I. A.C. (2nd and 37th Infantry Divisions).
XII. A.C. (3rd and 26th Infantry Divisions and 4th Guard Reserve Division).
XVII. A.C. (35th and 36th Infantry Divisions and 1st Guard Reserve Division).
XI. A.C. (38th Infantry Division and Wernitz Division).
XVII. Reserve Corps (Landwehr Division von Breughel and 14th Landwehr Division).
Dickhuth Corps.

—was quite ready on July 13th for the attack on Prasznicz and the enemy positions on both sides of that place.

Thanks to exemplary Staff work the attack succeeded perfectly. The army broke through the Russian positions and reached the Narev on the 17th. Here there was naturally a certain pause. Pultusk and Rozan were taken on July 23rd; Ostrolenka on August 4th, and the river was crossed on a broad front. The right wing turned towards Novogeorgievsk and Zegrze.

The 8th Army had likewise begun to advance, and after severe fighting had also reached the Narev, where it met with stubborn resistance from the Russians. The object of this fierce resistance of the 12th and 8th Armies was naturally only to give the Russian troops time to retire from the Warsaw salient.

As we had expected, as soon as the Russian High Command realized that the break-through of the 12th Army was not to be resisted it had given orders for the evacuation of Poland.

The Russians stationed opposite Woyrsch's Group and the 9th Army were already considerably weakened by the forces that they had had to send to the south. Both armies now began to attack. The Woyrsch Group met strong rear-guard detachments on the Ilshanka and at Radom, which it defeated and drove beyond the Vistula. To the north of the Pilica and on the front of the 9th Army there was no heavy fighting. The Russians gave up the area west of the Vistula and hurried back to Warsaw.

In the meantime, about the middle of July, the Niemen Army, on the left wing of the forces that had been placed under the Commander-in-Chief, had again begun an offensive, and was advancing victoriously.

The 10th Army also pressed forwards on Kovno. and drove the Russians behind the Liesna segment.

About this time General Ludendorff was again summoned to G.H.Q. He pointed out that the offensive of General Gallwitz had led only to the results that the Commander-in-Chief had foretold, and that to continue this offensive would not produce any better results than it had done already. He repeated the suggestion to take all the available troops from the Woyrsch Group and from the 12th and 8th Armies, shift them to the 10th Army, take Kovno and then make an attack on Vilna with all these forces.

These operations might even yet have had great success. Whether it would still have been possible to inflict on the Russians an overwhelming defeat —that is, a defeat which would have turned the Tsar's thoughts towards peace—must remain an open question.

G.H.Q. again rejected these suggestions, and ordered the continuation of the offensive in the direction already begun. Nevertheless the Commander-in-Chief held fast to his idea of taking Kovno and of pushing the left wing of his troops as far forward as possible. G.H.Q. reinforced the 12th and 8th Armies by sending each of them a Division from the West; the Commander-in-Chief sent to the 12th Army two more Divisions from the 9th Army.

The Russian High Command had apparently 1812 in their mind during this retreat; they not only destroyed all communications, but they also burned towns and villages and drove the people and cattle away towards the east with the retreating army. For some unaccountable reason they seemed to believe that in this way they would cause us more than temporary difficulties, otherwise their conduct would have only been useless cruelty towards their own people. It is a strange thing that, even now, comparisons with 1812 often appear in German periodicals and newspapers. The people who write them do not realize that the difficulties that Napoleon had at that time in his campaigns have been overcome by modern means of communications and transport. If Napoleon had had railways, telephones, motors, the telegraph and an air force, he would have been in Moscow to-day.

Except for temporary difficulties with regard to quarters, these proceedings were in many ways an advantage for us. Take for example the burning of Brest-Litovsk, where afterwards the Commander-in-Chief had his Headquarters for nearly two years: although it was burnt down we were able to find quarters there, while the 80,000 inhabitants, for whom we should have had to provide, were not there. And the entire evacuation of the town quite relieved us of the risk of espionage, and of other dangers.

After having received the above-mentioned reinforcements the 12th Army recommenced its advance. The forces under Mackensen also pressed forward from the south. G.H.Q. would not give up the idea of trying to outflank various sections of the Russian Army; but these attempts, as the Commander-in-Chief had foreseen, had no success.

By the end of July, Cholm and Lublin were taken. The Woyrsch Group and the Kövess Group stormed the bridge-head at Ivangorod, and at the end of July Woyrsch crossed the Vistula north of Ivangorod in the very sight of the Russians. This crossing was a bold military exploit, which however did not lead to any great success; on the contrary, the units that had crossed the river were fiercely attacked by the Russians and found themselves in a difficult position for a time.

Before the advance of the 9th Army the Russians evacuated the outposts of Warsaw and the town itself at the beginning of August. On August 5th the 9th Army occupied Warsaw.

On that same day the Woyrsch Group and the 9th Army were removed from the area under the Commander-in-Chief on the Eastern Front, and were placed under the immediate control of G.H.Q. as the Army Group of Prince Leopold of Bavaria. Any tactical reason for this new rearrangement of the areas of command was unknown to me at the time, and I was never able afterwards to find out the reasons that had prompted it. On the contrary, when difficulties occurred on the Eastern Front, in 1916, not only were these units again put under the Commander-in-Chief, but the sphere of his authority was extended, after some opposition by the Austro-Hungarian High Command, as far as the Carpathians. I can therefore only suppose that these measures were taken by G.H.Q. owing to the dissensions that existed between them and the Commander-in-Chief.

After the occupation of Warsaw the whole of the Army Group of Prince Leopold of Bavaria crossed the Vistula between Ivangorod and Warsaw and continued the pursuit of the Russians towards the Bug, north of Brest-Litovsk, while the Mackensen Army Group remained based on Brest-Litovsk.

After crossing the Narev the 12th Army took a southern direction, in the hope of being able to cut off some Russian units near Warsaw. This hope proved vain, as the Commander-in-Chief and General Gallwitz had foretold it would, and they also turned eastwards, while the 8th Army, after taking Ostrolenka, marched on Lomza.

General von Beseler, the conqueror of Antwerp, was commissioned to invest and take as quickly as possible Novogeorgievsk. He was assisted by his very able Chief of Staff, General von Sauberzweig.

Owing to excellent leadership and the energetic attacks of the besieging army, which consisted entirely of Landwehr and Landsturm troops, the fortress fell on August 19th.

The Russian High Command had doubtless over-estimated the value of the ring of frontier fortresses when they decided to continue the defence of Novogeorgievsk and to leave a garrison of 80,000 men there. The bitter experiences they had had with Novogeorgievsk and Kovno were probably the causes that afterwards made them decide not to attempt the defence of the strong fortress of Brest-Litovsk.

Notwithstanding all the difficulties of the task, in the beginning of August the Commander-in-Chief decided to take Kovno. Two batteries of 42 cm. guns were all the heavy artillery he had at his disposal, as the chief part of our heavy artillery had to be brought into action against Novogeorgievsk. G.H.Q. gave us no ammunition; but, owing to economy in the past, General Ludendorff had a small stock of ammunition, which he placed at the disposal of the 10th Army.

It was only by thinning the line of its Front in other parts, and by weakening it in an almost unpermissible manner, that the 10th Army could obtain the necessary number of troops for the attack. However, the troops had such a strong feeling of superiority over the Russians that the leaders, General von Eichhorn and his Chief of Staff, Colonel Hell, as well as General Litzmann, the leader of the assaulting troops, were quite willing to take the risks upon themselves.

On August 6th the infantry was pushed forward nearer to the fortress, on the 8th the artillery opened fire. Although the Russians defended themselves fiercely, by the 15th General Litzmann had driven them behind the line of forts; on the 16th a company, taking them by surprise, broke in from the banks of the Niemen. The result of the fighting that followed was that the line of forts was taken, and on the 17th General Litzmann crossed the Niemen and took the town and the eastern forts. After the fall of the western line of forts the Russians gave up all attempts at resistance, and hurriedly retreated on Vilna. The bridges across the Niemen, especially the railway bridge—the loss of which was most unfortunate for us—were naturally blown up. On the other hand the railway tunnel had been only slightly injured, and with the help of the material we had captured we were soon able to establish communication with Vilna by means of trolleys, which was of great importance for the continuation of our operations.

After the fall of Kovno, General von Eichhorn pushed the troops that were on his left wing across the Niemen and sent them along the railway line towards Vilna. It was characteristic of the conditions of the means of communication in Tsarist Russia that there was no metalled road, not even a proper highroad between Vilna, the chief town of the Vilna government, the residence of the Governor, and the important garrison and industrial town of Kovno.

General von Eichhorn sent the right wing of his army, under General von Hutier, to continue the advance in the direction of Olita. Weaker units were sent through the Augustovo forest towards Grodno. They were in touch with the left wing of the 8th Army, which, after the fall of Osoviec, was advancing on Grodno.

General von Hutier drove the Russian rear-guard, which fought fiercely, into the wooded country towards the Niemen, and forced them over it; he reached Olita on August 26th, crossed the Niemen at the end of August, and pressed on to Vilna along the railway. The Russian resistance became stronger here. Nevertheless Hutier's advance made itself felt southwards and the Russians evacuated Grodno.

The left wing of the 8th Army took the south-west Front on September 1st, and after severe street-fighting the town was taken on September 2nd.

East of Grodno we met with strong opposition on Lake Osiery. To the right of the 8th Army the 12th Army had reached the Svislocz by this time, and the Army Group of Prince Leopold of Bavaria had crossed the Bialoviez forest.

On the extreme left wing of the Niemen Army the position was now as follows: General von Below had been able to hold the line that had been reached in June: the Dubissa as far south as Schaulen; the Wenta and the Windau as far north as Hasenpot. In the beginning of July the already mentioned reinforcements sent him by the Commander-in-Chief began to arrive. With their arrival General von Below received an order to re-commence the advance, and to begin by cutting off the enemy forces stationed at Schaulen.

For this purpose General von Below collected the I. Reserve Corps and formed a strong attacking force out of his left wing, leaving the rest of the Front quite thinly manned, and began operations about the middle of July. The strong left wing was to advance in the direction of Mitau, and to envelop the enemy stationed at Schaulen from the north, while the I. Reserve Corps advanced to the south.

The Russians were again taken by surprise by

our offensive. As always, they defended themselves energetically, and one of their attacks on our 6th Reserve Division in the direction of Okmiany forced this Division to retire towards the west. However the pressure from the south soon obliged the Russians to desist from their attack on the 6th Reserve Division and in their turn they had to retire.

On the 17th the left wing defeated the Russians at Auz, and after several days' fighting at Schaulen the whole of the Russian 5th Army was driven back in the direction of Ponjewicz. Ponjewicz was taken on July 29th, and Mitau on August 1st. Even the weak right wing crossed the Dubissa and one detachment pushed on against Kovno.

To the south of Riga the Russians halted at a large fortified bridge-head. On the other hand we succeeded in driving the Russians to the north bank of the river between Üxküll and Friedrichstadt. With this the attacking power of the Niemen Army was brought to an end. Its weak forces were extended over a very large area, and reinforcements were difficult to send owing to the conditions of the roads; besides which the Commander-in-Chief had been obliged to send the larger number of the transport to Gallwitz's 12th Army. However, this successful advance of the Niemen Army, notwithstanding its weak forces, only proves that the Russians would not have been able to repel an advance made by the forces of the Commander-in-Chief and the attack ordered by G.H.Q. in the direction of Kovno—Vilna, supported on the left wing by the advance of the Niemen Army.

It was only in the middle of August that the Commander-in-Chief was permitted to continue his offensive in the direction of Vilna. This was naturally too late for him to be able to obtain any

decided advantage over the Russian Army; consequently it became only a question of local successes.
G.H.Q. permitted the siege-troops from Novogeorgievsk and some Divisions of the Reserves that
had been taken from the 8th and 12th Armies to
be sent to the 10th Army. The bulk of the troops
that could be released, as a result of the converging
movements of the advancing armies, were destined
for the West and for the Serbian theatre of war.

In the meantime, half way between Kovno and
Vilna, the 10th Army had had fierce fighting. The
Russian High Command had sent to the Northern
Front part of the troops that were retreating from
Poland. The enemy forces that were here facing
the left wing of the 10th Army, though part of a
connected line towards the north, were weak, and
it was easy to break through their line. The chief
necessity for a further advance of the left wing in the
direction of Vilna—Minsk was to cut the railway
lines from Dünaburg and Molodeczno that were on
the flanks and the rear of the attacking forces.

The Niemen Army therefore received the order
to advance on Dünaburg as soon as the 10th Army
renewed the attack; the strong cavalry of the 10th
Army was told to proceed towards the railway line
near Polozk, and especially to the Molodeczno
junction.

The movement of reinforcements took an end-
lessly long time. The railway, Wirballen—Kovno,
was in a far from effective condition, and needed
first to be put in order; the roads were bad and
the horses were tired and worn out. The renewed
attack could only begin on September 9th.

General von Eichhorn and Colonel Hell, his Chief
of Staff, were very hopeful, and they also infected
General Ludendorff with their optimistic anticipa-
tions. The line was broken through quite success-

fully, the cavalry reached the railway line, the 1st Cavalry Division went even as far as Smorgon; the Russians were obliged to give up Vilna, but then the advance stopped : it had been begun too late. At that time the Russian retreat from Poland was so far successful that the Russians could simply divert Divisions from their fronts that lay farther to the south.

The 1st Cavalry Division fought like heroes in a battle at Smorgon. They were attacked by superior Russian forces, but they thought they would be able to hold Smorgon and that they must hold it until the infantry came up; but owing to the bad roads it arrived too late, and after having sustained heavy losses the Division was obliged to evacuate Smorgon.

The Russian High Command also brought up strong forces by rail to the country round Dünaburg. The Niemen Army was unable to take Dünaburg. The attack was brought to a standstill here also.

Now the Russians began attacks on the whole Front of the 10th Army and on the right wing of the Niemen Army. Their attacks were everywhere repulsed; our troops succeeded in a few places in taking some more ground.

General Ludendorff realized that the operations must be stopped; success was now impossible. The entire German offensive was suspended, the left wing of the 10th Army was drawn back, and in conjunction with the Army Group of Prince Leopold, who in his advance northwards had reached Minsk —Baranovici, took up winter positions on the line Beresina—Kovno—Lake Narocz—Lake Drysviaty —Novo-Alexandrovsk—Düna. For a short time fighting continued near Lake Narocz, and more especially before Dünaburg, where the I. Reserve Corps still continued to hope to be able to capture the bridge-head; but gradually quiet settled down on the whole Front.

The High Command of the Austro-Hungarian Army felt very justly that it was inconvenient that the Russian lines should be less than two days' march to the east and north-east of such an important railway junction as Lemberg. General von Conrad had therefore planned an attack from the country round Homel on the gap that really existed in Volhynia between the southern and south-western Russian Fronts, in order to force back the north wing of the Russian south-west Front, and thus free the rest of Galicia from the Russians.

The German G.H.Q. had approved of the Austrian Commander-in-Chief's plan, and after the fall of Brest-Litovsk at the end of August they had consented to the withdrawal from the Mackensen Army Group of the 4th and 1st Austro-Hungarian Armies, which had been sent to assist in that operation. Unfortunately, in this undertaking General von Conrad had his usual want of success. The idea was right, but the instrument failed him. The attack was driven back by a Russian counter-attack.

The campaign of 1915 was ended for the Commander - in - Chief, Eastern Front, when the permanent positions were taken up.

The Entente's plan to bring the war to an end by a simultaneous attack of the Russian masses on Prussia and the Carpathians had failed. The Russians had been beaten along the whole Front, and they had sustained losses from which they were unable to recover. But it had not been possible to defeat the Russians so completely as to compel them to sue for peace. And yet (I wish again to emphasize this fact) the possibility of doing so had existed.

If G.H.Q. had decided in July 1915 to transfer all the available forces to the 10th Army, to take Kovno and to make a strong attack in the direction of Vilna—Minsk, at a time when the Russian troops were still in Poland to the west of Warsaw, the defeat of the Russians must have been a decisive one for the results of the war. The Germans would not have met with any special difficulties in making such a break-through, as the German weak forces, without any assistance from G.H.Q., took Kovno and broke through the Russian lines.

On the Russian side there was now a change in the Chief Command : the Tsar gave in to the persuasions of his consort, dismissed the Grand Duke Nicolai Nicolaievich, and took over the Supreme Command himself.

The first measure is a question open to dispute; it is quite true that the Grand Duke had caused incredible loss of human life, without attaining the slightest tactical successes. On the other hand, he was a good soldier, who kept strict discipline. He was respected in the army, and feared in the higher grades of the service, and especially at the Front, for the strict measures he had introduced to maintain discipline. Perhaps he would have found ways and means to prevent the Bolshevik propaganda from penetrating into the army.

The Tsar's second measure, the undertaking the Chief Command himself, can only be called a mistake. The work of a Commander-in-Chief in our days requires the whole attention of a very capable man; a monarch of a great country has not the time to devote to it, as the business of his government requires both time and work from him daily. Either the leadership of the army or the government of the country must suffer if he tries to do the work of both.

CHAPTER X

LONG before the fighting was drawing to an end in the summer of 1915, German G.H.Q. had already sent to the Danube any forces that could be spared from the German Front, to be brought into action against Serbia. Other units were dispatched to the West, and arrived there just in time to repulse the mighty attack made by the Entente.

The campaign against Serbia was necessary, first, to relieve the pressure on Austria; second, in order to clear a direct way to Constantinople to send assistance to our Turkish ally, who was fighting desperately. The negotiations with Bulgaria had at last been settled. The Bulgarians, who had been robbed by the Serbs, the Greeks and the Rumanians of the fruits of their victory over the Turks in the second Balkan War, were burning for revenge, and hoped by joining the Central Powers not only to obtain it, but also to get Macedonia and the Dobrudja.

Before the commencement of the campaign there had again been a slight difference of opinion between G.H.Q. and General von Conrad. General von Conrad aimed at the entire destruction of the Serbian Army; he proposed that the bulk of the Bulgarian troops should not be concentrated on the Timok, but farther south, so as to make it possible to cut off the entire Serbian Army that was being driven to the south by the armies of Mackensen and Kövess. Unfortunately German

G.H.Q. rejected this plan. In consequence of this, the left wing of Mackensen's army and the right wing of the Bulgarian Army very soon came into collision; difficulties and stoppages occurred, and part of the Serbian Army was able to escape.

It also seems incomprehensible that the campaign was not continued and Salonika captured as General von Conrad had recommended. It is not a fact that an advance on Salonika was technically impossible—which was the reason that General von Falkenhayn gave Conrad for not making one. The opinion of the Director of Field Railways, Gröner, who was sent to Serbia specially to examine the matter, proves quite clearly just the contrary; it is equally useless to point to the neutrality of Greece as the cause : the neutrality of Greece was violated when the Entente landed troops at Salonika. If we had driven the troops that had been landed there into the sea we should not have increased the difficulties of the position for Greece; on the contrary, they would have been diminished.

I cannot share the opinion given by General Ludendorff (page 133 of his book) that, if Salonika had been taken, the Serbians, English and French who had been there would probably have fought on the West Front, while we on our side would not have sent any Bulgarians there, and therefore to take or not to take Salonika was unimportant.

In the councils of the Entente there were different opinions as to whether the bridge-head of Salonika was still to be held after the attack from that point for the support of Serbia had failed, owing to the victory of the 2nd Bulgarian Army.

The capture of Salonika would probably have caused the Entente to give up their plans against Bulgaria, and it would have been possible to employ the Bulgarian troops elsewhere. They might have

been brought into action against Rumania, and
Rumania might have been forced either to join
the Central Powers or at least to pursue a policy
of benevolent neutrality.

Thus the Salonika Front continued to exist, which
forced us to keep troops in Macedonia, and at last,
in 1918, caused the entire collapse of our Bulgarian
ally.

The limited objective that General von Falkenhayn had in view for the Serbian campaign—to
open out a way to Constantinople—was certainly
attained, and even before the railway connection
with Constantinople had been opened, in the middle
of January, as the Entente forces left Gallipoli on
January 9th.

General von Falkenhayn consented only with
reluctance to Conrad's plan of occupying Montenegro and Albania in order to clear the air in that
direction and to prevent the Entente from making
use of Montenegren territory as a military base for
operations against Serbia. The execution of this
plan met with no difficulties, and on January 11th
the heights of Lovcen were stormed, and Skutari
was taken on January 30th.

In the meantime the Russians had attacked us
again about Christmas. This time it was the
extreme southern wing that attacked the Southern
Army, commanded by Linsingen, and the Austro-
Hungarian 7th Army, under Pflanzer-Baltin. While
the Southern Army repulsed every attack, the army
of Pflanzer-Baltin in the Bukovina fought with
varying success, which continued until the middle
of January. It was only with difficulty that their
army was able to maintain its position.

At the end of October the Commander-in-Chief
removed his Headquarters to Kovno.

During the advance the 12th and 8th Armies

had been so pushed together that at last there was space for only one Army, and the 12th remained. It stood on the Niemen, as far north as the railway line Grodno — Molodeczno. General von Fabeck took over the command from General von Gallwitz, who had gone to Serbia. To the north of the 12th Army the 10th Army held the line as far as the Disna. Before Dünaburg a special group was formed under the command of General von Scholtz, the former Commander-in-Chief of the 8th Army. From this point the Niemen Army, under General von Below, reached to the sea.

In order not to allow the name of the 8th Army —which was so closely connected with the fights in East Prussia, and especially with the battle of Tannenberg—to disappear, the Niemen Army was now named the 8th Army, and also because the name " Niemen Army " was, owing to its present position, no longer appropriate.

South of the position held by the Commander-in-Chief, the Army Group of Prince Leopold was stationed, which stretched to the district south of Minsk. From this point southwards the Front was formed by the Austro-Hungarian Army Commands, with the Army Group of Linsingen on their left wing.

As soon as the fighting had ceased, the work of constructing positions was carried on with the greatest energy. At the same time the reconstruction of the lines of communication in the rear, especially the railways, was also undertaken; and General Ludendorff also created the admirable administrative organization of the Eastern Command.

As the Russians, when they retired, had carried off with them the whole of the apparatus of government, everything had to be created anew. These difficulties, however, had one advantage : there were no officials who could put obstacles in the way of the new administration.

The administrative district under the jurisdiction of the Commander-in-Chief stretched much farther south than the military front extended, as it comprised the district occupied before by the 12th Army and now belonging to the provisional district of the Army Group of Prince Leopold of Bavaria, which included the forest of Bialoviez. The splendid organization for the exploitation of timber that was established there by the Commissioner of Forests, Escherich, who became so widely known after the war, can be cited as a good example of what was done.

I myself had nothing to do with the administration, and therefore, when the fighting gradually subsided, I had more free time, which I employed in visiting the Fronts and in becoming acquainted with them in detail. During these visits to the army I saw all the most important sections of the Front. Wherever I spoke with the troops in the trenches I was often greatly moved by what I heard; I learned the sorrows and cares of the men, and I was often able to help them.

Personal intercourse with the officers of all ranks also gave me valuable hints. Thus, when I visited the Niemen Army, the conversation turned for the first time on the possibility of capturing the Riga bridge-head. General von Below drew my attention to the ford at Üxküll, and was the first to speak about operations at that point. Unfortunately we were unable to carry them out in the spring of 1916, and they had to be postponed until August 1917.

CHAPTER XI

THE year 1915 had brought no decisive action on any of the Fronts. We had maintained our positions in the West, and in the East we had had great successes. The decision that, in my opinion, might have been obtained in the East had never been attempted by the German G.H.Q. The Austro-Hungarian Army Command had driven back all the attacks of the Italians; by the Serbian defeat their rear had been freed; their self-confidence was increased in consequence of events on the Russian Front, especially as Pflanzer-Baltin's weak army had succeeded in keeping its positions without any German help. Now the question arose in both Allied Headquarters as to how the campaign of 1916 was to be continued.

In December 1915 General von Conrad had already requested German G.H.Q. to send him nine Divisions to Galicia in order to enable him to release a similar number of Austrian Divisions from that Front, which he wanted to send to the Italian Front to make a decisive attack on the Italians. General von Falkenhayn had refused.

German G.H.Q. did not agree with the opinion that an attack on Italy, and even a great defeat of the Italian Army, would have any considerable effect on the general course of the war. On the other hand, they did not feel themselves strong enough to attempt decisive operations on any one of the Fronts, as General von Falkenhayn has

specifically stated in his book. It is quite possible
to agree with him, as far as the negative portion
of his explanation goes, that we were too weak,
both in troops and material, to attempt a decisive
attack or to break through any one of the enemy
Fronts.

In the East we had missed our chance, as has
already often been asserted. As long as such considerable German forces were employed in the
East it was impossible to bring together sufficient
Reserves in the West to make it feasible to effect
a break-through on a large scale.

I cannot agree with General von Falkenhayn's
conclusion from these facts, that it was therefore
necessary to attack the strongest enemy—the French
—at one point of the Front. The French could not
give up this position for reasons of prestige—they
were therefore obliged to concentrate all the forces
they could muster at that point. To attack the
French without having the intention of attempting
to bring about a decisive action, but only with
the hope of weakening them, was a mistake. The
unfortunate Verdun attempt had cost the French
much loss of blood, but our losses were also very
great indeed, and in the end the French could justly
reckon Verdun as a French victory. Operations
that have only a limited object must be undertaken
only when their success is certain. Verdun could
have been a success for the Germans only had they
been able to take the fortress.

The tragic side of this, as of so many other opportunities of this war, is that a success was nevertheless
possible for us if the attack had been made in the
proper way—that is, if the attack had been made
simultaneously on both sides of the Meuse. The
attack on the eastern bank alone was fated to come
to a standstill as soon as it got under the flank fire

from the other bank. The French were really about to abandon at least the eastern bank in consequence of our attack. When, however, the III. Army Corps was brought to a standstill by the flanking fire from the western bank they changed their plans. What the reasons were that had prevented the attack on both banks I do not know; if it were want of troops, then the attack should not have been made at all. My standpoint is different to General von Falkenhayn's: I would not have rejected General von Conrad's plan. If it were impossible to deal a decisive blow on the main Front I would have transferred the operations to Italy, the secondary theatre of war, but I would have made an attack there on a grand scale. Judging by the success that the 11th German Army really had in 1917, if the attack General von Conrad had proposed making from Arsiero—Asiago had been executed simultaneously with a similar attack from Flitsch—Tolmein it might have led to a decisive defeat of the Italians. Naturally it is impossible to say if such a defeat would have caused the Italians to sue for peace, still, despite the pressure that England exercised on the Allies, the outbreak of internal troubles might have led to it. If we had succeeded in continuing our offensive to the line Genoa—Venice the results would have been very great, not only for Italy but, through its effects on the Western Front, for France also.

Of course Austria-Hungary had the chief interest in a great campaign against Italy; but we were so closely united—for better or for worse—with the Dual Monarchy that there was no use abusing our allies for their defective assistance; on the contrary, we ought to have tried to raise the self-confidence and prestige of the Austro-Hungarian Army.

The first condition for a great attack on Italy was naturally the certainty that both the chief Fronts in France and Russia would hold, as we had to be prepared, in such a case, for the Entente to attack on a large scale on both these Fronts, in order to relieve the pressure from Italy. The most critical point would be the Austro-Hungarian sector of the Eastern Front. It would have been possible to extend the command of the Commander-in-Chief in the East as far as the Carpathians, as it was afterwards done in the year 1916. He would then have been in a position to send German reinforcements to the most important places on the Austro-Hungarian Front to strengthen the line and to place his scanty Reserves behind the lines in such a way that they might intervene at the right moment. Only once during the whole war were we taken by surprise on the Eastern Front by a Russian attack—it was on the Aa, in the winter of 1916-1917. With this exception we were always warned by the wireless messages of the Russian Staff of the positions where troops were being concentrated for any new undertaking.

Naturally this extension of the area under the Commander-in-Chief would not have pleased the Austro-Hungarian High Command. The proposal would, at first, have met with opposition: it was only owing to the pressure of circumstances that the plan was carried out in 1916. If, however, it had been explained to General von Conrad that it was only under these conditions that the offensive against Italy could be made with German assistance, and he had realized that only in this way could he strike such a destructive blow against Italy, the old hereditary enemy of Austria, I certainly think he would have been willing seriously to consider submitting to a German Supreme Command.

However, as circumstances really were at the time, Falkenhayn's jealousy of Hindenburg and Ludendorff would probably have placed more difficulties in the way of increasing the sphere of authority of both those generals than Conrad's scruples of allowing a great portion of the Eastern Front to pass under German command would have done.

In fact, a consultation—which would have been most desirable—on the proposed operations never took place between the Chiefs of the General Staffs. It is true that General von Conrad had communicated his Italian projects when he had asked for the assistance of German troops, but General von Falkenhayn left our allies in complete darkness about his own plans.

The German attacks on Verdun were at once answered by attacks of the Entente on all the Fronts to relieve the pressure there. The Italians attacked on the Isonzo, for the fifth time in vain—and the Russians began an attack on a large scale on the Eastern Front. Their attack was made in grand style, in the second half of March, and with such an expenditure of ammunition as we had not as yet seen in the East. It is, therefore, probable that this attack was not simply made to relieve the pressure at Verdun, but was part of the Entente's general plan of attack for 1916, that had been prepared with the object of breaking through our lines. But it had probably been begun sooner than they had intended, with the object of relieving the Western Front. It is otherwise not possible to suppose that without this compulsion they would have begun so early as March, in a time of "roadlessness," as the phrase goes. In Russia the period—which often lasts for weeks—when the colossal quantities of snow begin to melt is called "roadless," as communications, except on the highways, which in Russia are few and far between, are rendered impossible.

The point of attack was well chosen. The chief assault was made between the lakes Viszniev and Narocz on the one side and Postavy on the other. This double attack was to envelop the German XXI. Corps from both sides, overrun it and thus make a wide breach through the line towards Vilna and Kovno. Secondary attacks—probably chiefly to detain the German Reserves and to divert the attention of the German Command—were made to the south of Dünaburg near Vidzy, at Dünaburg and at Jakobstadt. The attack began on March 15th with a drum-fire such as we had never experienced in the East before.

From the 18th to the 21st, and later again on the 26th, there were infantry attacks, that were conducted, as usual, with the utmost bravery and determination, and with complete disregard for the loss of life.

Unfortunately, a Baden Reserve regiment was overpowered between the two lakes. This produced a temporary crisis at that point. However, somewhat farther to the rear, the 10th Army succeeded in parrying the blow and closing the line again. All the other attacks were repulsed with great losses for the Russians.

Our thin lines fought as usual admirably. Naturally there were some exciting moments at Postavy, but there is never a battle without such moments. Towards the end of March the attacks subsided. With the exception of a small area near Lake Narocz the German positions had all been retained.

By the beginning of April, quiet set in along the whole Eastern Front. At the end of April we recaptured our lost positions on Lake Narocz. This attack of the 10th Army, which was preceded by an admirably carried-out artillery preparation, can serve as an example of all our subsequent attacks in the East. The artillery preparation was in charge of the commander of the artillery of a Landwehr Division, the retired Lieutenant-Colonel Bruchmüller. This artillery officer, who afterwards became famous not only in the East but in the whole army, was then discovered.

I consider Bruchmüller to be quite a genius in his way. He had a gift, which I have never seen possessed by any other artillery officer, of knowing, as if by instinct, the exact quantity of ammunition that it was necessary to discharge on any single point to render it ready to be stormed. The troops also soon noticed that an attack which had previously been prepared by artillery under Bruchmüller's command was a sure thing, and they advanced with full confidence in the success of any undertaking that had been prepared by the artillery of Bruchmüller and his Staff.

From all the reports that came in, it appeared that notwithstanding the attacks that had been repulsed at Postavy—Narocz, the Russian Headquarters was planning an attack on the Front of the Commander-in-Chief. Large concentration of troops and preparations for an attack, the reports said, were being made at Smorgon, at Dünaburg, and at the Riga bridge-head.

G.H.Q. had placed several Divisions from the south Front at the disposal of the Commander-in-Chief in the East. These Divisions, as well as our own Reserves, were stationed at the points necessary for meeting the expected attack, and we awaited with full confidence the Russian preparations for an offensive.

The Commander - in - Chief would have been better pleased if he had been able to forestall the

Russian attack by an advance from our side. The most desirable point of attack for us would have been Riga. It was impossible to do so with our own forces, even with the above-mentioned Reserves that G.H.Q. had sent us: we should not have been strong enough. The numerical superiority of the Russians was enormous. The bridge-head of Riga was the most sensitive point on the Front of the Commander-in-Chief. If the Russians had succeeded in making an attack from that bridge-head somewhere in the direction of Mitau the whole of our Eastern Front under the Commander-in-Chief would have had to retire.

As a preventive against such an attack the Headquarters Staff began, therefore, to consider the plan, originally suggested by General Otto von Below, of crossing the Düna at Üxküll. Had G.H.Q. been in a position to give us some six additional Divisions it might have been possible to carry this plan into effect. It offered not only the possibility of capturing the Riga bridge-head, but likewise of dealing a severe blow to the whole Russian Army. If we succeeded by a surprise attack in crossing the Düna at Üxküll and then of making a thrust northwards as far as the sea, the main body of the Russian garrison at the Riga bridge-head would be cut off. The fall of Riga would be a moral victory, and the German positions from Üxküll to the sea would be considerably shorter than they were, so that the need for more troops was only temporary; they would soon be free, and besides, the Commander-in-Chief, East, would be able to spare some of the forces he had owing to the much shorter line of his Front.

On the other hand, the Russians would be obliged to concentrate more Reserves at that point and it would probably have prevented them from resuming the offensive, at least for a time, on the Eastern Front.

The fall of Riga could not have produced a battle that would have decided the fate of the campaign, but it would have been a fine success that would have raised the spirits of the army, and could have been obtained with probably but little loss, and would have contributed to the gradual defeat of the Russian Army.

About the end of May, H.M. the Kaiser, accompanied by the Chief of the General Staff, came to Kovno on a visit to the territories under the administration of the Commander-in-Chief. The latter explained the Riga plan, and asked for the six Divisions that were needed. Unfortunately, His Majesty was obliged to refuse the request. General von Falkenhayn explained that he required all the troops at Verdun. Verdun was a great success, and it was to be presumed that during the continuation of the fighting the bulk of the French Army would be ground down in the mill of Verdun.

General Ludendorff and I were not of that opinion; but our opinion was not sufficient to alter the decision already taken.

Whether G.H.Q. was able to give the six Divisions is difficult to decide, but I think it would have been possible, as a few weeks later, at the collapse of the Austrian Front, they were obliged to send— and sent—about the same number of Divisions to support it.

In May the grinding battle of Verdun was continued in the West. With this exception both on the Western and Eastern Fronts there was quiet; only in Mesopotamia fighting was going on after the Turks had succeeded at the end of April in taking Kut el-Amara.

On May 15th General von Conrad began his offensive in Italy. For weeks he had had to wait on account of the weather. With a powerful rush the Army of the Archduke Eugene broke out of the line Rovereto—Trieste, swept the Italians from the mountains and burst through the enemy's line of frontier forts between Arsiero—Arsigo.

By the end of May the army was fighting for the last mountain ridges that still barred the way to the plains and which were obstinately defended by the Italians.

It was only a question of days, or even of hours, before the struggle for this passage would have been over.

The Staff of the Commander-in-Chief were discussing future prospects with the Austro-Hungarian liaison officer when, on June 4th, the great battle that took place in the southern half of the Eastern Front against the Austro-Hungarians completely changed the fairly favourable picture of the year 1916.

As it became known by Colonel Blood's article in *The Quarterly Review* of October 1920, the Entente had intended to make a general attack on the German Army during the summer of 1916, which was to begin on July 1st, in the West on the Somme, in the East at Baranovici—Smorgon.

The chief attacks against Baranovici—Smorgon were to be supported by auxiliary attacks at Riga and also at Luck, Tarnopol, and on the Dniester. It has already been stated that these Russian concentrations of troops and preparations for an attack on the Front of the Commander-in-Chief had been noticed, and correctly understood.

The Austro-Hungarian attack in Italy caused the Russians, in response to a request made by the Italians, to begin the intended auxiliary attack on the Austro-Hungarian Front before they had intended, and it unexpectedly brought the Russians their most brilliant victory in the whole campaign.

When, on June 4th, the Russians, who were numerically scarcely superior to the Austro-Hungarian troops, and who had neither concentrated their forces at any special point for the attack nor made any great artillery preparation for it, fell upon the 4th Army at Luck and the 7th in the Bukovina, both these armies gave way helplessly without offering any serious resistance. The retreat of the 4th Army, more especially, soon assumed the character of a rout. Unfortunately the leadership of General von Linsingen and his Chief of the General Staff, Stoltzmann, was not equal to the situation; it entirely failed, and was the cause mainly of the extent of this disaster.

On June 7th the Russians took Luck, on the 13th their vanguard reached Stochod, south-east of Kovel. During the first three days more than 200,000 Austrians were made prisoners.

This unexpected success caused the Russian Headquarters to change their plans. They gave up the attack that had been planned on the Front of the Commander-in-Chief in the East, which after the experiences they had had in March at Postavy they were probably not looking forward to with much confidence, and they gradually took troops away from our Front and sent them to the south to exploit the success they had already achieved there. This decision is comprehensible, but it was not right. If, on the contrary, the Russians had now attacked the German Front with all their forces, regardless of the losses they might incur, they would have prevented the Commander-in-Chief from sending forces for the support of their allies, and without this help the crisis would probably have developed into a complete defeat of the Austro-Hungarian Army.

The measures taken by the Commander-in-Chief would have had greater effect if the conditions of the Command on the Eastern Front had been more homogeneous. And although the personal relations with the Army Group of Prince Leopold of Bavaria and with Woyrsch's Group, which was chiefly affected by the Russian attack, were excellent, especially with Colonel Heye, the Chief of the Staff of Woyrsch's Group, with whom a constant exchange of ideas took place, still all sorts of friction occurred, owing to the wish of G.H.Q. that all intercourse between the various sections of the army should be effected through them and not directly.

On the receipt of the first reports of the collapse of the Austro-Hungarian 4th Army the Commander-in-Chief had several Divisions prepared to be transported to the south, although at that time he had to reckon with the possibility of strong Russian attacks. The Army Group of Prince Leopold of Bavaria made similar preparations.

The troops that were sent were naturally not sufficient. G.H.Q. found themselves obliged to send strong forces from the Western Front for the support of the allied army. Once again we have the picture we have seen so often before: if G.H.Q. had given the Commander-in-Chief the six Divisions he asked for in order to capture the Riga bridgehead at the proper time it is probable that the entire Russian attack would not have taken place, and the summer of 1916 would have ended with a great German success on the Eastern Front; now they were obliged to give the six Divisions in order to avert a great disaster that menaced the whole of that Front.

To take strong forces away from the West when, to judge by all the information that came in, the Entente's great attack on the Somme was imminent, was a difficult decision to make, but it was not to be avoided. General von Conrad had instantly stopped the whole of the Italian offensive and he had dispatched troops from the Italian Front to the East. The first thing that had to be done was to stop the attack at Luck. As soon as the first reinforcements arrived, G.H.Q. tried to stop the Austro-Hungarian troops by making a counter-attack, but the resisting power of the Austro-Hungarian 4th Army was too much shaken. The first German troops were carried off in the retreat.

The next German reinforcements that arrived first formed a new Front on the Stochod and stopped the Russian pursuit. The next troops that came joined up with the remains of the 4th Army near Kisjelin, and south of that place, in the district round Gorochov, combined with them to form a strong attacking force, and began an advance from there. As, on the one hand, the reinforcements arrived only in driblets, owing to the defective state of the railway communications, and, on the other, the critical position did not admit of a delay, the offensive was begun with insufficient forces, and they had no decisive success. At all events the Russian advance was stopped here. It was an advantage for us that the Russian attack had been made without proper preparation, and had no strong Reserves in its rear, and therefore was quickly brought to a standstill by the resistance opposed to it.

The position of the 7th Army in the Bukovina resembled that of the 4th Army, though it was not quite so bad. The Front was broken through in several places, the Russians took Czernovitz, and had reached the line Dniester—Kolomea—Kimpolung by the end of June. The line of the Austro-Hungarian Front that, before the Russian attack, had occupied the narrow strip of land between the Rumanian frontier to the east of Czernovitz and the Dniester was, owing to the retreat, greatly increased in length. Owing to the bad means of communication it was difficult to send them reinforcements, which were long in arriving, although both from the German and the Austro-Hungarian sides everything was done that was possible to hasten their arrival. It was lucky for us that the Russians suffered from the same difficulties of transport, and here also the want of preparation for the attack and the absence of Reserves prevented them from following up their success with energy.

On June 13th the Russians began a fierce attack on Woyrsch's Group at Baranovici. This was followed by a series of exciting days. But with the exception of a small breach made in the line of one of the Austro-Hungarian Divisions the group was able successfully to repulse all the attacks. However, they had to employ their last Reserves for this purpose, and the Commander-in-Chief had likewise to send the last of the troops he had at his disposal to assist them. By doing this the Commander-in-Chief ran a certain risk, as the Russians who were facing his Front, although they had begun dispatching troops to the south, were still quite strong enough to attack him. In fact the Russians did attack this Front at Lake Narocz, Smorgon, Dünaburg, Friedrichstadt, and at the Riga bridgehead. Most of these attacks were little more than demonstrations and they were easily repulsed. Their object was only to mask the dispatch of Russian forces to the south, and to prevent us from sending reinforcements there too. Only at Riga was the attack fiercer; by making a strong thrust the Russians were at first able to capture some territory. However the bravery of the troops and the good leadership of the 8th Army soon regained the lost positions.

The Reserves that had been sent to the south from the Front of the Commander-in-Chief gave renewed energy to the attack on the Brussiloff Front. The ground that had been gained by German counter-attacks in the Luck angle had partially to be given up. General von Böhm-Ermolli, the Commander of the Austro-Hungarian 2nd Army, was obliged to retire with his left wing and centre to the Galician frontier.

The Russian attacks on the Styr, to the north of Luck, were also successful. The Austro-Hungarian troops gave way here. General von Linsingen found himself obliged to draw back his left wing beyond the Stochod. The right wing of the Army Group of Prince Leopold of Bavaria had likewise to retire to the south of the Pripet.

The position had become very critical for the whole of the Eastern Front. The uncertainty concerning our allies was what mostly told on our nerves. Nowhere was it certain, if the Russians attacked, that they would be able to hold out. We scraped together all the Reserves we could find, thinned the quieter Fronts, and obtained in this way a few regiments. By these means we were able to send some reinforcements to Linsingen's Army Group to make it possible for him to hold the Stochod. He succeeded, and the chief crisis was thus tided over.

Count Bothmer, the Commander of the German Southern Army—the Chief of whose General Staff was Colonel von Hemmer, a very able man—also found himself obliged, at the beginning of June, owing to the complete failure of our allies, to draw his right wing back to the south of the Dniester, but in his new positions he repulsed every Russian attack, as he had done before in his old ones.

The events that had occurred thus far proved the unsuitability of the divided High Command, as well as the necessity of combining the Allied Front more closely. Wherever German troops were stationed, or where the Austro-Hungarian troops were intermixed with German ones, every Russian attack was repulsed, and our Front had been held. Wherever the allied troops had alone held a long Front they had failed.

The Commander-in-Chief pointed this out. At the end of June, Field-Marshal von Hindenburg and General Ludendorff were summoned to G.H.Q. in the West. They again pointed out the necessity of an absolute combination of the chief command on the whole of the Eastern Front, as it was possible only by those means to manage with the limited number of Reserves we possessed. They also proposed to send more German troops to the Austrian Front. In order to do this, weak Austrian Divisions could be posted at quiet places on the Eastern Front, and by so doing German Divisions could be freed to be employed on the Austro-Hungarian Front.

The first proposal, of having a single Commander-in-Chief on the Eastern Front as far as the Carpathians, they were unable to carry through. As General von Falkenhayn mentions in his book, he never even suggested the question to the allies; he tried to obtain a German High Command on the southern half of the Eastern Front under General von Mackensen. Such a subdivision of the High Command on the Eastern Front would of course not have been of much assistance.

The dispatch of Austro-Hungarian Divisions to

the Front of the Commander-in-Chief was effected to a limited extent. The first that arrived was a war-worn Infantry Division, which was stationed in the neighbourhood of Lake Narocz, and for which General von Linsingen was given in exchange the 10th Landwehr Division.

At the end of July, Field-Marshal von Hindenburg and General Ludendorff were again summoned to G.H.Q. The difficult position on the Eastern Front demanded energetic measures. The fall of Brody, news of which had just arrived, caused most of the trifling objections to be silenced. They were unable as yet to decide to make a complete job of it, and to extend the Front of the Commander-in-Chief, East, as far as the Carpathians; they decided, however, to place under his command the whole Front as far as the district south of Brody—that is, to include the Army Group of Böhm-Ermolli.

The Army of Pflanzer-Baltin, the Austro-Hungarian 3rd Army and the Southern Army were formed into a new Army Group, under the command of the Archduke Heir-Apparent Karl. He was given as Chief of the General Staff the German General von Seekt.

Although these new arrangements of the Chief Command were only half-measures, still they denoted an improvement.

The Commander-in-Chief began his new duties by first visiting the new positions that were now under his command in order to acquaint himself with the state of affairs on the spot. The command of the 10th and 8th Armies was combined into an Army-Group Command, and taken over by General von Eichhorn, who retained the command of the 10th and his Headquarters at Vilna.

The 12th Army was transferred to the Army Group of Prince Leopold of Bavaria.

Before there was time for personal conversations with the leaders of the southern portion of the Eastern Front the Russians recommenced the attack along the whole Front.

On July 25th and 27th the Russians, in great numbers, made a fierce attack on Baranovici; but they were repulsed.

Linsingen's Army Group had been continuously fighting on the Stochod. From July 28th to August 1st fierce attacks were made on this Front, which, quite regardless of the losses they sustained, the Russians were determined to break through at all costs. The position was critical, but, on the whole, the line held out. The attacks had also spread to the southern part of Gronau's Army Group, which adjoined the left wing of Linsingen's Army Group; but they were all repulsed at once. It was thought probable that the attacks would be extended farther south, and that they would spread to the Army Group of Böhm-Ermolli and to the troops under the command of Archduke Karl.

The Staffs we visited were consequently in very low spirits.

General Ludendorff, who had to arrange for the removal of the Staff from Kovno to a place more suitable for the Headquarters of the newly extended sphere of the Commander-in-Chief, had taken only the smaller and exclusively military Staff with him and had gone with them temporarily to Brest-Litovsk. Geographically, Brest-Litovsk was the most suitable place for the new Headquarters, but the town had been entirely burned down and could not provide quarters for the whole Staff of the Commander-in-Chief. The only part of the town that was still in existence was the officers' quarters in the Citadel; they were dirty and neglected, but could be rendered habitable in a short time. The space available was just sufficient for the military section of the Staff, but the administrative section had to remain in Kovno. Until the necessary cleaning up could be done, and arrangements made, we lived in our train at the Brest-Litovsk station.

On August 3rd and 4th General Field-Marshal von Hindenburg, General Ludendorff and I went to Kovel to see General von Linsingen, and the next day to Vladimir—Volynsk to the Commander-in-Chief of the 4th Austro-Hungarian Army, Colonel-General von Tertsczanski, and then to Lemberg, to the 2nd Austro-Hungarian Army to see General von Böhm-Ermolli and his Chief of Staff, General Bardolff.

On the way back to Brest-Litovsk we spoke also to Generals von der Maritz and Litzmann, the Commanders of the Groups of Austro-Hungarian and German troops that formed part of the Linsingen Group. The German Generals described the position as very serious. The Fronts were thin, powerful Russian attacks were to be expected, most of the Austro-Hungarian units were unreliable, but everywhere we found firm determination and confidence that the line would hold.

The reports of the Austro-Hungarian leaders were also not calculated to throw a more rosy light on the picture. General von Tertsczanski admitted quite openly that his troops had not the necessary *morale*, and that they were scarcely in a position to resist a strong Russian attack.

The same unsatisfactory picture was given by General von Seekt of the condition of the Army Group of the Archduke Heir-Apparent Karl. General Ludendorff had summoned General von Seekt to Lemberg for a consultation.

Böhm-Ermolli and Bardolff were a little, but not much, more confident. Only on one point all four were of one mind: in the request for German troops in order to intermix them with the Austro-Hungarian units.

The Commander-in-Chief was unable to assist much in that way at first. The strong Russian attacks at Riga had been repulsed for the time, but it was not impossible that they would be renewed.

As has already been remarked, Riga was the most sensitive spot of the whole of the Northern Front; if the Russians could succeed in breaking through there, the whole of the Front would have to retire. We were unable to take away the 1st Landwehr Division that we still had at our disposal there. With great trouble we had been able to draw from the rest of the Front three battalions more, and a section of artillery, under Major-General Melior, to form a Reserve and also one reinforced Cavalry Brigade.

During the consultations at Lemberg, General Ludendorff had promised to send Melior's Force to the 2nd Austro-Hungarian Army, so that for the whole Front from Lemberg to Riga all the Reserves that the Commander-in-Chief in the East had at his disposal was one Cavalry Brigade. This Brigade was afterwards also sent to the 2nd Austro-Hungarian Army.

G.H.Q. had three Divisions still at their disposal. These had been newly formed during July from parts of units sent to the West from other Fronts, and they were destined for the Eastern Front. They had likewise the disposal of a Turkish Army Corps that Enver Pasha had promised. The arrival of this Corps could, however, not be counted on, as only one train a day had been assigned for its transport. It was afterwards placed at the disposal of the Southern Army under Count Bothmer, and in conjunction with it fought splendidly.

We would gladly have provided the German Divisions. General Ludendorff begged that they might be sent quickly. Unfortunately G.H.Q. delayed for several days before they were dispatched. In consequence of this the Commander-in-Chief was prevented from averting a misfortune that befell the Army Group of Böhm-Ermolli.

In the meantime the Russian Headquarters had come to the conclusion that it was hopeless to try to break through the German Front, and their next attacks were made south of the Pripet. During the days from August 8th to 10th, Linsingen's Army Group and the left wing of Gronau's Group were again subjected to fierce attacks. Most of these attacks were repulsed, except at two places, Toboly and Kisielin, on the western bank of the Stochod, which the Russians succeeded in taking and retaining.

Simultaneously with these attacks the Russians attacked the 2nd Austro-Hungarian Army and the Archduke Karl's Army Group. The right wing of the Austro-Hungarian Army was broken through and had to give up its positions on the Sereth. It was only now that G.H.Q. placed two of the three Divisions—the 195th and 197th—at the disposal of the Commander-in-Chief, and they were brought into action under the command of General von Eben. They succeeded in stopping the retreat of the Austro-Hungarian troops at Zborov, and after hard fighting and severe losses they were permanently brought to a stand.

Melior's Force had already previously been brought into action.

Unfortunately the Russians also had succeeded against the Archduke Karl's troops. They broke through his lines at Tlumacz and took Nadvorna and Stanislav. As the Austro-Hungarian troops had given way on both his wings, Count Bothmer was obliged to withdraw the Southern Army, which had repulsed every attack of the Russians, beyond the Zlota-Lipa. The Russian attacks on the Carpathian passes were all driven back by the help of German troops. Nevertheless the impression produced by this great defeat of the Austro-Hungarian Army near the Rumanian frontier was so great that it removed the last hesitation Rumania still had of joining the enemy. Her attitude became with every day more suspicious, and it became necessary to reckon on her coming in on the other side.

After the Commander-in-Chief's round of visits to the Staffs that had been newly placed under his command we passed several days in our train at the Brest-Litovsk station and then, about the middle of August, removed to the Citadel. When I unpacked my trunk I little thought that my stay there would last nearly two years. There was an enormous amount of work that devolved upon every department of the Staff. Not only had General Ludendorff undertaken to keep tactical order in the East, but also to raise the conditions of training in the Austro-Hungarian Army, and he went into the matter with his usual energy.

On August 29th I had to be at a conference in East Prussia. Shortly before I left Brest there was a telephone call from the Chief of the Military Cabinet, Baron Lyncker, summoning Field-Marshal von Hindenburg and General Ludendorff to G.H.Q. Owing to their departure I had some hesitation about absenting myself at the same time, but as I was to be away only one night I decided to go ; and it was in Insterburg that on August 29th I received

the news that General Field-Marshal von Hindenburg had been appointed Chief of the General Staff
of the Army in the Field and General Ludendorff
to be First Quartermaster - General. The new
Commander-in-Chief in the East was General Field-
Marshal Prince Leopold of Bavaria, and I was
appointed his Chief of the General Staff.

Thus ended a period of two years during which
I had worked together with General Ludendorff, an
epoch of much work and anxiety, but also a time of
many achievements. During the whole of the period
no discordant note had ever troubled the work we
had to do together, and I believed and hoped that
the friendship which was established between us by
the experiences of those hard years could never be
shaken. It has often been asserted that I had taken
it amiss that General Ludendorff had not taken me
with him to G.H.Q. I wish to deny most emphatically all these rumours. I leave it an open question
whether our union, which during two years had
been without the slightest friction, would have been
for the general good if it had been continued longer.
For me the nomination as Chief of the General Staff
of the Commander-in-Chief in the East was naturally a great distinction and a better post. It gave
me a position of responsibility.

My new distinction nearly came to a premature
end. The special train that was taking me on the
29th from East Prussia back to Brest-Litovsk, by a
mistake of the engine-driver, ran into a leave-train
to the north of Bialystok. There were quite a
number of injured. I myself escaped with only
a painful shaking.

CHAPTER XII

BEFORE I begin a new chapter of my reminiscences as Chief of the General Staff I wish to say a few words on two questions, although I had no influence on either their development or solution. These questions, however, were often discussed by the Staff of the Commander-in-Chief, especially when statesmen, or persons who thought they were statesmen, and politicians from home came to visit us: they are the Polish question, and the problem of the submarine war.

I do not know who first suggested the idea of creating a Polish Kingdom; I think it was Baron Burian, who eventually signed the agreement with the Chancellor of the Empire, Bethmann-Hollweg. It was a stupid idea—it deprived the Tsar of any possibility of concluding a separate Peace—and it was quite superfluous. There was not the slightest reason for the Central Powers to touch on the Polish question. The creation of a General Government of Warsaw by Germany and a General Government of Lublin by Austria-Hungary were already mistakes, as they seemed to give to these Polish provinces which had been taken from Russia a special status. It would have been better to have treated these provinces in the same way as the other portions of the Russian Empire occupied by the allied armies, and to have simply made them the zones of occupation of the army in question.

150

General Ludendorff had often talked with me about the idea of founding a new Polish Kingdom, and he always declared that in answer to questions regarding this matter he had said he could agree to the plan only if the Poles could assist the Central Powers with an army that, at first, must be at least four Divisions strong. I was sceptical about Polish auxiliary troops, but at that time we were so much in want of Reserves that, from a military point of view, we looked with pleasure on any accessions we could obtain.

The advisability of the formation of a Polish Army was encouraged by those who were of the opinion that it was a pitiable idea that so numerous a nation as the Poles should allow their freedom and independence to be obtained only by the efforts of others, without themselves making any sacrifices in the cause. It is well known now that we soldiers deceived ourselves, and the politicians did not make the military demands one of the conditions of the political bargain.

With regard to the question of the U-boats, no man of sense can be in doubt that in our struggle for the existence of Germany we not only had every right, but that it was our bounden duty, to bring them into action without any consideration for others. It is absurd to talk of inhumanity, and so on, when all know that England had already begun the hunger blockade against German women and children. There was no possibility for us Germans to escape from the consequences of this blockade, while the Americans had no need to take their pleasure trips in the precise zones blockaded by Germany. From the very beginning I was only afraid that we might begin the U-boat war too soon —that is to say, we would not have sufficient submarines to be able to continue this warfare. I often think of a discussion I had on this question with the President of the Union of Landowners, Dr Rösicke, in Kovno, when he came to visit the Field-Marshal. During this discussion he reproached me with want of patriotism, etc., when I objected to bringing the unrestricted submarine warfare into immediate action.

Later events proved that I was right. We began too soon—that is, with too few U-boats—and the results were very similar to those produced by our gas warfare. We showed the adversary what a dangerous weapon we possessed at a time when the weapon was not strong enough to prevent him from taking the necessary measures to defend himself from it. I do not doubt that the U-boat war might have been completely successful if from the beginning we had applied all our available power to the construction of an unlimited number of submarines.

If, as Admiral von Tirpitz says in his book, the Navy Department had determined from the beginning not to employ the fleet for a great decisive naval battle, it was quite useless to continue the construction of battleships during the war.

CHAPTER XIII

THE CONDITIONS OF MY NEW COMMAND

On August 30th I took over the duties of Chief of the General Staff of the Commander-in-Chief, Eastern Front. As my successor to the post of Senior Officer on the General Staff I had suggested to G.H.Q. the choice of two officers on the General Staff of the Eastern Front who possessed the necessary seniority, and were, in my opinion, the most suitable for this appointment. They were Lieutenant-Colonel Keller and Major Brinckmann; both these men had special military capacities and extensive knowledge, extraordinary powers of work and were keenly optimistic.

At first Lieutenant-Colonel Keller was appointed, but he remained only a short time and then became the Chief of Linsingen's General Staff. His post was then held by Major Brinckmann, who afterwards became very widely known owing to his participation in the Peace negotiations of Brest-Litovsk and in the Armistice negotiations in the West.

The new Commander-in-Chief arrived next day. Already before the war I had become acquainted with H.R.H. Field-Marshal Prince Leopold of Bavaria during the great manœuvres, when I had met him several times, and having heard his criticisms I knew that he was a clever soldier and a distinguished Commander. During the two and a half years that we worked together I found that these two qualities were his most conspicuous characteristics. The Prince was an impassioned soldier, a keen sportsman and rider, and the last *Grand Seigneur* I ever met. In the most difficult situations he retained a clear mind and iron nerves. During that whole time we never had any differences over military questions, and I can remember only one case when the Prince did not reply to me with the amiability he usually showed to everybody. During the battle at Zloczov—Tarnopol, in July 1917, H.R.H. had forced his way to the Front, and he would have been best pleased if he could have been in the front line of infantry. We had taken up our positions with the 1st Guard Division on a small mound from which a general view of the battle could be obtained. The Russians began to direct their artillery on this mound. I felt it was my duty to beg the Prince to change his position, as there was not the slightest use in our remaining there any longer, and it was to be expected that in a few minutes a strong artillery fire would pour on the spot where we were standing. The Prince enjoyed danger. In answer to my energetic insistence he replied, in an almost unfriendly tone: " You begrudge me the smallest pleasure."

From the other members of the Staff, General Ludendorff took only Major von Bockelberg with him to his new sphere of work. He had been Assistant Quartermaster-General, and his place on the Staff of the Commander-in-Chief was now taken by Major Hoffmann, an officer of great military capacity, tremendous power and love of work, and an iron sense of duty.

The Administrative Department remained as formerly under the Chief Quartermaster-General, von Eisenhart-Rothe. There was a small superficial difficulty here, as Eisenhart-Rothe was already a General, while I, his chief, had only just been promoted to the rank of Colonel. This difficulty was quickly overcome, as General von Eisenhart consented to work under me. We worked together without the slightest friction until, on my recommendation, General von Eisenhart was appointed Quartermaster-General to the Commander-in-Chief. General von Eisenhart combined wide knowledge and judgment with a special capacity for all administrative questions. In character, in a just feeling of responsibility, and in demeanour, he was a perfect example of an old-fashioned Prussian officer, in the best meaning of the words.

H.R.H. took up his private quarters in the small abandoned estate, Szkoki. Every morning at about eleven o'clock he came to the office to hear the report; he had his midday meal at home, and in the evening at half-past seven he came to the mess dinner to the officers' quarters. He informed me, however, that from 5 A.M.—his usual hour of rising both in summer and winter—he was always at my disposal at any time if he were required.

The position on the Eastern Front could be looked upon as, in general, safe at that time, though of course we had to expect fresh Russian attacks at any moment. The 195th and 197th Divisions, under General von Eben, which had been sent to reinforce the Austro-Hungarian 2nd Army, had effectually succeeded in bringing it to a standstill. The last Russian attacks on Woyrsch had also been successfully repulsed. There was still a certain tension in the Linsingen Army Group on the Stochod, though Colonel Hell, Linsingen's Chief of Staff, was quite confident for the future. The position was not quite so secure with the Archduke Karl's Army Group, and there were hardly any forces at our disposal to repulse our new enemy—Rumania.

In the West, fierce battles were raging on the Somme and at Verdun, and were producing great gaps in the effectives of the German Army that could never be made good. For the first time the feeling of the absolute superiority of the German soldier was lost, and signs of war weariness and despondency began to be observable in certain quarters. The general situation was much more serious when Field-Marshal von Hindenburg and General Ludendorff undertook the Supreme Command than it had been at the first change of that post after the battle of the Marne.

During the two years he had been Commander-in-Chief, General von Falkenhayn had squandered the capital of a proud army and the national enthusiasm without having attained a single success. Ludendorff's energy was able to master these difficulties. The unfortunate Verdun adventure was liquidated; the line of the Somme was held, though with loss of territory; the Archduke Karl's army was supported, and the force necessary for the Rumanian campaign was called into existence. The chief burden of the last task fell to the Commander-in-Chief in the East. Although, as already mentioned, the situation of the Linsingen Group was not quite secure, we gave as many troops as could be spared, and even more. We drew off some regiments from quiet parts of the Front and created new Divisions. The risks that this involved had to be borne, and H.R.H. the Commander-in-Chief and I were quite willing to bear them.

Once again it was proved that the Russian Army had produced no great leader, no man of real strategic understanding. Instead of attacking us again along the whole Front, and occupying us in that way, to hinder us from removing troops for other Fronts, Brussiloff's offensive was absolutely stopped. The Russians dispatched their Reserves to the south to take part in the Rumanian offensive.

At the time that the Supreme Command of the Allied Armies was undertaken by German G.H.Q. the various commands were regrouped, and the sphere of the Commander-in-Chief on the Eastern Front was also slightly increased. The Southern Army of Count Bothmer was placed under his command. This army and the Austro-Hungarian 2nd Army formed the Army Group of Böhm-Ermolli. Unfortunately the 3rd Austro-Hungarian Army, which was stationed to the immediate north of the Carpathians, was not as yet included in this arrangement.

However, even without this section, the Front was large enough to occupy the whole of a man's working power. Even when there was no fighting my days passed in the following manner. In the morning I went to the office at eight o'clock, where I found the morning reports, which usually meant the issue of instructions; about eleven o'clock H.R.H. the Commander-in-Chief came in to hear my report, which took up a shorter or longer time according to circumstances. At one o'clock I went straight from the office to the mess-room to lunch; from two to three I took a walk of an hour, and then returned to the office, where I remained until it was time to go to the mess dinner at half-past seven. H.R.H. remained after dinner for about half-an-hour in conversation with the members of the Staff and the guests who always were present. At nine o'clock he drove back to Szkoki, while I and the other members of the Staff returned to the office, where we usually were occupied until one o'clock. If any important fighting was in progress the working day was longer, and the time of rest was often broken by telegraphic or telephonic messages. Unfortunately my present occupations did not give me time to visit all the sections of the Front—as I had been able to do while I was G.S.O., Ia— and become acquainted with them by personal inspection. My work did not admit of such long absences. I therefore requested the Central Department of the General Staff to provide me with a very capable General Staff Officer, whose business it should be to keep in direct touch with the troops, and get closely acquainted with all the most important positions. I was very fortunate in this matter: the Central Department sent me an officer who had really remarkable capacities for the execution of this difficult task. Major Wachenfeld possessed both great tactical understanding and military insight, combined with the amiability and tactful reticence that were absolutely necessary for the fulfilment of his difficult task. He was untiring in making his inspections; he gave valuable encouragement to the troops at their posts, and made it possible for the Commander-in-Chief to give orders for any necessary improvements in our fortified positions.

At the beginning of September Field-Marshal Hindenburg and General Ludendorff went for a short time from Pless to the Western theatre of war, in order to be able to consult on the spot about the new position of affairs, especially on the Somme and at Verdun. Shortly after this visit I came for one day to Pless for a consultation on questions regarding the service. The relations between General Ludendorff and myself were still, at that time, of the most friendly and confidential nature. He spoke quite openly of the serious position in the West, and that much had been neglected in the construction of the positions, and many mistakes had been made. He said that G.H.Q. and the War Office had not exerted sufficient pressure on the working capacity of our industries for the production of the necessary war material, especially of ammunition, and that, in general, there had been a complete failure of a united effort of G.H.Q. and the Civil Administration. After a long conversation on tactical and technical details we naturally discussed the question that at the time was occupying the minds of most men—the question of how it would be possible to end the war in a reasonable manner. In reply to my question as to how General Ludendorff supposed it would be possible to bring the war to an end he said:

"For the moment I see no possibility; the Entente are now counting on winning the war, and judging by the general position they have the right to do so. Therefore at the present moment we can do nothing. If we succeed in defeating the Rumanians, and in repulsing all the attacks in the West, which, unfortunately, I can only hope we may, it will be more possible to talk about peace. And I can give you my word that if the slightest possibility offers itself of concluding a fairly reasonable Peace I shall grasp it with both hands."

I returned to Brest-Litovsk much relieved in mind.

Meanwhile the campaign in Rumania took its course—with the exception of a few slight frictions —much as G.H.Q. had anticipated.

G.H.Q.'s appreciation of our Commander-in-Chief's co-operation in the victorious conduct of the Rumanian campaign found its expression in the following telegram that General Ludendorff addressed to me:

December 12th, 1916.   PLESS.
COLONEL HOFFMANN, HEADQUARTERS EAST.

Sincere thanks to you and the members of the Staff for your congratulations. The Victory in Rumania could only have been won because we had won the battle of the Somme in the West, and in the East the tremendous battles on the southern half of your Front, and because we had received from you constant reinforcements for Transylvania and Rumania.

About the turn of the year the German troops approached the Sereth. It was evident that the advance would stop there. In the meantime the Russians had concentrated very considerable forces at the Rumanian frontier. About Christmas 1916 I wrote a letter to General Ludendorff, in which I explained that in my opinion the offensive movement in Rumania, that had now become quite a frontal advance, would be entirely stopped about the New Year on the Sereth. If it was desired to continue the campaign, and finally dispose of Rumania, in my opinion there was only one thing to be done, and that was to give up the attacks in the south and to make a thrust from the north. If G.H.Q. was in a position to send the Commander-in-Chief in the East four to six Divisions—it would be simplest to send a part of those already fighting in Rumania—I thought we could carry through the attack. I proposed that the reinforcements, and all the forces the Commander-in-Chief could collect, should be concentrated in the neighbourhood of Zloczov. The Russian position was to be broken through there, and the offensive was to be continued through Tarnopol along the main railway towards Odessa. The bulk of the Russian

Army in the Carpathians would by this movement be brought into an untenable position, and I thought that by these operations a great success would be attained. I considered that a break-through at Zloczov would be easy to effect, and I proposed it should be made exactly as we carried it out in July 1917.

General Ludendorff replied that he was quite of my opinion with regard to the advance in Rumania, which would come to a standstill on the Sereth, as well as with the operations I proposed, which would probably be successful. Unfortunately the preliminary conditions were not obtainable—especially the dispatch of reinforcements to the Eastern Front. For the moment, nothing could be given from the West, and it was impossible to transport troops quickly from Rumania owing to the condition of the Rumanian and Hungarian railways.

I must say a few words about an event that occurred in the autumn of 1916, and which at the time was generally underrated by most men. I mean the death of the Kaiser Franz Joseph, who closed his eyes on November 21st, 1916. He was the last bond that still united the divergent states that formed the Austro-Hungarian Monarchy. His successor, who had been brought up as a simple cavalry officer, and whom the murdered Heir-Apparent had purposely prevented from occupying himself with political questions, now found himself facing an impossible task. The worst of it was that the young monarch, encouraged by an ambitious wife whose whole sympathies were on the side of the enemy, and who hated Germany and the Hohenzollerns, and surrounded by irresponsible counsellors who flattered his vanity, began by wanting to undertake the control of both the political and military situations. The first thing he did was to supersede in a somewhat summary manner the Archduke Frederick, who had been until then the Commander-in-Chief of the Army. The Emperor appointed himself Commander-in-Chief. Although the Archduke Frederick had played no great part, he had given full liberty of action to Conrad von Hötzendorff, the clever Chief of the General Staff, and he had always given him the support of his Imperial name. In all the frictions and differences of opinion that occurred between the allies, his quiet, amiable and distinguished manner had always been a conciliatory influence. One of the first military measures of the new Emperor was to have G.H.Q. transferred from Teschen to Baden, near Vienna. The Emperor wanted to get away from the influence of the German G.H.Q. in Pless, which he found too near. Conrad protested but without success. In this, as in every other military or political question, the General gave his opinion in the clear and positive manner he always had done, and in consequence he was obliged to give up his post in the shortest possible space of time. His successor, General von Arz, was a more conciliatory personage, who contented himself with being his Imperial master's confidential servant, and not what Conrad had been, a responsible Commander-in-Chief.

The position of the Chief of the General Staff degenerated in the hands of its new holder, especially as he was always obliged to accompany the Emperor, who constantly travelled about from one part of the Front to another, and could never be quiet; so he, too, could display his efficiency only in travelling about. I had only one opportunity of conversing for some time with the Emperor Karl. On the occasion of his first visit to the Linsingen Army Group I had to receive His Majesty, by order of the Commander-in-Chief, who was absent at the time, and in connection with several inspections I was invited to dinner, and passed two hours in the Imperial Court train. The Emperor, who at that time had not the weary, careworn look that showed itself towards the end of the war, was still fresh and active. He carried on an animated conversation during these two hours, and gave his opinion on military matters, making it quite clear that he did not know what he was talking about.

About Christmas 1916 I found myself obliged to transfer the Administrative Department of the Commander-in-Chief in the East from Kovno to Bialystok. When I became chief of this Department I had left it as General Ludendorff had organized it. Every fortnight or three weeks the Quartermaster-General came over to Brest-Litovsk—sometimes, if necessary, accompanied by the different heads of departments—to make his report, and to receive my instructions or those of the Commander-in-Chief on any difficult question that might have arisen.

In the autumn of 1916 a certain number of irresponsible people had made attempts to take away from the Commander-in-Chief the control of the Administrative Department, and to put it directly under the Quartermaster-General. As I did not consider these endeavours practical—but on the contrary I was of the opinion that the Commander-in-Chief must remain complete master of his area—I wrote to General Ludendorff, explained to him my reasons, and asked for his decision. General Ludendorff agreed with me, and gave orders that all should remain as heretofore. However I considered the above-mentioned change of quarters for the Administrative Department as advisable, so as to have it nearer to hand. It was thus possible for the Quartermaster-General, accompanied by the necessary officials from the various departments, to come to Brest-Litovsk every week to make their reports.

The opinion of the Commander-in-Chief on the Eastern Front with regard to the Peace proposals made by the Central Powers in December 1916 was never asked, either officially or privately. He would certainly have been against such a step, which was calculated only to augment the weakness and indecision in those circles which from the very beginning had always been doubtful of the favourable results of the war.

The blunt refusal that the Entente gave to these proposals of the Central Powers caused us to begin the unrestricted U-boat warfare on February 1st, 1917. I have already given my opinion on the question of the submarine warfare; I am quite positive, first, that Germany had unquestionably every right to carry out an unrestricted U-boat warfare; and, secondly, that it was our duty to employ every weapon we possessed to achieve the final victory. It was England who had begun the extension of the war to women, children and non-combatants by the blockade measures she had taken. There can be no doubt we had the right to defend ourselves with similar measures. The outbreak of American indignation against Germany for preventing Americans from coming to England, or going in safety anywhere else they desired, sounds almost childish. With the same right the Americans might demand that a battle should be broken off, and the artillery fire stopped, when a few Americans took it into their heads to go for a walk on that particular battlefield.

Unfortunately by our first attempt at submarine warfare we gave the English the time and opportunity of inventing effective means of opposing it, and then we also neglected to employ all our powers in the construction of U-boats.

The assurances of the Admiralty that it would succeed in less than six months in reducing England to submission were, therefore, too optimistic. In order even to form an opinion as to what the causes of this optimism were, and if it was right to run the risk of an American declaration of war, it would be necessary to have more details than I possess as to what the navy knew about the enemy's means of resisting this mode of warfare, and why they hoped to attain the desired results in spite of them.

With the decision to commence unrestricted U-boat warfare the chief centre of the war was temporarily transferred from the land to the sea. On land, orders were given to stand on the defensive and to incur as little loss as possible during the months required to reduce England to submission. For these reasons the troops were drawn back in the West from the salient between Arras and Soissons to the so-called Siegfried Line. By this measure it was possible to follow up and retard the enemy's plans of attack, and we compelled our adversary to make new and wearisome preparations in order to execute his plan, for which more difficulties were thrown in his way by the entire destruction of all means of communication and all possibility of finding quarters; while on our side, in consequence of the shorter line, we were able to economize in the number of troops required to defend it.

Of course the destruction involved in this withdrawal caused shouts of rage in the whole of the enemy Press. However, every professional soldier, even in the enemy army, will acknowledge that they were quite imperative. I do not doubt for a moment that the English and French would have taken the same measures if the case had been reversed. I need only recall to my memory, at this point, the destruction of the Rumanian petroleum wells by the English.

CHAPTER XIV

THE WASTED OPPORTUNITIES OF THE RUSSIAN REVOLUTION

In the spring of 1917 the position of the Central Powers was not as serious as it had appeared at the end of August 1916. Still it was bad enough. The Eastern Front was quite secure, but it was impossible to send considerable forces from it to the West in order to make an offensive possible on that Front. Owing to the severe fighting on the Somme and at Verdun the Western Front had received a slight moral shock; there was no longer the same confident tone as formerly. The superiority of the massed effect of the enemy's war *matériel* was beginning to make itself felt. Our industrial capacity could not compete with that of something like the whole world.

The feeling at home became worse: the food conditions grew more difficult, the high wages that, in accordance with the Hindenburg programme, were being paid to the workmen at home, or to the men who had been discharged and sent home, had a depressing effect on the army. There certainly was great injustice in paying high wages to a man who had been recalled from the Front because he no longer bore, with his comrades, the hardships and dangers of the trenches, but was at home quietly practising his trade. Ludendorff's idea, when he first introduced the Laws of Compulsory Labour, was evidently that work at home for the war was as much service as military service in the trenches,

167

and must be remunerated in the same way. Then
America joined the war. And although America
had no army at the time, and the Admiralty,
in their usual optimistic way of looking at things,
declared to everybody that even if it were possible
for America to create an army she would never be
able to transport it to Europe, still there was a large
number of serious people who declared that from the
moment America joined the war it was impossible
for Germany to issue from the struggle victorious.

In March 1917, at that moment of great difficulty, an event of world-importance took place
which gave Germany once again the possibility of
a military victory: the beginning of the Russian
Revolution. The Tsar had realized that Russia
was unable any longer to support the burden of the
war, and by continuing it he would expose his state
to severe internal convulsions. He was therefore
considering the question of a separate Peace. In
this, however, he calculated without taking into
consideration the will of England. The British
Ambassador in Petersburg, Sir George Buchanan,
had received orders to prevent a Russian separate
Peace at any price, and he acted in accordance
with his instructions when he joined Kerenski
and Gutschkov in deposing the Tsar.

It was evident that such an event would produce
a great effect on the *morale* of the Russian Army.
The idea naturally occurred that it would be a good
thing to accelerate the collapse of the Russian Army
by a few strong thrusts on the Eastern Front. However, on the one hand the Commander-in-Chief
in the East had not the necessary means to do so,
and on the other our Foreign Office entertained the
delusive hope of being able to enter into negotiations
with the new ruler, Kerenski, that would eventually
lead to peace.

Now, when it is possible to examine the conditions more clearly, one is obliged to regret that the first alternative was not adopted, and early in the Revolution, when the Russian soldier was inclined to take advantage of what, for his understanding, were the natural consequences of the Revolution—that is to say, to lay down his arms and go home—that we did not attempt to shake the Russian Army by a general attack on the whole of the Front. If we had succeeded in this, no power on earth would have been able to stop the process of disintegration that would then have set in, or to bring that host into order once more.

It is well known that owing to our inactivity Kerenski was able to carry away the army with his persuasive eloquence, and to induce them to continue the struggle, and thus to hold eighty German Divisions on the Eastern Front during the whole of the summer of 1917, and to keep them busy too.

In order to encourage the belief in his intention of concluding a separate Peace, and to lead our Government farther astray, Kerenski ordered his agents abroad to enter into negotiations with the German representatives. As a proof of this I can cite the following fact. About this time I was for one day in Berlin for a business consultation, and while there I received an intimation from the Foreign Office that I was to have an interview with the deputy Erzberger, who was to return that night from Stockholm. I met Herr Erzberger that night, and he told me that in Stockholm he had had negotiations with the representative of the Minister-President Kerenski and had nearly succeeded in obtaining the signature to a separate Peace with Russia. I was to hold myself in readiness to start with him at a moment's notice for a Peace

Conference in Stockholm.   I was somewhat sceptical, but of course I could not deny the possibility
of such a step.   In fact it would have been the most
comprehensible thing that Russia could have done,
to have concluded a separate Peace with Germany.
If they had done so then they would have been
spared the experience of a Bolshevik Government and
the blood of many millions of murdered citizens.

The Commander-in-Chief was, however, not able
to abstain entirely from hostilities.   Of the two
bridge-heads on the Stochod which the Russians
had retained after the hard fighting during the
Brussiloff offensive, only one, the smaller one at
Witoniec, had been recaptured in the autumn of
1916, while the larger one at Toboly was still in
their hands.   It formed a constant source of danger
for us.   In consequence of this the Commander-in-
Chief had already made preparations in March to
retake it.

The attack was to be made when the thaw would
cause inundations in the Stochod lowlands and the
bridge-head with its four bridges would be entirely
cut off.

The thaw set in early in April, and transformed
the Stochod lowlands, to the rear of the bridge-head,
into a lake about 1000 metres wide.   It would have
been a mistake from a military point of view not to
take advantage of such a favourable moment for
making an attack, as it would be impossible to send
reinforcements from the eastern bank, nor could the
troops that were stationed at the bridge-head escape
our attack.   The Commander-in-Chief explained
the situation and received permission from G.H.Q.
to make the attack.

The attack was executed by the 1st Landwehr
Division, under General von Jacoby.   Several

weeks before, the Commander-in-Chief in the East had sent Lieutenant-Colonel Bruchmüller to the Division as Artillery Commander and Adviser. It was possible to take from the Front only about 300 guns and 100 Minenwerfer to be held in readiness for this attack. As the number of guns was insufficient to make an attack on the whole bridge-head, it was decided at first to move against only the southern half; and then on one of the subsequent days, if possible on the next day, to capture the northern half.

The attack began at three o'clock on the afternoon of April 3rd. Thanks to the admirable direction of Bruchmüller and of the Commander of the Minenwerfer Brigade, Lieutenant-Colonel Heuschkel, the effects of the artillery fire were so overpowering that the Russians made scarcely any resistance. The infantry charge that followed immediately after this rain of projectiles surprised most of the Russians in their shelters. After the southern half of the bridge-head had been captured so quickly, and with comparatively so little loss, the attacking party proceeded, without having orders to do so, to storm the northern half, and took that too.

The success of the day was astonishing, as besides quantities of war material we took 10,000 prisoners. Owing to the understanding with the Government that there should not be any important engagements on the Eastern Front the Chief Command was quite perplexed how to give an account of these events in the daily Army Report. It was therefore silent about the magnitude of the success. This naturally caused great indignation among the troops that had taken part in the attack and it could not be understood by them, especially as on the following day the Russian Army Report gave an account of the battle in all its details and particulars.

Although at that time the new Russian rulers showed no signs of having any intention of making peace, but on the contrary, on every possible occasion, both Kerenski and the new Minister of Foreign Affairs, Miliukov, reaffirmed their adherence to the alliance with the Entente, and the will to continue the war to a victorious conclusion, the German Government continued to entertain hopes that the Revolution would possibly bring about a separate Peace. In accordance with their wish, after the success at Toboly, G.H.Q. forbade the Commander-in-Chief to take any further action for the time.

In February G.H.Q. were removed from Pless to Kreuznach. One of the reasons that induced them to make that change was, first, that they expected the Entente's great attack in the West to begin in the middle of February, and they wanted to be nearer to the scene of action; and, secondly, the chief advantage of Pless, the proximity of the Austrian G.H.Q., no longer existed, since they had been transferred to Baden, near Vienna.

General Ludendorff ordered me to come to Kreuznach on April 17th to make a personal report. I gave him my views on the Russian Army and its fighting strength; I told him the *morale* of the army, and consequently its fighting power, had naturally been much shaken by the Revolution, but that it was impossible to count on seeing it run away before a possible German attack; on the contrary, the Russian Army would be certain to defend itself. The Commander-in-Chief had not, at the time, the Reserves necessary for making an attack on a grand scale. If G.H.Q. wished an attack to be made on one or several points of the Eastern Front, in order to make the Russian line give way and cause the disintegration of the army, they would have to provide their own Divisions for that purpose.

G.H.Q. could not think of doing this at the time, as all the Reserves were required in the West. There were no signs of a possible Russian advance to be noticed as yet.

During the rest of our conversation General Ludendorff made no secret of his uneasiness, caused by the internal conditions, and especially by the entire want of decision shown by the Chancellor of the Empire.

Then we spoke of the possibilities there might be in the future if, owing to the Revolution, or to an attack that the German Army made, the Russian lines were broken through, and the Commander-in-Chief in the East were able to send a sufficient number of troops to the Western Front, which, together with the Western Army, would make a grand offensive thrust on one or other point of the enemy Front, and by a successful break-through bring about the decisive battle of the campaign.

We were both agreed that every means must be employed to attain this object. In answer to my question of when, and how, General Ludendorff proposed to make such an attack, he said that the thrust in the West could not be made as it could in the East. To break through in the West was much more difficult, and it would probably be necessary to try at various points, in order to find out where the enemy was weakest, and at which point an attack should be made with all our strength.

I was not of that opinion, and I told him my mind quite freely. My opinion was, and I have not changed it, that there is only one form of tactics possible, however great or small the fighting power of the combatants may be. If you wish to take upon yourself the difficult decision of making an attack, you must concentrate all the forces you possibly can collect at the point you consider the most favourable for that object. This is, of course, a gamble—it is staking everything on a single card.

At the end of our conversation, which was as friendly as all our previous meetings had been, General Ludendorff pointed out to me that there were certain forces at work which were trying to undermine the good understanding that existed between us. I took this news as a joke; I could not believe such a thing could be possible, as we were both working for the same end with all our strength: for the success of the German arms.

The Eastern Front remained inactive during May and June. Already in June there were increasing signs that Kerenski was not in the slightest degree thinking of peace. On the contrary, all the reports that reached us pointed towards Russian preparations for an attack on a large scale. Such preparations could be noticed at Riga, at Dünaburg, at Lake Narocz, at Smorgon, and also along the whole of the Galician Front.

It was about this time that Germany had recourse to a new medium of warfare. This was a species of still stronger poison gas—the so-called Yellow Cross. Privy Councillor Haber, to whom we owe the invention of the first poison gas, and who was also the inventor of the Yellow Cross gas, told me after the war that when he had invented the Yellow Cross he went to G.H.Q. and made a report of his invention to General Ludendorff. The difference that existed between the Yellow Cross and the gas that was already in use was that the latter had forced the opponent to use masks, while for the new Yellow Cross the masks would be of no protection in the long run. The deposits from the Yellow Cross settle on the clothing, eat away the material and cause unpleasant burns. For a time it is possible to find protection from these effects if the soldiers are able often to change their clothes.

In his report to General Ludendorff, Privy Councillor Haber suggested that use should be made of the new gas if it was certain that the war could be brought to an end in a year's time. He could guarantee that the enemy would not be able to imitate it in less than a year, so that for a year we would have the possibility of alone being able to use it. If, however, the war was not finished by the end of a year, Professor Haber thought it would be irretrievably lost for us, if we employed the Yellow Cross in our warfare, as by that time our opponents would have succeeded in imitating it. Thanks to their great industrial capacity they would then be able to produce enormous quantities of it, and they would in their turn be able to bombard us with it. Protective measures—such as macintoshes, and a change of two or three uniforms—we should be unable to supply, as we should not have the necessary materials. Consequently the enemy would not even need to attack: he would simply gas us out of each position.

As a matter of fact, Professor Haber made a mistake on one point: our opponents did not succeed in imitating the Yellow Cross in a year, but in sixteen months. At the beginning of the Armistice the French alone had 5000 tons of this gas ready, and to their great sorrow they were unable any longer to employ it against the German troops.

General Ludendorff was therefore running a great risk when he introduced the use of the Yellow Cross; for although we all hoped that in the course of a year we should be able to defeat Russia, and to release the bulk of the German Eastern Army for the decisive battle in the West, we could not be sure of it.

We naturally tried, by means of propaganda, to increase the disintegration that the Russian Revolution had introduced into the army. Someone at home who had connections with the Russian revolutionaries exiled in Switzerland hit on the idea of employing some of them in order to hasten the undermining and poisoning of the *morale* of the Russian Army. He applied to the deputy Erzberger, who approached the German Foreign Office. And thus it came about that Lenin was conveyed through Germany to Petersburg in the manner that afterwards transpired.

I cannot say if German G.H.Q. was cognizant of this measure. The Commander-in-Chief in the East knew nothing about it. We only heard of it months after, when the foreign newspapers began to reproach Germany about it, and asserted that we were the fathers of the Russian Revolution. This assertion, which is as false as so much of the enemy propaganda, cannot be denied emphatically enough. As I have already said, the Russian Revolution was *engineered* by England; we Germans, who were at war with Russia, had unquestionably the right, when the Russian Revolution did not lead to peace, as at first had been expected, to augment the disorders of the Revolution both in the interior and in the army.

In the same way as I send shells into the enemy trenches, or I discharge poison gas at him, I, as an enemy, have the right to use propaganda against him. On the other hand, at the same time as Lenin, there appeared in Russia a number of Bolsheviks who until then had lived as political refugees in England and Sweden.

As I have already said, I personally knew nothing of the transport of Lenin through Germany. However, if I had been asked, I would scarcely have made any objections to it, as at that time nobody could foresee the fatal consequences that the appearance of those men would have for Russia and for the whole of Europe.

CHAPTER XV

THE Commander-in-Chief on the Eastern Front did not share the hopes of the Foreign Office that a separate Peace could be concluded with the Russian Provisional Government. By the end of June the Russian preparations for an attack became more and more apparent, and when the Russian attack began in Galicia on July 1st it was no surprise for us. At the time of the recommencement of hostilities by the Russians, G.H.Q. again had their hands free. General Ludendorff telephoned to me, and asked if I still thought it would be possible to break through the Russian line in the direction of Tarnopol, as I had formerly suggested, and by such an action parry the Russian attack. He also asked what reinforcements would be needed for the purpose. I answered joyfully in the affirmative, as a German offensive along the railway line Lemberg—Tarnopol would necessarily bring the Russian attack that had just begun in Galicia to a standstill. The more forces the Russians concentrated for their attack on the Fronts of the Austro-Hungarian Army and the Southern Army the greater must be our success.

As the lowest possible demand I asked for four Divisions; G.H.Q. gave us hopes that we might get six.

The Commander-in-Chief began to make energetic preparations for the attack. General von Eben, the leader of the Zloczov sector, was entrusted with the execution of this plan (Major Franz was the

178

Chief of his General Staff). The artillery preparation was again in the charge of Lieutenant-Colonel
Bruchmüller.

The artillery preparation and the bringing up
of troops would take about a fortnight, so that we
calculated July 15th would be the earliest date
for the attack. Already on July 1st the Russians
began their offensive. The Russians broke into the
Austrian positions between Zborov and Brzeczany.
By good luck the first troops that had been sent for
our attack had already arrived. They were sent at
once into action, and on July 2nd they re-established
the position. All the other Russian attacks, which
were made with great dash, failed.

On July 4th, strong attacks were made against
the Southern Army, which after many days'
fighting ended with a complete success for Count
Bothmer's army.

On the 6th and 7th, attacks were begun to the
south of the Dniester on the Austro-Hungarian 3rd
Army. This army had at last been placed under
the Commander-in-Chief on the Eastern Front. We
had placed a German Division at their disposal, and
we had intended that this Division should remain
as a supernumerary Reserve to meet, by a counter-
attack, any Russian break-through on the Austro-
Hungarian Front, and drive the Russians out again.
Only a few days before the attack the Commander-
in-Chief had come in person to the army to assure
himself of the condition of the troops and of the positions. He returned quite satisfied with the general
position. Unfortunately the Austro-Hungarian
Command had not left the German Reserve Division
as a supernumerary Reserve, but had taken it
into action at once, and when the Russian thrust
took place on the 6th there were no troops in
reserve, and no troops at their disposal to make a

counter-attack. The German troops were involved in the retreat, the front of the 3rd Army gave way and fell back beyond the Lomnitza. Kalusz fell into the hands of the Russians. This caused the situation to become very critical. If it were not possible to hold the Lomnitza or to recapture Kalusz, and the retreat of the 3rd Army went still farther back, Stryj, the chief base of the Southern Army, and the oil wells of Drohobicz would be in danger.

The Commander-in-Chief was obliged to support the 3rd Army by sending them German troops, and the question arose whether it would be possible to make the Zloczov attack on July 15th, as had been arranged.

The Bavarian Cavalry Division that had just arrived, with the Reserve Jäger Guard Battalion and the Reserve Guard Light Infantry Battalion, as well as an Infantry Division, were diverted to the 3rd Army. It was also decided for the present to keep to the plans for the attack from Zloczov. If the worst came to the worst—that is, if the German reinforcements were unable to support the 3rd Army —it was always open to us to send southwards all the German troops that would have collected by the 15th to the west of our Front in the district round Zloczov, and strike at the flank of the Russians attacking from the other side of the Lomnitza.

By the intervention of the Bavarian cavalry the Russian advance was stopped, and the position at Kalusz was re-established, so that the attack from Zloczov could be undertaken. It was a pity we had had to give up some units to the 3rd Army, especially the reinforced Bavarian Cavalry Division. The Commander-in-Chief had planned that a specially equipped Cavalry Corps should be thrown across the Sereth, immediately after the break-through from Zloczov had been effected, to pursue the retreating Russians east of the Sereth, in a southern direction. This Corps would probably have had a a great success.

The attack had to be postponed for several days because continuous rains, that had lasted some days, had rendered the clayey soil of Galicia quite impossible for any heavy vehicle, except on the highroads. At last, early on the 19th, the advance was able to begin. The chief thrust was led by the 1st and 2nd Guard Infantry Divisions, and the 5th and 6th Infantry Divisions, under General Kathen. Two days before the Commander-in-Chief had come to Zloczov, so as to be on the spot to intervene if that were necessary. Thanks to Lieutenant-Colonel Bruchmüller's admirable artillery preparation the break-through succeeded perfectly on a width of twenty kilometres. The first day our thrust penetrated to a depth of fifteen kilometres beyond the enemy's line.

Thus, as I have already said, this battle, which in the Reichstag was spoken of as an encouraging success, was, merely by chance, fought on the day the Reichstag was sitting. It is true that during the day General Ludendorff had asked me to give him news of the battle, before 6 P.M.— the time when the Imperial Chancellor intended to give information about the progress of these operations.

The watch-tower from which the Commander-in-Chief and I watched the fight was connected by telephone with G.H.Q., so that at 5 P.M. the Imperial Chancellor could in a few minutes, through G.H.Q., be made acquainted with the exact position at the Front.

During the next few days the attack went on as it had been planned. Tarnopol was taken on the

25th, and, as had been predicted, the whole of the Russian Front, as far as the Carpathians, began to waver. Our nerves were again somewhat strained when, on the 21st, a strong Russian attack at Kovno, south of Smorgon, succeeded in breaking through the Front, and drove back a Landwehr Division, which, however, fought magnificently. For the moment we were unable to help. A Division that we had been able to dispense with at the beginning of the Russian retreat was at once ordered to march to the point in question, but naturally days would elapse before it could arrive. Until that time the 10th Army had to help itself, and it was able to do so. By strong artillery fire, the Russians, who had broken into our positions, were held there, and at last they were obliged to give up the captured trenches. The *morale* of the Russian Army had suffered greatly by the Revolution. Earlier our position would have been somewhat worse.

At the beginning of the Russian retreat in Galicia the allied troops—the Southern Army, the Austro - Hungarian 3rd Army and the Austro-Hungarian 7th Army — got as far as the Carpathians. In the first days of August the pursuit got as far as Zbrucz, and with the exception of quite small areas the whole of Galicia and the Bukovina were cleared of Russian troops. Unfortunately then the operation stopped. For our German troops the distance from our base was too great, and fresh drafts did not come up. The Austro-Hungarian forces more to the south had not the necessary power of attack to develop the success any farther. An attempt of G.H.Q. to develop the success of the Zloczov break-through against the Rumanian Army, which had been the reason for sending the German Alpine Corps to the Rumanian Front as reinforcements, was never carried out, as the Rumanians on their side attacked and had even temporarily local successes.

In the first days of August, when it became clear that before the railways were repaired a continuation of the pursuit in Galicia was not to be thought of, General Ludendorff called me up. We were both of the opinion that these repairs would require a considerable time, and that it was a pity to leave the troops inactive for so long. General Ludendorff said that with the present development of the position in the West he could not foresee how long he would be able to leave us the Divisions that had been sent us as reinforcements for the break-through at Zloczov, but on the other hand it was very desirable to deal the Russians another blow soon in order to hasten as much as possible the disintegration of their army. He therefore wished to know if I thought that, with the forces that had been placed at our disposal, the old favourite idea of the Commander-in-Chief on the Eastern Front, of a crossing of the Düna and the capture of Riga, would be feasible. If it were, he would try to leave the Divisions on the Eastern Front for a short time. I naturally said yes.

I had already sent for Lieutenant-Colonel Bruchmüller while the operations in Galicia were in progress, and I had ordered him to go to the 8th Army in Mitau and to make the necessary artillery reconnaissances for the crossing of the Düna at the point that General Otto von Below had suggested to me long ago, and which I myself had reconnoitred at the time.

Unfortunately it took a long time before we could extricate the troops from the Galician Front, get them to the railway, and move them to Mitau. It was only possible to have them ready by the end of August. We passed several days of great suspense, wondering if we would be able to keep the troops or if we would have to give them up before the taking of Riga.

In the West the great battle of Flanders had been raging since July 31st, and it was just in the last days of August that there were fierce attacks and serious crises. Twice General Ludendorff telephoned to me that he required the troops, twice that he was still able to do without them. At last we had the certainty that we would be able to keep them, and we began the final preparations for the attack.

The Commander-in-Chief went, as usual, to the scene of action in order to be able, if necessary, to intervene personally. The execution of the attack was entrusted to the 8th Army, under General von Hutier (his Chief of Staff was General von Sauberzweig). For this attack three General Commands—the 11th Infantry Division and two Cavalry Divisions—had been assigned. The real thrust was made by three Divisions—the 19th Reserve Division, 14th Bavarian Infantry Division and 2nd Guard Infantry Division — under the General Command 51. The Commander was General von Berrer, who unfortunately was afterwards killed on the Isonzo. After Bruchmüller's 170 batteries and 230 medium and heavy Minenwerfer had done their work the three Divisions making the thrust were to cross the river, at first on pontoons and then on bridges; each Division was to cross by one bridge.

On September 1st, at 4 A.M., the gassing of the enemy positions began; after daybreak, at 6 A.M., the preliminary bombardment; at 9.10 A.M. the first pontoons left the bank. The work of the artillery was again irreproachable. At the beginning of the attack only a few of the enemy guns were fired, and their shooting was bad and irregular. As soon as the first of the infantry reached the northern bank the work of putting up the bridges was begun. It was only the bridge situated farthest to the east that came under some enemy fire during its construction, and also while the troops were crossing it afterwards, but there were only slight losses. On the whole, the crossing was almost ridiculously easy. The first who crossed the central bridge was H.R.H. the Commander-in-Chief, who, as always, hurried to the Front to accompany the troops in their attack. Our thrust met with fierce opposition only on the Little Jägel, which, however, was soon broken. The result in prisoners and booty was smaller than we had expected. Long before our attack the Russians had already evacuated, of their own free will, the western part of the Riga bridge-head, and they evacuated the remainder with feverish haste when the attack began. I regretted very much that we had not been allowed to make an attack on Riga two years earlier, as the Commander-in-Chief had wished. The Russians would not have evacuated the bridge-head then, and the whole of its large garrison would have fallen into our hands. I have never doubted that at that time the crossing of the river would have been effected quite as successfully as on September 1st, 1917, though with somewhat greater losses.

The army was very enthusiastic, and wanted to advance and continue the offensive as far as Petro-grad. From a military point of view this would not have been difficult if G.H.Q. could have left us the reinforcements. But this unfortunately was not possible. After a few days the 8th Army had to be stopped in order to send part of the troops to the West, and the greater part to Italy.

The joy with which we were received in Riga itself was quite touching. The inhabitants had suffered very much from the excesses of the troops, whose *morale* and discipline had sunk very low owing to the Revolution, and also from the hatred of the Letts, and they were thankful to breathe more freely when the German troops occupied the town and brought quiet and order with them.

The Commander-in-Chief had therefore to rely on his own forces for any further development of the operations on the Eastern Front. The objectives could therefore only be limited, as the fights at Zloczov and Riga, and especially on the Little Jägel, had proved that though the Russians had suffered in their *morale*, and that they had no longer the same power of resistance as formerly, they would still defend themselves. Two small undertakings presented themselves without being sought: one was the capture of the bridge-head at Jacobstadt, where the Russians were still on the south side of the Düna; the other was the occupation of the islands of Ösel, Moon and Dagö. The first undertaking was proposed by the 8th Army, the second was necessary if we wished to remain in the undisturbed possession of Riga, and it also meant a stronger menace to Petrograd.

For the capture of the bridge-head at Jacobstadt Lieutenant-Colonel Bruchmüller and the necessary amount of artillery was left with the 8th Army. As usual, Bruchmüller carried out the placing of his artillery and the preliminary artillery bombardment in a masterly manner, and on September 21st the bridge-head was easily taken. The preparations for the occupation of the islands required a longer time, as the fleet was to take part in it, and naturally it had no experience in the operation of landing troops. On the other hand, the naval authorities were glad, after so long a time, to be able once again to have the opportunity of taking an active part in the war otherwise than by the U-boat warfare. The continued inactivity of the High Sea Fleet, the crowding together in one place of such numbers of human material, favoured the propaganda of the disaffected elements. Already for some time past there had been unsatisfactory reports about the moral atmosphere in the fleet, especially in connection with the cases of mutiny that had occurred during the summer on some of the ships. The legal inquiry and the discussions in the Reichstag on this subject had caused it to become generally known.

In order to consult about this scheme I went once to Berlin and, shortly before it began, to Libau. The Commander-in-Chief had entrusted the leadership of this expedition to General von Kathen. He had the 42nd Infantry Division and a Cycle Brigade placed at his disposal.

At the beginning of October the preparations were at last concluded, but unfortunately contrary winds delayed the commencement of the undertaking. It was only on the 11th that the transport flotilla, convoyed by a part of the High Sea Fleet, left the harbour of Libau, and it landed on the 12th in the Taggar Bay on the northern side of the island of Ösel. The island was well protected by a chain of permanent batteries. The landing, especially on the northern side, took the Russians by surprise. It was effected without much opposition. The troops that had landed pushed forward rapidly through the island to the south and the east, and by a bold stroke seized the embankment opposite the island of Moon, and the next day they occupied without much resistance the islands of Moon and Dagö.

Afterwards I became very well acquainted with the Russian defender of the island, Admiral Altvater, who belonged to the Bolshevik Armistice Commission, as an expert. He told me at that time the Bolshevik propaganda had spread so widely among the troops that it was impossible to think any longer of a real defence. The troops simply melted away before his eyes.

While we were winning easy victories in the East over the Russian Army, which was becoming more and more disorganized, the fierce fighting of the battle of Flanders raged in the West, where our troops were able to maintain their positions only with difficulty.

In the Italian theatre of war, since August, attacks were also being made on the Austro-Hungarian Army. In the actions that took place during August and September, and which go under the general name of the 11th Isonzo battle, the Italians had certain successes to the north and the south of Görz. Here also it was very evident that the strength of the Austro-Hungarian troops was exhausted. It might be feared that if there was a 12th Isonzo battle they would quite collapse. German G.H.Q. were therefore requested to send them help. Here again two questions arose, whether the help was to be in the form of a strong thrust, which would relieve the Austro-Hungarian Army on the Isonzo Front, or if we were to begin operations on a large scale in order to deal the Italians a shattering blow.

General Ludendorff explains in his book why only the first of these questions could be considered at the time. From these explanations it appears that G.H.Q. had likewise considered the second question—that is, a simultaneous attack from Tyrol and on the Isonzo Front. General Ludendorff goes on to say that the only reason against it was that Germany was not able to spare sufficient troops, but only six to eight Divisions, which for such a double thrust on a large scale would be insufficient. I am not quite of that opinion. The Eastern Front, at that time, could easily have spared considerable forces if we had been asked to do so. It was not to be expected that the Russians could be roused into another attack, so that the risk of even a considerable weakening of the Eastern Front was not very great. If one remembers how small was the Italian power of resistance against a German attack it is almost impossible to realize what the success of the larger operation would have been.

CHAPTER XVI

THE ARMISTICE IN THE EAST

In the meantime the destiny of Russia was pursuing its course. The officers were deprived of their rank and discharged. Soldiers' Councils were organized. With this destruction of discipline the army was done for; the regiments degenerated into armed hordes which no longer possessed any sort of military value. The ruin of the army went hand in hand with the internal decomposition. After one unsuccessful attempt, the Bolsheviks succeeded in getting all the power into their own hands. One of the first measures of the new Government was the dispatch of a wireless message, on November 26th, in which the Commissary Krylenko, who had been promoted from corporal to Commander-in-Chief, inquired if German G.H.Q. were willing to conclude an Armistice.

General Ludendorff telephoned to me, and asked: " Is it possible to negotiate with these people?" I answered: " Yes, it is possible to negotiate with them. Your Excellency needs troops and this is the quickest way to get them."

I have often thought since that it might have been better if the leaders of the German State and Army had refused to have any sort of negotiations with the Bolshevik usurpers. By giving the Bolsheviks the possibility of concluding a Peace, and thus satisfying the longing of the people, we also gave them the opportunity of getting themselves into power and staying there. If Germany had refused to negotiate with them, and had insisted on representatives of the Russian people and a Government constituted by free election, the Bolsheviks would not have been able to remain in power. Still, I think, no man of sense will reproach us for having accepted Krylenko's proposal for an Armistice.

G.H.Q. accepted Krylenko's proposal, and on December 2nd the Russian Armistice Delegation crossed our lines at Dünaburg and proceeded to Brest-Litovsk. The Commander-in-Chief received orders to conclude an Armistice. H.R.H. the Commander-in-Chief entrusted me with the direction of the negotiations. A few days before, von Rosenberg, who afterwards became Ambassador, arrived in Brest-Litovsk to represent the German Foreign Office. He had instructions only to be present at the negotiations and to see that certain points to which the Foreign Office attached importance were not neglected. G.H.Q. looked upon the conclusion of an Armistice as an entirely military question. Representatives of the Allied Powers also arrived. They were Lieutenant-Colonel Pokorny, for Austria-Hungary; Adjutant-General Zekke represented Turkey, and Colonel Gantscheff was sent by Bulgaria.

The conditions that were to be demanded had been settled in principle by G.H.Q. some time before, and they had been sent to the Commander-in-Chief. They were dictated by our desire to end the war on one Front, and contained no conditions that were unjust or humiliating to the Russians. Hostilities were to cease and each side was to retain the positions they held.

On such a basis the conditions of an Armistice could have been settled in a few hours with any normal adversary. With the Russians it was not quite so simple. The Russian Delegation was composed of Joffe (who afterwards unfortunately became so well known to us), Kameneff (Trotzky's brother-in-law), and Madame Byzenko (who had already achieved a certain amount of fame through the murder of a Minister), a non-commissioned officer, a sailor, a workman and a peasant. These were the members of the Commission who were entitled to a vote.

Admiral Altvater and a certain number of Staff Officers were attached to the Commission. They had no vote and had only to act as experts. Karachan was the secretary of the Commission. It was not difficult to house this Commission in some of the huts that we occupied in the Citadel of Brest-Litovsk. With regard to their food, I asked the Commission whether they would prefer to have their meals in the Staff Officers' mess-room or to have their food sent in to them. The Russians accepted the first proposal. I had one of the large huts arranged for the meetings of the Commission. It was here that we first met the Russian delegates. H.R.H. the Commander-in-Chief greeted them in a speech of welcome and informed them that he was empowered by the Allied Chief Commands to conclude the terms of an Armistice, and that he had appointed me to conduct the negotiations. Joffe replied in a few words.

Then the negotiations began. The first condition the Russians made was that of entire publicity. They demanded to have the right, at the conclusion of each consultation, to make known by telegraph or wireless the exact text of what each party had said. I had nothing against this; but in order to avoid the publication of erroneous interpretations, on one side or the other, I suggested the appointment of an Auxiliary Commission which would draw up the minutes of each meeting immediately after it had taken place, and when these minutes had received the approval of both sides this text would be used for publication. The Russians agreed to this. Then we had to listen to a long propagandist speech similar to many others that Trotzky inflicted on us. It concluded with a demand to all the Powers engaged in the war to end the struggle, to conclude an Armistice, and then settle the terms of a general Peace.

My reply to this consisted of the question whether the Russian Delegation was authorized by their Allies to make such proposals to us. The military representatives of the Quadruple Alliance were present and they were willing to enter into negotiations. The Russians had to confess that they had no such authority. I therefore proposed that they should keep within the limits of the authority they possessed, and that we should proceed to the negotiation of a separate Armistice with Russia.

Other Russian attempts to change the negotiations into propagandist channels I was also able to check. A little difficulty arose when Admiral Altvater suddenly demanded the evacuation of Riga and of the islands in the Moon Bay. Considering the state of affairs, I felt that this demand was an incredible piece of assurance, and I therefore refused curtly and emphatically to consider it at all. In a pamphlet that one of the Russians experts published afterwards, I noted that all the officers of the General Staff were unanimously against Altvater's idea, as it could not be supposed that we would agree to such a proposal. It was therefore quickly suppressed after my refusal.

The Russians laid great stress on the condition that all the German troops stationed along the Eastern Front should remain there, in order to prevent us transporting them to the West. There was no difficulty about agreeing to this. Before the negotiations had begun in Brest-Litovsk, the order had already been given to send the bulk of the Eastern Army to the Western Front. Consequently I was easily able to concede to the Russians that, during the Armistice that was about to be signed, the Germans would not send away any troops from the Eastern Front except those that were already being moved, or that had already received orders to go.

Certain difficulties were caused also by the question of intercourse between the two armies. With the object of propaganda in view, the Russians naturally laid great store on the most extensive and unhindered intercourse between the trenches, while our interests were exactly contrary. I therefore proposed, as it seemed quite impossible to prevent all intercourse, that it was to be limited to certain places. In this way it would be possible to exercise some control, and to intercept the greater part of the propaganda literature that might be expected.

The further demand for the free admission into Germany of all Bolshevik propaganda and literature I was obliged to refuse, but I said I was quite willing to assist in the export of this to France and England.

After much negotiation we at last succeeded in making a draft Armistice scheme which was largely in accordance with the German plan. Then, during lunch, Joffe explained that in order to obtain power to sign a definite treaty for an Armistice he must go back to Petrograd. Although this delay was unwelcome, I did not share the suspicion of some of the Allied representatives that Joffe's demand was only a manoeuvre to break off the negotiations, and that the Delegation would probably not return at all. I was not mistaken, however: the Delegation returned at the appointed time, and the suspension of hostilities that had been arranged for the time of their absence was changed into an Armistice by the signing of the treaty by both parties.

As the Delegates took their meals with us in the mess we had the opportunity of getting to know what sort of men some of them were. I had, of course, placed those members of the Commission who had a vote higher than those who were merely experts, so that the workman, the sailor and the non-commissioned officer sat in higher places than the Admiral or the officers. I shall never forget the first dinner we had with the Russians. I sat between Joffe and Sokolnikov, who is now the Commissioner of Finance. Opposite me was the workman, who was evidently caused much trouble by the various implements that he found on the table. He tried to seize the food on his plate first with one thing and then with another; it was only the fork that he used exclusively as a toothpick. Almost opposite me sat Madame Byzenko, next to Prince Hohenlohe, who had on his other side the peasant, a typical Russian figure with long grey curls and an enormous, untrimmed beard. He drew a smile from the orderly who was serving the wine, and had asked him if he would take claret or hock, when he inquired which was the stronger, as he would prefer to have that.

Joffe, Kameneff and Sokolnikov all appeared to be extraordinarily intelligent, more especially Joffe. They all spoke enthusiastically of the task that lay before them, the task of leading the Russian proletariat to the heights of happiness and prosperity. They all three did not doubt for a moment that this must happen if the nation governed itself according to the teaching of Marx. The least of Joffe's visions was that all men should live in comfort, and that a few—among whom, as I gathered, he himself would be numbered—should live in something more. To be sure, they all made no secret of the fact that the Russian Revolution was only the first step towards the happiness of the world at large. It was naturally impossible for a state governed on communistic principles to continue to exist when it was surrounded by states governed by capitalistic systems; therefore the object they were all striving for was a universal revolution.

It was during these conversations that the first doubts arose in my mind as to whether it had been right for Germany to enter into negotiations with the Bolsheviks at all. They had promised their people peace and happiness. If they were able to take peace home with them, would not their position be greatly strengthened in the eyes of the masses who had longed for peace for years? Other doubts came into my mind during the conversations I had with the officers, especially with Admiral Altvater. I talked much with him about the extraordinarily fine Russian Army, and wondered how the Revolution could have so completely corroded it. Altvater replied:

" The influence of Bolshevik propaganda on the masses is enormous. I have already often talked with you about it, and complained that at the time I was defending Ösel the troops actually melted away before my eyes. It was the same with the whole army, and I warn you the same thing will happen in your army."

I only laughed at the unfortunate Admiral. He was murdered some time after that.

CHAPTER XVII

THE PEACE OF BREST-LITOVSK

The fulfilment of the terms of the Armistice that had been signed at Brest-Litovsk met with opposition on most parts of the Front. It was not that the Russian troops did not want an Armistice, but because both on the Southern Front and in the Caucasus the Bolshevik Delegation was not recognized as possessing the authority to conclude an Armistice. Of all the Commissions that had been appointed to carry out the conditions of the Armistice only one was able to reach its appointed place, and that was in the northern sector, where it was able to reach Dünaburg. All those that had to go south could not cross the frontier for the time.

The Armistice was concluded with the view of bringing about a Peace between Russia on the one side and the Quadruple Alliance on the other. In order to carry this intention into effect the representatives of the four Powers assembled in Brest-Litovsk. The Secretary of State, von Kühlmann, came as the representative of the German Empire. By an order of G.H.Q. I was appointed as their representative to assist the Secretary of State. I was placed under his authority, and I had only the right of bringing the wishes or the opinions of G.H.Q. forward for discussion and, if necessary, to protest against any measures taken by the Secretary of State. I wish this to be well understood, because public opinion is inclined to make G.H.Q. and myself, as their representative, responsible for all that took

197

place in Brest-Litovsk, and more especially for the Peace that was dictated there. That is wrong. It is Count Hertling, who was at the time Chancellor of the Empire, and the Secretary of State for Foreign Affairs, who are alone responsible for the negotiations, and for the signature of the Peace.

Count Czernin, a clever, distinguished man, whose nerves were unfortunately entirely shattered, came as the representative of the Dual Monarchy. He was firmly convinced that Austria-Hungary would crumble to pieces if they could not obtain peace very soon. The one thought that completely mastered him was the wish at the very least to come to some arrangement with Russia and to be able to take a Treaty of Peace home with him.

The Bulgarian mission was headed by their minister Popoff, an unimportant personage, with a limited political horizon and, perhaps just in consequence of this, great obstinacy. The clever Minister-President Radoslavov and the Turkish Grand Vizier Talaat only appeared on the scenes later.

The representatives of Turkey were at first the Ambassador in Berlin and former Grand Vizier, Hakki, an unusually clever and skilful diplomatist, and the Secretary of State for Foreign Affairs, Messimy Bey.

The leaders of the Russian Delegation were at first: Joffe, Kameneff and Professor Pokrovsky.

To house and feed these numerous missions (they numbered together about four hundred people) was naturally no easy matter. However, thanks to the ability of the Quastermaster-General and of the managers of the various officers' messes, these difficulties were overcome. In the former Russian theatre, which had almost escaped destruction, a hall of sufficiently large dimensions was prepared for the general meetings; while for the smaller assemblies the smaller room we had used for the negotiations of the Armistice was at our disposal.

Shortly after the arrival of Kühlmann and Czernin I was called upon to be present at a consultation that took place between them for the settlement of the first steps that were to be taken. The first thing to be done was to send the Russians an answer to their Peace proposals, which, like their proposals for an Armistice, were addressed to all the belligerents, and suggested that all should meet at a round table to negotiate terms for ending hostilities. The Russian proposals spoke of a Peace without annexations.

Secretary of State von Kühlmann's standpoint was that Germany would accept this proposal if the Russians were able to induce the Entente States to agree to such negotiations. In his opinion the settlement of the question of the border states, Poland, Lithuania and Kurland, did not come into the category of annexations, as the legally appointed representatives of these states had decided of their own free will, a long time previously, to separate themselves from Russia and to place the settlement of their future status in the hands of Germany or the Central Powers. Count Czernin was naturally anxious to accept the proposal of a Peace without annexations, and he certainly ought to have been pleased to enter into negotiations on such a basis with the enemy Powers, who had decided on the partition of Austria-Hungary.

The two statesmen had decided to send an answer agreeing unreservedly to a Peace without annexations " if the Entente Powers would also agree to negotiate a Peace on similar terms." I did not like this answer. First, because, by adopting the Russian style, it contained a number of expressions that went against my feelings; and, secondly, because at bottom it was a lie. It was entirely based on the conditional phrase: " If the Entente," etc. I considered it would have been more correct to have kept strictly to facts, by answering the Russians that the Central Powers were willing to enter on negotiations for a general Peace, as they had proved by several proposals they had already made, and by the resolutions of the German Reichstag, but as the Russian Peace Delegation had no legal right to speak for the other Powers of the Entente, and until the Russians were able to produce credentials that would entitle them to do so, it would be possible for them to negotiate only a separate Peace with the Quadruple Alliance.

I mentioned my scruples to the Secretary of State. He, however, stuck to his decision. As he had gone with the Chancellor of State to G.H.Q., before coming to Brest-Litovsk, I had to suppose that during the consultation of the Supreme Civil Authority and the High Command a decision had been arrived at with regard to the *modus procedendi*, so I had to submit.

When it came to the signing of the answer to the Russians the Bulgarians made difficulties. Minister Popoff declared that they—the Bulgarians—had been promised certain portions of Serbia and the Dobrudja, and they could not think of endangering their claim to these promised territories by putting their signature to such an answer. They had entered into the war with the object of annexations and they had no intention of resigning them. It was in vain that Kühlmann and Czernin lavished their persuasive eloquence on Popoff; even when they had explained to him a hundred times that there was no danger, that it was done only to make a good impression at the very beginning of the negotiations, that it was impossible to suppose England and France would agree to enter into negotiations for peace, and that all the explanations that the Central Powers were giving now would be invalid if the Entente were not ready to negotiate — still he obstinately stuck to his " No."

General Gantscheff, the second Bulgarian representative, showed himself more amenable and more sensitive to this diplomatic logic. He sent a detailed telegram to Tsar Ferdinand, and he was able to obtain from him an order for Popoff to sign. Messimy Bey was also in doubt about signing, but he was more easily persuaded by Kühlmann and Czernin than the Bulgarian could be. On December 24th the answer was delivered to the Russians. Some expressions in this Note, that appeared to me too humiliating, I had succeeded in having deleted or altered.

The Russians were triumphant, and telegraphed their satisfaction to Petrograd. By mutual consent we had now to wait ten days, to give the Entente time to notify if they wished to participate in the Peace Conference.

Secretary of State Kühlmann and Count Czernin suggested to the Russians that they should not remain inactive during these ten days, but should organize a number of Commissions and proceed at once to the settlement of various secondary points of the Treaty of Peace. The Russians agreed to this. Joffe and some of the members of the Delegation had the intention of again returning to Petrograd during that time. He hinted that when he came back he would probably be accompanied by the Commissioner for Foreign Affairs, Trotzky.

From the conversations we had I received the impression that the Russians had misunderstood the offer of our diplomatists, and that they supposed a

Peace without annexations would give them back the Polish, Lithuanian and Kurland governments. My impression was confirmed by a conversation Major Brinckmann had with the Russian Lieutenant-Colonel Fokke. Fokke said quite positively that immediately after Peace had been signed the German troops would retire beyond the old frontier of 1914. I told the Secretary of State that I considered it impossible to allow the Russians to go back to Petrograd under such misapprehensions. If in Petrograd they not only led their Government, but also large circles of the people, to believe that the Peace they were about to sign would guarantee to Russia the old frontiers of 1914, the admission that they had misunderstood it, and that the Note of the Central Powers must be understood differently—in other words, that they had been deceived—could only result in frantic indignation on the Russian side. I therefore considered it was quite time to undeceive them on this point, and I offered to do so.

The Secretary of State saw that I was right, and agreed with me. Count Czernin agreed too.

That morning during lunch I said to Joffe, who sat next to me, I perceived that the Russian Delegation had understood the meaning of a Peace without forcible annexations differently from the meaning attached to it by the representatives of the Central Powers. The latter took up the standpoint that it was not a forcible annexation if portions of the former Russian Empire decided, of their own free will, and by a determination of their existing political representatives, on a separation from the Union of Russian States, and on being united to the German Empire, or any other State. The Russian rulers themselves had given these rights to the different states by their declaration of the Self-Determination of Nations. This applied to Poland,

Lithuania and Kurland. The representatives of the three states had announced their withdrawal from the Union of Russian States. The Central Powers did not consider it an annexation if the future fate of these states were decided by a direct understanding with their representatives, to the exclusion of the Russian State.

Joffe looked as if he had received a blow on the head. After lunch we had a conference that lasted several hours. The Russians were represented by Joffe, Kameneff and Pokrovsky—the Germans by the Secretary of State, Czernin and myself. In this conference the Russians gave free vent to their disappointment and indignation. Pokrovsky said, with tears in his eyes, it was impossible to speak of a Peace without annexations when about eighteen governments were torn from the Russian Empire. In the end the Russians threatened to break off the conference and depart. Count Czernin was beside himself. He had brought with him instructions from the Emperor of Austria not to allow the Conference of Brest to fail on any account, and if the worst came to the worst, and the German demands endangered its continuation, he was even to make a separate Peace with the Russians. His nerves completely gave way, and he not only spoke very excitedly with the Secretary of State of his intentions of making a separate Peace, but he also sent his military adviser, Field-Marshal Csicsericz, to my office, to threaten me in the same manner, evidently hoping to make an impression on the German Headquarters in this way. I could not understand the Count's excitement. In my opinion there was no question of the negotiations being broken off by the Russians. The Russian masses were longing for peace, the army had crumbled away — it consisted now of mere insubordinate armed hordes—and the only chance the Bolsheviks had of remaining in power was by signing a Peace. They were obliged to accept the conditions of the Central Powers, however hard they might be.

I therefore answered Field-Marshal Csicsericz's threat of a separate Peace very calmly: that I thought this a brilliant idea, as it would release our twenty-five Divisions that till then I had been obliged to keep on the Austro-Hungarian Front, for the support of their army. By a separate Peace the right wing of the German Army would be automatically covered by Austria-Hungary, so that the military position of the German Eastern Army would derive special benefit by such a measure.

Kühlmann, the Secretary of State, also received Czernin's threat of a separate Peace with great calmness. He told me that he had requested a written statement of the standpoint of the Austro-Hungarian Government, and it appeared to me that he was not loth to have such an instrument in his hands in case G.H.Q. seemed inclined to go too far. The excited discussions, and the still more excited exchange of telegrams, of these days had at first no results, as we were obliged to wait quietly to see if the Russian Delegation would return from Petrograd or not, though the only one of us all who doubted this was Count Czernin.

During this pause Count Czernin went to Vienna and Secretary of State Kühlmann to Berlin, and by his request I accompanied him.

When I was announced to General Ludendorff I was received very coldly and with the angry question: "How could you allow such a Note to be dispatched?"

I explained that I had supposed, and I was bound to suppose, that the general outline of the negotiations had been discussed and settled between

G.H.Q. and the Chancellor of the Empire and the Secretary of State during their conferences in Kreuznach. General Ludendorff denied this, but admitted that I had the right to suppose this had been done.

Even now it is a mystery to me that G.H.Q. and the leaders of the Government had not arrived at such an understanding during the conference they had had on December 18th. It is impossible to settle the lines for so difficult a task as a Treaty of Peace by casual conversation on both sides.

In connection with my conversation with General Ludendorff I had to report myself to the Kaiser in the Bellevue Palace. His Majesty took great interest both in the Armistice, which had been concluded, and in the negotiations that were in progress. I had to describe to him minutely all that had occurred and the personalities of all who had taken part in the negotiations, and as my report was not finished when the lunch hour approached I was bidden to lunch. After the meal His Majesty continued the conversation on the question of the Eastern Front, and alluded to the Polish difficulties. He demanded my opinion on the Polish question. I hesitated a little, and begged His Majesty to excuse me from giving it, as my opinion differed from the views of G.H.Q. and I did not wish to put myself in opposition to them. His Majesty replied: " When your Chief War Lord wishes to hear your opinions on any subject it is your duty to give them to him, quite irrespective of whether they coincide with the opinions of G.H.Q. or not."

I was an enemy of any settlement of the Polish question which would increase the number of German subjects of Polish nationality. Notwithstanding the measures that Prussia had taken, during many decades, we had not been able to manage our fellow-subjects of Polish origin, and I could not see the advantage of any addition to the number of citizens of that nationality. To add to Germany a broad strip of borderland with a population of about 2,000,000 Poles, as G.H.Q. demanded, would, in my opinion, be only a disadvantage to the Empire. I considered the so-called Germano-Polish settlement as still worse. In my opinion, the new Polish frontier ought to be drawn in such a way that it should bring to the Empire the smallest possible number of Polish subjects and that there should be only a few unimportant corrections of the frontier. To the latter I reckoned a small strip of land near Bendzin and Thorn, so that in any subsequent war the enemy artillery would not be able to fire straight into the Upper Silesian coal-mines or on to the chief railway station of Thorn. I also reckoned on including the heights of Mlava, for the better defence of the Soldau district, and, lastly, the crossing of the Bobr, near Osowiec, which had caused us so many headaches.

The increase in Polish inhabitants, which would amount to about 100,000, could not be helped. But beyond that not a man.

During this conversation His Majesty agreed with me.

On January 2nd there was a consultation between the Government and G.H.Q. in the General Staff, and afterwards a Privy Council in the Bellevue Palace. I was ordered to attend both. I tried in vain to see General Ludendorff for a moment previously, to inform him of the report His Majesty had demanded of me.

At the Privy Council the first subject of discussion was the progress of the negotiations in Brest-Litovsk. Secretary of State von Kühlmann made a statement of what had been done as yet, and how he expected the further negotiations would progress, to which His Majesty assented. Then the Kaiser began to speak on the Polish question. He had had the new Polish frontier drawn on a map in accordance with my report, and said that he considered this the right one. He could not refuse to take into consideration the serious objections there were to the settlement proposed by G.H.Q. and which, on his demand, had been laid before him by me, in consequence of which he must retract the consent he had previously given to the project of G.H.Q. General Ludendorff contradicted these objections in a somewhat vehement manner. His Majesty's decision could not be definitely given at once, and he earnestly entreated that G.H.Q. might be permitted to lay the case again before His Majesty. General Field-Marshal von Hindenburg seconded this request. His Majesty brought the somewhat painful scene to an end by saying: " I therefore await a further report from G.H.Q."

The Privy Council had not settled anything definitely or decisively. The Secretary of State had not been told quite clearly what position he was to take up at Brest, nor had the Polish question been decided. His Majesty the Kaiser had only approved of what Kühlmann had done so far, and he had authorized him to continue on the same lines. The difficult problem of the border States remained unsettled. It is true that G.H.Q. had advised a more rapid and energetic method of negotiation at Brest, by which the fate of the border States that were already in the possession of Germany would be settled by their being definitely separated from Russia and assigned to the Central Powers. However, Kühlmann succeeded in carrying his point of trying to have the separation of the border States not made by the way of annexation, but by

the more amicable method of Self-Determination.
After this meeting, on the evening of January 2nd,
we started again for Brest-Litovsk.

It was quite clear to me that General Ludendorff
would be very much offended with me for differing
so completely from them on the Polish question,
and I was not deceived. Already the next day I
was telephoned to from Berlin, and informed that
Hindenburg and Ludendorff had made it a question
of confidence. They both threatened to resign and
demanded that I should be recalled. The Kaiser
gave in on the Polish question but refused to alter
the personal one. He protected me, as might have
been expected.

Besides these facts, which were only told me, I
felt the resentment of G.H.Q. personally in a series
of orders and questions that were sent me in a form
which showed me great men can also be very small
sometimes.

At the end of the first week in January the Russians returned from Petrograd. I had never doubted
that they would do so. The former leader, Joffe,
returned, but not as the head of the deputation;
his place was taken by Trotzky. There were two
versions of the reason for this change: one report
said Trotzky had been furious that Joffe had not
seen at once the craftiness of the Central Powers'
answer and that this was the cause of his being
superseded; he was retained in the Delegation only
on account of his local and personal knowledge of
Brest-Litovsk and its inhabitants, which he had
acquired during the weeks he had been there and
which the Delegation wanted to utilize. The other
version said that Joffe had really been enraged at
the hypocritical offer of peace made by the Central
Powers and that he had refused to continue the
negotiations. It was against his will, and only at

Trotzky's request, that he had given in, and had consented to accompany the Delegation and assist it with his personal knowledge.

Trotzky was certainly the most interesting personality in the new Russian Government: clever, versatile, cultivated, possessed of great energy, powers of work, and eloquence, he gave the impression of a man who knew exactly what he wanted and who would not be deterred from using any means for the attainment of his end. The question has been much discussed whether he came with the intention of concluding a Peace, or if, from the very beginning, he only wanted to find the most conspicuous platform from which to spread his Bolshevik theories. Although propaganda played such a prominent part in the whole of the negotiations of the following weeks, I still think that Trotzky at first wanted to try to make peace, and that it was only afterwards, when he had been driven into a corner by Kühlmann's dialectics, for which he was no match, that he thought of bringing the conference to a spectacular finish by declaring that, though Russia could not accept the conditions of peace offered by the Central Powers, nor even fully discuss them, they hereby declared the war at an end.

Even before the negotiations had begun, a new group of participants presented themselves in Brest-Litovsk. They were the representatives of the Ukrainian Peasant States, whom the Rada had sent in order to make a separate Peace for the Ukraine, basing their demand on the declaration of the Petrograd Soviet Government regarding Self-Determination. Kühlmann and I received the Ukrainians with pleasure, as their appearance offered a possibility of playing them off against the Petrograd Delegation. To Count Czernin, however, their arrival was merely a new source of anxiety, as it could be foreseen that the representatives of the Ukraine would make demands about the political rights of their fellow-countrymen who were living in the Bukovina and East Galicia.

With Trotzky's arrival the unconstrained intercourse that had existed until then outside the meeting hall came to an end. Trotzky requested that the Delegation might have their meals in their quarters, and prohibited all private intercourse and all conversations.

At the very beginning of the negotiations there was a slight collision. Herr Trotzky seemed to consider the platform in Brest-Litovsk not large enough for his propagandist designs. He demanded that the scene of the negotiations should be removed to Stockholm. His chief object in this demand was the wish to get away from Brest-Litovsk, the Military Headquarters in the war zone, where it would be impossible to get into direct contact with the dissatisfied elements of the Central Powers, with whose help the inflammatory portions of his speeches would be underlined and carried to wide circles of the people for propaganda purposes. Naturally the Central Powers refused this demand. Then a battle of words began between Trotzky and Kühlmann, that lasted several weeks, and led to nothing. It was only gradually that it became clear to all parties concerned in the negotiations that Trotzky's chief object was to preach the Bolshevik doctrines, that he was only speaking to the gallery and did not set the slightest store by any practical work to be done. Simultaneously with his speeches, wireless messages were sent to "all," inciting to revolt, to disobedience, to the murder of officers. I protested energetically against this. Trotzky promised to desist, but these inflammatory wireless messages continued to be sent.

The negotiations went further and further from their real object, and turned into theoretical discussions. Trotzky's tone became with each day more aggressive. One day I therefore pointed out to Secretary of State Kühlmann and Count Czernin that it was impossible to attain our object in this way: that it was absolutely necessary to bring the negotiations back to a basis of facts, and offered at the next opportunity to represent to the Russians what the position really was, and why we were assembled there. As always, the Secretary of State was quite of my opinion. Count Czernin, whose nerves became worse every day, as he felt that he never came an inch nearer his object of returning to Vienna with a Treaty of Peace, had some objections to make, as he still hoped by amiability and diplomatic cleverness to get round the Bolshevik gentlemen. At last he also gave in. It was decided that at the next favourable opportunity Kühlmann would pass the word on to me, and I should say whatever I thought necessary.

The opportunity came sooner than we had expected. The next day Kameneff, Trotzky's brother-in-law, made a speech, by Trotzky's order, which infuriated all the officers present. It was a piece of amazing insolence; the Russians might have had a certain right to speak in that way if the positions had been reversed—that is to say, if the German Army had been defeated and lay defenceless on the ground, and the Russian armies had been in victorious possession of German territory.

A glance at the Secretary of State showed me that his patience also was exhausted. He desired me to speak, and I explained to the Russians on the one hand the exact position, and on the other the difference there was between their words and their deeds—how they made great speeches about freedom of conscience and freedom of speech, self-determination and other beautiful things, and how in fact they permitted no sort of freedom within the circle of their power : how they had dispersed with bayonets the Constitutional Assemblies that went against them, how they had expelled by force of arms the National Assembly of the White Russians in Minsk, in the same way as they had now turned out the freely elected Rada of the Ukrainians. I said that the question of the border States was settled, as far as German G.H.Q. was concerned : they took the view that the legal representatives of these States had decided on separation from Soviet Russia, and that no further vote was necessary. I spoke seated, and absolutely quietly; I neither raised my voice in any way, nor did I thump with my fist on the table, as reports had it.[1]

When I finished there was profound silence. Even Herr Trotzky, at the first moment, could not find a word in reply. It was difficult to find anything to say against it, as all I had asserted was in strict accordance with facts. The meeting was quickly adjourned.

The actual effects of my explanations were not as great as I had expected. At the next meeting Trotzky confined himself to saying a few meaningless words of defence and scarified my speech as a mere expression of military propaganda. After this he still avoided touching on anything that might have led to practical results, and continued his dialectical fireworks. Unfortunately the Secretary of State also failed to take advantage of the position created by my speech to force the meetings to begin practical work.

[1] Compare my description with the report given by Karl Friedrich Novak in his book, *The Collapse of the Central Powers* (Chapter: " Brest-Litovsk "), which was written from details given by those who were present, and is quite truthful on every point.

Through the Chief of the Operations Section I had had my motives in making that speech explained to General Ludendorff, and I had begged him to give me his opinion on it. General Ludendorff approved of my action, and encouraged me to do all I could to shorten the negotiations and bring them down to realities. Not having been able to attain any real advance by my interruption of Trotzky's flow of eloquence, another way was open to me; this was negotiation with the Ukrainian Delegation.

The Ukrainian representatives did not hold themselves aloof from us as Trotzky did. They had their meals with us in the officers' mess-room, and they conversed with us quietly about their objects and their wishes. I had the impression that we would soon be able to come to terms with them. I therefore offered Count Czernin, who was naturally the most important personage in these negotiations with the Ukrainians, my services as intermediary. In this I acted in accordance with the opinion I held that the conclusion of a separate Peace between the Central Powers and the Ukraine would naturally also force Trotzky to emerge from his reserve. The young representatives of the Kiev Central Rada were not sympathetic to Count Czernin, and he did not like to negotiate with young Messrs Liubinski and Sevruk, who were scarcely past their student years, on a footing of equality. I proposed that the Count should authorize me first to find out privately from the Ukrainians under what conditions they would be willing to conclude a separate Peace with the Central Powers. Count Czernin gave me this authority. After a certain amount of persuasion on my part the two Ukrainian gentlemen at last divulged their wishes. They extended to the annexation by the Ukraine of the districts round Cholm, and also the Ruthenian portions of East Galicia and the Bukovina.

As I considered an independent Polish State to be a Utopia, and I still hold that opinion, I had no hesitation in promising the Ukrainians my support with regard to the Cholm lands. On the other hand, I looked upon the demand for Austro-Hungarian territory as a piece of impudence, and I gave the two young men to understand as much, in a somewhat curt manner. They had evidently expected my reply, as they assured me most amiably that they would require to obtain new instructions from Kiev to be able to continue negotiations on the basis resulting from our conversation.

Count Czernin's position became very difficult about this time owing to a food crisis that broke out in Vienna in consequence of the want of foresight of the Austro-Hungarian Government. In order to prevent a state of famine, Berlin had to be asked for aid. Notwithstanding its own need, Berlin assisted, but in consequence Count Czernin naturally was deprived of the possibility of threatening to conclude a separate Peace with Trotzky, or even trying to do so. On the other hand, the separate Peace with the Ukraine, which I had looked upon as a measure that might force Trotzky to sign a Peace, now became, as a means of obtaining bread, a vital necessity for Count Czernin. It was a bad thing for Austria that it was impossible to hide her desperate position from the Ukrainians.

In the meantime, fresh instructions arrived from Kiev, and were submitted to me at another consultation. The Cholm district was *conditio sine qua non*. It apparently had dawned upon the authorities in Kiev that the defeated side could not demand the cession of territory from the other party. They therefore renounced all claim to any part of East

Galicia and the Bukovina, but they demanded that these districts should be formed into independent Austro-Hungarian Crownlands under the Habsburgs. I had the impression that the Ukrainians would not recede from these conditions, and that the critical position of Count Czernin was well known to them. Czernin's difficulties were twofold: if he consented to the cession of the Cholm district to the Ukraine he was threatened with the deadly hatred of the Poles; if he agreed to the creation of Ruthenian Crownlands he introduced the principle of self-determination among the mixed nationalities of the Austro-Hungarian Empire, while on the other hand, the cession of the Cholm district without consultation of the population was in exact opposition to the principles of self-determination.

Czernin's indisposition entailed a delay of two days, after which he authorized me to continue negotiations with the Ukrainians on the basis of their demands and, if possible, come to a settlement with them.

In the meantime the negotiations with Trotzky went on in the same aimless manner.

Apparently the Russian Commissar realized the danger with which he was threatened by our negotiations for a separate Peace with the Ukraine, for he suddenly asserted that the Ukrainian representatives, whom till then he had recognized, had not the right to carry on a separate negotiation in the name of the Ukraine, as the frontiers between Soviet Russia and the Ukraine had not been fixed as yet. On this question and some others he said he must consult the Petrograd Government. He proposed a further interruption of a few days in the negotiations, as he was obliged to go to Petrograd.

Of course this was not the reason for his journey to Petrograd. I concluded that he wanted to convince himself how far the Bolshevik rule had become stabilized in Petrograd; whether, in consideration of the wishes of the people, he would have to conclude a real Peace with the Central Powers, or if he could break off the negotiations with the sensational coup he did in fact use. Kühlmann went to Berlin to render an account of the negotiations to the Reichstag, and Count Czernin went to Vienna in order to obtain sanction for the conditions of peace with the Ukraine.

After the return of all the delegates, in the early days of February, Trotzky tried to prevent the separate Peace with the Ukraine in another way. He brought two Ukrainians with him, Medviediev and Shachrei, who were sent not by the Central Rada, but by a new Bolshevik opposition government that had been formed in Kharkov. The representatives from the Central Rada protested against this attempt at checkmate, and there were lively encounters between the Ukrainian and the Russian delegates. In an excellent speech Liubinski laid before the Bolsheviks the whole list of their sins. In his answer, Trotzky contented himself with hinting that the power of the Central Rada had vanished and that its representatives could look upon their room in Brest-Litovsk as the only space of which they had any right to dispose.

Judging by the reports from the Ukraine that I had before me, Trotzky's words seemed unfortunately not to be without foundation. Bolshevism was advancing victoriously, the Central Rada and the Ukrainian Provisional Government had fled. Kühlmann and Count Czernin decided, however, despite these transitory difficulties for the Ukrainian Government, to adhere to the arrangements. The difficulties were transitory in so far as at any time we could support the Government with arms and establish it again. They therefore refused to recognize the Ukrainian representatives whom Trotzky presented, on the grounds that, in the beginning of January, Trotzky himself had recognized the Ukrainian Delegation as the representatives of the people.

During those days I often admired the young Ukrainians. It is certain that they knew that the possible help from Germany was their last hope, that their Government was but a fictitious conception; nevertheless, they held to the demands they had succeeded in obtaining, and they did not give way a finger-breadth in all their negotiations with Count Czernin.

The Peace with the Ukraine was signed. It was a hard blow for Trotzky, as it was clear that now the negotiations with him must be brought to some sort of conclusion.

In the meantime, despite my protest and notwithstanding all Trotzky's assurances, the propagandist appeals to the world, and more especially to the troops, were sent out as usual. It was at this time that an appeal was addressed to the troops in which they were incited to murder their officers. Until now only G.H.Q. had urged that Trotzky should be disposed of finally, but after this Kühlmann received a telegram from His Majesty instructing him to send an ultimatum to Trotzky demanding a settlement within twenty-four hours. However, just at that moment Kühlmann had the impression that it might be possible to bring Trotzky to a settlement of the negotiations, as Trotzky, no doubt under the influence of the Peace with the Ukraine, had, for the first time, approached the question of peace in a practical way. He had sent to ask the Secretary of State if it would not be possible, by some means, to arrange that Riga and

the islands that lay before it should be retained by
the Russian Empire.

The Secretary of State was in a difficult position.
He did not hesitate for a moment to sacrifice himself for what he thought right: he telegraphed
in reply that the moment was ill-chosen to send
an ultimatum for such a short period and that he
earnestly advised that it should not be presented. If
His Majesty insisted on its delivery, the Government
would have to find another Secretary of State.
He would await an answer until four-thirty that
afternoon; if by that time no further orders about
the ultimatum were received he would pass on
to the order of the day. Nothing occurred until
four-thirty, and Kühlmann kept the order for an
ultimatum in his pocket. He had tried to nail
Trotzky down with this Riga proposal. He had sent
the Ambassador von Rosenberg to Trotzky to suggest
that he should state in writing that he was willing
to negotiate on the basis of Riga and the islands
remaining Russian. After some hesitation Trotzky
refused. On the other hand he perceived that he
could no longer go on simply making speeches and
proposals, and that the Central Powers would now
demand acts. He evidently also thought that he
had produced sufficient effect with his propaganda,
and now sought for an opening which would enable
him to bring the Brest negotiations to an end in a
way that would produce the greatest possible effect.
In the meeting of February 10th he announced
that, although he would sign no Treaty of Peace,
Russia would consider the war at an end from that
time; she would send all her armies to their homes,
and she would proclaim the fact to all the peoples
and all the States.

The whole congress sat speechless when Trotzky
had finished his declaration. We were all dumb-

founded. That same evening the Austro-Hungarian and the German diplomatists had a meeting to consult on the new position, at which I also was summoned to assist. The diplomatists of both countries were unanimous in asserting that they would accept this declaration, as, although no Peace had been signed, the conditions of peace were established between the two countries by this declaration. I was the only one against it. We had made an Armistice with the Russians with the object of arranging the terms of peace. If peace were not concluded the object of the Armistice was not attained, and therefore the Armistice came automatically to an end, and hostilities must recommence. Trotzky's declaration was, in my opinion, nothing more than a denunciation of the Armistice.

I was unable to bring the diplomatists round to my opinion. One of Czernin's assistants, the Ambassador von Wiesner, with a complete mis-understanding of the situation characteristic of this diplomatist, had already telegraphed to Vienna that peace was concluded with Russia. I apprised G.H.Q. of the results of these conversations, and received a reply that the High Command was quite of my opinion. It is well known that the High Command of the Army was also able to persuade the Government and the Foreign Office to accept their point of view.

On the eighth day after the negotiations had been broken off so abruptly by Trotzky, the Eastern Army resumed the offensive. The demoralized Russian troops offered no kind of resistance—if it were possible even to call them troops, as it was only the Staffs that still remained; the bulk of the troops had already gone home. We simply swept over the whole of Livonia and Esthonia, and took possession of them. Our troops were greeted everywhere as deliverers from the Bolshevik terror, not only by the Baltic Germans, but likewise by the Letts and Esthonians.

Two days after our advance had recommenced a wireless message was received from Petrograd announcing that the Russians were ready to renew the negotiations and conclude a Peace, and also begging that the German advance might be stopped. It had very quickly been proved that Trotzky's theories could not resist facts. The German Army advanced only as far as Lake Peipus and Narva, in order to release at least all the Baltic members of our race from the Bolsheviks and all their crimes. Then the advance was stopped, and the Bolsheviks were informed that they might send a delegation, authorized to sign a Peace, to Brest-Litovsk. Almost immediately the delegation, under the leadership of Sokolnikov, arrived. The representatives of the Quadruple Alliance, who had dispersed to all the points of the compass, also hastened back. But in the same manner as on the Russian side, so also on our side there appeared, one may say, only the second fiddles. Kühlmann, Czernin, Talaat, Rodoslavov, had gone in the meantime to Bukharest for the opening of the Peace Conference with Rumania and did not return, but sent their representatives. The Ambassador von Rosenberg came as the representative of Germany.

This time also the negotiations were carried on in a very extraordinary manner. At the first meeting von Rosenberg proposed to discuss at once each of the paragraphs of the draft of a Treaty of Peace he had brought with him; Sokolnikov replied to this proposal with a request that the whole draft might be read out to him. When it had been read to him he said that he did not demand the discussion of the single points, and that the Russians were willing to sign the draft that had been presented to them. The only reason such a proceeding could have had was the intention to prove more completely that they were forced into signing a Peace that was dictated to them. As propaganda has often asserted that I was the author of this " Peace of Violence " I wish again to state emphatically that I had not the slightest influence on the drafting of this Treaty of Peace; I became acquainted with its contents, for the first time, when it was publicly read aloud in the presence of the Russian Delegation. The definite acceptance of it by Sokolnikov took place at a private meeting of the diplomats at which I was not even present.

Of course the greatest propaganda with this " Peace of Violence " was made by the Entente. I would only ask the Entente why they did not alter this treaty when they had won the war and completely changed the political conditions of Europe by the Peace they dictated? The Peace of Brest-Litovsk was declared as annulled, but its chief conditions remained unchanged. It never occurred to the Entente to return to their former ally— Russia—Poland, Lithuania, Livonia, Esthonia and Bessarabia. The only thing that was changed was the dependent position of the provinces that had been taken away from Russia.

We were also obliged to take up arms again on the southern section of the Eastern Front. True to their principles to respect the rights of self-determination only when they were to their own advantage, the Russian Bolshevik Government had begun hostilities against the Ukraine, and their Government, the Rada. The Ukrainian Government was overthrown and ejected.

If the Central Powers, who had made peace with
the Ukraine for the sake of bread, wanted to get
bread, they would have to go and fetch it.

After the Peace had been signed, the Ukrainian
representatives made no secret of the desperate
position in which their Government was placed, and
quite openly begged assistance from Germany. In
my opinion it was a logical necessity for us to accede
to this request. Having taken the first step we had to
go on; we had recognized the Ukrainian Government as having the right to exist, and we had concluded a Peace with them : we had therefore to see
that the Peace we had signed was carried out, and
for this purpose the first thing we had to do was to
support the Government that had concluded the
Peace with us.

Therefore our troops marched into the Ukraine.
Our advance, chiefly along the railway lines, went
rapidly forwards, although we met with opposition
in many places. The Bolshevik bands that had been
sent to occupy the Ukraine defended themselves,
and, besides, we had many fierce engagements with
the Czecho-Slovak Divisions, whom we met here for
the first time. However, resistance was suppressed
everywhere, and our troops marched through the
whole of the Ukraine as far as the Steppes of the
Don.

At first the Austro-Hungarian troops had hesitated to join the advance. The Austro-Hungarian
Government wanted peace and the cessation of
hostilities, and it was with difficulty that they could
be persuaded that in the present circumstances a
state of peace was impossible; that above all if
they wanted to get corn, which was more needed by
them even than by Germany, it would be necessary
to go and fetch it. We therefore began the advance
alone, but the Austrians followed us very soon, and

then a race for the great object began between us, which was often not without friction. While Kiev fell quite without dispute into the German sphere of interest, the Austrians took possession of Odessa and the Odessa railway.

One of the conditions of peace with Soviet Russia naturally concerned the resumption of diplomatic relations. In the meantime I had become sufficiently well acquainted with the Bolsheviks to know the danger there would be in allowing a Bolshevik Embassy to be established in Berlin or consulates to be opened, which would serve as centres for Bolshevik propaganda against Germany. Not for a moment had the Bolsheviks left it in doubt that their object was a World Revolution and that they considered the revolutionizing of Germany was the first step towards it. They used every opportunity for propaganda. Radek, a member of the Peace Delegation, even went as far as having propaganda leaflets thrown out of the railway coaches to be distributed among our soldiers. I therefore sent a special warning that a Bolshevik Embassy should not be allowed in Berlin; I explained my reasons to G.H.Q. and proposed that, as long as the state of war lasted, the two ambassadors, both the Russian and the German, should have their residence in the Headquarters of the Commander-in-Chief, Eastern Front. Here I would be able to keep in check any excessive activity on the part of Herr Joffe. In any case, in this way it would be possible to prevent his having any very close connection with the German communists. As far as I know G.H.Q. quite agreed with my proposal, but it met with opposition from the Foreign Office and came to nothing. His Excellency Kriege, the Director of the Legal Department of the Foreign Office, swore to Joffe's sincerity, and was burning with a desire to continue in Berlin the negotiations he had begun with him in Brest-Litovsk. Events proved that I had been right in my fears. It was too late when Secretary of State Solf had the case that contained propaganda literature broken open. He locked the stable door after the steed had been stolen.

CHAPTER XVIII

1918

THE military activity of the Commander-in-Chief on the Eastern Front can be looked upon as concluded at the end of the German advance into the Ukraine, as the small encounters with the Bolshevik bands caused no great trouble. The administrative work was also insufficient to occupy the whole working power of my Staff and myself, and, furthermore, General Ludendorff removed various matters from the control of the Commander-in-Chief. Thus General Gröner was sent to Kiev to found a large Germano-Ukrainian business organization there. This organization was brilliant on paper, but it produced small results. It will probably never be known if the Ukrainian Delegation had over-estimated the existing stock of corn, or whether the peasants hid the remaining stocks of wheat. I think the latter was the case. Whatever may have been the cause, our organization was unable to procure any considerable quantities of corn. I think that without having a large central organization we should have been more successful if we had engaged a large number of Jewish dealers and commissioned them to buy the corn for us in the open market. We were no longer allowed any influence on the political conditions in Kiev, and we had not the slightest influence on the fall of the existing Government and the setting up of the Hetman Skoropadski in its place.

We had the same fate in the Baltic provinces as

in the Ukraine. Here also the Commander-in-Chief was asked, in the most amiable way, to refrain from interfering, and the 8th Army was commissioned to execute the plans of G.H.Q. for the Baltic provinces. The new Chief of Staff of this army, Lieutenant-Colonel Frantz, enjoyed General Ludendorff's special confidence. It is useless to criticize the German policy for the border States, as events drew a thick line through all that Germany had intended to do in the East. I wish only to observe that I personally did not approve of the plan of taking away from Russia all the Baltic provinces. A great Power such as Russia was—and must again become —would in the long run never be able to permit Riga and Reval, which may be called the doorkeys to its capital, Petrograd, to be taken away from it. And besides, the percentage of the population in Livonia and Esthonia of German origin is not so great as to vindicate the establishment of a purely German rule there.

On May 1st, 1918, the Commander-in-Chief removed his Headquarters to Kovno, and the Administrative Department returned there too. We had nothing more to do on the southern half of the Front. For the management of internal affairs it was most desirable that the whole Staff should be united in one place.

In the meantime, until the beginning of March, all the troops that were capable of fighting were dispatched from the Eastern Front to the West. For the first time during the whole war we were in superior numbers on the Western Front. Now General Ludendorff had the difficult decision placed before him whether he was to use this superiority to make a great and decisive offensive, and, if he decided on this move, when and where the attack was to be made. Judging by our experiences in the West—where the great Entente offensives had been begun with enormous numbers of troops and quantities of material, and had been carried out quite regardless of the losses of human life, but still had never ended in a decisive success—some of the German leaders were of the opinion that a German offensive would also fail to attain a great success. It might have been possible to suppose that with a friendly Russia in the rear, from which the starved-out Central Powers could obtain provisions and raw materials, they would have decided not to attack in the West, but to await the attack of the Entente. However, these preliminary conditions did not exist at all. The news that came from Russia grew worse every day: atrocities of every description, the massacre of many thousands of the educated and propertied classes, plunder, robbery, and such complete disorder that all regular commercial relations were quite out of the question, was what we heard in every report. If it were desired to follow the suggested plan of suspending action in the West until the Central Powers had received supplies from the East it would be necessary first of all to establish conditions in the East which would produce the necessary preliminary conditions. Every day we received piteous entreaties for help from all classes of the Russian population. The greater number of the reports we received from the delegates we had sent to Russia asserted it was impossible that we could look on inactive at the atrocities of the Bolshevik rulers. Nevertheless everybody must agree that it was a difficult decision for us to make : to denounce the Peace that had just been concluded and again recommence hostilities against Russia. I must confess that at first even I was not able to favour such a decision. The weight of the Russian Colossus had pressed politically too heavily on Germany for over a hundred years for a feeling of relief not to be experienced that the might of Russia had been destroyed for many long years by the Revolution and the Bolsheviks' rule. But the more I heard of the Bolshevik atrocities the more my opinion changed. In my opinion it was impossible, as a decent man, to stand inactive and allow a whole nation to be butchered. For this reason I got into touch with different representatives of the old Russian Government. Besides, a real state of peace did not exist in the East: we still had a weak but consecutive line of troops along the Front facing the Bolshevik bands; there was shooting almost every day; we did not know what was going on in real Russia; the true purpose of the Czecho-Slovak legions was veiled in utter obscurity. As always during war time, the most exaggerated reports of their numbers and their plans reached us; it was reported that England furnished them with money, and that with England's support they wanted to march from the East on Moscow and take possession of the Government. If that happened Germany would again be surrounded. For these reasons, in the spring of 1918, I supported the opinion that it would be best to clear the situation in the East—that is, to denounce the Peace, to march on Moscow, to form another Russian Government, to grant them better conditions of peace than the Brest-Litovsk Treaty had given them—for instance, at first, Poland might be returned to them—and to conclude an alliance with the new Government. The Eastern Front would not have required any additional troops for this purpose. Major Schubert, who was our Military Attaché in Moscow at the time, was the first to support the idea of decisive action against the Bolsheviks, and he considered that two battalions would be sufficient to restore order in

Moscow, to overthrow the Bolsheviks and establish a new Government in their place. Although I looked upon his views as somewhat too optimistic, the Divisions that we still had would probably have been sufficient to carry out this plan. At that time Lenin and Trotzky had no Red Army at their disposal. They had their hands fully occupied with disarming the old army and dispatching the soldiers to their homes. Their power was supported only by a few Lettish battalions and a rabble of Chinese coolies, who had been armed, and were employed at first, and still are, as executioners.

For instance, we could have advanced on the lines Smolensk—Petrograd, and once arrived there we could have formed a new Government, which should simply maintain the fiction that the Tsarevitch was still alive, and we would have appointed a Regent for him. I thought at the time of the Grand Duke Paul, with whom, through his son-in-law, Colonel Durnovo, the Commander-in-Chief in the East had been in connection. The Provisional Government could then have been transferred to Moscow, where, in my opinion, it would have been a simple matter to sweep the Bolshevik Government away. If we had done this, Russia would have been spared unspeakable misery and suffering and the lives of millions of her people. How far such events would have cast their shadow over Germany and the West must be left to the imagination. It would doubtless have been immense if German politics and the German High Command had come to this resolve before Ludendorff had made his first offensive in March 1918.

There can be no doubt that the possibility of establishing orderly conditions in the East, of concluding an alliance with a new Russian Government, and pursuing a waiting policy in the West, had never entered General Ludendorff's mind. He was determined to bring about a decision by an attack in the West, and he was convinced that the attack would succeed and that the German Army would conquer. On the other hand, there were two dangers that were involved in a waiting policy in the West, and which, as time passed, would certainly become more pressing, which were: the increasing numbers of American troops and the menacing possibility that the enemy would succeed in imitating the new gas. From the military point of view nothing can be said against the decision to attack. It remains to inquire if it was properly carried into effect, and here we find two matters open to criticism. The attack was not made solely at the point that was considered most favourable for a breach in the line to be made, and it was not made with the whole of the forces available. The point that was considered as the most favourable was the southern wing of the English Army to the north of the Somme. All the available forces ought to have been hurled at that one point. Instead of which, attacks were made both to the north and the south of the Somme.

In his essay, that appeared in 1922, entitled, *As it Really Happened*, Captain Wright shows us that in spite of this the German attack of March was almost victorious, and we missed winning the war by only a hair-breadth. However, as we did not succeed in taking Amiens, and thus separating the English and French Armies, we only almost succeeded—we did not win the victory. Our offensive met with the same fate that the numerous enemy attacks had experienced; it had only dented the enemy Front, but it had not broken through.

The troops that G.H.Q. had at their disposal in the spring of 1918 were, without doubt, good. It has been proved that both the communists and the socialists had used every expedient to undermine the *morale* of the troops. By the reports I received from many hundreds of officers whom I questioned on the subject in the spring of 1918 this agitation had not had any great effect on the troops at the Front. On the lines of communication the position was worse. The poison that was being spread there penetrated at first but slowly into the troops at the Front, and it was only under the influence of the severe fighting during the summer of 1918 that the decay set in, which brought about the disintegration of the proudest army that has ever been known in the history of the world.

At the moment when G.H.Q. saw that they would not get Amiens, that they had not been able to break through the enemy's Front, they ought to have realized that a decisive victory on the Western Front was no longer to be expected. If this first attempt, which had been made with the best forces they possessed, had failed, every succeeding attack, that could only be made with ever-diminishing forces, would likewise have no chance of success. On the very day on which G.H.Q. gave the order to break off the attack on Amiens it was their duty to apprise the Government that the time had arrived to proceed to Peace negotiations, and that there was no longer any prospect of bringing the war to an end by a decisive victory on the Western Front.

I do not know if, in April 1918, it would have been feasible to obtain a reasonable Peace, but I think it would have been possible. It would certainly have been a better one than the Peace of Versailles. In any case, we ought to have refrained from any further offensives. They only cost us terrible losses—both in men and material—which we could no longer replace. Even then it would not have been too late to carry into effect the Russian plan of the Commander-in-Chief on the Eastern Front. It appears to me doubtful whether the Entente nations would have had the energy to continue the war if we had established a new Government in Russia in May or June, and concluded an alliance with it. While we remained on the defensive in the West our Government would have offered to make a Peace in which the restoration of Belgium would have been guaranteed, and perhaps a few districts in Lorraine sacrificed.

The continuation of the offensive required measures that were hazardous considering the fighting value and the *morale* of the army at the time. The demands on individual Divisions became intolerably great; the time that they had to remain in the front line without being relieved was too long; good substitutes were not to be found; G.H.Q. searched for men and scraped them together, wherever they could be found, and they were sent to the Front to fill up the ranks, regardless of anything else. Thus all the younger men were taken out of the Eastern Divisions and sent to the West. There was special need of well-trained artillery Reserves, so that all the men who were fairly well fitted for service in the field were taken away from every battery in the East. I am convinced that it was especially this transfer of men from the troops on the Eastern Front to the West that had the most fatal consequences. It was quite evident that the Bolshevik propaganda was working. Although the old discipline held the body of troops together, and the army as a whole was reliable, still, it was unfortunately impossible to prevent individuals who were dissatisfied that they had been torn from their units, and sent from a quiet Front into fresh fighting, from passing on the poison which they had imbibed in the East from Bolshevik theories. In this way disintegrating elements were transferred to the Western Front, and fell upon only too fertile soil in the men who were overstrained by continuous heavy fighting.

In the same way as General Ludendorff refused to see that the unsuccessful March offensive had definitely deprived the German Army of all prospect of a great victory, so also he closed his eyes to the threatening signs that were visible on the Fronts of our allies. It is true the Turks had still been able to resist the attacks near Jerusalem during April and May, and they had retained their positions there, but the English superiority was daily making itself more felt. Marshal Liman von Sanders foresaw the events that inevitably were bound to occur before the autumn. He described the position and asked for help. The German G.H.Q. paid no attention. Moreover no attention was paid to the numerous warnings that came from the Bulgarian Front. With the exception of a few battalions, all the German troops that had formed the backbone of the Macedonian Front had been taken away for the great battle in the West. A German victory in the West would have naturally also saved the Bulgarian Front; as this victory did not take place they ought, at least, to have thought, in the summer of 1918, of sending new German forces to the Bulgarian Front. There were troops available on the Eastern Front. For although the Divisions we had on the Eastern Front were composed chiefly of old Landwehr and Landsturm units, and unsuitable for the Western Front, I am convinced that they would have done their duty on the Bulgarian Front.

Thus we drifted into hopeless disaster. Added to this, nobody among the people knew how serious the situation really was. The announcements of victory sent out by G.H.Q. after the March attack, the honours that were bestowed on the members of G.H.Q. and the leaders who had taken part in the attack, caused not only the greater part of the nation, but also the greater part of the army, to believe that all was going well. We—the Eastern Command— heard nothing of the heavy losses that the offensive had cost, we did not know that Germany was no longer in a position to make good these losses. All in the army were convinced that the Western Front would at any rate be able to hold out. It was only in the summer that the position became clear to me.

CHAPTER XIX

BEFORE concluding, I wish to recapitulate once more my opinions on the chances Germany had had in the World War, and the reasons why they were not fully utilized.

In August 1914 we ought to have won the war in the West in a canter, if Count Schlieffen's original intentions had been carried out—that is to say, if, after breaking through Belgium, the right wing had been reinforced and lengthened by all the available forces. That this was not done, but on the contrary that troops were taken from the right wing for the Eastern Front, was unquestionably a mistake of the first G.H.Q.

But even then the repulse on the Marne ought not to have taken place. That the crisis in which the 2nd Army found itself was not met by energetic action; that the decision of the 1st Army to get out of this difficult position by an attack was not supported; but on the contrary, through that unfortunate mission of Lieutenant-Colonel Hentsch, with his ambiguous verbal order and his doubtful authority, the miracle of the Marne, which the French were unable to understand, was possible, is another blunder on the part of the Commander-in-Chief, Moltke.

After the repulse on the Marne it was once more possible to try to make a dash forward, instead of letting the Front be strengthened for a trench war. This would have been possible if a decision had been

235

taken to transport at least ten to twelve Army Corps from the left to the right wing, and with them to make a grand combined attack on that side. That this plan, which was suggested by General Gröner, was not executed is the fault of the succeeding High Command.

As the war was now not to be won in the West, it was necessary to attempt a decision in the East, where events had developed in such a manner that such a decision might be possible. In the late autumn of 1914 and in the summer of 1915 two favourable opportunities occurred, that might have led to the complete defeat of the Russian Army. Both these opportunities General Falkenhayn let slip. He is also responsible for the offensive at Verdun, the defective conduct of the Serbian campaign, the failure to take Salonika and the refusal to make a combined offensive against Italy. After the opportunity of so completely defeating Russia that she would have been obliged to make peace had been missed, it was essential to realize once and for all that, according to all human calculations, Germany could never win the war.

From that moment all the endeavours of the Government ought to have been directed to the obtaining of a Peace with the *status quo ante,* and the exertions of G.H.Q. ought to have been to prevent any reverse, so that the army might remain in possession of the conquered territories. I believe that such a Peace might have been obtained in 1917 if we had quite definitely resigned all claim to Belgium.

Contrary to all expectations, an event occurred at that time which offered the German Empire once again the chance of emerging victoriously from the war. This was the Russian Revolution, which eliminated the numerically strongest opponent and gave us the numerical superiority on the Western Front, notwithstanding the enormous numbers of our opponents.

There were two possibilities of profiting by the new position of affairs: either we could decide to put Russia in order, to make an alliance with a new Russian Government, and to bide our time in the West (by this proceeding, it is true, we could not achieve a great victory, but we could never be defeated); or else to employ the superior numbers we possessed in order to make a great decisive attack. General Ludendorff decided on the latter possibility. He wanted to conquer, but he did not employ the whole of the forces he possessed, nor was he fortunate in the way he brought them into action. The great attack to break through did not succeed; instead of realizing then that the last chance of victory had been forfeited, instead of acting solely on the defensive from that moment, and of letting the Government know that it was high time to try, by diplomatic means, to attain peace by negotiation, he continued the offensive until the last strength of the army was exhausted. In this way Ludendorff found himself obliged to ask for an Armistice within twenty-four hours, and he left Germany defenceless before the cold hate of England, France's fanatical desire for revenge, and an imbecile, Wilson.

THE TRUTH ABOUT
TANNENBERG

CHAPTER I

GENERAL VON PRITTWITZ und Gaffron, the Commander of the German 8th Army, to whom, at the outbreak of war, fell the task of defending the Eastern Frontier of the Empire against the Russian hordes, was faced with an extraordinarily difficult task.

The way to set about it had, indeed, been expounded to us by our great chief of the General Staff, Count Schlieffen, in numerous war games and staff exercises.

Count Schlieffen had again and again emphasized the fact that a success could be achieved only if the inferior German forces concentrated in East Prussia were so manœuvred as to take advantage of the lie of the country—*i.e.* the unavoidable cleavage of the enemy advance by the Masurian Lakes—and strike with all available strength at the first Russian army that came within reach.

There is a certain tragedy in the fact that if the 8th Army had kept to the exact programme laid down by the gifted strategist they could probably have completely destroyed, in two energetic strokes, both Russian armies advancing on East Russia.

If we assume that General Prittwitz, when he saw that the Russian Vilna Army would come within reach sooner than the Warsaw Army, had moved not only the XVII. but also the XX. Army Corps from the southern frontier of East Prussia to the north, leaving the defence of the southern frontier to Landwehr and garrison troops, and, with a strongly echeloned left wing, had taken up a position roughly on a line from Angerburg to the north of Insterburg, and thus, outflanking the northern wing of the Vilna Army, had attacked it on August 20th, he would in all probability have quickly won a complete success.

If, subsequently, the Russian Warsaw Army had advanced across the frontier, the position from our point of view would have become more and more favourable the farther this army penetrated into German territory. The 8th Army would have swung to the south-west, fallen on its right flank, and driven it on to the Vistula towards Thorn.

Steps should, of course, have been taken to avoid the isolated frontier fighting and attacks by the I. Army Corps. If it had been decided to make a concentrated attack on the Russian Vilna Army there would have been no reason for trying to delay its advance; on the contrary, the more quickly it was allowed to get within the reach of the 8th Army the more quickly would the decision have been reached, and any possibility of danger from the Warsaw Army would have been by so much diminished.

But, as is well known, the High Command of the 8th Army did not carry through the great Schlieffen plan.

They left the XX. Army Corps and the 70th Landwehr Brigade on the Southern Front. A suggestion by the Q.M.G., General Grünert, that the Landwehr Brigade at least should be moved up to the north, was not approved by General Count Waldersee, the Chief of the General Staff. Moreover, the latter had formed an incorrect idea of the disposition of forces in the Russian Vilna Army. He took the view that the main body would advance south of the Rominten forest, as a result of which he thought that their right wing would be moving south of the Königsberg—Kovno railway, perhaps even reaching that line. What can have given him this impression I do not know.

As a consequence of this erroneous idea, in attacking the Russian Vilna Army under General Rennenkampf, on August 20th, the Germany Army did not envelop its left wing, but made a frontal attack. However, we were successful on both wings. The XVII. Army Corps in the centre met with a reverse. The Corps had made a premature and violent attack, without adequate artillery preparation, against prepared Russian positions, and were repulsed with heavy losses. Whether a dispatch from the I. Army Corps to the XVII. Corps on the forenoon of the 20th, stating that the I. Corps was pressing a successful attack, and that if the XVII. made a determined thrust in the direction of Szirgupönen (10 kilometres south of Gumbinnen) they were certain to win great success—whether this had any influence on the XVII. Corps is, of course, very hard to establish.

I myself, in the course of the forenoon, twice telephoned an order to the Command of the XVII. Corps that they were to advance, deeply echeloned to the right on Goldap. I well remember our amazement when the news came in that the Corps was defeated and the position serious, and it became apparent that the Corps then stood with its rear towards Goldap, and that it had no Reserves whatever. The fact that this neglect of the enemy forces at Goldap brought no ill consequences was entirely due to the determined and independent handling of the Divisions of the I. Reserve Corps. In any case, it is not easy to show that the above-mentioned request of the I. Corps to the XVII.

Corps contributed to create a false impression in the mind of the commander of the latter Corps, General von Mackensen, that the enemy opposing him was preparing to retire, and that his business was to prevent this movement by a rapid stroke. Had this not happened, and if the Corps had advanced, according to orders, deeply echeloned to the right, they might not have been hurried into an attack without adequate artillery preparation.

In spite of the somewhat clumsy conduct of the battle, and the defeat of the XVII. Corps, the situation on the evening of August 20th was extremely favourable for the continuation of the attack on the 21st.

On the front of the I. Army Corps, General von François had had to halt his victorious troops by the afternoon, and give them a rest, as they were entirely exhausted by marching, fighting and the heat, and urgently in need of a breathing space.

On the southern wing, General von Morgen stood ready with the 3rd Reserve Division to launch an attack at daybreak of the 21st against the flank and rear of enemy forces which had already been defeated the day before by the I. Reserve Corps.

Even without the knowledge of the state of affairs on the Russian side that we have to-day—namely, that Rennenkampf's army was on the point of collapse, that his whole Staff was calling for a retreat, to avoid overwhelming disaster—on the 21st we could count on a complete success which, in the course of two or three days, would give the 8th Army complete freedom of manœuvre and enable it to concentrate all its forces on attacking the enemy advancing from Warsaw.

General Grünert and I were also of the opinion that the Gumbinnen battle promised well, and should be fought out without regard to the possibility of any danger from the Warsaw Army. Furthermore, the unit more particularly threatened by the Russian advance from the direction of Warsaw—*i.e.* the XX. Army Corps—not merely asked for no assistance, but on the contrary were quite calm and confident, and emphasized the fact that there was no need for anxiety; they reckoned on being attacked by about three enemy Corps in two or three days, and expected no support.

CHAPTER II

Such was the position of the Gumbinnen battle towards the evening of the 20th. All the more devastating was the news that reached us, about seven in the evening, of Colonel-General Prittwitz's decision to break off the fight and withdraw the army behind the Vistula. That General von Prittwitz had been considering this decision for some hours previously had not been known to me. He had said nothing of it to his Staff.

The position in the south, opposite the Warsaw Army, was, on August 20th, as follows: the plan of operations for the 1st (Vilna) and 2nd (Warsaw) Armies, inspired as it was by the urgent appeal of the French for a quick stroke, provided for an attack by these two armies from the east and the south, without waiting for the Reserve formations to come up, to envelop from the north and south the German forces there, which they rightly assumed to be inferior in numbers, cut them off from Königsberg or the Vistula, and destroy them. The plan of General Jilinski, the Commander on the Russian North-west Front, provided for the Vilna Army to cross the frontier earlier than the Warsaw Army, to remain on the move and attack the German Army wherever they might find it. The Warsaw Army, which was to cross the frontier two days later, was then to strike at the German rear and envelop from the left the forces engaged against Rennenkampf and cut them off from the Vistula. The time-table

246

laid down by Jilinski for the advance of the two armies did not provide for the bad state of the roads on the Southern Front. The interval of two days between the attacks of the two armies had consequently to be extended. A further postponement of the time when the 2nd Russian Army was to attack was due to the efforts of its commander, Samsonoff, to push his army farther west, so as to be able more effectively to carry out the task of enveloping the German forces and cutting them off from the Vistula.

On the afternoon of the 20th, the XX. Army Corps reported that they estimated the enemy forces which had reached the frontier on the line Chorzele—Friedrichshof at 2 to 2¼ Army Corps, and two Brigades of frontier troops, and that the General-in-Command, von Scholtz, proposed to move his Corps towards Neidenburg and delay the Russian advance by an attack on their left wing. About seven o'clock in the evening a further report came in from the commander of the frontier troops at Soldau, General von Unger, to the effect that at least an additional Russian Corps advancing from Warsaw had reached a point south of Mlava. The position of the XX. Army Corps and the garrison troops at Soldau was consequently serious. There could be no further question of an attack at Neidenburg, nor could the XX. Corps now deal with the situation by an offensive. On the other hand, the forces at the disposal of General von Scholtz were strong enough to remain on the defensive and hold up the Russian armies advancing from the Vistula long enough to allow the battle at Gumbinnen to be brought to a successful conclusion. On August 20th I was standing with General von Grünert, between six and seven o'clock in the afternoon, outside our office door in a house on the main street in Neidenburg, and discussing with him the favourable prospects for the development of this battle, when the further news came in from the XX. Army Corps Front. At the same moment the Commander - in - Chief, Colonel - General von Prittwitz, and Count Waldersee appeared from their quarters next door; they had received the news at the same time as we had. General von Prittwitz asked us to come into the office, and there said: " I suppose, gentlemen, you have also received this fresh news from the Southern Front? The army is breaking off the battle and retiring behind the Vistula."

General Grünert and I raised objections. We pointed out that the Gumbinnen battle was going well in spite of the reverse on the XVII. Corps Front, and that it was to be expected that in two —or at latest three—days we should have won a complete victory. The 8th Army had more than this time at their disposal because the advance of the Russian Warsaw Army could be held up for several days by the relatively strong forces on the southern frontier of East Prussia. The Commander-in-Chief brushed our objections aside rather curtly with the words that he and the Chief of the General Staff alone were competent to conduct operations and take tactical decisions, and were responsible for them, not the Q.M.G. and the G.S.O.,I. However, we both called attention to the fact that no preparations had been made for a retreat behind the Vistula, that the left wing of the Russian Warsaw Army was actually nearer the Vistula than the 8th Army now engaged at Gumbinnen, and that measures must at least be taken to hang up the advance of that same wing, or else the 8th Army would run the risk, against which the orders for advance had issued particular warning, of being cut off from the Vistula, and forced into the fortress of Königsberg. General von Prittwitz persisted in his decision, and left the office. General Count Waldersee asked me to put out the order for the retreat of the 8th Army. I again pointed out the impossibility of carrying out the retreat behind the Vistula without engaging the Warsaw Army, and asked for his instructions on the framing of the order. General Count Waldersee saw the justice of our objections. In a further conversation with General von Prittwitz, who in the meantime had reappeared in the office, it was established that it was in fact necessary to strike against the left wing of the Russian Warsaw Army so as to give the 8th Army freedom to manœuvre and to move.

It was decided that the I. Army Corps should be put on the Königsberg—Dirschau—Graudenz railway, the 3rd Reserve Division on the Angerburg —Osterode line, and that these three Divisions should be brought up on the right wing of the XX. Army Corps with a view to an attack at that point. The I. Reserve Corps and the XVII. Corps were to retreat on foot along a wide front, first behind the Alle, and then into West Prussia. It was not possible at that moment to issue any further orders for these Corps. The disengagement of those Corps now in active conflict with the Russians must inevitably be difficult, and the Commander of the Russian 1st Army would certainly press us heavily as soon as he learned of our retreat. General von Prittwitz then determined to drop the idea of the retreat behind the Vistula, to send the XVII. Corps and also the I. Reserve Corps to support the XX. Corps, if it proved possible to disengage them from Rennenkampf's army, and resume the fight this side of the Vistula.

The *Imperial Archives* (vol. ii., p. 103) gives the

21st as the date of this discussion and decision to transfer the I. Army Corps and the 3rd Reserve Division to the right wing of the XX. Corps, with a view to an offensive at that point, but the writer is wrong. The I. Corps Transport was moved behind the Vistula for technical reasons as the result of a discussion with the Director-General of Railways on the Eastern Front, Major Kersten, who happened to be at Headquarters. It was to be shifted to the east bank again at Graudenz. It is all perfectly clear from the Army Command Order, No. 8, August 20th, 9.30 P.M.: " I. A.C. to the line Goslershausen—Strasburg—Bischofswerder—Freystatt. 3rd Reserve Division to Deutsch-Eylau, both in support of the XX. Corps." The error in the *Imperial Archives* seems to me the more inexplicable as, in addition to the usual documentary evidence, they had at their disposal the written statements of the persons concerned, including my own.

How, therefore, did it come about that General von Prittwitz was recalled?

During the interval in which the Commander-in-Chief left the office he had, without informing any of the members of his Staff, got on the telephone to G.H.Q., as well as to Headquarters in the Field, and in his agitated and depressed state of mind had told everyone that the army was retiring behind the Vistula. He went so far as to tell General von Moltke that he could hold the Vistula only if reinforcements were sent. When, at the instance of General Grünert and myself, he altered his mind, in his agitated state he forgot to mention his telephone conversation to the Chief of Staff or to the G.S.O.,I., so that his altered decision might be made known to G.H.Q., etc. As no one but General von Prittwitz himself knew about these conversations, nothing was done. That was how G.H.Q. came to recall the Commander-in-Chief and his Chief of Staff, although, by his orders of the evening of August 20th, he had made preparations for the subsequent battle of Tannenberg, and given the preliminary instructions without which the battle would have been impossible. According to the narrative in the *Imperial Archives* this telephone conversation between General von Prittwitz and General von Moltke did not take place until the 21st. General von Moltke recorded this in writing five days later. I think it probable that General von Moltke made a mistake about the date. After the decision had been reached to attack the left wing of the Russian 2nd Army, on the evening of the 20th, and the appropriate preliminary orders had been issued, General von Prittwitz could not possibly have telephoned on the 21st about retreating behind the Vistula, when, owing to the better news then coming in to Headquarters, a much more cheerful feeling prevailed, and the Commander-in-Chief could not then have been overcome by nerves or lost his head.

On August 21st, H.Q. were shifted to Bartenstein. Reports were coming in to the effect that we had disengaged ourselves from the Russian 1st Army without mishap. Opposite the XX. Corps, which General von Scholtz had concentrated in a position on either side of Gilgenburg, the Russians had made only a little progress with their east wing; the west wing had come to a standstill. Colonel Hell, Chief of Staff to the XX. Corps, to whom I telephoned about the new plan, was absolutely calm and confident. A further piece of good news was that the 1st Cavalry Division had got into touch once more, after successful fighting, in which the Russians had lost heavily. There had been a certain amount of anxiety at G.H.Q. that the Cavalry Division which had been pushed forward against Rennenkampf's rear, and could not have heard of the retreat of the 8th Army, might be lost.

On August 22nd, H.Q. moved to Mühlhausen, on the Elbing — Königsberg railway. On this day, too, the news that came in was, generally speaking, favourable. Rennenkampf's army seemed to have suffered more heavily in the Gumbinnen battle than we had thought. They were not pursuing us at all. The entraining of the troops was proceeding without a hitch.

In the morning Colonel Hell rang up, and expressed anxiety about the left wing of the XX. Corps. The Russians were so strong that they might be able to outflank this wing and attack it with superior numbers before the I. Corps had reached its destination, and we were thus enabled to attack. He therefore requested that the 3rd Reserve Division should not be detrained at Deutsch-Eylau but at Allenstein, and put into the line not on the right but on the left wing of the XX. Army Corps. This request was approved by H.Q., and the destination of the 3rd Reserve Division accordingly altered.

On the afternoon of the 22nd I rang up the Chief of Staff of the I. Corps, Colonel Freiherr von Schmidtseck, to find out how the railway movements were going on. Colonel von Schmidtseck said something like this: " Why, what do you mean? Don't you know what has happened?" I said I did not, and asked him to enlighten me. Whereupon he answered: " If you don't know, then I don't feel called upon to tell you: you will hear soon enough." I was on the point of referring to the Chief of Staff, Count Waldersee, to report this singular interview, when the Director-General of Railways on the Eastern Front, Major Kersten, came in with a very startled expression, and showed me a telegram announcing the arrival of a special train, with a new Commander-in-Chief, General von Hindenburg, and a new Chief of Staff, General Ludendorff. General Count Waldersee had just heard the news, and carried it to the superseded Commander-in-Chief. The telegram from the Imperial Cabinet, placing General von Prittwitz and Count Waldersee à *disposition*, came in half-an-hour later. The manner in which these two officers, who had been much thought of in peace time, were sent home, was uncommonly abrupt. However, Prittwitz's conduct in telephoning in that agitated way, without telling any member of his Staff, was inexcusable.

CHAPTER III

THE NEW HIGH COMMAND

THE orders that emanated from the new High Command, or rather from G.H.Q., related mainly to the arrival of reinforcements. Whether von der Goltz's Schleswig-Holstein Landwehr Division was then ordered up I do not know. A mixed Brigade from the fortress of Thorn, under Lieutenant-General von Mühlmann, was sent on foot to Strasburg and the neighbourhood. For this latter step the sanction, or an order, of G.H.Q. was not necessary. After the final orders to march had been given, the areas of the various Commands, as well as the fortresses with their garrisons, were under the High Command of the 8th Army. The suggestion to withdraw troops from the fortresses had already been made to General Prittwitz, but he had not approved. General von Morgen, for example, who, when advancing from Lötzen, had taken with him a heavy battery from the Lötzen garrison, had been ordered by the indignant Commander-in-Chief to send it back. A second order followed, to the effect that the Corps composing the 8th Army were to be handled independently until the arrival of the new Commander-in-Chief in the Eastern theatre of war on August 23rd. The I. Reserve Corps and the XVII. Army Corps then issued orders for a rest on the following day. The statements of the *Imperial Archives* on this point (vol. ii., p. 113) make it appear that this period of rest was ordered by G.H.Q. — *i.e.* General Ludendorff — on tactical grounds. That is, as I have just said, an error. As regards the order itself, I cannot think it was the case that the exhaustion of the troops was such that a rest was necessary before they could carry on. The reports of the Generals-in-Command, in reply to inquiries by G.H.Q., make no mention of any such exhaustion. On the other hand, it was a matter of great urgency to get the two Corps away from Rennenkampf's army as far, and as quickly, as possible, so as to give them freedom of movement towards the south. We shall see in the course of the battle that this day of rest had to be made up by forced marches later on. Thirdly, the High Command received an order to move to Marienburg to meet the new Commander-in-Chief at two o'clock on the afternoon of August 23rd. H.Q. were accordingly moved back. They had intended to stay a day longer in Mühlhausen and then to go somewhere behind the right wing— *e.g.* Riesenburg. The idea of moving back to Marienburg was not a happy one. It could have been avoided if G.H.Q. or the new Chief of Staff had had a talk on the telephone not only with the individual Army Commands, but also with Eastern Headquarters as hitherto constituted.

It is stated in the *Imperial Archives* that when the High Command reported in Strasburg the feeling was one of depression and discouragement: this was certainly the case, and was the natural consequence of all the circumstances of the change in the command.

After the officers had reported, General Ludendorff dismissed most of them to their posts, but ordered the First General Staff Officer to remain and give him an account of the situation. I did so, and found him extremely surprised that all the instructions and orders necessary for the intended attack on the

Russian Warsaw Army had already been given. And during the discussion of the best means of conducting the battle, which I dealt with in my statement, General Ludendorff and I were in complete agreement. Whether it was possible to throw the I. Reserve Corps and the XVII. Army Corps into the battle depended for the moment on whether Rennenkampf would pursue. I also mentioned, in this first interview, the proposed advance of the I. Army Corps towards Seeben—Usdau.

CHAPTER IV

THE ADVANCE BEFORE THE BATTLE

THE general position in the Eastern theatre of war was at this time as follows.

The commencement of the Austro-Hungarian offensive could be expected in about a week. Woyrsch's Landwehr Corps, which was under the 8th Army Command, and had been advancing on our allies' left wing, had got as far as the neighbourhood of Piotrokov without a fight. A telegram from the Austrian Chief of Staff, General von Conrad, again requested that the German 8th Army should make a thrust across the Narev in the direction of Sielce, so as to work in conjunction with the Austro-Hungarian Army. If General von Prittwitz had followed the Schlieffen plan, and disposed the whole 8th Army for an attack on the 1st Russian Army, and carried the attack through, then by the 23rd he would have probably finished with that Army, and could have moved against the 2nd Russian Army, turned its left flank and forced it back on the Vistula and Thorn. It would then have been feasible to have carried out the movement that Conrad wanted, and joined hands with the Austro-Hungarian Army in a victorious advance. How differently would the Russian campaign have then turned out! But, as the situation stood, such an operation was, of course, outside the bounds of possibility.

The Russian Warsaw Army—at least five Army Corps and five Cavalry Divisions—had crossed the frontier of South-Eastern Prussia, on a broad front, on the evening of August 22nd; they had reached the great Soldau—Ortelsburg road, and continued their advance on the 23rd. Their centre had so nearly reached the line of the XX. Corps that an engagement would have been possible on the 24th.

The XX. Army Corps, reinforced by the 70th Landwehr Brigade and the garrison troops, amounting to about three and a half Divisions, stood in prepared positions on a line south-west of Gilgenburg—Lahna. The detraining of the 3rd Reserve Division at Allenstein was nearly completed.

The movement of the I. Army Corps had been delayed owing to technical difficulties connected with the railways; by noon on the 23rd only the 1st Grenadier Regiment had arrived, and the whole of the combatant troops had not arrived until the evening of the 25th. Opposite Rennenkampf's army lay the I. Reserve Corps and the XVII. Army Corps, together with the 1st Cavalry Division, on and to the west of the Nordenburg—Insterburg road. The 1st Cavalry Division was completely exhausted and in urgent need of rest, which could not, of course, be sanctioned.

Rennenkampf's army had not yet made itself felt, and the bulk of the force still apparently lay on the battlefield of the 20th. However, we could scarcely rely on Rennenkampf continuing in a state of complete inactivity; we had to assume that he would advance as soon as his cavalry had reported the evacuation of the Angerapp position along the entire Front. Still, his inaction hitherto gave us grounds for hoping that he might dally a little longer and that it would be possible to move sections of the I. Reserve Corps and the XVII. Corps to take part in the decisive battle against the Russian Warsaw Army. Accordingly the I. Reserve Corps received orders to proceed on the 24th by forced marches through Schippenbeil and cover as much ground as possible in the direction of Bischofstein —Seeburg, while the XVII. Corps was at once to cross the Alle at Friedland and then swing southwards towards Bartenstein. The High Command did not then believe it would be possible to get the XVII. Corps down; they counted on leaving this Corps together with the 1st Cavalry Division behind the Alle, to be used against Rennenkampf's army in case of necessity. In any case, both these Army Corps had to make up by forced marches for the time lost in the before-mentioned day's rest. The 6th Landwehr Brigade in Lötzen received orders to fall back and join the I. Army Corps.

CHAPTER V

THE FIRST FIGHTING

ONLY the centre Corps of the Russian 2nd Army —the XIII. and the XV.—had been ordered to advance on August 23rd, and the XIII. was in fact to advance against the line Jedvabno—Omulefofen and the XV. on Lykusen — Seelesen. The movement of the XV. Army Corps led to the engagement with the 37th Infantry Division. This Division, reinforced by parts of the 70th Landwehr Brigade, was attacked on the line Lake Kovnatka—Lahna —Orlau. At Lahna and Orlau especially there was violent hand-to-hand fighting, which, however, came to an end late in the evening, with complete success for the 37th Infantry Division. Only the town of Lahna, which lay in front of our position, remained in Russian hands.

The XX. Corps Command had ordered the 3rd Reserve Division to proceed from Allenstein towards the northern end of the Lanska Lake, with the idea of striking to the east of the lake against the flank of the Russian force then attacking the 37th Infantry Division. This bold stroke had, however, to be held up, as reports came in of the advance of the Russian XIII. Corps through the forest country to the north-east of Neidenburg in the direction of Kurken. Moreover, the orders issued by the 8th Army to the XX. Army Corps, which were based on the consideration that the reinforced XX. Corps must hold on alone until the 26th against the superior Russian forces, and were to the effect that the XX. must economize their strength while the 3rd Reserve Division retired on Allenstein, were not favourable to any offensive tactics, which, having regard to the relative strength of the forces involved, could not have been successful. Accordingly, General von Scholtz decided to move his left wing back, so as to withdraw from these further enemy attacks to be expected early on the 24th, and to move the 3rd Reserve Division towards Hohenstein in defence of Kurken, which was then threatened with envelopment. The 37th Division received orders to swing backwards in conjunction with the left wing of the 41st Division at Thurau on to a position astride the Mühlen Lake, with their left wing in the neighbourhood of Paulsgut. Although the order for the withdrawal of the Division was not given until very late, the disengagement from the enemy was successfully achieved in the darkness, and the movement carried out without any considerable fighting.

The Headquarters of the 8th Army shifted on the morning of the 24th to Riesenburg, and the actual Staff went early on the same day to Tannenberg, when a conference with General von Scholtz and Colonel Hell took place. These two officers' attitude was grave but confident. They were both under the impression that the effort to beat off the Russian attack had just succeeded after heavy fighting, and that the retreat during the previous night had embarrassed the enemy. A continuation of the enemy attacks must be anticipated in the course of the afternoon of the 24th or, at latest, on the morning of the 25th, as a result of which the Russians, who were already reported to be advancing on Kurken, would in all probability advance through Schwedrich to Hohenstein. General von Scholtz accordingly proposed that the left wing should be still further withdrawn and that the whole XX. Corps should start a turning movement backwards on to the line Gilgenburg — Mühlen. He suggested moving the 3rd Reserve Division towards the left wing to the neighbourhood of Kgl. Lichteinen. If the Russians proposed to make a flanking attack on this position they would have to reach out pretty far to the north. The Corps would thus gain time to hold out at least until the 26th, on which day the I. Army Corps was to take a hand. The High Command agreed to these proposals, except that orders were given that the 3rd Reserve Division should not be immediately moved to the wing, but should for the present be allowed to remain unattached near Hohenstein. The Crown Prince's Grenadier Regiment, the first that had arrived from the I. Army Corps in Löbau, was, at the request of the XX. Army Corps, placed at the disposal of that Corps.

The position on the evening of the 24th was as follows. The 5th Landwehr Brigade, under Mühlmann, had reached a position somewhere between Strasburg and Lautenburg. Strong forces of Russian cavalry were reported on its flank and in front of it. The transport of the I. Army Corps had been still further delayed as a result of the premature retirement of the Königsberg main Reserve and the consequent necessity of entraining the Corps at a point still farther back. On the new Front of the XX. Corps there had been no serious engagements, but an attack on the whole Front was to be expected early on the 25th. For this purpose the Russians had about seven Divisions at their disposal—*i.e.* they would outnumber the XX. Corps by two to one. Any further retirement by that Corps was not to be thought of, and it accordingly received orders to meet the attack, and hold the position to the last man.

From the point of view of the High Command the position that evening was the most difficult in the whole battle. The decision was undoubtedly right. As General Ludendorff reported to G.H.Q., a further retreat by this Corps would have the same effect as a defeat.

The 5th Landwehr Brigade was placed under the command of the I. Army Corps and received orders to get to Lautenburg by 10 A.M. The troops of the I. Army Corps that had already arrived there were sent forward at the same time as far as Rybno. In the event of an overwhelming Russian attack against the reinforced XX. Corps these forces could take the Russian advance in the flank.

In the meantime the Russian VI. Corps had been detached from the main body of the 2nd Russian Army, had continued the advance from Ortelsburg, and was now marching on Bischofsburg in two columns. The Russian II. Corps was advancing on Angerburg, east of the Masurian Lakes. Rennenkampf's army was slowly advancing from the Angerapp, but had again come to a standstill by midday.

The Eastern Group of the German 8th Army—*i.e.* the I. Reserve Corps, the XVII. Corps and the 6th Landwehr Brigade — had the chance of attacking, with superior numbers, the isolated Russian VI. Corps marching northward. This involved enormous forced marches, and the consequences of that day's rest became painfully apparent. The I. Reserve Corps was to start out early on the 25th, advance through Seeburg together with the 6th Landwehr Brigade, which was under the same command, and attack the enemy wherever they found him. One Division of the XVII. Army Corps was to reach Bischofstein by a forced march of about fifty kilometres, the other was ordered to

advance on Gross-Schwansfeld. It seemed at that
time doubtful whether it was possible to get this
second Division of the XVII. Army Corps into
the battle to the south. It would probably have
to join the 1st Cavalry Division in holding up
Rennenkampf's advance.

On August 25th there was a succession of encouraging news and events.

Above all, we heard that G.H.Q. had placed at
the disposal of the 8th Army the Holstein Landwehr
Division that had been stationed on the Danish
frontier, and that it would begin to arrive on the
27th. The High Command did not settle a place
for the detrainment of the Division, but sent it in
the general direction of the right wing.

In front of the XX. Army Corps the night had
for the most part passed without incident, and there
was not a sign to suggest an imminent attack.

CHAPTER VI

THE WIRELESS MESSAGES

AT this juncture two Russian wireless messages, not in cipher, were picked up. The first, sent out by Rennenkampf's army, reached the Army Command in the early morning, and was to the effect that the Russian 1st Army would not reach the line Gerdauen—Allenburg—Wehlau until the 26th. From this it was clear that Rennenkampf's army could not take a hand in the battle with the Russian 2nd Army. The second message contained an order for pursuit issued by Samsonoff, who had interpreted the rearward turning movement of the XX. Corps as a general retirement of the German forces opposite him in the direction of Osterode.

The Headquarters' Staff met General von François for a conference early on the 25th, on Hill 168, to the south-east of Montovo. At this moment the wireless messages containing Samsonoff's objectives had not yet come in. Headquarters reckoned that by the morning of the 26th, at the latest, the XX. Army Corps would be attacked by superior Russian forces. They also took the view that the I. Army Corps attack should begin as soon as possible so as to avoid the risk of any mishap on the XX. Corps Front. Accordingly, Colonel-General von Hindenburg gave General von François the verbal order to attack Usdau, which was the objective I had suggested in my first report, at 5 A.M. on August 26th. General von François raised various difficulties, as much against the time as the direction of

265

the attack. He pointed out that by the time the High Command wanted the attack to start, the fighting troops of the Army Corps would not all have arrived—to say nothing of the ammunition columns. He did not feel he could be responsible for carrying out the attack prematurely before his Corps was complete. Equally he thought that the direction of the attack was open to criticism. He would prefer to move his men farther south, envelop the right wing of the opposing forces, and then attack. General Ludendorff replied to General von François' objections in the name of the Commander-in-Chief, and disposed of them by repeating the order to attack early on the 26th: the direction likewise remained unchanged—viz. a frontal attack and break-through at Usdau.

General von François' objection to attacking before his Corps had been completely assembled was entirely justified. In spite of this, the attack would have had to materialize if the Russian Army had attacked the XX. Corps on the evening of the 25th or the morning of the 26th. At that time the High Command were unaware that they did not intend to do so. Ludendorff's summary treatment of the objections probably was inspired by the feeling that, in view of the independence General von François had shown in the days before Gumbinnen, the new High Command must lose no time in making clear that they were not disposed to permit any departure from their orders. As regards the direction of the attack, General von François was in favour of an envelopment. The experience of the Gumbinnen battle had clearly proved the shattering effect of an enveloping movement on the Russian soldiery, and the failure of the XVII. Corps had equally clearly demonstrated the dangers of a frontal assault. The High

Command would indeed have gladly given effect to his suggestion of an enveloping movement, but from the news then to hand regarding the enemy it was clear that there were strong Russian forces still kept back in the Soldau—Mlava area. So that for the purposes of an enveloping movement the troops would have to be pushed down south of Mlava. Against this there were two objections: in the first place, there was not time enough, as the precarious position of the XX. Corps called for a speedy attack; in the second place, a so widely extended enveloping movement would have stretched beyond breaking-point an already weak attacking line.

When General von François was proceeding to Löbau, the High Command stopped at Montovo railway station to telephone to Headquarters and ask for any news that had come in meanwhile. It was here that I was in the meantime handed the intercepted wireless message from General Samsonoff to the Russian XIII. Corps containing the objectives for the main body of the Corps on the 25th. This order was some little time in reaching me, and I only received the transcript when Colonel-General von Hindenburg and General Ludendorff had already left. I hurried after them, had my car driven up level with that of the Commander-in-Chief and handed General Ludendorff the telegram while our cars went on. The Commander-in-Chief stopped east of Löbau, and we proceeded to study the order by reference to the map. The most important point was that the Russian attack would probably not take place until the 26th. In addition to this, the order confirmed the information we already had as to the strength of the Russian forces, and, apart from this, we were very glad to know the exact objectives of the individual enemy Corps.

General Ludendorff at once sent copies of the message to the Generals commanding the XX. and the I. Corps. General Grünert took a copy to General Scholtz and one to General von François.

The certainty that the Russian attack would probably not begin until the 26th, and perhaps later, was naturally a great relief to General von Scholtz. He could now count on the I. Corps starting its attack in time. He was accordingly relieved of any anxiety about his right wing, but the steadily continuing envelopment of his left wing made him uneasy. He therefore suggested to the High Command that the force under Unger should be withdrawn from his right wing, replaced by the 1st Grenadier Regiment of the I. Army Corps, shifted to his left wing and posted behind the Drewenz sector. He could then keep the 3rd Reserve Division concentrated behind his left wing, to deal with any possible attempt at envelopment. This proposal was approved.

CHAPTER VII

SAMSONOFF'S MISAPPREHENSION OF HIS POSITION

AUGUST 25TH passed without serious fighting. By the evening the position had still further cleared up. Mühlmann's Landwehr Brigade had found Lautenburg occupied by Russian cavalry — an incident which was naturally calculated to raise the confidence and courage of the Landwehr who were going under fire for the first time. The outposts of the I. Army Corps had reached Kielpin and Rybno, three battalions of infantry and the bulk of the cavalry and artillery had not yet arrived, and could not arrive before early the next morning. The XX. Corps had been regrouped as indicated above, and the forces stood thus: the 1st Grenadier Regiment of the I. Army Corps, now attached to the XX. Corps, between the Rumian Lake and Gross-Damerau Lake; the 41st Division between Gross-Damerau Lake and Logdau, there joining the 37th Division, which reached to the Chaus Lake; farther to the north were the 70th Landwehr Brigade and garrison troops under Unger, behind the Drewenz; and lastly, the 3rd Reserve Division at Reichenau. The Russian advance against the XX. Corps proceeded very slowly; Waplitz was not occupied until between three and four of the afternoon. The Russian XIII. Corps was reported to be continuing its advance northwards on either side of the Lanska Lake, and the Russian Commander-in-Chief seemed to suspect nothing of the storm that was brewing in front of him. It was

269

clear from the intercepted wireless messages that he was counting on a general German retreat. In pursuance of his order to cut off the German 8th Army from the Vistula, Samsonoff had decided to close up his left wing and push it forward along the line Allenstein—Osterode. However, the Corps on his extreme right wing—the VI.—was ordered by Jilinski's Group Command not to proceed towards Allenstein, but to stay in the neighbourhood of Bischofsburg to act as a covering force against Lötzen. So that Samsonoff really had only three Corps at his disposal for the coming battles. These were to march only a short distance to the north on the 25th, and this movement entirely miscarried owing to a misunderstanding between the XV. Corps and the 2nd Division under its command. These tactics were completely at variance with the position. As Samsonoff assumed that the German forces opposite him were in retreat, and as he, moreover, had been ordered to intercept the retirement behind the Vistula of the German troops defeated by Rennenkampf, he should, on the contrary, have hurried forward with all the forces at his disposal. The explanation lies in the condition of his troops. The Russian 2nd Army was completely exhausted as a result of over-long marches and inadequate supply services. For example, the XIII. Corps had covered 250 kilometres in twelve days on deep sandy roads. All the Generals to a man told Samsonoff that the troops could do no more. He agreed, and proposed a day's rest, which Jilinski was nevertheless forced to refuse. From Samsonoff's reports, too, he did not anticipate severe fighting on that Front, but he believed that Rennenkampf had much stronger German formations opposing him, and that he would again have to engage them on this side of the Vistula. Samsonoff was accordingly informed that a day's rest for his army could be sanctioned only when he had reached the line Allenstein—Osterode; for it was not until then that the retreat of the German forces opposing Rennenkampf could be threatened.

In the course of the 25th, Samsonoff abandoned the view that the Germans opposite him were in retreat towards the Vistula. The regimental numbers of the garrison troops, which were composed of Landwehr and Reserve formations, as well as the reports of railway movements on the right wing, suddenly gave him the idea that sections of the XVII. Army Corps, the I. Reserve Corps and the XIX. Corps had arrived, or were arriving, near and to the west of Gilgenburg. To meet the German thrust to be expected at this point Samsonoff formed a special group on his left wing under General Artamonov, the General commanding the I. Army Corps, consisting of the I. Army Corps, the 3rd Guard Division, the 1st Light Infantry Brigade and two Cavalry Brigades. Artamonov received orders to anticipate the German stroke by an offensive on his part. On the morning of August 26th, of the I. Russian Army Corps some four regiments were in the neighbourhood of Usdau and two regiments were to advance farther south to Heinrichsdorf. The 3rd Guard Division reached Soldau, the Light Infantry Brigade was still coming up, and the two Cavalry Divisions stood east and south of Lautenburg.

CHAPTER VIII

DIFFERENCES BETWEEN GENERAL FRANÇOIS AND THE HIGH COMMAND

THE attack ordered by the High Command for the morning of the 26th was never carried out. At 8 A.M. on the morning of the 25th General von François had received the verbal order to attack. The written order, which was a repetition of the verbal order, did not reach him until about midnight of the 25th-26th. General von François had apparently hoped that, on the ground of General Samsonoff's intercepted wireless message and the quiet state of the Russian lines on the 25th, the High Command would yield to his objections, and postpone the attack until the remaining troops of his Corps had arrived. On this ground, preliminary orders for the troops to be got in readiness early for the first attack on the heights to the northwest of Seeben had not been issued. The Corps order issued at midnight—that the 1st Infantry Division was to be in possession of these heights by 4 A.M., and at 10 A.M. was to attack Usdau, and that the 2nd Infantry Division was to advance at 7 A.M. from Kielpin to Gr.-Tauer Lake, and the 5th Landwehr Brigade at 7 A.M. from Lautenburg, through Heinrichsdorf, towards the district north of Borchersdorf—could not now be carried out up to time.

It was not until 8 A.M. that the van of the 1st Infantry Division reached the section of the Welle to the west of Seeben. The Divisional Commander drew up his troops there ready for an attack, but at once reported that he could not begin his attack on the entrenched heights of Seeben without a thorough artillery preparation. But as the Division had at this time only four batteries at its disposal, it was obvious that the whole attack must be subject to considerable delay. General von François, who had in the meantime got into telephonic communication with the XX. Army Corps, and had been informed by them that the general position on their Front did not justify a premature attack, agreed with the opinion of his Divisional Commander, and gave orders that the 5th Landwehr Brigade and the 2nd Infantry Division should not, for the time being, cross a line from the Kl.-Tauer Lake to Gr.-Koschlau. General von François reported to the High Command that the attack on Usdau must be delayed owing to the belated arrival of the troops. As a report from the I. Army Corps at 7.30 A.M. had stated that the attack on the heights of Seeben was proceeding, although with insufficient forces, the High Command assumed that the delay in question would be a matter only of hours, and fixed the attack on Usdau for twelve o'clock punctually. To their extreme surprise, General von Francois reported, in reply to this order, that not even the heights of Seeben had been taken.

In the face of the probably unfriendly reply of the High Command as a result of this first intimation of the real position, General von François gave up any further opposition to the views of the High Command and ordered the attack to be carried out with the troops then available. The right wing of the I. Army Corps reached the line Heinrichsdorf —Grallau railway station, and between noon and 1 P.M. the 1st Division took the heights of Seeben, which had been occupied only by advanced sections of Russian troops; they continued the advance and fought their way forward to the line Meischlitz— Gr.-Grieben.

General von Conta, the Commander of the 1st Division, did not think it possible to carry out his orders and attack Usdau on the same day. His troops, which had been on the march since the early morning, were very tired. The artillery preparation for the attack had lasted so long that he could not have sent his men forward until the evening. To try to develop their success that day was out of the question. General von François shared this view, and determined to postpone the storming of Usdau until the morning of the 27th.

If at this point the question is asked which side was right—the High Command, who adhered to their decision that the attack should be made on the 26th, or General von François with his passive resistance, which delayed the decisive attack on Usdau by twenty-four hours — the following considerations must be taken into account: for the I. Army Corps to carry out an attack on a prepared position before all the fighting troops of that Corps —and more especially its artillery and ammunition columns—were in position could only have been justified and necessary if the reinforced XX. Corps had already been attacked by superior Russian forces on the 26th and was in danger of being overwhelmed. From the news of the enemy that was to hand this was not the case. The High Command would have done better to have listened to General von François' repeated representations and on their own account postponed the attack until all the troops of the I. Army Corps had arrived. But the method adopted by General von François to secure the postponement of the attack cannot be approved. And yet the conclusion cannot be avoided that the postponement that actually took place became of capital importance for the progress of the whole battle. If he had followed the letter of his orders, taken the heights of Seeben on the early morning of the 26th and attacked Usdau at 10 A.M. on the same day, by which time only four batteries of the 1st Division were in position, this attack would very likely have met with disaster. But if the break-through at Usdau had not succeeded, then the attack by the XVII. Army Corps and the I. Reserve Corps in the course of the succeeding day would have resulted in the retreat of the 2nd Russian Army, and it would have escaped destruction.

CHAPTER IX

By an Army Order of the evening of the 25th the reinforced XX. Corps was instructed to support the attack of the I. Army Corps by advancing its right wing in the direction of Gr.-Grieben—Jankowitz, and in addition to hold themselves in readiness to take the offensive along its whole Front as the attack by the I. Army Corps progressed. During the night the XX. Corps Staff had already received a telephone message from General von François and Colonel Hell informing them that they must not count on an early attack by the I. Army Corps in the direction of Usdau, and as a result of this they had rightly checked the advance of their right wing.

The Russians made no movement that morning: according to the reports that came in there was a gaping chasm between the Russian troops at Usdau and the Russian forces confronting the southern wing of the XX. Corps. At 1 P.M. the High Command decided to take advantage of this blunder on the part of the Russians and attack with the powerful right wing of the XX. Corps between the Gr.-Damerau and Mühlen Lakes. The support of the I. Army Corps in the direction of Usdau was for the time being abandoned.

When the Army Order was received by the XX. Corps Command, a report had just come in that strong Russian forces were advancing against the positions of the 37th Division and the 70th Landwehr

Brigade on either side of the Mühlen Lake. Accordingly the Corps Command decided to use only the 41st Division and the southern Brigade of the 37th Division in carrying out the attack as ordered.

The attack, which began between 3 and 4 P.M., caught the 2nd Russian Division by surprise in the flank as it was marching northward, and ended in the evening, on the line Ganshorn — Faulen — Mühlen, with a complete success for the three attacking German brigades.

On the extreme left wing of the reinforced XX. Army Corps the 3rd Reserve Division received orders to cross the Drewenz in the direction of Hohenstein. General von Morgen, the Commander of the 3rd Reserve Division, had the impression that in moving thus on Hohenstein he would be advancing against the Front of the Russian XV. Corps, and that his Division would then simply have to make a frontal attack. He accordingly decided to take his own line, remain close to Reichenau and there await the Russian advance, and then deliver a blow at their flank. He did not, however, report this departure from the orders given to him, so that the Corps Command and the High Command still believed, at 6 P.M., that the 3rd Reserve Division was moving on Hohenstein.

The training of our Generals to make independent decisions has, as can be seen, its disadvantages. It is possible that the feeling that in the great tactical exercises in peace time the so-called " Patent Solution " was constantly a departure from the orders issued had a certain effect on our Generals at the beginning of the war. If the 3rd Reserve Division had advanced in accordance with orders they would probably have engaged the northern wing of the Russian XV. Corps, enveloped and attacked it, and perhaps inflicted a check on it.

The Russian XIII. Corps could not have come up in support, as it was on the eastern side of the long line of lakes.

On the 26th the German Eastern Group met and engaged the Russian VI. Corps. As has already been said, by the 25th both Corps had done a great deal of forced marching, the effect of which was increased by the necessity of leaving the main highroads to the hordes of fleeing inhabitants, who were conveying with them their movable effects and their live stock, and using the sandy by-ways. The I. Reserve Corps had reached the neighbourhood of Seeburg by the evening, and the 6th Landwehr Brigade coming from Lötzen had reached Lautern. Of the XVII. Army Corps, the van of the 36th Division had reached Bischofstein after a march of 50 kilometres, and the van of the 35th had reached Gross Schwansfeld after an even longer march. The 1st Cavalry Division was standing to the west of Gerdauen.

The High Command had hitherto intended to leave the 35th Infantry Division, as well as the 1st Cavalry Division, to cover Rennenkampf. It was not until the afternoon of the 25th that it was decided to bring this Division also into the main battle, and orders were given that the XVII. Army Corps and the I. Reserve Corps, with the 6th Landwehr Brigade under the same command, were all to attack the Russian VI. Corps. The two Corps Commands had already got into touch, and had independently determined on the method of advance. The I. Reserve Corps was to advance to the attack on the 26th from Seeburg, on a broad front, in the direction of Wartenburg, and the XVII. was to move east of the Gr.-Lautern Lake and the Daday Lake against the enemy flank. The attack by the I. Reserve Corps was to strike and

hold the enemy if he showed any intention of trying to move from Bischofsburg in the direction of
the main army towards Allenstein. The concerted
arrangements of the two Corps Commands did not
work out quite successfully. General von Mackensen
assumed that the I. Reserve Corps would start
early, and accordingly, in spite of his troops' fatigue,
he ordered an early advance. General von Below,
on the contrary, was disposed to allow for the
fatigue of his troops, and gave orders that the Corps
need not be ready before 10 A.M. He wanted, in
this way, to give the XVII. Corps time to come up,
and he did not imagine that this Corps was in a
position to get on the move so early.

General Blagovjeshtshenski, the General commanding the VI. Russian Army Corps, had orders
to move on the 26th from the neighbourhood of
Rothfliesz and Bischofsburg and get into touch
with the right wing of his army in the direction of
Allenstein. He imagined that the German forces
were in retreat towards the west, and when the
leading Division, the 4th, unexpectedly fell upon the
van of the XVII. Army Corps in the neighbourhood
of Lautern he assumed that this was a force thrown
out to protect the flank of the Germans in retreat
from Rastenburg towards the west. Proceeding
on this assumption he advanced to the attack on
Lautern.

The XVII. Army Corps received the first reports
of the Russian advance from the 6th Landwehr
Brigade, which, on its march north of Lautern to
join the I. Reserve Corps, crossed the track of the
XVII. Corps. General von Heineccius, the Commander of the 36th Infantry Division, decided,
in the face of the Russian attack now developing
against him, to keep strictly to the defensive so as
to wait until the rear Division of the Corps, the

35th, came up, and the I. Reserve Corps arrived
on the scene. This took some time in both cases,
so that the left wing of the 36th Division was for
a short time hard pressed by the Russian attack.
The 35th Infantry Division, which General von
Mackensen had dispatched in the direction of
Gross-Köllen to attack and envelop the enemy
right wing, did not arrive. In the face of the utter
exhaustion of the troops, it had to be ordered a rest,
and when the advance-guard finally reached Gross-
Köllen they had to have another rest. The news
that came in to the German side about the Russian
forces gave the impression that the whole Russian
VI. Army Corps had been put into the battle to
the east of the Gr.-Lautern Lake. When the
I. Reserve Corps had taken up its position on the
line Alt-Vierzighufen—Kirschdorf without getting
any sight of the enemy, General von Below, in
agreement with the XVII. Army Corps, sent only
sections of the 36th Reserve Division through
Klein-Bössau against the left flank of the Russians
engaged to the east of the Lautern Lake, and in
immediate support of the 36th Infantry Division;
he moved the main bulk of his army towards the
southern extremity of the Daday Lake, so as to cut
off the retreat of the Russian VI. Corps. The
Commander of the 4th Russian Division saw himself forced, in order to cover his attack on the left
wing towards the north, to move up forces to the
neighbourhood of Klein-Bössau. These, of course,
attracted still stronger forces of the I. Reserve
Corps against them, and finally the main body
of the 36th Reserve Division and the 6th Landwehr Brigade were attacking at Klein-Bössau, and
flung back the enemy, who defended himself desperately. In the course of this the Russians were
hemmed in to the east of the Bössau Lake, with

the lake in their rear, and a certain number must have been drowned. This is probably the origin of the legend, that has been current for years, to the effect that at the battle of Tannenberg Hindenburg drove thousands of Russians into lakes and marshes and left them to their fate.

The I. Reserve Division, as it continued its march, came in contact with the advance-guard of the rear Division of the VI. Russian Army Corps, which General Blagovjeshtshenski had diverted from their advance westward and sent northwards in support of his 4th Division. The reports to the effect that the whole Russian VI. Corps was in action at Lautern were false. The inclination of troops always to regard the enemy opposite him as stronger than he actually is, as well as the constant difficulty in the early part of the war of correctly estimating formations now up to war strength, were the causes of this mistake.

The Russian 16th Division retired before the advance of the German 1st Reserve Division. The Russian 4th Division, under the pressure of a threat to its flank, had already begun its retreat from Bössau by the afternoon. The infantry attack by the 36th Division, which was launched after a prolonged artillery preparation, found only abandoned positions. General Blagovjeshtshenski led his Corps through Bischofsburg to the south.

The possibility now offered by the tactical position of entirely destroying the Russian 4th Division could not be used by us; the contributory causes were the late arrival of the 35th Division of the XVII. Army Corps and the long interval before the I. Reserve Corps was ready to attack. The fundamental cause was the total exhaustion of the troops of both Corps as a result of the excessive forced marches that were necessary to make good the day's rest I have already mentioned. So the only order preliminary to the battle of Tannenberg issued by General Ludendorff, without his having heard the views of the High Command, was proved to be rather unfortunate.

The I. Reserve Corps and the XVII. Corps expected to be attacked again on the following morning. Airmen had reported a prepared Russian position south of Bischofsburg. It was to be assumed that the Russian VI. Corps, perhaps still further reinforced, would put up a renewed resistance here. The position was made more difficult by the fact that, according to reports from the military authorities at Lötzen and an intercepted wireless message, the Russian II. Corps was now moving through Angerburg with the object of joining hands with the Russian 2nd Army west of the Mauer Lake towards the south. Although the position might become very precarious for both German Corps, in case the Russian VI. Corps put up any considerable resistance, both Corps Commands had agreed to attack again early on the 27th: the XVII. was to make another frontal attack, and the I. Reserve Corps was to envelop the enemy's left wing. The High Command at once approved this decision. It could have done nothing else. The slightest delay could only have made things worse. In his discussion of the situation with Colonel-General von Hindenburg, General Ludendorff seems to have lost his nerve a little; what else can be the explanation of Hindenburg's observation on page 87 of his book: " Is it surprising that grave thoughts filled every heart: if the strongest wills showed signs of weakening, and doubts found their way into the clearest heads? Should we not strengthen our forces against Rennenkampf, and not make a serious effort against Samsonoff? Were it not better not to try to destroy the Narev Army, but make sure of avoiding destruction ourselves? We overcame the inner crisis, held by the decisions we had taken, and tried to find a solution by an attack with all our forces."

If, indeed, the decision once taken could not be revoked, everything of course pointed to the urgent necessity for speed.

On the 27th the I. Reserve Corps and the XVII. Army Corps started their advance southwards to attack the reported enemy positions. The 6th Landwehr Brigade and a small section of the XVII. Army Corps were left near Lautern in immediate readiness to cover the rear of the advance. The High Command ordered both Corps, as soon as they had disposed of the VI. Russian Army Corps, to turn in a south-westerly direction against the right flank of the Russian 2nd Army. At midday a report came in that the Russians had evacuated the position south of Bischofsburg and were continuing their retreat. About the same time news came in from Allenstein that strong Russian forces had arrived there and occupied the town.

The High Command thereupon instructed the Reserve Corps, then on the march in the direction of Passenheim, to turn west with the main part of its forces and make for Patricken, south of Wartenburg. The further disposal of the I. Reserve Corps, whether in a westerly or south-westerly direction, was reserved for the moment. The Corps Command was also instructed to send forward a mixed section of all arms, which was to reach Passenheim without fail the same day and bar the defile there. General von Below passed on this latter order to the XVII. Army Corps, with the request that they would carry it out, as his own troops were too tired; and the XVII. did so. The main part of the Corps reached the neighbourhood of Mensguth, but small sections continued the pursuit until late into the night, and one of them reached Passenheim after midnight. The news from Rennenkampf's army was to the effect that the most southern Russian Army Corps, the II., had reached Rastenburg. Farther to the north the High Command believed the enemy infantry to be on the line Schippenbeil—Friedland. The Russian cavalry got as far as the Heilsberg and Preussisch-Eylau area. The weak Landsturm formations along the railways could not, of course, put up any serious resistance.

CHAPTER X

ON the morning of the 27th the battle was decided
on its western wing by General von François'
break-through at Usdau, and its exploitation.
The Russian High Command had reached
Neidenburg on the 26th. The Commander-in-
Chief, Samsonoff, had come back to the view that
he had only weak German forces in front of him,
which he ought to attack as speedily as possible, so
as to cut off from the Vistula the troops retreating
before Rennenkampf. This attack was to be carried
out by the XIII., XV. and half the XXIII. Corps.
The VI. Corps was to advance through Allenstein
against the left flank of the German forces, and the
reinforced I. Corps was to cover his own left flank.
Samsonoff had already been informed, on the evening of the 26th, of the German advance against his
left flank in the direction of Usdau, and also of the
successful stroke of the 41st Infantry Division against
his own 2nd Infantry Division to the south of
Mühlen. However, he assumed that Artamonov's
reinforced I. Corps would be strong enough to repel
the attack on Usdau and successfully support the
2nd Division.

He still held to his decision to attack when he
received the report of the reverse of the VI. Army
Corps at Lautern—Gr.-Bössau. This report must
have startled him considerably. On the evening
of the 26th he had before him the news that

about three Divisions were moving against his left wing, that vastly superior forces had defeated the leading Division of his VI. Corps and forced it to retire. Even if he knew nothing of the strength of the forces holding the Drewenz sector, the mere length of the line held by the Germans on their side of the river—reaching north to the Hohenstein —Reichenau road—must have indicated that there were considerable German forces facing him, which were actually so strong on the southern wing that they could attack and overwhelm his 2nd Division. So that Samsonoff's decision to attack on the 27th must be regarded as a blunder. It can, perhaps, be explained only by the fact that Samsonoff said to himself : " Even if the German troops outnumber me, my business is at all costs to prevent them retreating and pin them down this side of the Vistula, and so make time for Rennenkampf to get here and deliver the decisive blow."

In pursuance of the order to attack on the 27th, the Russian XIII. Corps—one and a half Divisions strong—marched on Allenstein, which it occupied without fighting. Reports that strong German forces had reached a point two miles to the east of Allenstein were not believed. It was assumed that they referred to Russian forces—namely, to the VI. Corps. There was no communication with this Corps, and, as a result, neither the defeat of the Corps on the 26th, nor its continued retreat to Ortelsburg on the 27th, was known. The latter information, it may be remarked in passing, did not reach the Russian High Command either. General Klujeff, the General commanding the XIII. Corps, in reply to a wireless appeal for help from the XV. Army Corps, sent a mixed Brigade to Hohenstein. The dispatch of the whole Corps, which Klujeff had himself proposed to the High

Command, and which had been approved by the latter in the course of the afternoon, was delayed by a succession of difficulties until early on the 28th.

The XV. Russian Army Corps, under General Martos, moved a Brigade from its right wing to its left in support of the 2nd Division that had been defeated on the previous day, and with the three remaining Brigades, together with the Brigade of the XIII. Corps sent up through Hohenstein, proceeded to attack the left bank of the Drewenz, which was held by the Germans. This attack failed. The Brigade sent in support of the 2nd Division got as far as a point near Waplitz, where it remained inactive; while the 2nd Division, which had been defeated on the previous day, and was no longer capable of serious fighting, retired on the line Bujaken — Frankenau — Neidenburg, where it was stopped by the General commanding the XXIII. Corps, General Kondratovich, and reinforced by a section of the 3rd Guard Infantry Division belonging to the XXIII. Corps.

The German Army Orders of the 27th ordered an attack on the entire Front, and the movement was in fact to begin at 4 A.M. The I. Corps, echeloned to the right as a protection against the forces still remaining to the west of Soldau behind the enemy's right wing, was to attack Usdau, and then with all available forces strike at Neidenburg, so as to roll up the Russian line in front of the XX. Army Corps. The XX. Corps was to give direct support from the north, so that the break-through could be carried out with the utmost speed. Apart from this, the attack ordered for the 26th was to be continued, in the course of which the 3rd Reserve Division was to hold on to Hohenstein and strike in the direction of Waplitz.

It was not until the Army Orders had been

issued that the High Command discovered that the position on the left wing of the XX. Army Corps was quite different from what they had supposed—that the 3rd Reserve Division had not advanced on Hohenstein but had remained behind the Drewenz.

The Staff of the XX. Army Corps took the view that they must reckon with a strong Russian attack early on the 27th by at least two Army Corps, and the chance of striking with the 3rd Reserve Division at the flank of this attack had been thrown away by that Division's failure to move on the 26th. They accordingly thought that an attack by the right wing was not at all desirable, but that it was practicable to move the 3rd Reserve Division along the Drewenz as far as the left wing of Unger's garrison troops and then remain on the defensive and await the Russian attack. The XX. Army Corps proposed to attack only with its victorious right wing, which should be strengthened by reinforcements from the south. General Ludendorff was not in agreement with these views and proposals, but he had to sanction them after raising various objections. Personally, I think that, as the situation lay, General von Morgen not having advanced on Hohenstein on the 26th, the Army Corps Staff could not have acted differently.

When the High Command Staff left Löbau, on the early morning of the 27th, to observe the progress of the battle from a small height at the southern end of the Damerau Lake, a report came in from the Staff of the I. Army Corps that the 1st Division had taken Usdau at 5 A.M., and that a pursuit had been ordered in the direction of Neidenburg, the 5th Landwehr Brigade being detailed to cover Soldau.

Unfortunately it soon appeared that this report

was false. The 1st Division had taken Gut
Meischlitz, and had mistaken it for Usdau.

General von François had directed the main body
of his Army Corps against Usdau—the left wing
of the 2nd Division from the south-west, and the
1st Division from the west and north-west. The
southern wing of the 2nd Division and the 5th
Landwehr Brigade were to remain on the defensive.
The XX. Army Corps had detailed a mixed detachment of six battalions, two squadrons and two
batteries, under General von Schmettau, to attack
Usdau from Bergling. The artillery attack ordered
for 4 A.M. and the infantry attack for 5 A.M. were
delayed. A part of the 1st Division artillery did
not arrive until the evening of the 26th, and did
not reach the Division until it was dark; and the
assembling of Schmettau's Force also was delayed.
When we reached our observation-point we saw
the town of Usdau, about 7 kilometres away, under
heavy German artillery fire, the Russian artillery
replying, and German infantry flinging back the
advanced parties of Russians along the whole Front.
The storming of Usdau did not take place until
11 A.M.; but the German artillery had done its
work so well that the infantry found little resistance.
General von François ordered the 1st Division to
pursue in the direction of Neidenburg.

The erroneous report of the capture of Usdau
had, in the meantime, led to an unpleasant reverse
on the southern wing of the I. Corps. When it
was received, the Corps Command ordered the
southern wing, which had hitherto been marking
time, to advance immediately. As they did so, a
strong Russian attack fell upon them from a south-
easterly direction. The 5th Landwehr Brigade
came to a standstill to the west of Skurpien, the
3rd Infantry Brigade, which was advancing on the

Gr.-Tauer Lake, was attacked by the Russians on the left flank and thrown back with considerable loss. However, it was found possible to rally most of the infantry in the neighbourhood of Heinrichsdorf.

At the news of this retirement, General von François rightly held up the advance of the 1st Infantry Division on Neidenburg, and diverted it to the south, so as to push back the enemy attacking from Soldau, and give himself a free hand for the following day. The Russian forces confronting our 2nd Division to the south of Usdau did not wait for the attack of the 1st Division and Schmettau's Force, against their flank and rear, but retired hastily on Soldau. The enemy rallied at the Soldau bridge, and General von Conta waited long enough to deal them a blow, and then pressed southward with all his forces. But the troops were so exhausted by the exertions of the last few days, and the heavy fighting, that a further attack could not be expected of them. Accordingly, in the afternoon, General von François ordered the cessation of the pursuit. The 5th Landwehr Division reached Hohendorf, the 1st, the area south of Borchersdorf, and Schmettau's Force reached Schönwiese.

General von François, reckoning on continuing the battle on the following morning, gave orders for the whole of his artillery to open fire at daybreak on the 28th against the existing Russian artillery positions round Soldau, and for the infantry to be ready to attack. The air reports that the Russians were not intending to resume the battle, or make a stand, but were retreating precipitately to and beyond Mlava, did not reach the General.

The XX. Army Corps Command had passed on the High Command's order for attack on the 27th, but with certain limitations. They intended that the right wing should pursue its successful

offensive, but it was to attack in conjunction with
the reinforced I. Army Corps. It would thus secure
its position to some extent, as it was to be expected
that the attack on Usdau would take a certain time,
and not until then could the two Corps expect
to move forward in complete unison. The 37th
Division, reinforced by sections of Unger's garrison
troops and the 70th Landwehr Brigade, was to proceed to the attack south of the Mühlen Lake. The
remainder of the garrison troops were to hold the
Drewenz line north of the Mühlen Lake, reinforced
by the 3rd Reserve Division on the left wing.

The 41st Division was unfortunate in its Commander. It started early, met with no considerable
resistance, and after a short advance stopped again,
as the Divisional Commander, in accordance with
his orders, wanted to wait for the arrival of the
I. Army Corps, or was not clear whether he ought
to make any movement in support of that Corps.
The advance of the 37th Division also took place
without meeting with any considerable enemy resistance. It reached, almost without a fight, the line
Konti Lake—Seythen—Thymau, and there stopped.
The two German Divisions found opposite them
only the remains of the two Russian Divisions
defeated on the previous day, which had hastily
started to retreat eastwards in the face of the
German advance.

During all this time the Russian XV. Army
Corps was moving to its expected attack on the
German positions to the north of the Mühlen Lake.
The Drewenz sector is very awkward country, as
the thick forests make it difficult to see far, and it
thus facilitated the concealment of the Russian preparations and advance to the attack. Mühlen and
the positions near by were under Russian artillery
fire since daybreak. Even farther north, opposite

the 3rd Reserve Division, which had arrived in the meantime near Kirsteinsdorf, signs of the imminent attack became observable. General von Scholtz decided to divert his two Divisions, which were advancing south of the Mühlen Lake, towards the southern corner of the Mühlen Lake, and then to take the Russians attacking Mühlen in the rear. There was some delay over the fulfilment of this order. The 37th Division, which had started for Waplitz at 8.30 A.M., had by 9 A.M. reached the area north of the Konti Lake, and had been then ordered to rest for an hour and a half. The 41st Division, farther south, had determined upon an attack on Usdau, and for this purpose had concentrated troops on its right wing. It was not until 11 A.M. that the Division learned that the Russians at Usdau were in retreat, and that the intended stroke had, therefore, become superfluous.

CHAPTER XI

FRICTION IN THE XX. ARMY CORPS

AFTER the capture of Usdau the High Command, at 11.30 A.M., issued orders for a movement which General von Scholtz had himself intended to carry out—viz. that the 41st and 37th Divisions should turn to the east of the Mühlen Lake and both advance against the rear of the attacking Russians.

This order was not carried out, for at the same moment General von Scholtz received a report that the Russians had broken through the German Front at Mühlen. North of Mühlen, German infantry and artillery were in retreat; the situation was, for the moment, a critical one. No more Reserves were available in any considerable numbers. General von Scholtz consequently decided to send the 37th Division direct to the spot where the line had been broken: so that he had only the 41st Division left for the thrust round the Mühlen Lake. The latter Division started at noon, but made a very dilatory progress, and towards evening came to a stop between Januschkau and the southern extremity of the Mühlen Lake. This premature halt was due partly to the exhaustion of the troops by the bad roads, and partly to anxiety as to sections of the defeated Russian 2nd Division which were still in the neighbourhood of their left wing.

But if we are to look for the real reason why an attack that the High Command had planned, and ordered the XX. Corps to carry out with the "greatest energy," came to nothing in this way, we must admit that the High Command were themselves responsible, in so far as they sent on the 26th a verbal message by General Grünert to the Corps Command to wait until the I. Army Corps had made itself felt. If the High Command had assumed that the attack of the I. Army Corps on Usdau would take place earlier than it in fact did, they should have realized that, owing to the mere distance of Usdau from the 41st Division, this modification of plan would severely hamper the XX. Corps for the time being.

In the meantime, it had been established that the report of the break-through at Mühlen was a false alarm. It was a mistake which a Signals Officer had passed on in good faith. The attack on the German positions at Mühlen, which did not materialize until about 4 P.M., broke down almost entirely under the fire of the defending troops. On the other hand a considerable Russian attack was impending through the Jablonka forest against the left wing of the Drewenz position. Reports mentioned a determined envelopment of the 3rd Reserve Division, and stated that sections of the XIII. Russian Army Corps were taking part in the operation. Since midday on the 27th, von der Goltz's Schleswig-Holstein Landwehr Division, which had been sent up by rail, had been in process of detrainment at Biesellen. Whether they were in time to be sent into the fighting in support of the left wing seemed doubtful. General von Scholtz consequently decided to transfer the main body of the 27th Division to the rear of the extreme left wing. As the marching powers of the troops were exhausted for that day, this movement was deferred until the morning of the 28th.

The Russian attack through the Jablonka forest by sections of the XV. and a Brigade of the XIII.

Army Corps did not take effect, as the Brigade in question went astray in the forest, and, as a result, the attacking troops were all withdrawn to its north-eastern edge.

Although in the centre of the battle, on the front of the reinforced XX. Army Corps, a great success was not to be looked for, owing to friction among the various Staffs, the 27th was the decisive day of the battle. On that day took place the victorious break-through at Usdau, and on that day the High Command became certain that, as a result of the victory at Bössau, and the consequent retreat of the Russian VI. Corps on Ortelsburg, they could secure the envelopment of the Russian centre by the I. Reserve Corps and the XVII. Army Corps.

At noon on the 27th the High Command Staff left their observation-point to the north of Usdau and went to the Headquarters of the XX. Corps, to urge a more energetic and speedier prosecution of the attack. The XX. Corps could not wait any longer for the I. Corps to co-operate, since the latter, as described above, was fully engaged in the direction of Soldau. It has been stated already that this movement did not achieve its object, and the 41st Division did not even succeed in reaching Waplitz by the 27th.

At the same time, prospects for the 28th were discussed with the Corps Command. On the 28th the results of the victorious battles on the wings must materialize. Now was the time to encircle and destroy the Russian centre group of about two and a half Army Corps. Of the Russian troops, the half of the XXIII. Corps on the southern wing had already been severely damaged, and the XV. had lost considerably in fighting power during the preceding battles. Only the XIII. was still intact. The High Command counted on this Corps being brought in on the right wing of the XV. with a view to an outflanking attack on the Drewenz position. Moreover, it was not impossible that General Samsonoff—after the reverses on both the wings, and the failure of the frontal attack that day —might break off the battle and begin to retire. As the situation had developed by the evening of the 27th, such a retreat would lead to an immediate and crushing disaster.

CHAPTER XII

THE Army Order for the 28th envisaged an attack at 4 A.M. by the reinforced XX. Corps, beginning with the right wing, in the direction of Hohenstein. Goltz's Landwehr Division, now completely detrained, was to attack at 5 A.M. from Osterode and Biesellen, also in the direction of Hohenstein. The I. Reserve Corps was to pass north of the Allenstein forest and attack the enemy's rear, and to send a mixed Brigade through Passenheim and Kurken to bar the Schwedrich defile. It was assumed that for the next day the I. Army Corps and the XVII. Reserve Corps would be engaged with the enemy at Soldau and Ortelsburg.

In the evening, however, as the result of a report from the I. Reserve Corps, this order was modified. The I. Reserve Corps reported that at noon of the 27th an entire Russian Division had reached Allenstein from the south. General von Below thought it necessary first to dispose of this enemy force, more especially to prevent it continuing its march towards the north and joining hands with the II. Russian Army Corps, which had reached Rastenburg. A movement of that kind would have completely severed the rearward communications between the I. Reserve Corps and the XVII. Army Corps. The General Commanding therefore proposed to march on Allenstein the next day, in conjunction with the XVII. Corps, and there attack the enemy. This proposal was approved, and General von Below was instructed to agree upon the future measures necessary with his G.O.C. XVII. Corps, as there was no telephonic communication with the latter. As a result of this alteration in the original orders for the I. Reserve Corps it was forgotten to repeat the express order to block the Schwedrich defile. The High Command assumed that the I. Reserve Corps Command would hand over this duty to the XVII. Corps, which would see that it was carried out in reasonable time.

At 7 A.M. on the 28th the High Command Staff took up a position of observation at Frögenau, at the Headquarters of the XX. Corps. Since 6 A.M. the noise of fighting could be heard from the east, but a thick mist prevented any glimpse of what was happening. The XX. Corps Command had ordered the 41st Division to advance to the attack so early that by 4 A.M. it had reached the line Luttken—Ganshorn, and from thence could proceed to attack Paulsgut. In giving this order the Corps Command thought that they could ignore the defeated sections of the Russian XXIII. Corps that still lay on the 41st Division's right flank. The Division was instructed to avoid any possible threat from the Bujaken area by marching northwards in the night, and detaching a strong rear-guard for action against the enemy's flank. As soon as the attack of the 41st Division made itself felt, the troops on the main Front were to attack under the orders of the Commander of the 3rd Reserve Division. The 37th Division was to stand ready to the west of Reichenau by 4 A.M., and attack in the direction of the Platteinen Colony. The time for this attack, as for the attack by the centre, was to depend on the progress of the 41st Division.

The 41st Division did not receive the order to

attack until 11.20 P.M. There was little time to get the troops ready for the advance that night. To march past the front of an enemy, who had indeed been defeated the day before, but was still on the spot, and deliver an attack to the north towards his rear, was a venturesome proceeding. The Divisional Commander also had grave misgivings about the proposal. His troops were tired. The reports that had come in did not give him a clear picture of the enemy's position either on his flank or in front. As, however, his representations against the advance on Waplitz, which he had again repeated that day, had merely met with unfriendly rejoinders from the Corps Command, he did not believe that another objection to an advance through Waplitz would be successful, and accordingly proceeded, though with reluctance, to carry out the operation. It ended in a complete failure. There was much delay over the preparations, as various bodies of troops lost their way in the bad forest roads. The advance then came upon enemy resistance on both sides of Waplitz, on the Maranse, and the movement came to a standstill at that point. Only the 2nd Battalion of the 58th Regiment succeeded in crossing the Maranse to the west, driving the enemy back and making progress towards the north. In consequence of the thick mist the Command did not hear of this success, and took no advantage of it. When the mist dispersed, Russian artillery from round Bujaken opened fire on the rear of the troops fighting on the Maranse. At the same time the Russian infantry advanced against the flank and rear of the right wing of the 41st Division. The position of the Division was untenable. The Divisional Commander advised a retreat to the point of departure—*i.e.* the area between the Konti and Thymau Lakes. That this retreat was successful, and did not lead to the capture of the greater part of the Division, is only thanks to the utter inactivity of the Russians. However, as a result, the Division got back— though with heavy losses—to the neighbourhood of Vronovo.

CHAPTER XIII

GENERAL VON MORGEN'S INDEPENDENT DECISION

THE Command of the XX. Corps and the High Command got no news of this reverse for the time being. The noise of fighting could be heard from towards Waplitz, but there were no signs of the 41st Division. The Corps Command accordingly wanted to hold up the attack from their main Front. The garrison troops in the front line were, as has been stated already, under the orders of the Commander of the 3rd Reserve Division.

According to reports received by General von Morgen during the night, the Russians had evacuated the Jablonka forest. The danger of being enveloped by the Russians on the left was obviated by the arrival of the 37th Division on the left wing. General von Morgen and his troops, who had not yet been in any fighting, were burning with eagerness to attack. General von Morgen knew that the Goltz Division had been on the march from Biesellen to Hohenstein since 5 A.M. On the one hand, therefore, he did not think it correct to wait too long for the 41st Division to materialize, and on the other, he felt it important to move his troops through the Jablonka forest as soon as possible, before it could again be occupied by the Russians. He therefore, on his own responsibility, gave the order to attack, and reported to the Corps Command at 8.30 A.M. that he had done so, and that his troops had engaged the enemy. The orders issued had not in many respects been coherent, and a further result of this became apparent at this stage, in so far as General von Morgen did not know that the 37th Division, in the course of its march from the right to the left wing, had left three battalions behind in the neighbourhood of Mühlen. The active regiment behind Unger's garrison troops accordingly received no order to take part in the attack made by these troops.

The Staff of the XX. Corps was not in agreement with General von Morgen's decision, but as the attack was already under way when the announcement arrived they could not stop it, and they accordingly ordered the 37th Division also to proceed forthwith from Reichenau in the direction of Hohenstein.

Unger's right wing did not reach Mühlen and his left wing made slow progress. On the other hand the 3rd Division drove the enemy back everywhere, by a purely frontal attack, and their left wing reached Hohenstein between 12 noon and 1 P.M. The XV. Russian Army Corps put up an obstinate resistance near Dröbnitz and Schwenteinen, but then began to give way near Hohenstein, as by that time the infantry of the Goltz Division had worked their way down to that place.

General Freiherr von der Goltz had not yet got his Division entirely together by the morning of the 28th. As the result of a collision on the railway he was short by five battalions and three batteries. But he had started with the forces that had already arrived—seven battalions, four squadrons and a battery—and, in spite of the report that the enemy were advancing from Allenstein in strength against his left wing, he had, in accordance with his orders, begun to move on the Russian position at Mörken to the east of Hohenstein. Athough the Hamburgers and the Schleswig-Holstein Landwehr attacked with great dash, the attack north of Mörken, which was supported by one battery only, came to a standstill. It was not until the left wing of the 3rd Reserve Division took Hohenstein, and its artillery caught the Russians at Mörken with a flanking fire, that the enemy evacuated the town and the adjoining positions. The entry of the 6th Reserve Brigade into the battle was none too soon for the Goltz Division; for in the meantime the advanced formations of the Russian XIII. Army Corps, coming from Allenstein, had reached the neighbourhood of Grieslienen, and began to fire on the flank and rear of the Goltz Division. At this moment the 37th Division was far back in the forests of the Drewenz sector, and it was not until midday, after they had heard the news of the victorious attack by the 3rd Reserve Division, that they began to advance along the main Hohenstein road. The attack evolved by General von Morgen's initiative had won a complete success by the early afternoon. Only at Mühlen did the enemy hold out.

This independent action was viewed with the greatest satisfaction by the High Command. We stood impatiently near Frögenau and waited for the XX. Army Corps to make a move. When the report came in of the severe defeat on the Front of the 41st Division—on the success of which the beginning of the frontal attack by the XX. Corps was to be dependent—our anxiety was naturally greatly increased, especially as at that time we had no report of how the I. Army Corps was getting on in the fighting round Soldau, or what the Russian XIII. Corps was doing at Allenstein. It was, of course, still possible that the latter might avoid the attack of the I. Reserve Corps by turning north-ward. At 8 A.M. a wireless message came in that cleared up this point. The XIII. Russian Corps was marching on Hohenstein and intended to reach Grieslienen by midday. It was obvious from the accounts of the fighting at Hohenstein and Mörken that Morgen's decision had not been taken and carried out a moment too soon.

About the same time as the intentions of the Russian XIII. Corps were cleared up a cheering report also came in from General von François. François had had his troops ready for attack towards the south by 6 A.M. But the news that had come in during the night had already thrown a good deal of light on the situation, and made it clear to him that he would probably not need to use all his troops in the attack. He had accordingly sent six squadrons and a battery in the direction of Neidenburg, and proposed to send the 2nd Infantry Division after them as soon as possible. He considered that the 1st Division with Mühlmann's troops would be enough to drive back the remainder of the Russians through Soldau. The 1st Division was then to follow the 2nd in the direction of Neidenburg. The High Command approved these proposals.

When, soon after this, the report came in of the retirement of the 41st Division, the High Command thought they had better come to the assistance of that Division as soon as possible, and ordered the 2nd Infantry Division to set out at once for Rontzken, to prevent a break-through by the Russians. Schmettau's Force also was to proceed to the same place. When the order reached the I. Army Corps the 2nd Division was already on the march towards the east, and the remaining troops, including Schmettau's, in process of attacking Soldau. The Russians put up very little resistance. They had destroyed the crossings over the Soldau, and the main body of their troops was in hurried retreat through Mlava to the south. General von

François carried on with the plan he had proposed to the High Command: he left only the Mühlmann Division near Soldau; Schmettau's Force and the 1st Infantry Division were sent off towards Neidenburg. Further news of the 41st Infantry Division —which was completely shattered and there was a certain amount of panic—compelled the High Command again to order the I. Army Corps at midday to send direct assistance to the 41st Infantry Division, which was in retreat through Vronovo; the rest of the Corps was to pursue the enemy in the direction of Lahna.

General von François writes in his article[1] on the battle of Tannenberg that the order to pursue towards Lahna had surprised him. The road led through the thick forest country of Kamusien, where manœuvring and artillery work was out of the question. Although the High Command's order concluded with a solemn adjuration that "the Corps could render the greatest possible services to the army if these intentions were duly carried out. All depends on the I. Army Corps!" General von François did not alter his order, but correctly maintained his determination to pursue the enemy through Neidenburg.

Shortly after midday the High Command began to get a clearer picture of what was going on. We discovered that, although the 41st Division was indeed defeated, yet it had been successfully extricated, and the Russians were not pursuing. The attack by the 3rd Division was making victorious progress. The Goltz Division had in the course of their attack reached a line immediately to the north of Hohenstein—Mörken. The High Command got the impression that the enemy was now defeated, and at 1.30 P.M. issued an order that the right wing

[1] *Reichsflagge,* September 17th, 1925.

of the XX. Corps should also move forward, and that the I. and XX. Corps should co-operate in the pursuit. The objective for the I. Corps was to press forward as far as possible through Neidenburg —Muschaken, in the direction of Willenberg, being the direction which General von François had already given to his troops.

When the 2nd Infantry Division, about 3 P.M., got to within about a mile of Neidenburg, enemy formations advancing from a northerly direction made themselves felt. The Division deployed against them, and drove them slowly backwards behind the line Sallusken—Rontzken, and there came to a halt. The enemy facing them was a Guard Regiment of the Russian XXIII. Corps, sections of the 6th Cavalry Division, and a few batteries. Schmettau's Force reached the area to the east of Neidenburg by the evening, rested there, and continued the pursuit during the night. They reached Muschaken at 3 A.M. The 1st Infantry Division reached the neighbourhood of Neidenburg late in the evening.

General von François' orders for the 29th were that Schmettau's Force should reach Willenberg, the 1st Division, Muschaken, and the 2nd, Grünfliess.

In the neighbourhood of Hohenstein fresh fighting developed in the afternoon, in the course of which Goltz's Landwehr Division was rather hard pressed. They were opposed by the Russian XIII. Army Corps, which was advancing from Grieslienen and towards the north: the latter gradually forced sections of the Landwehr Division out of the Kämmerei forest, from which they had supported the attack on Mörken by their fire, and actually occupied Mörken, through which the victorious Landwehr had marched southwards, and had left undefended.

About 3 P.M. the 37th Division also had, in the meanwhile, got near Hohenstein. The Division did not, however, make any attempt to attack the Russian XIII. Corps that same afternoon. Whether, in fact, the exhaustion of the troops by their march through the Jablonka forest was so great that they were not capable of fighting, or whether it was partly due to the circumstance that the Division was waiting for the I. Reserve Corps to fall upon the Russian rear, seems doubtful. By the evening the Division stood outside Hohenstein, and sections of the Landwehr which had been ejected from the Kämmerei forest had joined up with it.

The 3rd Reserve Division had immediately followed up the pursuit of their defeated enemy. They tried to steal a march on the Russians, who were retiring on Schwedrich, by a circling movement to the south and an advance through Nadrau. But the attempt was not successful. They came to a standstill in the evening before Nadrau, which was still occupied by the Russians. One Brigade of the Division was diverted by the High Command to a more southerly direction, so as to take the enemy in the rear, who, from reports sent in by the 41st Division, was still holding his ground.

General von Scholtz had, at 1.30 P.M., already ordered a pursuit along the whole Front. The order could not be carried out by the 41st Division, who were to advance in the direction of Orlau: they were at the end of their strength and remained where they were to the west of Vronovo. Mühlen was taken at 3 P.M., after an attack by the three battalions of the 37th Division that had been left behind, and the troops got as far as the Ganshorn— Paulsgut area.

CHAPTER XIV

As a result of the High Command's order to the I. Reserve Corps to communicate to the Staff of the XVII. Corps the instructions for the co-operation of the I. Reserve Corps and the XVII. Army Corps against the enemy at Allenstein, the Chief of Staff of the I. Reserve Corps had gone in person to the Headquarters of the XVII. Corps, to represent the views of that Corps to General Mackensen. As has been stated above, telephonic communication between the High Command and the Command of the XVII. Corps was not possible. Accordingly the High Command had sent Major Drechsel as liaison officer. Although the latter transmitted the order that both Corps were to combine in attacking the enemy at Allenstein, but that sections of the XVII. Corps were to continue the pursuit in the direction of Ortelsburg, so as to secure a decision without fail by the following day, and that accordingly the I. Reserve Corps should attack the enemy at Allenstein and not wait for the rest of the XVII. Corps, which was to come up later; and although General von Mackensen was, to begin with, very strongly against giving up his pursuit of the enemy, wheeling his Corps round and marching on Allenstein; for reasons that cannot now be established both Corps Staffs came to an understanding that was not in the least appropriate to the real state of affairs.

The XVII. Corps, accordingly, turned, marched

308

round north of the I. Army Corps through Wartenburg, and northwards towards Allenstein. Only a mixed force continued the pursuit of the defeated Russian VI. Army Corps through Mensguth, in the direction of Ortelsburg. All the other troops available were put into the advance through Wartenburg.

The I. Reserve Corps, contrary to the instructions of the High Command, did not start until 10 A.M.; which meant that it could not reach Allenstein until about 2 P.M. When the Corps was already on the march a report came in that there were now only weak enemy forces at Allenstein. General von Below correctly assumed that the Russians had marched away in the direction of Hohenstein, and not to the north, and decided to take a more southerly line. Somewhat later he received an order from the High Command to the effect that, as the XIII. Russian Corps was on the march from Hohenstein to Allenstein, the shortest route would be to the line Stabigotten— Grieslienen. The order contained no instructions for the XVII. Army Corps, as the High Command was not clear where the XVII. Corps was at that moment. They imagined that part of it was pursuing the enemy towards the south, and part was following with the I. Reserve Corps.

So far as I remember, it was assumed as a matter of course that the I. Reserve Corps would inform the XVII. Army Corps of the change in the situation, as the co-operation of the two Corps followed naturally from their combination. However, it was of course a blunder that the XVII. Corps was not then instructed to march southward in full strength so as to complete the encirclement of the defeated Russians.

The Staff of the I. Reserve Corps did not for

the moment think of the XVII. Corps. It was not
until midday that General von Below got into
communication with them, and rightly suggested
that they should turn about once more and march
through Passenheim southwards. It was, of course,
very trying for General von Mackensen, after he
had, at the suggestion of the I. Reserve Corps, just
abandoned the pursuit of the defeated enemy and
marched on Allenstein to the right of the defeated
Corps, now to have to wheel round again and march
round behind the I. Reserve Corps to the south
once more. He accordingly rejected the proposal
of the I. Reserve Corps. He was determined to
persist in the direction he had taken, to march
towards Stabigotten to the scene of the fighting
and, as the senior General, he requested that the
I. Reserve Corps should leave the main road from
Allenstein to Stabigotten free for the advance of
the XVII. Corps. He gave his troops a brief rest
and sent a Staff Officer by aeroplane to the High
Command to announce his intentions and ask for
direct orders.

When the latter reached Army Headquarters
at Frögenau with his report he found a far from
friendly welcome. The High Command learned
from him, in the first place, that the I. Reserve Corps
had somehow started very late, and could not reach
Grieslienen in time, and, secondly, that General
Mackensen's request to the I. Reserve Corps to
leave the road free for him would still further delay
the movement of that Corps, so that it became
questionable whether any attack could take place
that day. The position of the Goltz Division
would inevitably be made very precarious. Just
about the same time as the Staff Officer's visit—
but not, so far as I remember, until he had started
his return flight — we succeeded in getting into

telephonic communication with the I. Reserve
Corps, as well as with the XVII. Army Corps.
The instructions given to the Staff Officer, as well
as transmitted by telephone, dealt with two points.
In the first place, the I. Reserve Corps was to
attack at Grieslienen that day without fail, and,
secondly, the XVII. Army Corps was to turn about,
collect every available man, and march south to
the Jedwabno area, so as to close the ring round
the Russian armies which the I. Army had begun
in the south along the Neidenburg — Willenberg
road.

It was no longer possible to get the I. Reserve
Corps up to the attack by the 28th. It had been
diverted from the highroad on to sandy tracks,
and its advance had been greatly delayed. The
XVII. Army Corps turned about and marched
back in its original direction. Small sections of
infantry on carts, machine guns, cavalry, and artillery hurried ahead of the columns, and late at
night reached the neighbourhood of Passenheim
and Ortelsburg. The Corps Command got to
Passenheim.

Although the events of the 28th had not befallen
as the High Command had intended, and hoped,
there was, of course, a very cheerful feeling about
on the afternoon of that day. It was clear that the
Russian Warsaw Army had been defeated with
heavy losses, and that the next few days would see
an even greater improvement in the situation. At
the same time it now became important to consider
what was to be done if the battle came to an end
here. Measures must be taken in good time to
disentangle all this confused concatenation of forces.
This was rendered necessary by the fact that they
would be needed in the near future for the attack
on Rennenkampf's army. The order for pursuit

that General Ludendorff issued on August 28th, at
5.30 P.M., at Frögenau, dealt with this aspect of the
situation.

When General Ludendorff was dictating the
order he began with these words: "Frögenau—
leave the exact time open." I suggested that instead
of Frögenau he might choose the historic name of
the town that lay in front of us, Tannenberg, which
he did, and this led later to the battle being named
after the place from which the final order was
issued. The order directed that the I. and XX.
Army Corps, as well as the 3rd Reserve Division,
should continue the pursuit in an easterly direction.
The Landwehr and garrison troops were to remain
where they were and reorganize. The Eastern
Group—*i.e.* the I. Reserve Corps and the XVII.
Army Corps—the High Command proposed to
hold back and send towards Allenstein and the
north, with a view to engaging the 1st Russian Army
in those parts. But the order was only actually
issued for the troops of the Western Group, as we
again had no clear picture of the situation of the
I. and XVII. Corps.

CHAPTER XV

THE BEHAVIOUR OF RENNENKAMPF

In the course of the afternoon, reports came in as to Rennenkampf's army—to the effect that Rennenkampf at last showed signs of marching to Samsonoff's support.

His advance was too late to avert the defeat of the 2nd Russian Army, but might still interfere with the conclusion of the battle. On that account the High Command's efforts to get a few Divisions behind the Alle as soon as possible, as a safeguard, was reasonable. The conduct of Rennenkampf during the entire day seems incomprehensible to our military standpoint; and nothing that has been published on the subject up to date gives any clear explanation of the matter. The heavy losses that his army had suffered during the battle of Gumbinnen, the belief that strong formations of the German Army had been withdrawn within the Königsberg radius, the notion that Samsonoff's army was opposed only by weak German forces, do not explain or excuse his inactivity. The Russians were exactly informed of the entire strength of the German forces in the Eastern theatre of war, and their business was, if it were at all possible, to overwhelm with their superior numbers the weak German forces this side of the Vistula. I cannot rid myself of the suspicion, that I mentioned to General Ludendorff at the time, that General Rennenkampf did not want to help General Samsonoff. They had been enemies since the Manchuria campaign.

Samsonoff regarded the inactivity and the bad leadership of Rennenkampf's Force as responsible for the fact that his, Samsonoff's, Siberian Cossack Division had not been able to hold the Yentai coal-mines in the battle of Liauyang. After the battle there was a pretty lively personal encounter between the two Generals on the railway station at Mukden. As Samsonoff shot himself at Tannenberg, as soon as he realized the extent of his defeat, and Rennenkampf was murdered by the Bolshevists at Taganrog, it will never be known whether my idea has any foundation or not. I should merely like to emphasize the fact that it explains at one stroke Rennenkampf's inexplicable behaviour. I of course assume that, if I am right, Rennenkampf did not imagine that his failure to make any move would consign Samsonoff's army to destruction.

After the issue of the Army Order the High Command went forward towards Mühlen to visit the victorious troops. Half way between Tannenberg and Mühlen we had to stop, as we were confronted with a stream of ammunition wagons, commissariat and ambulance carts, approaching us in the wildest disorder. It was an excellent example of a panic among the ammunition columns and transport. Near Mühlen, Russian prisoners were being brought back by Landwehr men with fixed bayonets. Someone had shouted : " They're coming "; another passed the word on : " The Russians are coming "; a third turned his cart round and made off; and soon they were all on the run. By General Ludendorff's orders we spread ourselves out in a long chain across and on each side of the road, and with levelled revolvers brought the business to a stop. But the whole road was so blocked with a confusion of wrecked wagons that we had to give up our idea of getting any farther.

CHAPTER XVI

THE CORPS FROM THE WEST

WITHOUT any request from the High Command, G.H.Q. had in the meantime placed reinforcements at our disposal for the operation against Rennenkampf. Already, in the night of the 26th, the head of the Operations Section, Colonel Tappen, had rung up. General Ludendorff called me to the telephone, and said: " G.H.Q. has just rung up, take the other receiver and let us both listen to what they want."

Colonel Tappen informed us that, in the next few days, three Army Corps—namely, the Guard Reserve Corps, the V. and the XI.—as well as the Saxon Cavalry Division from the West, would be transferred to the Eastern theatre of war, and asked where the High Command wished to have them sent. In reply to this inquiry, General Ludendorff answered that these reinforcements were not absolutely essential to us, and they would, moreover, be rather too late for the battle now in progress. We expected this battle to end victoriously in a few days, and then the 8th Army would proceed to deal with Rennenkampf. He accordingly asked that the reinforcements should be sent only if they could be entirely dispensed with in the West. If they were needed for a decision in the West, then we could manage without them.

The question as to why G.H.Q. came to offer us these Corps and did, later on, send us two Army Corps and one Cavalry Division, I find still quite inexplicable. General von Prittwitz had certainly asked for reinforcements in his private telephone conversation with General von Moltke. The new High Command never again referred to the question; on the contrary, G.H.Q. were well aware that the 8th Army had a certain prospect of victory over Samsonoff. Moreover, the reference in the *Imperial Archives* (vol. ii., p. 203) to the fact that the Austrian Chief of the General Staff had shown disappointment at the non-arrival of the Reserve Divisions, originally intended for East Prussia, does not seem to me to justify the decision. It must really have been the case, however unbelievable it may seem to-day, that, as General Tappen says in his book, the news from the armies in the field, until August 25th, gave G.H.Q. the conviction that the great decisive battle in the West had already been fought, and had terminated in favour of the German Army.

On the evening of the 28th we were waiting in the new Headquarters at Osterode for the final reports from the I. Reserve Corps regarding the issue of the attack at Grieslienen, so that we might be in a position to issue fresh orders for the disposition of this and the XVII. Corps behind the Alle. It was not until 10 P.M. that the disappointing news arrived that there had been no attack by the I. Reserve Corps that day, that the Kurken defile had, by a blunder, not been occupied, and that probably the Passenheim—Jedwabno district stood open for a Russian retirement towards the east, as it was more than unlikely that the XVII. Army Corps would get so far by that evening. The High Command had to give up the idea of immediately disposing the I. Reserve Corps and the XVII. Corps behind the Alle, so as to finish off the battle which had been held up by the misunderstandings

of the past day. We had to take the risk of letting
Rennenkampf come a great deal nearer during the
next twenty-four hours. However, I should like
to emphasize the fact that at this time the High
Command were not anxious about the possibility
of Rennenkampf's appearance on the scene. Our
only trouble was that we were afraid that considerable sections of Russian troops that we had
hitherto regarded as cut off might succeed in
escaping in a south-easterly direction.

The I. Reserve Corps was forthwith instructed
to send one Division early in the day through
Grieslienen to Hohenstein, and the other towards
Jedwabno, taking a line south of Wuttrienen. The
Corps cavalry were to proceed to Ortelsburg; but,
as it seemed rather weak, Ludendorff decided to
send forward at 3 A.M. a brigade of the 1st Cavalry
Division, which was then at Roessel, as fast as
possible to Ortelsburg. Sections of the XVII.
Army Corps reached Passenheim, Ortelsburg and
Jedwabno in the course of the night, but the High
Command did not know it. We assumed they were
far back in the neighbourhood of Wartenburg. The
Corps was ordered to be ready to move from its
place of bivouac at 6 A.M. Thus, if it should prove
necessary to move against Rennenkampf's army, it
could start its march in that direction very early
in the morning. On the other hand, it was equally
ready to move southward.

In the night of the 28th-29th, first, a wireless
message came in to the effect that Rennenkampf's
army was at last showing signs of advancing in
support of Samsonoff; secondly, there was a final
communication from G.H.Q. to the effect that two
Army Corps and a Cavalry Division would be transferred from the West to the East. This time, also,
while Colonel Tappen was talking to General

Ludendorff, I held the second receiver. Colonel Tappen said that two Army Corps would be sent, not three, as had been previously intended, as the V. Army Corps was needed in the West. General Ludendorff again observed that we could manage without these reinforcements in the East, and that the Guard Reserve Corps and the XI. Army Corps had better stay in the West if they were needed there.

At 6.30 A.M. a report came in that the XVII. Army Corps had not received the Army Order of the previous evening—that they were to wait for further orders in the neighbourhood of Wartenburg—and that during the evening and the succeeding night they had advanced much farther southwards. The High Command decided to leave them there, but ordered them not to go beyond Ortelsburg and Passenheim. Now that the XVII. Corps was no longer available, the only troops that could be used against Rennenkampf's formations, that might possibly be advancing to the attack, were the garrison troops under Unger, in the neighbourhood of Waplitz, and Goltz's Landwehr Division, which were ordered to concentrate at Hohenstein, and there to await orders. On the other hand, there would very soon be further troops available at Hohenstein, where, since the early morning of that day, the 37th Division had been attacking from the west and the I. Reserve Corps from the east. General Ludendorff decided to go to Hohenstein in person, so as to straighten out the situation on the spot and talk to the Generals Commanding. I accompanied General Ludendorff on this expedition, and I shall not forget the scenes of enthusiasm among the troops, and the impression made by the thousands of assembled prisoners.

The fighting in the neighbourhood of Hohenstein

on the 28th had lasted until late in the evening, and began again at daybreak. At 6 A.M. the 37th Division, a Brigade of the 3rd Reserve Division and sections of the Goltz Division attacked those parts of the XIII. Russian Army Corps that still held their ground near Mörken and the Kämmerei forest, and forced them back eastwards on to the two Divisions of the advancing I. Reserve Corps. The fighting came to an end about 10 A.M., with extraordinarily heavy losses to the Russians, and 8000 men were taken prisoner at Grieslienen. The main body of the XIII. Corps, owing to the delay of our I. Reserve Corps, had been able to escape capture at this point. It had started to retreat in the course of the night in a south-easterly direction on to the line Kurken — Jablonka. General Samsonoff had by the evening finally realized the futility of his attack, and had given orders for the three Corps to retreat.

By General Ludendorff's order the 37th Division was concentrated at Grieslienen, and a Division of the I. Reserve Corps was to concentrate at Allenstein. But it was possible to collect only one Brigade. Three Brigades of the Corps were engaged in the pursuit and it was not at the moment possible to get the troops together.

The XX. Corps Command had given orders for the 41st Division to pursue the enemy as far as Jedwabno, and the 3rd Reserve Division through Schwedrich—Kurken, in the direction of Waplitz, south of Passenheim.

The 41st Division, which had become very cautious as the result of its defeat, advanced very slowly, allowed itself to be held up by weak enemy formations and got only as far as the Orlau district. The 3rd Reserve Division got as far as Kurken with continuous fighting.

To the south of the main Neidenburg—Willen-berg road the position had, in the meantime, turned out as follows. General von François reckoned on the Russians making a serious attempt to break through in the direction of Neidenburg. He had sent forward Schmettau's Force, as well as his cavalry and some artillery, as fast as they could move, with the order to get to Willenberg at the earliest possible moment, but apart from that he now proposed to concentrate the two Divisions nearer Neidenburg. The first was to go only as far as Muschaken, and the second as far as Grünfliesz. In the course of its advance the 2nd Division met with a certain resistance from sections of the Russian 2nd Division, and did not reach Grünfliesz until the early hours of the afternoon. The 1st Division artillery took part in this fighting from positions to the north of Neidenburg, but the infantry was kept in readiness to the east of Neidenburg to deal with the expected attempt to break through. However no such attempt was made. On the contrary, the Russians could be seen moving backwards in an easterly direction. Accordingly General von Conta, who was in command of the 1st Division, pushed forward sections of his infantry towards Muschaken.

The cavalry detachments had ridden farther on, and had already captured Russian supply columns, ammunition trains and several thousand prisoners on the road to Willenberg. Schmettau had started off again after a rest of only a few hours, and by 7 P.M. had got to Willenberg, where numerous Russian supply columns and ammunition trains fell into their hands. When it became apparent that the Russians did not intend to try to break through in any considerable force at Neidenburg, General von François rightly pushed his 1st Division forward farther eastwards, and ordered it to occupy

the cross-roads between Muschaken and Willenberg,
with mixed detachments, and so prevent the surrounded Russians from breaking through to the
south.   In the course of the night numerous small
engagements occurred in this area, in which Russian
attempts to break through were frustrated.

The reports that came in during the 29th seemed
to make it probable that Rennenkampf's army was
at last advancing to the assistance of Samsonoff.
His cavalry had advanced some distance in force,
had reached Roessel and Bischofstein, and was
pressing forward northwards towards Wormditt.
Although this movement could not avert the fate of
the Russian troops surrounded in the forest country
to the north of the Neidenburg—Willenberg road,
measures had to be taken to deal with the advance.
On the evening of the following day, formations
were ready to deal with the army of the Niemen:
the I. Reserve Corps, the 37th Division, Goltz's
Landwehr Division, as well as the 6th Landwehr
Brigade duly left in the Lautern area, unknown to
the High Command.

In the course of the 30th more troops would
be inevitably set free.   It was to be assumed that
if Rennenkampf still intended to fight he would
advance in the general direction of Allenstein.
By the Army Order for the 30th, accordingly, the
I. Reserve Corps, the 37th Division and the 6th
Landwehr Brigade were ordered to begin by constructing a fortified position each side of Allenstein,
facing to the north-east. Goltz's Landwehr Division
was to bar the line of lakes north-east of Osterode
against any further forward movement of the
Russian cavalry.   The High Command were
convinced that it would be possible to hold up the
Russian attack at this point until the troops then
engaged on the field of Tannenberg should be set

free and the reinforcements should arrive from the West. These troops could then be sent against one or both enemy flanks, and the stroke would, in particular, be more effective against Rennenkampf's left flank the farther he moved it forward to the west. So what we had hitherto feared we now hoped for —namely, a full-dress advance by Rennenkampf's army.

For the rest, the Army Order provided for a speedy liquidation of the battle. The XVII. Army Corps barred the way in the east, the 41st Division and the 3rd Reserve Division were driving farther eastwards the Russian hordes who were in the meantime scattered in confusion among the forests, and the I. Army Corps was to co-operate in this movement along the main road to Willenberg. The garrison troops and the 70th Landwehr Brigade were allowed a day's rest in the neighbourhood of Hohenstein. General von Mühlmann, the Commander of the reinforced 3rd Landwehr Brigade, had requested that he might be allowed to advance from Soldau to Mlava, and drive in that direction the weak Russian forces that still faced him. The Army Order sanctioned this request.

On the evening of the 29th the General commanding the XV. Russian Army Corps, General Martos, was brought in as a prisoner to Osterode. The High Command were, of course, in very cheerful mood. Now that, thanks to General von Mackensen's correct initiative, the Russian egress to the east had been barred in time, it was hoped that large numbers of Russians would be found within the trap. I must, however, make it clear that we did not reckon upon the total of prisoners that was actually reached later. In this connection I should like to relate a small episode. Two days later I was driving over the battlefield, on official duty, with the Cavalry General, Count Dohna, who happened to be at our Headquarters, and as we saw a railway station crowded with Russian prisoners, waiting to be sent back, we fell into an argument over the number of prisoners actually made. Count Dohna said: " Well, how many prisoners do you think there will be?" I answered: " We have no exact reports, but I should estimate at least 30,000 to 40,000." Count Dohna thought this figure too high, and said he thought the total would not exceed 20,000. By way of a joke I offered him a wager— viz. that he should pay me one mark for every prisoner over 20,000, and that I should do the same for every unit by which the total fell short of 20,000. But, unfortunately, Count Dohna would not accept the wager.

CHAPTER XVII

ON the 29th, reports had already come in to General von François that the enemy forces defeated at Usdau and Soldau had again begun to approach the frontier. The General commanding the I. Army Corps had accordingly instructed his Divisions to send out reconnoitring parties in a southerly direction, and see that Janovo was occupied. He also assigned his Corps only limited objectives for the future pursuit on the 30th. The 1st Division was to push a little farther east, so as to make room for the 2nd Division in the neighbourhood of Muschaken. The future movements of the Corps were to be held up until General von François issued a further order, which was to depend on the results of an air reconnaissance to the south early on the 30th.

Although, therefore, the recrudescence of enemy activity in the rear of the I. Army Corps had already come within the bounds of possibility, an air report, dropped at 10 A.M. on the Neidenburg market-square, to the effect that about four Russian Divisions were advancing on the Mlava—Neidenburg main road, and that their advance-guard had reached a point just south of Neidenburg, was somewhat unexpected. The position of the German I. Army Corps was a rather unpleasant one. In front of them, in the forest country north of Muschaken, there were still considerable enemy forces which might be expected to make every possible effort to break through; they could hear the noise of fighting to the south; and greatly superior enemy forces were advancing in their rear. Just about the same time as the report was dropped, the first Russian shells fell on the Neidenburg market-square.

But General von François, with his fearless energy, was the right man in the right place. He had never, from the very beginning, had much respect for the Russian power of attack, and in this case, at least, he was absolutely right. He determined that he would on no account break the encircling line to the north, and would move only such forces as were absolutely necessary to maintain himself in the south. He gave orders that the weak outposts to the south of Neidenburg should hold the high ground there, and that the 2nd Division should concentrate every man they could collect to the south in the neighbourhood of Gregersdorf. It was not known whether and, if so, how far, the 5th Landwehr Brigade had advanced in the direction of Mlava, so orders were given for it to move from there against the enemy's flank and rear, or if it had not yet got as far as Mlava it was to march on Kandien and from there make an attack on the enemy's flank.

General von François issued these instructions in the market-square at Neidenburg, and then went on to Gregersdorf to visit the sections of the 2nd Division that were being collected there. He was then informed that the High Command had also taken measures to deal with the enemy's attempts to restore the situation. The same airman who brought the report to Neidenburg also had dropped a similar one at the Headquarters of the High Command. General Ludendorff proposed to the Commander-in-Chief that the Goltz Division, Unger's garrison troops, and the 3rd Reserve Division should start for the point of danger at once.

These reinforcements were naturally more than sufficient to avert the Russian thrust, but they could not take any active part in the fighting until the following day. Until then the weak forces near Neidenburg had to do the best they could.

One battalion each of the 45th and the 41st Regiments, and one battery each from the 16th and 37th Field Artillery Brigades, under Major Schlimm, carried out their task of holding the heights south of Neidenburg as long as possible, in a most admirable manner, and they held out until the late afternoon against the certainly slow and hesitating Russian advance. They were supported by the fire of twenty batteries that General von François gradually brought up round Gregersdorf. It was not until night fell that Major Schlimm's Force had to fall back in the face of a threat of envelopment and evacuate Neidenburg. The town was occupied in the darkness by the 3rd Russian Guard Division. The Mühlmann Brigade, on receiving news of the Russian advance, had not pursued their march to Mlava, but wheeled round with a view to an attack in the direction of Kandien. They reached Gr.-Koslau by the evening, and from that point their artillery came into action with considerable effect. It had, however, no longer any direct influence on the fight put up by Schlimm's Force: their successful resistance had averted any danger to an encircling operation. By the morning of the 31st all the reinforcements were on the march; the High Command had put them as a whole under General von François' orders.

General von François gave an order to attack on the 31st, but the enemy was no longer there. The Russian leader, the General commanding the I. Russian Army Corps, General Artamonov, had already decided in the course of the night to turn about and march off with his entire force. Whether he had lost courage, or whether he had received reports of the approaching German reinforcements and did not want to meet them, remains undecided. If he had succeeded in quickly overrunning Schlimm's Force, and had the nattacked the seven battalions of the 2nd Division who were gradually collecting round Gregersdorf, the position of the I. German Army Corps might have become unpleasant. Perhaps he might have made a breach through which considerable numbers of his surrounded comrades could have extricated themselves. But as he did not even succeed in reaching Neidenburg before darkness fell, one can only approve his decision to withdraw before the attack that threatened for the next day, involving as it did a most unpleasant threat to his flank from Gr.-Koslau. When the 41st Division reached Neidenburg in the early morning they found the town evacuated and saw no sign of any enemy. Only the Mühlmann Brigade, which had advanced early as far as Saberau, was able to use its artillery with good effect against the retreating enemy columns. It could not attack as it had no material for constructing bridges across the Neide.

By the evening of the 29th, fighting had broken out also in the east, in the neighbourhood of Ortelsburg. Here, too, the Russians made feeble efforts to come to the help of their surrounded comrades. On that evening the Russian 4th Cavalry Division had again occupied Ortelsburg, but, after setting fire to the town, retired before a regiment of the 35th Infantry Division and the 1st Cavalry Brigade which entered Ortelsburg just about the same time. On the morning of the 30th about one Division of the Russian VI. Army Corps, as well as the 4th Cavalry Division, again attacked the town

by an enveloping movement from the east and
north, and put the German Infantry Regiment,
which had no artillery at its disposal, into a rather
awkward position. In the course of the morning,
cavalry from the I. Army Corps from Willenberg,
as well as sections of the 35th Division, relieved the
situation. By midday the Russians abandoned their
efforts here too, and finally retired to the south.

With that the battle came to an end. The surrounded Russian forces did not make any really
serious attempts to break through to the south. I
am of the opinion that German troops, if surrounded,
could not have been prevented from forcing their
way out. And yet on the section Muschaken —
Willenberg, fifty kilometres long, there were only
twenty-nine battalions available to bar the way. I
might compare the only occasion on which the
Russians succeeded in surrounding troops and the
totally different conduct of the German Command
and the German troops — i.e. at Brzeziny, where
General von Litzmann was at the head of the
German troops, and got them out. The Russians
simply strayed about aimlessly within the circle,
from time to time made a dash against the enclosing
lines, but retired back into the forests before the
fire of the weak forces that faced them, and finally
surrendered in thousands to the far weaker German
forces. Thus one battalion of the 43rd Regiment
made 17,000 prisoners. Early on the morning of
the 30th, after an airman had reported that large
numbers of troops he could not account for were
assembling in the open country near Willenberg,
General von Schmettau shortly afterwards reported
that with his weak forces he had already taken
11,000 prisoners and did not know where to leave
them. The actual total of the prisoners taken—
92,000—was not known to the High Command

until much later. The 8th Army now wheeled round and marched to attack Rennenkampf, in conjunction with the two Army Corps arriving from the West, and had other things to think of than the results of victory. We only learned the details during the campaign in Southern Poland.

CHAPTER XVIII

I SHOULD like to make a few remarks on the plan and development of the battle.

Seldom has a battle given rise to so many myths as Tannenberg. According to popular legend, Field-Marshal von Hindenburg worked out his plans of this battle a generation ago. He is said to have explored the country when he was General Staff Officer to the 1st Division, with the rank of captain or major, and averted the carrying out of schemes for draining the lakes and marshes in that district, and applied his long-cherished plans to drive the Russians into lake and marsh at Tannenberg, where thousands died a horrible death of suffocation. Another version describes him hurrying in a special train from Hanover to the Eastern frontier, receiving reports at stations by the wayside, and issuing his orders accordingly. All these stories are a complete fabrication. Tannenberg was not the work of a single individual: it was the result of the magnificent training and education of our commanders, and the incomparable exertions of the German soldiers.

The decision to stop the retreat at Gumbinnen and attack the right wing of Samsonoff's army was taken under the Prittwitz regime. The consequent dispositions, and therewith the preliminaries of the battle at Tannenberg, were determined before there was any idea of the change in the command. The only order that General Ludendorff issued before

330

he reached the East was for the abolition of the High Command as then existing, and approving a day's rest for the XVII. Army Corps and the I. Reserve Corps. And this last measure was, as I have tried to show, somewhat unfortunate. When the new High Command reached Marienburg they had no fresh instructions to issue: their orders were simply in effect to " carry on."

As regards the development of the battle, it cannot be denied that a succession of most important events resulted, not from the orders of the High Command, but from the individual initiative of the subordinate leaders. At a point which was decisive for the brilliant success of the battle—the break-through at Usdau — General von François indisputably did a great service in putting off the attack until he had in position all his fighting troops, and more especially his artillery. If he had advanced a day earlier, when his troops had only partly concentrated, and without extensive artillery preparation—as the High Command wanted him to do—against the prepared Russian position at Usdau, who knows whether he would have succeeded? And without his success the whole future progress of the battle would have been imperilled. Not quite so important, but extraordinarily fortunate in its consequences, was General von Morgen's equally independent decision to attack on the 28th without waiting for the arrival of the 41st Division. As the latter did not appear at all, but for Morgen's decision the advance of the 3rd Reserve Division would probably have been so long delayed that Goltz's Landwehr Division would have been defeated before help came to it from the XX. Army Corps Front. Correct, and fortunate in their results, were General von François' and von Mackensen's movements which led to the encirclement of the Russians. Correct also was General von François' decision not to carry out the order to march in the direction of Lahna, but to send his cavalry and Schmettau's Force at once along the main road to Willenberg, and follow with his Corps. General von Mackensen also rightly recognized, as he swung his force round at Allenstein, the importance of cutting off the enemy to the east, and pushed forward sections of the Corps by forced marches as far as Passenheim and farther south.

If we try to give an exact answer to the question who deserves the most credit for the victory at Tannenberg, we must also briefly consider the conduct of the enemy, without whose blunders the success would not have been possible. I have already commented on the conduct of Rennenkampf's army. I have also mentioned that in my opinion it was because of an ancient feud with Samsonoff that Rennenkampf did not want to help him. He was supported in this by the conduct of the Army Group Command, whose instructions to him to go to the assistance of the Warsaw Army were belated and far from insistent. Moreover, during the whole of this period he never succeeded in getting a clear picture of the distribution of the German forces. Samsonoff himself was throughout equally in the dark as to the forces facing him and the intentions of the Germans. His first vigorous push was completely right. He agreed with the Army Group Command and Russian G.H.Q. in supposing the German 8th Army to be in rapid retreat towards the Vistula. Nor can he be blamed for persisting in this idea when he became aware of a concentration of German forces on the left flank—*i.e.* in the area to the north-west of Usdau. For it was natural that, if the Germans proposed to retire behind the Vistula, they should use all their available force to attack and hold up the left wing of the Warsaw Army, which was nearer to the Vistula than they. He accordingly collected on his left wing forces that he hoped would be strong enough to meet this attack. His conduct becomes incredible only after he had been defeated on both his wings. After the VI. Corps had been defeated at Bössau, and after the I. German Corps had broken through at Usdau, his persistence in adhering to his decision to attack in the centre was a blunder, and led to the great disaster. Whether he was influenced by the fact that Rennenkampf had just brought off a victory, and he, consequently, could not bring himself to give an order for retreat, is merely a matter for speculation.

The task of the German Command was greatly lightened by the interception of the Russian wireless. Incredible as it may sound, the Russians sent their battle orders "in clear" from their wireless stations without reflecting that our stations, and more especially the main station at Königsberg, picked them up and sent them on to the High Command.

And here I will conclude my brief account of Tannenberg. I hope that I have succeeded in showing that the credit for the victory is not due to one individual, and that it is futile to answer the eternal controversy in newspapers and speeches as to who was the victor of Tannenberg conclusively and with one name, which varies according to the prejudices of the disputant.

The battle was not planned out on the so-called Cannae principle, in the sense the word is used by Professor Hans Delbrück, for at its beginning no one could suppose that it would prove possible to use the German eastern wing to envelop the

Russians. This possibility appeared in course of time only as a result of Rennenkampf's absolute inactivity. After that the battle became a Cannae.

The decision to fight the battle was taken under the command and on the responsibility of Colonel-General von Prittwitz; and the logical and inevitable fulfilment of that decision, which led to the great victory, took place under the command and on the responsibility of Colonel-General von Hindenburg.

THE SPRING OFFENSIVE OF
1918

THE SPRING OFFENSIVE OF 1918

GENERAL LUDENDORFF, after much inward strife, had determined to carry out a great offensive on both sides of the Somme.

There were two matters in particular that made it urgent to seek a decision quickly and by means of an offensive. The first was the arrival of the American Army in France, and the second was the fear that our enemies would manage to reproduce our new poison gas. The resources needed for the great offensive stroke were ready to his hand, as, in my opinion, the German Eastern Army was now set free. Moreover, the military and political leaders of the Entente must also have reflected that the coming spring offensive would be in the nature of a game of *banco*, of which the stake would be the issue of the war and the fate of Europe.

It would have been natural for German G.H.Q. to approach the Government once again and say somewhat as follows:

"As a result of the breakdown of Russia we have the necessary number of Divisions and heavy batteries from the East at our disposal, so that we can attempt a great decisive battle in the West with good prospect of success. But before we decide on this great stroke we conceive it our duty to ask the Government to consider whether it may not be possible, in view of our threatened attack, to induce the Entente states to enter on Peace negotiations."

A necessary preliminary to this would, of course, have been a revision of the G.H.Q. Peace terms.

The intention of G.H.Q. to hold Belgium and to add strips of purely French territory to the Lorraine iron-fields was naturally unacceptable to France and England, and could be achieved only if we succeeded in utterly defeating them. If G.H.Q. adhered to these war aims, then "absolute" war in the sense in which Clausewitz used the word, and a battle of extermination in the grand style, became inevitable. The question that now emerges, after the event, is: "Did General Ludendorff clearly realize that this was the final decision—' to be, or not to be '—and did he take his measures accordingly?"

The first question is, of course, hard to answer. My interview with General Ludendorff on April 17th, 1917, in which he made no mention of a great decisive action, but talked of partial offensives and of "probing" the opposing line to see where it was weakest, suggests an answer in the negative. And a similar answer must be given to the second question. The conduct of the March attack does not display the firm will to seek a decision at one point and there make a decisive break-through on a limited Front.

The weakest point of the enemy Front was undoubtedly Gough's army on the southern part of the English Front. Having decided to attack it, the proper thing to do was to strike north of the Somme, in the direction of Amiens, with our left wing on the river. It should have been made quite clear that the object was to reach Amiens in one movement. Beyond Amiens the Somme would be a serious impediment; the occupation of this town would cut the communications between the English and French armies. In accordance with previous experiences of "break-through" battles, the entire heavy artillery should have been massed at the point in question and several armies piled up one behind another ready for attack. The next point to consider was how best to prevent French G.H.Q. from coming quickly to their allies' assistance. This could have been done by the threat of a grand attack against the French Front itself. If some twenty or thirty Divisions had been massed opposite, say, Rheims, it stands to reason that Marshal Pétain would have reflected rather carefully before he sent his Reserve Divisions north at the first English appeal for help. The necessary forces were available. Ludendorff had only to transfer more troops from the East, for as these Divisions were not to attack, but merely to create their effect by their presence, Divisions of a poorer quality could have been used.

BOLSHEVISM

BOLSHEVISM

WHEN in due course—in the autumn of 1917—a group of communists of mainly non-Russian origin succeeded, during the confusion and disorder consequent upon the Russian Revolution in Petersburg, in getting the upper hand and seizing power, there was not a soul in the world who would have believed that their regime would be more than temporary. The German G.H.Q., when the wireless message asking for an Armistice was received from Petersburg, at once felt misgivings about entering into relations with the new possessors of power, mainly from a doubt whether their authority was extensive enough to allow them to negotiate in the name of the whole nation. Moreover, I had the most serious misgivings against having any dealings with the ultra-radical group of Bolshevists, as there was of course a danger that the first effect of Germany's recognition of a revolutionary Government as one authorized to conduct negotiations would help to settle it in the saddle, and so prolong the duration of its regime. However, we had no choice: they were the first who declared themselves ready to discuss Peace terms with us, and we had to snatch at the opportunity. It was with this in my mind that I said, in reply to General Ludendorff's question whether we could negotiate with these people: "Yes, I believe we can."

If we had been completely aware of the state of affairs in Russia, and especially in the Russian Army, we should have known how utterly broken

343

was that host, once so proud, and how the masses had only one wish, and that was peace, and we should certainly have declined to open negotiations with the Bolsheviks. Then a less radical Government would probably soon have made its appearance, which must inevitably have made peace. The Russian Empire would then have been spared a period of the most bloody and oppressive tyranny, and the civilized world a conflict with a force that threatened it in its very foundations. For that is what Bolshevism, as embodied in its representatives, gradually became, by reason of the almost unlimited resources of the Russian Empire that stood at their disposal. During the Armistice negotiations, when the members of the Russian Delegation took their meals in common with the Staff of the Eastern Headquarters Command, the first doubts began already to arise in my mind in the course of my conversations with Herren Joffe and Kameneff. They increased in strength when Herr Trotzky then appeared to conduct the Peace negotiations in Brest-Litovsk and began to pour out his interminable harangues. Unfortunately, our Diplomacy realized too late that Trotzky had not the slightest intention of concluding a Peace, but that his sole object was to proclaim from that conspicuous platform the principles of Bolshevism *urbi et orbi*. That theory and practice were two different things— that people whose mouths were full of the ideas of freedom, equality and self-government were in practice ready to use the crudest force and the extremest terrorism—the world did not, or could not, see. I cannot otherwise explain the fact that my well-known speech, calling Herr Trotzky's attention clearly and calmly to the contradiction between the party's words and their deeds, aroused such fury in circles whose politics inclined towards the Left in Germany, and especially in Austria.

After the Peace had been concluded the Bolshevists' business was to establish their regime. The first thing to be done was to get rid of the remains of the old army, in which there were still to be found a large number of adherents of the old order, and create a force on which the new possessors of power could completely and entirely rely. They achieved the first object by simply sending the men home, and offering them 100 roubles for handing over their rifles before they went. Most of them so yearned for a sight of their wives and children, of whom many had heard nothing for years, that it is easy to understand that the majority of them were very ready to use the permission to go home. The men of the Reserve, which consisted largely of peasants, were offered a further inducement: they were told to hurry home as the land was about to be distributed among the peasants, and whoever was too late would be passed over, or would find the best parts of the expropriated estates in other hands. A large number of the loyal officers were murdered in the early days of the Revolution by the inflamed and perverted soldiery. They were systematically pursued and exterminated. Special battalions of foreign troops were formed as a mainstay of the new regime and a nucleus of the subsequent Red Army. In the first place, thousands of Chinese coolies were used, who had been imported in the later part of the war as labourers, and, secondly, Letts, who had not been able to get home, as their country was still occupied by the Germans. In this way the so-called Red Army was built up: there were no Soldiers' Councils and the discipline was very strict. And their officers, whatever their rank, were, and are, under the control of Bolshevik

Commissars, members of the Tcheka, distributed throughout the army as well as in all the professions in Russia. The Extraordinary Commission for Combating the Counter-revolution, " Tchreswüt-chainaja Commissija," abbreviated into " Tcheka," was created on the pattern of the old Russian Ochrana, the well-known Russian secret police, and took over the majority of its personnel, naturally only under Bolshevik leadership. As soon as the authorities in Moscow had the instrument of the army ready to their hand, they proceeded to the conquest of the whole of Russia and to the overthrow of the still existing White opposition : Koltchak, Denikin, Judenitch, Wrangel, Semicnov and Ungern-Sternberg were overthrown one after the other, and all Russia was made Bolshevist without consulting the people and without a ballot. From the purely military point of view it is amazing how it was possible for the newly formed Red Army to defeat the from time to time considerable forces of the White Generals and sweep them out of existence. More than one factor contributed to this. The most effective was the subtle, skilful, disintegrating Bolshevist propaganda among the White troops. Next in importance was the dissension and mutual ill-will among the White leaders, their clumsy policy and, at the end, the failure of the former allies of Imperial Russia to give them adequate support. If, as an example of what might have been done, Denikin had taken over the command of the troops opposing the Bolshevists in the Baltic, among whom were Germans; and if they had advanced through Dünaburg in cooperation with his own troops; and if, at the same time, he had met the wishes of the Bolshevists by immediate and far-reaching land reforms, instead of putting them off with promises of satisfaction later when the Tsar had come back, he might very well have succeeded. As it was, his troops broke down before the Bolshevists' propaganda.

There were two lines of this. The peasant population behind the Front were stirred up by being repeatedly told: " You will get no land if the Tsar comes back: none of the Tsars who have ruled Russia for hundreds of years has given you land." At the Front they worked the national propaganda: " We Bolsheviks are the defenders of holy Russia against the White Generals in league with France and England, who are selling her." As regards the military assistance given by the Entente, one had rather the impression that the Entente contributions were on a starvation basis. The reproach that many Russians make against England in particular—that she was delighted that the war had relieved her not merely of Germany but also of Russia, and that she was not sincerely anxious for the restoration of the old Imperial Russia—cannot be entirely dismissed. The harsh criticism, common in England and in military circles, of Russia's military services is not justified. The Russian Army did what it could. That it was badly handled, and consequently defeated, was due to the lack of a really great leader.

Thus the Bolshevists succeeded in overcoming a critical moment and extending their control over the entire Russian Empire as it had been. The power thus attained was established by an iron grip; all suspected of any inclination to the old regime were murdered, and Tcheka tribunals were started everywhere. In order to conceal from other countries the true character of the Bolshevist Government, these proceedings were accompanied by a number of excellent laws and provisions, which never came into operation, but were intended solely to serve as propaganda.

It goes without saying that the astute possessors of power in Moscow had no illusions on the fact that it is impossible in the long run to govern an empire on a communistic foundation while the neighbouring states are run on a capitalistic basis. Joffe, Kameneff and Sokolnikov made it quite clear in their conversations that they were convinced of this point. The aim of the Bolshevist movement is the abolition of the capitalistic regime over the whole earth—" World Revolution " was always the undertone of their remarks. The first step towards achieving this result quickly was the Bolshevising of Germany. If they succeeded in introducing Bolshevism among us, and reviving the campaign against the Entente, they counted on the Entente armies, more especially the French Army, being broken up by Bolshevik propaganda. That this was not impossible may be seen from events at Odessa.

When in due course, partly as a result of Joffe's collaboration and support, the revolution broke out in Germany, Moscow hastened to send to Berlin the most suitable men for carrying on the move- ment, especially Joffe and Radek. When the railway carriage containing them and certain other agitators was not allowed to pass through the Ober-Ost district, Radek proceeded to Berlin alone, in uniform and with the forged papers of a released German prisoner of war. We all know that in the middle of January, 1919, whether or not Bolshevism got the upper hand in Berlin hung by a hair. There was no constitutional authority to oppose to Liebnecht's fiery utterances or to the calculated policy of the far cleverer Rosa Luxemburg. The army had completely collapsed, and it was thanks to the energy of only a few individuals that we avoided disaster. When in the spring of that year the extreme elements in Munich succeeded in establishing a regime of councils, the greatest danger to Germany was over. The more sensible survivors of the old army had banded themselves together everywhere, formed free corps, and placed them at the disposal of the Government for the maintenance of order. It was, therefore, possible to bring help to Munich from without. The Spartacus riots in Berlin also were successfully suppressed under the Police President, Eichhorn. But Moscow made many attempts to seize upon power. We all remember the continual disorders, the eternal strikes, and all the rest. Hand in hand with all this went a propaganda adapted to patriotic Germans, and especially to the younger people—I mean the so-called Higher Bolshevism. Russian emissaries were very active among the patriotic youth of the country. They said something like this: " You Germans trusted to the lying promises of President Wilson, and believed that on the basis of his Fourteen Points you would get an honourable Peace: you accepted the conditions of absolute disarmament laid down in the Armistice agreement, and you see yourselves entirely betrayed and oppressed. It is the will of France to destroy Germany utterly. There is only one thing you can do: throw yourselves into the arms of Russia and the Russian popular regime. The Entente is not in a position to carry the war into the vast expanses of Russia. The advance of the enemy army must come to a stop somewhere between the Rhine and Moscow. Then the propaganda against this unrighteous continuation of the war will begin, and the French and English armies will rise against their Governments."

In any case there was a good deal of sense in this reasoning. If one considered that the devastation of war could be brought into Germany, that millions of Germans would be likely to die of hunger, the military effect would probably have been as predicted. The probable consequence was the Bolshevizing of the whole of Europe and the downfall of Western civilization. In spite of this, the propaganda found many adherents, especially in professional and student circles and among the young officers. They did not, and still do not, take Bolshevism seriously enough. They only read the marvellous programme of the Moscow Government, such as, for example, the radical reform of the administration of justice, which looks very pretty on paper, but they do not realize that there is an insurmountable obstacle between the theory and practice, the words and the deeds, of the Bolshevists.

As a result of my relations with Russia, and especially of my intention—well known in Russian circles, but unfortunately never to be realized—of coming to the rescue of that ruined country, left in the lurch by its allies in the summer of 1918—my idea being to march to Moscow and substitute a new regime for the Bolshevist reign of terror—as a result of this, I say, many Russians of nearly every shade of political opinion came to see me after the conclusion of peace. Among them were even Bolshevist agents who, especially after the signature of the shameful Peace of Versailles, painted in highly glowing colours the advantages of Bolshevism for Germany. One of them went a step farther. He said that, last of all, the whole Bolshevist world must turn against England, and that Bolshevism could not come into its own until the British Empire had been destroyed.

From the moment that Moscow realized that the improving conditions in Germany gave them no more prospect of winning over our country to Bolshevism, and thus securing a speedy outbreak of the World Revolution, the Bolshevists turned all their strength against the English world-empire. The power of the adversary was such that the fight must inevitably be prolonged and Bolshevism prepared to deal with it. The most important matter was to gain time so that the Bolshevist propaganda might become effective. All their political and commercial dealings were dictated by the necessity for gaining time. The Bolshevists had just as little intention of concluding the commercial treaty as Trotzky had of concluding a Peace at Brest-Litovsk. It is, generally speaking, quite natural that they cannot go on deceiving humanity as to their intentions. A normal thinking man cannot imagine how time, money and labour were wasted for months, and how individual paragraphs were disputed for days though they had firmly intended never to ratify the draft treaty.

A typical example of Moscow dealings was their establishment of relations with the Roman Curia. When the possessors of power in Moscow were not yet absolutely secure in their position they were nervous lest the Romish Church might raise its voice from its pulpits in defence of the many thousand murdered victims whose only guilt was not being proletarians. Accordingly the following proposal was made to the Curia. It was pointed out that by the death of the Tsar and the abolition of Tsardom in Russia the Russian Church was deprived of its Head. This was accordingly a very favourable opportunity for His Holiness the Pope of bringing the great schism in the Christian Church to an end. The Curia was asked to treat with Moscow on the subject, and negotiations actually proceeded for many months. In point of fact the Bolshevists never had any intention of allowing the Roman Church any rights in Russia; they merely wanted to get a little breathing space, and in that they succeeded. For some time there was no condemnation of Bolshevism and its regime from Roman Catholic pulpits. It was only when Roman Catholic priests in Russia began to be persecuted and shot that the deceptive nature of the negotiations was realized.

All the commercial negotiations came to the same sort of end. There were, of course, a few exceptions, and a few foreign merchants did actually manage to sell goods to Soviet Russia. But upon a nearer view it becomes apparent that what was actually sold was always material for the use of the army, or railway material which can hardly be disassociated from it. The Bolshevist negotiations, more especially with the states which had not recognized the Bolshevist regime as legitimate, had of course the subsidiary aim of obtaining such recognition. It is naturally of the greatest importance for the possessors of power in Moscow to be recognized, for in the event of a collapse of their regime they would then be able to live abroad wherever they liked on the money they had put by for that purpose without running the risk of being handed over as traitors to the new Russian Government. Moreover, recognition would provide the possibility of setting up Embassies, Consulates and Trade Delegations, and thus create an exactly equal number of propaganda centres in the adjoining states. In order to be able to satisfy the growing need for propaganda abroad an institute was called into existence in Moscow, in which, besides propaganda, especial attention was paid to the languages of all the Asiatic peoples, for their next intention was to mobilize Asia against England. That they succeeded in doing so in a far-reaching manner even a superficial observer could not deny. The whole of Asia was in a ferment. That the disorders in China were due mainly to the Bolshevist propaganda of Joffe, and later of Karachan, admits in my view of no doubt. It must indeed be admitted that the corrupt officialdom of the old Chinese Empire, which has merely grown a hundredfold worse since the metamorphosis of this state into a Republic, offered a favourable field for the propaganda. India is in open revolt against England. Mohammedans and Hindus have found a common basis. The enthusiast Ghandi is certainly no Bolshevist, but his fight to free his co-religionists from England is a fight that comes within the frame of Bolshevism, and was accordingly lavishly supported by Moscow. The passive boycott of English goods, the restoration of the old Indian home-spinning industry, must have caused anxiety in that country at such a crisis of unemployment. For " unemployment " is the vital problem of the present British Government. If they do not succeed in mastering this difficulty, then a Labour Cabinet will once more appear in Baldwin's stead, and that would mean, in its ultimate consequences, the beginning of a victory for Bolshevism.

In point of fact the Bolshevist agitation against English predominance was child's play. Bound by no scruples of morals or decency, they simply promised every one of England's many hundred subject-races whatever they wanted. " Your enemy is England alone; free yourselves from her and you will get all that your heart desires." In the other English possessions the same active propaganda was carried on. I remember the serious strike movement in Johannisberg, in the course of which about seventy Russian agitators were arrested, as well as, some years earlier, the murders of numerous English officials in the great Egyptian railway. Moreover, the late Egyptian disorders and the murder of the Sirdar are undoubtedly traceable to Bolshevist influence.

Latterly, too, in the French North African colonies much has been heard of the quick growth of a communistic movement. General Liautey has more than once made representations to his Government regarding his great difficulties in this matter. Whether this is a case of direct agitation from Moscow, or whether the inflammable matter spread by itself from Egypt, I cannot say. It is natural that in the Entente colonies, since the Great War, in the course of which coloured troops were used to fight against the white races, account must now be taken of wider aspirations among the natives. But this, and the growing troubles of America over the nigger question, would lead me beyond my theme.

Thus, if England continues to carry on her war against Bolshevism as she has done hitherto, she must inevitably succumb. Her difficulties in all parts of the Dominions and Colonies will grow; the world markets for English goods, which by the breach with Russia and the peoples subject to the Bolshevist regime must have already diminished by the loss of some 200,000,000 customers, must grow smaller still, and unemployment, far from diminishing, will increase. The only salvation lies in the abolition of the centre-point of Bolshevist agitation —*i.e.* the establishment of another Government in Moscow which, whatever may be the form of sovereignty, will re-establish the conception of private property as the principle of free trade. It is a very widespread error to assume that the mass of the Russian people are Bolshevistically inclined, and are satisfied with the Bolshevist regime. The assumption arises mainly from the fact that in that vast country there is little resistance to the Moscow tyranny, and there have been only a few local risings and sporadic opposition. That cannot, indeed, be denied; but it is not a consequence of general satisfaction, but of a ruthlessly carried-out reign of terror, the like of which the world has never seen. The mass of the old Intelligentsia is dead or has fled abroad. Such as remains does not venture on the slightest word of criticism for fear of being denounced and handed over to Bolshevist justice. The state of feeling on the land we do not know in detail, but it is quite out of the question that the peasant can be, in fact, a Bolshevist, and that he can subscribe to the doctrine that the land is a national possession of which he has only temporary enjoyment. If, for the time being, we hear no more of agrarian troubles and peasant risings, it must be due to the fact that the peasant resistance is broken. On the other hand, we hear of districts where the Local Authorities still possess weapons, and have so successfully used them against the Reds that they have been left in peace. However, all those who know Russia and Russian conditions are agreed that the country cannot by itself throw off the Russian tyranny. It is too weak. The Russian labourer and citizen has far less freedom than under the Tsarist regime. Strikes are counter-revolutionary and punished by death. At the moment Russia has not one Tsar, but many, compared with whom the regime of Ivan the Terrible may be described as mild. Release from this system can come only from without, and by the agency of one or more of the Great Powers. The Russian emigrants, whom in the early years of the Bolshevists we were inclined to hope would be able to get together an army, stir up local risings in Russia, and then help them to a decisive issue, have completely failed. It appears from a study of their Press that their most important activity is quarrelling with each other. The individual groups reproach each other for the military collapse and the Revolution. The Monarchists are divided into three groups: one of them supports Nicolai Nicolaevitch, who is competent and honourable, but too old; while the other supports the Grand Duke Cyril, or another son of the murdered Grand Duke Paul. Against the Grand Duke Cyril—apart from his conduct in the early days of the Revolution—(he was known to have been one of the first to hoist the Red Flag, and speculated on becoming President of the Republic)—it is urged that he is not eligible for the throne according to the ancient Russian law, as when he was born his mother did not yet belong to the Orthodox Russian Church. There are other objections to the third candidate, and in the midst of these disputes the emigrants forget that the bear whose skin they are dividing has not yet been shot.

From this side no help can come to the Russian people. Properly speaking, it is the duty of the Entente States to help their former ally, who spent herself in fighting for them and collapsed in so doing. In French and English accounts of the war and of its progress it is noteworthy that little importance is attached to the tremendous Russian battles, their heavy losses and final defeat. It is not recognized that they were of any service; on the contrary there is constant complaint of their failure, and reproaches for the German inclinations of the murdered Tsaritza and the treachery of the Russian Generals. For anyone like myself, who fought in the East from first to last, such reproaches are merely childish. It is, however, possible that they are believed in the countries concerned, and that consequently England and France feel relieved of the responsibility for putting their broken allies on their legs again. Thus Russia cannot hope for any help from the good will of others, but it is perhaps possible that as a result of the experiences of these last few years English policy may be forced to the conviction that peace and order cannot be restored in the Colonies until the source of the propaganda and sedition in Moscow is stopped up.

MOSCOW, THE ROOT OF ALL EVIL

THE PROBLEM OF BOLSHEVISM

GERMAN PUBLISHERS' NOTE

THE following Essay was composed by General Hoffmann at the end of the year 1922, and was then to be published by us.

In January 1923 the French occupied the Ruhr, and in the resulting state of high tension the publication of the Essay was postponed.

In the meantime the course of events showed how right had been General Hoffmann's view of the situation, and how he foresaw its inevitable development. His Essay is just as much to the point—or even more so—as it was then. So we are making it public now.

General Hoffmann has added a few fresh and explanatory observations of a military and technical character on the uprisings of the peoples in Asia and in Africa.

BERLIN, 1925.

NOTE

SINCE the end of the war a steady diminution in productive capacity has become more and more observable in the European States. The States who won the victory in that mighty struggle are suffering in this way just as much and, in some cases, more than those who were defeated. As four years have now elapsed since the state of war came to an end, it is no longer possible to seek the causes of this phenomenon entirely in the effects of the war. Moreover, the States who were successful in the war have themselves not yet overcome its effects.

The belief that we shall sooner or later get away from the effects of the war, and that a new period of prosperity will set in—at least in those States who were successful in the war—must disappear. It is becoming more and more certain that this commercial decline, now so general and so persistent, arises from the very condition of Europe as reconstituted by the Peace Treaties.

HOFFMANN, Major-General.

BERLIN, *Christmas* 1922.

PART I

THE statesmen who had believed in the summer of
1919 that they could decide the future development
of Europe had not realized that the developments
of commerce in general, and industry in particular,
based on the inventions of the past century and the
establishment of international trade communications, must necessarily subvert the principles of
state-craft.

When the States of Europe were still, in their
true character, essentially agrarian, after a period
of hostilities the victors could take provinces away
from the vanquished and exact tribute from them.
This represented a clear gain to the victorious
nation, while the conquered race had to bear all the
losses.

Modern industrial States on the other hand—
even though their character as National States is not
thereby disturbed—constitute commercial entities
that mutually supplement each other. They are
absorbing each other's production of raw material,
half-manufactured and manufactured goods, and
this production is reduced in value as soon as it
begins to be deprived of a market.

The interdependence of European commercial
activity had increased in the course of the past
century as the result of certain specific conditions.
The continent of Europe, the climate of which is far
from favourable, could not itself possibly produce
in sufficient quantities the raw materials that were

needed for the great industrial development based on the recent discoveries in Europe. But the British Colonies imported these raw materials into Europe, to be worked up by the manufacturers not only of England but of the whole of Central Europe, and especially Germany.

Thus the increasing import of raw material from the British Colonies made this European industrial development possible. The further this development progressed the greater was the need of raw material. At the same time it was important for those parts of the British Empire producing raw material that the industrial development should not merely take place in the Motherland, but also in the rest of Europe, and especially in Germany, as the possibility of the expansion of English industry is naturally limited. English capacity for absorbing the raw materials produced in the British Colonies could never equal that of the whole of Europe. The prosperity of the industries of Europe as a whole and the prosperity of England and her Colonies were in this way mutually dependent.

On the other side, as a result of this industrial development, the population increased so fast in the now thoroughly industrialized States of Europe that the products of the soil were increasingly insufficient to support it. However, the food-supply of the European people was secured by the fact that in exchange for their overplus of manufactured goods they could import foodstuffs from such areas as produced them in excess of their own needs. As a consequence, the gigantic agricultural area of the East of Europe and the West of Central Asia— Russia — had become, together with the corn-producing area of other continents, of importance to the economic life of Europe as a whole. Russia's surplus of agricultural products meant a much larger and cheaper food-supply for the industrial States of Europe.

All over Europe, as well, agricultural and industrial production had increased in mutual dependence. The rate of this increase of production was quicker than that of the increase of population. According to the principle of that classic of English Economics, Adam Smith—" As production stands in a higher or lower ratio to the number of the consumers, so will the total of those consumers be better or worse supplied with necessities and amenities " —the standard of living of the European people as a whole had continually increased.

If the statesmen who laboured at Versailles had realized these connections, they would have felt some hesitation in applying political principles that were appropriate in the time of agrarian States to industrial States of modern times. They must have seen that the indemnity exacted from their defeated enemies by successful industrial States may become very dangerous to those who demand it. If such indemnities have the effect of ruining the defeated States, and thereby destroying them as markets for the victorious States, then the industrial production of the victorious State itself suffers damage. This damage becomes the more pronounced the heavier the tribute levied from the vanquished. It will be the more deeply felt in the conquering State, in so far as its industrial production is the more highly developed, and as the population, whose increase is, and has been, dependent on the expansion of that production, is absorbed in its disposal in exchange for foreign foodstuffs. In this way, the effects of an indemnity may be such as to cause greater loss to the economic life of a State than the amount of the indemnity.

But the most serious aspect of the position is, as

I have pointed out, that in certain of the European industrial States the population has become so numerous as the result of industrial prosperity that the agricultural produce of these countries is quite insufficient to support it. The paralysis of industrial production in States of this kind deprives millions of people of the barest subsistence.

The statesmen who worked out the Peace Treaties of the year 1919 did not realize all this. They did not, consequently, realize that when the war was over it was not a question of surrendering this or that province by one State to another, but of the restoration of the economic life of Europe as a whole. They did not grasp that all European States without exception would suffer the same defeat if the machinery of European economic production could not be set in movement once again. If that was not done, then it was a mathematical certainty that millions of people in Western and Central Europe would perish by starvation, hunger-riots and civil war, according as the population figure of the industrial States exceeded the number of inhabitants that could be fed by home agricultural products. The problem whether these millions are to survive or not is the true problem of the European future.

The work of the statesmen after the World War should have been inspired by constructive ideas. Instead of this it was destructive.

The destructive character of this policy, which was in fact pursued by the Entente statesmen before the war was actually over, had inevitably an even worse effect, as it everywhere shattered the constitutional structure in the defeated States. It was on the endurance of this structure that the commercial activity of the European peoples and the commercial activity of the whole of Europe mainly depended.

It is not reasonable to believe that the commercial activity of a State is independent of its military power, and of the relation of this military power to adjoining States. European economic life was very considerably conditioned by the military equilibrium between the European Powers.

The burden of this military equipoise made the Powers mutually suspicious. This was a guarantee of the binding force of the international law that was needed for the commercial development of Europe. The armies and fleets of the Great Powers by their mere existence prevented any rash attempts by the smaller and greedier States of Europe. In this way peace and the economic life of Europe were secured in a time of quite exceptional development, and over a quite exceptionally long period of time.

In the domestic life of States the existence of the armed Power was of importance for commerce. It guaranteed the authority of Governments within the national borders and therewith the security of the administration of justice.

As a result of all this the exchanges in Europe were stable. This was to the benefit of the general economic life of Europe, which cannot dispense with a dependable inter-relation of exchanges.

The destructive tendency of the Entente policy had the more distressing effect as one inevitable result of the gigantic struggle of the World War was to destroy the stability of the States of Europe and, with it, the economic life of that Continent. Owing to the fact that the Entente statesmen completely paralysed their defeated enemies, the economic life of Europe suffered damage that extended far beyond the injuries inflicted by the war. The revolutions then made the situation much worse. They destroyed the habits of economy and further diminished productivity.

NEGATIVE RESULTS OF THE ENGLISH DIPLOMACY

IT is only natural that the effects of the destructive policy as pursued by the Entente statesmen comes most clearly to the light of day in the most highly developed of the Entente States—England. They are obvious in the paralysis of English industry and in the resulting unemployment. The Peace Treaties of 1919 were the finishing touch to financial and industrial ruin in a large number of European States. But at the same time the nations concerned lost their purchasing power of the raw materials, half-manufactured and manufactured goods which were produced in the victorious States, and in their Colonies, more especially the English Colonies.

Before the war Germany was not merely England's commercial rival but at the same time perhaps the most valuable customer of the British Empire. The Revolution in Germany destroyed, as it did everywhere, the economical administration of the German State finances, and diminished commercial productivity in Germany. The German State finances were then further overburdened by the Allies' Reparations claims. Our attempts to meet these claims were the main cause of the rapid disappearance of German purchasing power.

Moreover, since the end of the war the Entente has made no serious attempt to bring Russia once more within the orbit of world commerce.

The policy of the English Government has accordingly had this result—that a large part of their former world market has either lost its purchasing power for English goods, or can no longer maintain it. Great commercial areas, such as Central Europe, and more especially—as a result of its high industrial development—Germany, are becoming of less and less account as customers for

English manufactured goods and for the raw
materials of the English Colonies. English policy
in this matter has had the same effect as Napoleon's
Continental Blockade, by means of which the
French Emperor proposed to force the Island
Empire to its knees. It is quite incredible that
a truly English Government cannot have foreseen
these results of their policy.

The Continental Blockade—a burden which
England imposed on herself—is the more serious as
English industry and English trade will hardly succeed in finding in the English Colonies a substitute
for her lost market on the continent of Europe. It
will scarcely be possible for the reason that the purchasing power of the English Colonies for English-
manufactured goods depends largely on those
Colonies being able to dispose of their raw materials
in the markets of the continent of Europe, and
more particularly in Germany, which is industrially
so highly developed. If, therefore, for whatever
reason, German industry is completely paralysed,
the producers of raw materials within the British
Empire will be directly damaged, and the outlets
for British industry will be, indirectly, more and
more limited, to that country's hurt, than at present
appears to be the case.

THE HEGEMONY OF FRANCE AND HER OVERBURDENED FINANCES

THE Peace Treaties have not had so unfavourable
an effect on France as on England. France is much
more of an agricultural State than the Island Empire.
Added to which, French industry is concerned
mainly with its task of restoring the devastated
areas of Northern France, which offer profitable
prospects. On the other hand, French industry is

just as hard hit as English industry by the consequences of the Peace Treaties, in entering upon the open competition of the world market.

If, therefore, French economic life has been less injured by the effects of the Peace Treaties, on the other hand French State finances are more heavily burdened as a result of these Treaties. Since the end of the war France has used the excuse of the expected indemnity from Germany to pursue an exceedingly costly policy of force. This system must be imperilled as soon as it becomes obvious that Germany's capacity is quite unequal to meeting the financial claims presupposed by French policy. Germany is even less capable of doing so, as the plain effect of French policy is permanently to weaken the German people and thus further to prolong their essential incapacity to meet the French financial demands.

Of course French statesmen must have been strongly tempted to an open policy of force after the conclusion of the Versailles Treaty. By the terms of this latter the disarmament of Germany had abolished the military balance in Europe. As a result of this, France was presented with a military hegemony over Europe; and it was further established by a systematic perfecting and strengthening of the French power on land, at sea, and in the air.

There was now on the Continent no military force to rival the French Army, led by experienced generals, lavishly equipped with the most modern material, and always mobilized for action. French predominance was indeed actually greater than it had been under Napoleon I., who at the height of his power had still to reckon with the military strength of Austria, the Russian Empire, and England.

Moreover, England would not now be in a position to carry any differences with France to the ultimate conclusion of a war with that country. The Channel is exposed to French guns, and England is just as accessible to French flying squadrons as is the English fleet at the mercy of French submarines. France, an agricultural country, to which in any case all Europe is open, has little to fear from an English blockade.

Germany would be of no service as an ally of England against France owing to her disarmament and the destruction of her munition works. Before England could mobilize only a few German Divisions, France would have secured decisive successes with her always mobilized armies and fully equipped flying squadrons. Besides, any conscientious German Government would have to reflect that the battlefields of such a war would be on German soil and in industrial areas, the destruction of which would mean starvation to millions of German working men.

Thus, the unquestionable hegemony on the continent of Europe conferred on her by the Versailles Treaty had been extended even further by the French Government through military alliances with Poland and other States; and Germany was completely hemmed in by these armed Powers. The result of this policy would seem to be demoralizing for France even if it did not at the same time overburden the finances of the country.

However, the effect on French finances must come to light as soon as it is shown that this policy, backed as it is by the hypothesis that there is tribute to be got from Germany, is really quite Utopian. The French Government does not, for the moment, realize that a policy based entirely on military force is doomed to a negative result if it does not succeed in securing the material foundations essential to its success. The weakness of the French policy of force lies also in this, that it is destructive not merely of the economic life of Europe but also of the resources of the French State and the well-being of the French nation itself.

ITALY, THE NEUTRALS, AND THE UNITED STATES OF AMERICA

ITALY likewise is suffering under the effects of the commercial stagnation in Europe. This country is, however, spared the difficulties over the exchanges that have affected the commercial life of the rest of Europe, and their extension greatly increased her prosperity. In Italy the Fascist leader, Mussolini, seized the helm of Government with great vigour. His task will be made much more difficult by his inability entirely to avert commercial troubles in Italy arising out of the commercial stagnation abroad, though careful treatment may somewhat diminish their effect. It is not possible to predict how things will turn out in Italy.

The other States who were on the Entente side during the war, and the Neutrals, are suffering more or less from the financial collapse of the States conquered in the World War, and now ruined by the Peace Treaties. The more definitely they have developed into industrial and commercial States, the more they are suffering, just as England is, from the shrinkage of the European market, the ruin of Central Europe, and the disappearance of Russia from the commercial world of Europe. Wherever we turn our eyes, in all these States we see stoppages of trade, paralysis of production, and unemployment.

What will be the effect on the United States of America it is not yet possible to say, as they represent to a certain extent a closed commercial area, whose supplies of raw material are consumed largely at home: still, even that country cannot dispense with markets outside its own borders. Moreover, America, as a commercial force, has grown and prospered on the basis of reciprocal trade relations with the continent of Europe, which, though this was not generally recognized, had become, before the war, a collection of interdependent Continental units. It is consequently natural that the commercial collapse of Europe must produce sympathetic results in the U.S.A. Such stoppages of trade as there are on the other side of the Atlantic have their foundations mainly in the European situation. They will become more and more insistent the nearer Europe approaches to political and military disaster. The statesmen of the U.S.A. should not be considering the balance of power in their relations with individual European States; the most important business before the American Government should be to see that the economic life of Europe be restored in its entirety.

I must accordingly repeat that as an accompaniment of industrial development the population of the European industrial States has enormously increased during the past century, and, in some areas, it is now so numerous that such States are no longer self-supporting in the matter of foodstuffs. The stagnation of industry, caused by the political disintegration of Europe in general, and, in particular, by the effect of the political treaties, which run counter to the simplest economic laws, must bring with it the most serious consequences. It diminishes the possibility of exchanging the surplus yield of industrial production in the industrial States against the surplus foodstuffs of the great agricultural districts. This difficulty is materially enhanced by the fact that the production of Russia, one of the great agricultural areas of the world, can no longer be taken into account. All this threatens the fundamental daily needs of millions of Europeans.

THE BOLSHEVIST OFFENSIVE

THIS danger, which is in itself overwhelming, is greatly increased by the aggressive policy of the Bolshevist possessors of power, who have seized control of the broad lands of Russia. The policy of the Soviet Government is directed against Europe, now in her various ways fighting hard against ruin.

When in the spring of 1917, in the middle of the World War, the German Government permitted a few of the Bolshevist leaders, then living in Switzerland, to pass through Germany, the position in our country was very serious indeed. The military effect of the growing Entente superiority in war material was then pressing hard on the German Army in France. The German troops in Eastern Europe and in Russia were consequently urgently needed on the Western Front.

The first Russian Revolution did not bring peace in the East to the German Government. Kerenski went on with the war. The Bolshevist leaders were then looked upon merely as extreme Socialist visionaries. The German Government hoped that these leaders, when they arrived in Russia, would increase the confusion in that country, and that, as a consequence, Russia would be forced to make peace at no very distant date.

No one thought it credible that the Bolshevist would get control over the Russian Empire, at any rate for any length of time. Human wisdom could not foresee that these destitute revolutionaries, who haunted the cafés of Switzerland, would be in a position to seize upon power in Russia, maintain it through the establishment of a bloody reign of terror such as has not been seen in history, and grow to become a danger to everything that the intellect and labour of men have won for centuries past.

While the eyes of Europeans were still turned spell-bound upon Germany, though the war had been over for years, and while their disputes and the questions of daily policy still absorbed their attention, the Russian Soviet Government, with a consistency as incredible as their ruthlessness, and with a complete disregard of all the fundamental needs of the Russian people, had extended and established their rule over the vast land of Russia.

The power of the Soviet Government rests on their Chinese battalions, which are excellently fed, admirably equipped, and highly paid, with the result that these one-time coolies are blindly devoted to the Soviet regime. The power of the Soviet regime is also based on the Red Army, which, likewise, has a preference in the matter of food, to the complete disregard of all the needs of the Russian people. This Red Army is on the one hand afraid of the Chinese battalions, and on the other, lest, in the event of the fall of the Soviet Government, they would have to go hungry like the rest of the Russian people. The Soviet Government can therefore depend on the Red Army. They have it, indeed, the more firmly in hand as they have taken the officers' families as hostages. In the Tcheka— the Extraordinary Commission for dealing with the Counter-Revolution—the Soviet Government has a further terrible and reliable instrument of their power. The army of spies collected under the Tcheka has been guilty of so many betrayals, and driven so many men to death, that every one of these brutes has to expect a dreadful fate from the vengeance of the Russian people if the Soviet regime should fall. The Intelligentsia either have been forced to serve as officials under Government, where they are closely watched by the Tcheka, or they have been hunted down and destroyed. All the movable wealth of the Russian people—jewels, gold, foreign bonds, the vast treasures of the Russian monasteries and churches—has been appropriated by the Soviet Government. It alone possesses the financial power in Russia. Together with the Intelligentsia, the Soviet regime has imprisoned and exterminated the leaders of the Russian workmen —the Mensheviks—and the Social Revolutionaries because these Labour leaders were trusted by the masses and could influence them. The Government has used brute force and the arguments of the machine gun against the workers and the peasants themselves, when they have dared to rise up in their despair. It goes without saying that the Soviet Government has completely abolished the freedom of the Press : and as it finally dispersed by machine fire the constituent assembly chosen by the Russian people, it is entirely independent of any expression of opinion from the nation it has enslaved.

By destroying agricultural and industrial productivity, the Soviet Government has delivered the Russian people over to starvation. The safety of the Soviet tyrants does, in fact, depend mainly on the hunger and misery of the people. They know that hunger and misery will make the Russian people incapable of resisting the terror. The Soviet tyranny is therefore completely opposed to any practical reconstruction of Russia. Under a regime of fear, industry can never grow. It needs freedom of movement and legal security. But if the Soviet Government showed the slightest sign of relaxing the rule of terror with which they keep Russia down, they would give the unhappy Russian people a chance to rise again, and they would perhaps be in a position to shake off these few hundred ruthless traitors who keep them to the ground.

So long, however, as every Russian has to spend a day's labour to get a crust of bread, so long is the Soviet regime secure. And the result of it all is that there is no way back for the Soviet Government. The blood of millions of victims, who had to be destroyed so that the Bolshevist lordship might be established, can never be forgotten. Moreover, the possessors of power in Moscow cannot, obviously, allow foreign capitalists to establish themselves in earnest in Russia and acquire influence.

It is a condition of the very character of the Soviet regime that the continued extension of their power even beyond Russia's borders is for them an imperious necessity. They know very well that sooner or later the European peoples must become clearly aware how little they can dispense with the productive area of Russia. Thus the Soviet Government foresees that the day will come when the European peoples will, under the urge of necessity, unite to make war on Russia, liberate the Russian workers and peasants by military intervention on the part of the great European Powers, and restore the country as a commercial unit.

The Soviet Government is accordingly compelled to try to anticipate this by spreading its power so far into Western Europe, and inflicting such damage on the Europeans through their Colonies, that when the day of realization comes, those peoples will no longer be capable of making war on Bolshevism. Thus Bolshevism cannot remain limited to Russia; it also must conquer Europe, or Europe will conquer Bolshevism.

The Soviet Government have a further advantage

in the fact that they control the vast productive area of Russia, with the effect that this vast Empire is cut off, as an exporting and importing unit, from European commerce as a whole. Europe's increasing necessities, arising from this fact, she cannot herself allay; and it is just those increasing necessities that, on the other hand, make the peoples of Europe ripe for Bolshevist propaganda. The Soviet Government, on its side, can afford to wait: they have no pressing difficulties and time is on their side.

At the same time the Soviet Government tempts the Governments and manufacturers of the European States with the possibility of trade relations with Russia. These efforts are of course the more successful in so far as the leaders of European commerce have everywhere begun to feel how sorely the commercial life of Europe is damaged by its dissociation from Russia. They are accordingly instinctively drawn to commercial relations with Russia.

The majority of the European Governments and the leaders of European commerce have, however, not penetrated the actual character of the Bolshevist system. They have not realized that the Soviet Government, which in the huge agricultural area of Russia will always find enough to satisfy its own needs, those of its dependents, and of the Red Army, can have no interest in the reconstruction of Russia; it is much more concerned to keep its own power unshaken by perpetuating the miseries of the Russian people. The European commercial magnates have not understood that, for the Soviet Government, the negotiations regarding trade relations are not an end in themselves, but only a means of realizing their political purposes.

If European merchants, with the approval of their Governments, enter into commercial relations with the Soviet Government, these merchants and manufacturers intend to do business, while the Soviet Government wants to gain time to allow the effect of Bolshevist propaganda to ripen. The business in connection with which negotiations have taken place between European merchants and representatives of the Soviet Government has scarcely yet reached any result, with the exception of purchases of war material, including locomotives, for the Soviet Army. But the Soviet Government has gained time in the process: so that success has been on the side of the Soviet Government.

The negotiations of the Soviet Government regarding trade relations are only a part of the Bolshevist propaganda. It would be completely wrong to think this propaganda is always recognizable as Bolshevist and Revolutionary. It figures as such only among the European working classes, where its effects are accordingly immediately recognizable.

On other occasions the Bolshevist propaganda stirs up racial passions, for every war in Europe, every further resort to arms on the part of the civilized States of Europe must, in these consequences, still further shake the structure of European trade, increase the misery in Europe, and thus enhance the prospects of a Bolshevist victory over Europe.

The Bolshevist propaganda in Asia and in Africa has been clever enough to rouse the religious and national passions of the native races, and incite them against England and also against France.

The Bolshevist offensive is primarily directed against England because the British Empire spans the world. If the Soviet Government could succeed in breaking this Empire, through a general rising of the English Colonial races, as a result the import and export markets in India, Mesopotamia and Egypt would be closed to world commerce; and then, in all human probability, the collapse of Europe, and therewith the victory of Moscow over the European peoples, would be almost inevitable.

POLITICAL STRATEGY

THE result of a careful consideration of the position as a whole, and its more important attendant circumstances, is scarcely encouraging. However, it is desirable to examine these circumstances without prejudice.

When the strategist is confronted with the task of considering military operations, he must at once and before everything get a clear picture of the situation as it really is. Only if that is done can the generals in the field reach correct and effective decisions. Just in the same way the statesman, who at the present time has to reckon with economic as well as political and military necessities, must get a clear, far-reaching insight into the situation so as to lay down his policy on the right lines.

It would have been wrong to think that the mental activity of the strategist is entirely the result of cold calculation. There are important *imponderabilia* over and above all calculations that must influence his judgments. In war, most especially, the confidence of the troops has to be taken into account. A cheerful, hopeful army can be called upon for greater efforts than one which is burdened by discouragement. So also the statesman, who is confronted with the task of putting a stop to the ruin of Europe and showing its peoples a new way to salvation, must reflect that the spectre of discouragement is brooding over all the peoples of the earth.

The nations who conquered in the World War are growing more and more disillusioned, and the future of the vanquished grows more and more black. Besides all the real dangers that threaten the European States, this general discouragement is a factor and a spiritual encumbrance that cannot be taken too seriously. If it is essential for a commander to banish discouragement from his army, from whatever source it may appear, then he must do as Frederick the Great did when his hopeless situation before the battle of Leuthen forced him to attack a far superior enemy—the statesman of the present must offer fresh and far-reaching aims to these disillusioned peoples. He must disclose mighty prospects for the future so that the spirit of confidence, that carries with it the certainty of success, may everywhere be reawakened.

Thus the task of the statesman is the same as that confronting the commander in the field. It calls for a recognition of the given situation, a definitely realized ultimate object based on a cool estimate of that situation, a clear view at all its stages of the road to be taken, strength of decision to reach that ultimate object, flexibility of mind to deal with difficulties and disputes, and finally, the utilization of all the spiritual forces which will be the *imponderabilia* of success.

From a consideration of the European situation it becomes inevitable and obvious that the ultimate aim of any statesmanlike plan can only be the restoration of the commonwealth of Europe. As the prosperity of every European nation is bound up with that of every other, in this period of industrial development none of the European Governments can restore prosperity to their own country if other States remain in a state of disorder.

Next we must consider the measures that seem successively appropriate for achieving this ultimate aim.

THE FIRST OPERATION: THE COMBINATION OF THE GREAT EUROPEAN POWERS

In the first place it seems to be necessary that an agreement should be reached among the great States of Europe, whose co-operation is essential in the mighty work of restoration. The effort to procure such an agreement seems by no means hopeless. The great States of Europe are feeling the pinch of commercial necessity. On the other side it is becoming more and more clearly recognized that the nations of Europe are much more dependent on each other, and will remain so, than anyone realized before the war.

It would therefore be quite natural to give expression to this essential mutual interdependence of the great European States in such forms as are demanded by their commercial needs. In this connection the question of the relation between France and Germany is of decisive importance, and becomes the more obviously so as France's political power grows more predominant on the Continent.

The French know that the German people are more numerous than the French. The German people has, moreover, remarkable industrial and commercial aptitudes, and its military efforts in the war exceeded all expectations.

Prominent Frenchmen have said to me that there were really only two possible alternative French policies vis-à-vis Germany. One was that France should try to keep Germany in subjection. This has been France's policy hitherto. Its result has, however, been disastrous for France. The French deficit has been constantly increased by the cost of such a policy of force. It must consequently be considered not unlikely that France will abandon this line of policy and try the second alternative.

And the second is a complete understanding between France and Germany. Such an understanding must, however, be so well founded that, by its very constitution, future wars between France and Germany would be out of the question. This could be achieved on the sole and only basis of a combination of interests between France and Germany. There is for France no third alternative between these two extremes: complete alienation from Germany, or equally complete understanding.

The President of the Board of the National Bank of Germany, Geheimrat Witting, has suggested such a combination of interests in an interview published in the French paper, *Le Matin.* Geheimrat Witting said:

" It is immediately obvious that France and Germany, especially as regards their ' heavy ' industries, are dependent on each other. France has the ore, and Germany has the coal. The necessity for both countries to supplement each other's industries is in some sort laid down by Nature herself, and this necessity would be met by a powerful combination of interests between England and Germany. If it were possible to get English industry to take part in this alliance of the West European Commercial Powers, so much the better. Unfortunately this essentially natural development is gravely hampered by the Treaty of Versailles. The successful functioning of commercial combinations of this kind is only possible on the basis of equal rights for all participants: and they must be so constructed that all participants are satisfied. But the Versailles Treaty has abolished all such equality between French and Germans."

I should like to express my entire agreement with Geheimrat Witting's observations, and I should think it an excellent thing if England would at once take part in such a commercial alliance, although I believe that, in any case, England could not for long keep out of such a combination of French and German interests.

Such a *rapprochement* between the three great industrial States of Western Europe would be strictly in accordance with the policy which the English Minister, Winston Churchill, has publicly advocated for years past, and which he has indicated as necessary for the salvation of every one of the great European States.

Apart from which, I think such a participation by England in a combination of interests between the great European States would be entirely natural. As a result of the unemployment in England, the English are gradually coming to realize that the destruction of Germany's commercial life will do more harm than good to England, as Germany is one of her best customers for English and Anglo-Colonial goods. The commercial competition of Germany would, however, be much lightened, from England's point of view, if it were associated with a German commercial combination with France.

It accordingly appears that the statesmen of the three great nations are raising their voices in favour of the commercial co-operation of the great European peoples on the basis of industrial combinations. Their influence is spreading. The opposition which had to be surmounted is everywhere disappearing. I might remark in passing that I have no specialist knowledge of the technicalities of industrial combinations. I must therefore confine myself to agreeing with the principle without proposing to give any opinion on the details of their establishment. But I should like expressly to emphasize what Geheimrat Witting has said on the subject of the Treaty of Versailles. Any agreement between the great peoples of Europe is unthinkable if full justice is not done to the national pride and deserts of each one.

Only if patriotic persons in France and in England, as well as in Germany, can be satisfied with the form and content of such an agreement could such an arrangement be feasible, and only under such conditions could it be fruitful. Patriotism is in no way synonymous with striving for hegemony over other peoples.

No one will doubt that Prince Bismarck was one of the greatest patriots that the German people has produced. And yet Prince Bismarck, once he had united the German people, did not strive after the hegemony over Europe. The Prince declared that the German Empire which he had created was satisfied and desired no further expansion. His policy, which is defined with plastic clearness in the publications of the German Government—*The Policies of the European Cabinets, 1874-1914*—is a single and speaking proof of this. History has given Prince Bismarck his due. In the Empire which was his creation the prosperity of the German grew to an unexampled maturity. Germany's authority in the councils of the nations was weighty, and Germany always threw that authority into the scale of peace. That, later on, the opportunity to secure the commercial progress of the German people by a far-reaching industrial policy was lost, is not the great Chancellor's fault.

I should like, however, to repeat, with every possible emphasis, that true patriots of all nations must not forget that the States of Europe are all attacked by the system of Bolshevism, and that every dispute between the great European States will facilitate the victory of the Moscow Soviet regime over Europe.

The prospects of success in every battle are diminished when it has to be fought on two Fronts. Accordingly every dispute between the European peoples diminishes their power of resistance against the Bolshevist danger. Only when the patriotic citizens of the great European countries stretch out a hand to each other against the Bolshevist danger can they master it. It is of course possible for them to reach out a hand to each other, because commercial needs are an essential bond that knit together the interests of the great States of Europe.

The presumption, indeed, is that full equality will be conceded to the German people *vis-à-vis* the other Great Powers of Europe and that the national dignity of the German people will receive the general respect it deserves.

The achievement of an accord between the great European States is the first and most difficult step on the way that is to lead Europe to a recovery.

THE SECOND OPERATION: THE LIBERATION OF RUSSIA

THE co-operation of the great European industrial States on the basis of a commercial combination will thus be the first operation necessary for the realization of the ultimate aim before us.

This co-operation between the great States of Central and Western Europe seems also necessary for a further and more particular reason.

American diplomats and business magnates have assured me that the mutual quarrels between the European Powers, and especially the continual friction between France and Germany, have destroyed the credit of the European Powers in the eyes of American financiers.

The United States would, it was explained to

me, gladly, apart from this, employ their superfluous capital in financing European industry, and
lend money to Europe. But the statesmen and
financial magnates of the U.S.A. are afraid that
Europe, owing to the continual disputes among
the Continental Powers, is destined to collapse
before Bolshevism. On the one hand, it would be
too risky for the American financier to lay out his
capital in any European State, and on the other,
American investments of the kind would do no good
anywhere.

A high American diplomat said to me emphatically that the U.S.A., which were beginning to feel
the effects of the commercial ruin of Europe, would
make financial sacrifices to introduce definitely
settled relations between the European States, and
thus consolidate the European market.

Notwithstanding all this, however, the co-
operation of the great States of Western and Central
Europe is not in itself adequate to realize the object
in view. It has been described how indispensable
to the economic life of Europe is the vast area of
Russia. The restoration of Russia as an economic unit, and its inclusion within the orbit of
European and world trade, is therefore necessary.
It also has been shown that the restoration of
Russia and her re-inclusion in the trade orbit is not
possible so long as the Soviet Government, the very
basis of whose existence would be attacked by such
a process, still controls this vast land. Having
regard to the forcible means by which the Soviet
Government holds the wretched Russian people
down, there is, humanly speaking, no hope that
the Russian people can by their own strength free
themselves from these tyrants who have fastened
iron fetters upon Russia. In any event, there must
be a clear understanding of what is to be done if

the hope of a political evolution in Russia, such as, contrary to my view, is still canvassed, is not fulfilled. The only thing remaining is for the Soviet Government to be overthrown by military intervention from without. Only then can the foundation stone be laid of Russia's economic restoration and her inclusion in the orbit of European and world trade.

I must emphasize the fact that this conviction of mine is the result of personal experience, and does not arise from any desire to conduct any further military operations. I have borne for more than four years the heavy burden of the responsibility for military operations. Every day we were confronted by decisions of far-reaching importance. I may say that some of the victories that I was privileged to win for my country will not be forgotten in history. I have certainly no desire to assume such responsibility again.

It is cold conviction that makes me realize that an armed conflict between the peoples of Europe and Bolshevism is inevitable. If there is any element of emotion in this judgment it is, in addition to my love for my own country, a deep sympathy with the unhappy Russian people, whose armies opposed me in this war. I find it quite incredible that the cultured nations of the world, who carry the badge of civilization and humanity on their banners, can look on inactive while this once so happy people in that prosperous land is being done to death.

The task of freeing the Russian people, and not least the Russian peasants and working men, from the tyranny of the Soviet regime, reconstructing the commercial life of Russia and, in addition, gathering in the immeasurable national treasures that are sleeping in the soil of Russia, is so tremendous that it exceeds the military and commercial capacity of any single one of the great European States. Not one of the European Great Powers, moreover, could concede to any of the others a predominating influence in Russia of the future. The solution of the problem is possible only by a combination of the great European States, especially France, England and Germany, with the ultimate aim of liberating Russia and restoring her economic life.

These Allied Powers must overthrow the Soviet Government by a combined military intervention, put in its place a constitutional Russian Government, restore the commercial economy of Russia to take its necessary place in the combined economic life of England, France and Germany, by the common efforts of the great European nations and the Russian people, and by the gradual restoration of Russian economic forces. Such a recovery may be hoped for after the overthrow of Bolshevism. In conjunction with all this the financial and commercial co-operation of the U.S.A. would be most valuable. Special economic concessions in Russia must be guaranteed to the U.S.A.

The financing of such an undertaking is not easy, but it will not be insurmountable if it is backed by the security resulting from a combination of the great European States and the power that such a combination would have at its command. Moreover, experts take the view that it would be quite possible further to finance this undertaking on the basis of the vast natural resources of the Russian State as soon as Russia is liberated from Bolshevism by the armies of the European Powers.

If, then, the commercial interests of the great European States were from the beginning bound up in mutual dependence with those of the Russian

people, this does not mean an exploitation of Russia
by Western industries. I am, on the contrary,
firmly convinced that no solution could be found
which would be so surely instrumental to the restoration of Russia, her recovery and prosperity.
Such an interlocking of interests would, moreover,
become closer and more indissoluble with every
year of common work. Common interests are a
stronger bond than any alliance. In such a development lies, humanly speaking, the greatest
attainable security against any future entanglement
in war.

I should like, in this connection, to call attention to one consequence of a military nature. The
military balance of power in Europe could hardly,
once it had been destroyed, be restored without a
murderous war. But if the proposed solution of the
Russian question be adopted, it would no longer
be necessary to restore it. The Great Powers of
Europe, bound together, and to the Russian people,
by closely interlocked interests, would no longer be
in a position to make war on each other. After
the pacification of Russia they would be able to
reduce their armies on the basis of mutual military conventions. In place of a precarious military
balance of power in Europe, as it used to be, we
should have a stable basis of allied military power
on which to found a new development.

In the course of discussions of all these questions
some have pointed out that the failures of Koltchak,
Denikin and other Russian commanders against
the Red armies of the Soviet Government give rise
to apprehension; and reference was made even to
Napoleon's defeat in 1812.

These objections are, in my opinion, unfounded.
The campaigns of the Russian Generals against the
Soviet Government were undertaken with forces

which from the very beginning were quite insufficient to maintain control over operations in the vast areas of the Russian Empire. Moreover, these armies were without a commissariat. They had to take supplies away from the Russian people instead of bringing them in. All this is enough to explain their failure without the one-sided political activities of some of the White Russian Generals.

An army intended for the liberation of the Russian people should take nothing from them, but on the contrary bring supplies in with them. The Expeditionary Force must accordingly not merely be provided with a commissariat for its own use, but must also be in a position to supply foodstuffs to the starving Russian people. Finally, a steady flow of manufactured goods, of which the Russian people are so urgently in need, must follow the Expeditionary Force. Agricultural machines, etc. —of which there is great need—must be sent into the country. The advance of the army must be followed by a powerful advance of the European industries; and in this connection the financial help of the United States would be of value.

The reference to the fate of Napoleon can be even less maintained. The Emperor of the French had no railway, no motor transport and no telephones. He was without any means of building up communications in his rear such as the art of war of our time has at its disposal. It was the insufficiency of such communications that wrecked Napoleon's armies, although they were not defeated. On the contrary, during the World War the German armies advanced deep into Russia. They also supported the hardships of a Russian winter because the needs of the troops could be supplied by means of lines of communications organized with all the facilities known to the modern art of war.

I am consequently convinced that the European army of intervention, well supplied with heavy artillery, flying squadrons, and every sort of modern war material, would defeat the Red armies of the Soviet regime wherever they found them. One point I must especially emphasize: an army of this kind must from the very beginning be strong enough, after completely securing its communications in the rear, to reach Moscow in sufficient strength to win the final victory. Nothing would be more dangerous than to offer battle to the Soviet Government with forces in any way too weak. If civilization's last card—the armed conflict of the great States of Europe with Bolshevism—must be played, there must be no possibility of failure.

I take the view, incidentally, that an intervention of this kind against the Soviet Government would be quite different from the fighting in the World War. As a result of the technical superiority of the European Powers and their armies, as compared with Soviet Russia and the Red armies of the Soviet Government, the losses of the European army would in all probability be small and their success certain. The sacrifices demanded by such an intervention do not bear any comparison with the distress inflicted on the peoples of Europe by the loss of Russia's gigantic productive area.

The efforts of the Soviet Government, which the European Powers with incredible shortsightedness have done nothing to combat, have been so effective that, unless appearances are entirely deceitful, the world is on the eve of a gigantic uprising of the Asiatic and African peoples against the dominance of Europe. These are dangers that threaten all the great States of the continent of Europe.

IMPONDERABILIA

I COME at last to the *Imponderabilia*, which must be considered. Here logic fails us: instinct alone can estimate their importance. To begin with, I think, as I have already emphasized, that it is necessary to give the peoples a new and potent aim. The tremendous work of reconstruction in Russia, whose soil is full of sleeping treasures such as are elsewhere to be found only in the American continent—a task that must be carried out by the friendly co-operation of the great powerful nations of Europe, in which they will find salvation and bring prosperity to the Russian people—is such an aim. Moreover, the nations are weary of the strife that lies behind us, and they long to turn away their gaze from the past and face a new future.

In whatever way the development may take place, the importance of the working man must in no way be neglected, for German working men did their duty during the World War, on the battlefield and in the factory; but it would be a mistake to believe that material hopes alone, however splendid they may be, will suffice to overcome the spiritual depression among the nations. The power of religion—whether it is manifested in the homely form of the Evangelical creed or in the splendid ritual of the Roman Church—must be reinvigorated if we are to succeed in finding the way upwards. But this reinvigoration of the Christian faith must be free from intolerance. Every other religious conviction, of whatever kind it may be, must be respected.

I confess to a doubt whether this realization will be driven home in time to the leading statesmen of Europe and the nations, and whether accordingly it will be possible to stop the machine before it reaches the abyss. And yet I have a feeling, that comes not from my understanding but from my instinct, that the great peoples of Europe, and not least the German people, are in themselves too healthy, that they have too much knowledge, ability and energy, not to reach out a hand to each other when the day of realization comes—and come it must—and fearlessly and resolutely set their feet upon the way of deliverance.

PART II

AHRENSHOOP ON THE BALTIC, *July* 1925.

I WROTE down the preceding survey of the position in Europe at Christmas in the year 1922 and gave it to my publishers. But the publication was suspended owing to the conflict over the Ruhr which then began.

Since then France's policy of force against Germany has been wrecked by the fact that it overstrained the financial strength of the French people.

In England, since the year 1922, the paralysis of industry has become increasingly burdensome and unemployment increasingly threatening. The attempt to combine England and her overseas possessions into a self-sufficient commercial unit, whose outward token was to be the Wembley Exhibition, was a failure. This is proved by the fact that the number of English unemployed has not diminished. It remained the same under Liberal, Socialist and Conservative governments in England. The U.S.A. have become increasingly aware of the importance of restoring the prosperity of Europe.

All the attempts of the European Governments and the great European industries to build up solid commercial relations with Soviet Russia have remained without success. On the other hand, the Bolshevist propaganda in Asia and Africa has made enormous progress. The great majority of the peoples of China are in a ferment. In India—in the Punjab and in Bengal—in Mesopotamia, and

395

in Egypt, revolt against the English domination is coming to a head. All this has been stirred up by Moscow. Moscow likewise is stirring up the Moroccan war against France, and the propaganda of the Soviet Government is undermining Syria, Tunis and Algiers. The uprising of the Asiatic and African peoples has begun.

On the other side of the picture the agreement between the German and French potash industry has become a fact. The cartel of the German and French heavy industry — the alliance between German coal and French ore—is ready in the rough.

The beginnings of the developments that I sketched out in the year 1922 have become realities.

I shall be expected, of course, to consider the Asiatic-African uprising from the point of view of a professional soldier. The Asiatic and African peoples which England has added to her Empire in the course of centuries have never in themselves entirely acquiesced in English rule. Every people that is ruled by foreigners finds that rule burdensome. It must, however, at once be admitted that all these native races would never by their own efforts have reached the same level of prosperity as they have done under English authority. But the latent dissatisfaction of these peoples has never become at all threatening to England. The Asiatic and African native peoples united in the English Empire are far too divided in race, in religion and in national character to have been able to combine in a common, or even partial, movement against that Empire. The greatest revolt against England — the Indian Mutiny—left no impress on the other native races of the British World Empire.

Since the Soviet Government has been in power in Moscow everything has entirely changed. The Soviet Government is a rallying-point for all the

Asiatic and African native peoples. Whereas before, as has been said, there has been no bond of union between these peoples, now—to use a military metaphor—they have in some sense a Headquarters Command.

Incidentally the policy of the Soviet Government is not one of much delicacy. Each one of the native races within the Empire has some ideal or other, and Moscow promises each and all of them the fulfilment of their particular ideal, the presumption being that the English dominance must be broken and the European entirely driven out of Asia and Africa. Moscow can give such promises the more freely inasmuch as it is no way forced to redeem them later on. Moscow has, indeed, no intention of assuming control over the Asiatic and African native peoples. If the Moscow propaganda inflames the Nationalistic passions of these peoples, that is merely for the purpose of getting the Europeans driven out.

The more the unrest in Asia and in Africa gains ground—whether it is of Bolshevist or of Nationalist character—the more will those markets which the European industries have created in Asia and in Africa tend to disappear. And this must intensify the unemployment and the commercial distress all over Europe. If, in addition, it has become more and more obvious that the European Governments are not intelligent or energetic enough to stem this commercial collapse, their authority will be undermined all over Europe, and the ultimate end will be—according to the calculations of the Moscow Government—that the European peoples will be ripe for Bolshevism. It is a new and disconcerting reflection—to make Europe ripe for Bolshevism by the process of reducing her Asiatic and African markets.

England has just put down by force the Moscow-inspired and anti-English rising in Egypt.

In England's conflict with the Egyptian movement there may be observed a fundamental difference as compared with former English Colonial wars. When Lord Kitchener destroyed the Mahdi's troops at Omdurman the fighting was over, the victory won and the Sudan conquered for England. Now, on the other hand, Bolshevism is behind the Nationalistic movement of a Colonial people, and if military force is employed against such a rising it appears to vanish. But it is not overcome, it still heaves beneath the surface. If England withdrew her troops from Egypt the movement would break out once more, as quick and dangerous as ever. The English troops which were accordingly retained in Egypt must be kept continually mobilized, without the English soldier clearly realizing what enemy it is that he has to face and without understanding what it is all about. When a body of men is sent to storm an enemy position they go cheerfully into the fight, even when losses are likely to be high, as soon as the soldier understands that when the enemy position is taken the victory is definitely won and the fighting over. But if, on the other hand, those men must continue in a state of tension, not knowing when it is to end, then in the long run their *morale* will give way and the troops will be accessible to the pernicious propaganda of Moscow. This is the more dangerous where native regiments are involved, as they are naturally affected by the same propagandist arguments as the native races.

England did, indeed, employ Indian regiments in Egypt, who had nothing in common with the Egyptians and could be trusted against them. But the threads of Bolshevist propaganda from the Headquarters at Moscow reach the Indian regiments in

Egypt just as much as the native Egyptians themselves. Moscow can therefore incite both of them against England simultaneously.

However, it may be assumed that England will continue successfully to hold down the Egyptian movement. But other and similar troubles, fanned into activity by Moscow, will start in the Far East. And when England has become involved there, troubles will burst out in Bengal, then in the Punjab, then in Afghanistan, and then in Mesopotamia, and English troops will have to be sent and left there. It will be an unending contest, in which England's power and resources will be exhausted.

As regards the movement in China, which is in general anti-foreign, but more particularly directed against England, the Moscow Soviet Government is indifferent as to whether it is Bolshevistic or Nationalistic, or whether one Chinese marshal is fighting another, and with what success. It must, however, be emphasized that one thing, and one only, is of importance to the Soviet Government—namely, that by the spread of unrest in China the Chinese market should be closed for European industrial production and that, as a result, the commercial difficulties and unemployment in Europe should be intensified.

Moscow pursues exactly the same policy in the French colonies. It is quite possible that France will in one way or another get the better of the rising in Morocco, although such a campaign in North Africa, where water is scarce and roads do not exist, is extremely arduous, and inflicts unusual hardships and sacrifices on the troops. But France must also be made to realize that a Colonial rising engineered by Moscow is quite different from previous Colonial wars : it is a never-ending conflict in spite of European military successes. And such a war must at last exhaust European troops.

In the French Press, reports are continually appearing of the establishment of Bolshevist propaganda offices on French soil. These offices, which quite obviously do not date from yesterday, distribute leaflets in which French soldiers are urged to desert. Leaflets have been found in these offices also inciting the Moroccans to a war of liberation against France.

The unrest in the Asiatic and African possessions of the European Great Powers will last as long as the threads of it are pulled by Moscow—that is, as long as the central organization in Moscow is not destroyed. An additional point is that France has begun to regard her army of native regiments as an important factor in her political reckoning. If this native army is infected by the Bolshevist propaganda, and instead of fighting for France turns against her, that would be an upheaval which no French Government could ignore.

A characteristic instance of how Moscow prepares the Bolshevistic revolution under the surface, and touches off the mines as soon as the Soviet Government consider the situation ripe, is the late situation in Bulgaria. Only a few circumstances adverse to the Moscow wire-pullers and the activity of a few energetic Bulgarians prevented Bulgaria being caught in the web of the Moscow conspiracy.

The Soviet Government is no less apt in the planning of Nationalist risings, intended in the last resort to serve the aims of Moscow, than it is in the preparation of Bolshevist revolutions. For this purpose they use *agents provocateurs*, who have to play the part of fanatical patriots.

The final result of this military survey may be briefly summarized: the more the European Great

Powers enter upon endless Colonial campaigns stirred up by Moscow, and so exhaust their strength instead of marching on the centre-point—Moscow —the more they are serving the ends of the Moscow Government. The more exhausted Europe becomes —because her military power will be involved and worn down in Colonial wars, and because at the same time her Asiatic and African markets will disappear as a result of them, and because as a consequence the commercial distress in Europe will be intensified—the more difficult will a truly decisive expedition against Moscow gradually become. But if the centre of infection at Moscow is destroyed in time, then the uprisings of the Colonial peoples against the Europeans will, for lack of central leadership, collapse of themselves. Bolshevism will furthermore lose all its prestige among Asiatics and Africans as soon as Europe can make up its mind to take that citadel of Asiatic tyranny—Moscow.

THE END

MAP OF
EAST PRUSSIA

Statute Miles

0   10   20   30   40

Railways ----- Canals

INDEX TO VOLUME II

MAJOR-GENERAL MAX HOFFMANN

WAR DIARIES

AND OTHER PAPERS

VOLUME ONE

TRANSLATED FROM THE GERMAN BY
ERIC SUTTON

The Naval & Military Press Ltd

Reproduced by kind permission of the Central Library,
Royal Military Academy, Sandhurst

Published by

The Naval & Military Press Ltd

Unit 10, Ridgewood Industrial Park,

Uckfield, East Sussex,

TN22 5QE England

Tel: +44 (0) 1825 749494

Fax: +44 (0) 1825 765701

www.naval–military-press.com

© The Naval & Military Press Ltd 2004

In reprinting in facsimile from the original, any imperfections are inevitably reproduced and the quality may fall short of modern type and cartographic standards.

Printed and bound by Antony Rowe Ltd, Eastbourne

GENERAL HOFFMANN

CONTENTS OF FIRST VOLUME

PREFATORY NOTE

THE following account of historical facts and events is based on detailed information obtained from General Hoffmann during a close friendship with the Author that lasted over many years; and it has been extensively confirmed and enlarged from other sources. Details of his military career have been contributed by a number of his brother-officers.

Hoffmann's account of the development of the battle of Tannenberg is confirmed by his manuscript diary of those days: it was long thought to be lost, but was discovered under a mass of papers after his death. There, too, are recorded in his own handwriting the original dispositions of the troops, and the orders that were drawn up and issued as a result of his decision to attack the Army of the Narev on the night of August 20th-21st. It is there plainly established that Colonel-General von Prittwitz's much-canvassed telephone conversation with Colonel-General von Moltke regarding a retreat behind the Vistula must have taken place on the 20th August, not the 21st. Without the latter's concurrence the orders quoted in Hoffmann's notebook could not have been issued. The Prittwitz Army Command must have approved them, and after such a rearrangement of his forces—especially only a few hours before they were to begin a sixty-kilometre advance east of the Vistula—on 21st August the General could not possibly have talked of retreating behind that river.

The exact wording of the orders for the disposition of the I. Army Corps in the night of 20th-21st August—

7

*the 3rd Reserve Division had in the meantime been ordered
to Deutsch-Eylau—reads as follows in Hoffmann's notes :*

" *Gosslershaussen—Lindenau, with advance posts at
    Strasburg.*
Bischofswerder—Freistadt.
*Amm.-Col. and transport Luskovitz; Schmettau's
    garrison troops, Marienwerder.*"

*This establishes the time and scope of the much-disputed
order.*

*In this connection it appears from further notes of
Hoffmann that the I. Army Corps had already received
orders to push forward troops with a minimum of equipment, etc., to the line Neumark—Weissenburg Railway
Station, which they were to hold.*

*At the same time the 1st Cavalry Division was sent to
Gerdauen, and received directions to keep contact with
Lötzen and Königsberg, while the XVII. Army Corps was
already on 21st August ordered to proceed to the east of
Schippenbeil. The 6th Landwehr Brigade was to march
through Rastenburg, Korschen, Bischofstein, and join
hands with the I. Reserve Corps.*

*All these dispositions prove the intention of the Pritt-
witz Army Command to secure a decision by an attack to
the right of the Vistula.*

KARL FRIEDRICH NOVAK.

INTRODUCTION

GENERAL HOFFMANN was always a simple and consistent figure in his daily life, in his successful career and in his magnificent services to the State, from the moment when the tall, lanky, almost narrow-chested young schoolboy received his Cadet's commission from the King of Prussia until that sad hour when untimely death fell upon the giant in his fifty-fifth year. What everyone felt in him from his earliest days—what, indeed, he made everyone feel who had anything to do with him—was his presence of mind. Not merely in the sense that he was always unperturbed in the face of things, people and difficulties which so often came upon him unexpectedly. It was more than this: he had a truly forceful spirit that gave him an inexhaustible, exulting and triumphing strength. Many people, especially in the Great War, thought his successes were due to constant, or indeed invariable, good luck. In point of fact this rare gift of fate had never failed him. When, in the year 1906, as a tall, strapping, rather wild young captain, while on a Staff tour with his Section, he solved some hypothetical tactical problem, the Colonel who was criticizing his performance cried out:

" Really, Hoffmann, you didn't deserve such luck! "

Hoffmann—he was always called " der Lange," for none of his brother-officers ever called him by his rank or name—laughed that boyish laugh of his, that he never lost until the day of his death, with due respect to his Commanding Officer, but he added slyly, and with gay gratification:

9

" Certainly, sir, but—in the long run . . ."
Of course there was more in it than mere luck
and ability. Intellect and luck made that great
career. But beneath it all was a solid foundation
of genius.

He was, in many ways, very unlike his youthful
brother-officers of the 4th Thuringian Infantry in
Torgau, or his associates at Neisse and, later on, at
Lyck. He was almost the worst athlete, horseman,
swordsman of them all. The only physical aptitude
in which he excelled them was in his terrifying
appetite. His capacity for sausages was unlimited:
he sat drinking in the Officers' Club, alone for the last
part of the time, until seven o'clock in the morning,
when he took charge of his company on parade.
On his return, and before breakfast, he would
wash down his sausages with a couple of bottles of
Moselle. He played a first-rate game of *hombre*,
but was inordinately lazy at his studies, though his
military knowledge was soon considerable, for he
learned by listening; all his life long his quick
insight grasped the essential point, which an absolutely obedient memory enabled him to hold fast.
Such a man, whose amiability was flavoured with
a gift of repartee, or rather whose lightning-quick
superiority of judgment was tempered by a disarming humour and graceful turn of thought, was
naturally given preference before the others to prepare himself for the *Kriegsakademie*. Whereupon
he instructed his orderly to stand a light every evening on the table in his window in such a way that
the passers-by in the street below might gaze with
admiration at the industry of the future strategist.
The strategist himself, however, spent his evenings
in the Officers' Club, and carefully extinguished

the light when he really came back to the house in the morning. None the less, he passed the Akademie examination with distinction. He was sent to Russia for six months to study. To begin with, he applied himself to a thorough study of the Russian language. When, after his return, he was appointed to the " Russian Section " on the Great General Staff his Staff career was thereby already decided.

His daily life still wore an air of indolent eccentricity. His purse was none too well lined, and his inclination towards lavish ways was even then pronounced, though, as a First Lieutenant or a Captain, he prudently observed: " A man must live economically, but he must also understand how to part with a twenty-mark piece gracefully upon occasion." However, he lived a far from careful life, with sundry cheerful boon companions, so much so that his Colonel one day shook his head and said, with especial reference to him:

" My corps of officers seems to consist mainly of the rich sons of poor fathers."

Count York von Wartenburg, the head of the "Russian Section," had been his first patron, and had asked for his services. When Lieutenant-General von Lindenau succeeded the Count, who had been a failure in the China War, Hoffmann then found an avowed protector on the Great General Staff. The new Chief, himself an uncommonly agreeable and cultivated man, bestowed his favour on the young Hessian, who combined the best characteristics of the irreproachable Prussian officer with a lighter, not altogether North German social aptitude, and sound knowledge, with an imperturbable capacity for putting it into practice. It was characteristic of Hoffmann's unconcern, so seldom disturbed by the most untoward incidents, that on one occasion when he had been ordered to accompany his patron and chief on a journey to Warsaw he left the passports at home; he was quite unabashed, and allowed the General, looking very thunderous, to depart alone, merely shouting after him that he would, according to orders, report himself in Warsaw on the following morning, although there was no other train that night; and on the following day, when the General had only just arrived, he did, in fact, walk into the room. For, since "a man must understand how to part with a twenty-mark piece gracefully upon occasion," he had taken a special train to Warsaw. He did more: he even charged up the cost of the train to the General Staff account. At this point, however, old Field-Marshal Count Schlieffen sent for him. A thunderstorm burst over the head of the officer who had forgotten his papers when travelling on duty. But once more his military ability was allowed to outweigh his thoughtlessness. Count Schlieffen, as an exceptional measure, passed Captain Hoffmann's claim for expenses—which, incidentally, the latter had in the meantime managed to raise from his father-in-law, in case of necessity.

In 1904 he sent Hoffmann to the Russo-Japanese War. The Captain was to report to the General Staff his impressions from Japanese Headquarters.

He travelled through the world with open eyes —a grown-up boy in spite of the dignity of his position. Indeed one of his best qualities was that he always remained a grown-up boy, whether he was using his study-lamp as an alibi or, later, when the doctor forbade him to drink wine, and Hoffmann acquiesced with resignation, and then privately called for Moselle at his club. He looked upon great cities of the East—their strident colours, their strange happenings and burning problems—with a keen, penetrating gaze, that was always clear and never deceived by dazzling contours. In the Field Headquarters of the 1st Japanese Army he lived a hard, unpleasant, God-forsaken and wearisome existence, for his naturally inquiring mind was oppressed by the monotony of the blind and lifeless isolation in the comfortless melancholy of the Yentai coal-mines. He conscientiously reported what seemed noteworthy to his soldier's eyes. Finally, he saw the fighting on the Yalu, went through the battles on the Shaho and outside Mukden, and walked through the streets of the conquered city of Port Arthur. But when the fighting in the field was over, his thoughts often strayed gloomily away, beyond the marching columns and the artillery fireworks, in the lassitude of homesickness, towards a deeper contemplation of the scene. Suddenly the war stood before him as a dreadful thing, age-long and senseless—men tearing each other asunder:

" It seems so futile when one sees thousands of men, who were thriving and well the day before, now lying maimed, mangled, and dead upon the field — the Russians mostly with the astonished question in their staring faces: ' Why did I die here anyway? What have I to do with this country, this strange land, whose name I have never heard? ' "

Always solitary, he believes that for once he understands his own feelings :

" The only bliss in life does really not consist in establishing the most practical method of delivering an infantry attack, and we grow old here waiting. I notice it only in the others, but I think if the others are becoming so horribly old, I must be doing so likewise. . . . Happiness is a gift not granted to many—perhaps I shall only be happy

on my death-bed—looking back. So long as I see
the ladder before me leading upwards, I am never
continuously happy for more than a few seconds
together. There are moments of happiness, but
then, unfortunately, comes the thought—I must get
forward.''

In the jottings in his diaries that he sent to his
people at home he almost entirely forgets tactics and
strategy, and tries — he, a soldier, undistracted
by the clash of weapons—to find the meaning of
the war, its why and wherefore, and the new
frontiers that may result from it, more soberly and
more from the historical point of view than the
statesmen at the Peace Table now that the enemy
were letting fall their weapons. What he then
wrote about Russians has been fulfilled. What he
said about the Japanese—the wisdom of a policy
of moderation—was confirmed almost immediately
after he had written it. It then became clear that
this boyish young officer, who never seemed to shake
off the subaltern, could, with those five wholesome
senses of his, grasp a situation and its component
elements, analyse them, set them forth and, finally,
extract the kernel of truth. It is impossible to say
whether it was maturity that so quickly gave him
this power, or whether it was simply the clearness
of mind which had been one of his christening
gifts. At all events, his lightning power of judgment was one of his most outstanding characteristics
all through his career.

He liked talking, and he knew that he talked
well. He was at once silent when he felt the power
of another mind. The giant then sat bent forward
and thoughtful. The Far East widened the horizon
of the young officer, who came from Torgau, Lyck
and Neisse, via the clatter of Berlin, into China's
many pasts. He listened silently, when the distant

echo of European industrial unrest reverberated as far as Peking, to the old Mandarin who clapped him on the shoulder at an Embassy dinner and said: " My dear young friend, we had that sort of thing in China two thousand years ago, and we have finished with it. You will have finished with it some time too."

He sat dumb, too, beside the other Mandarin who talked to him about the Boxer troubles, and the meaning of Foreign Missions:

" What would you say if we, too, sent missionaries and, while we were forcing our way into Germany armed to the teeth, wanted to set up our altars in the Kaiser-Wilhelm Memorial Church in Berlin? "

And he nodded approval to the third Mandarin as the latter, with deferential courtesy, excused himself to an aristocratic young gentleman who was talking a great deal about his two-hundred-year-old family:

" Unfortunately we Chinese understand nothing about that. Our older families go back two or three thousand years. . . ."

The young Captain came back to his German home with much varied knowledge and all manner of forebodings. In the Far East he had seen the vast face of conflicting worlds, the perilous abyss of races and of peoples. Germany had not, for a long while, seemed so large, so overwhelmingly powerful when he realized that one may travel for weeks and weeks away from Germany and pass through many strange, different, not less powerful peoples, into far-off mighty continents. In front of the tea-house in Shimonoseki, in which the Japanese and the aged Li Hung Chang signed the surrender of Port Arthur to Russia—the German Ambassador had demanded it, quite unnecessarily thrusting himself forward as spokesman for Germany, France and Russia—in front of the tea-house at Shimonoseki, the Staff Captain said to himself on his departure from Japan:

" I hope we shan't have to pay for this piece of folly."

The Staff Captain had been promoted direct to Lieutenant-Colonel, omitting the intermediate step, when he set out for East Prussia in the World War. Japan now sent Germany an ultimatum demanding Kiaochow. The terms were precisely those of the ultimatum regarding Port Arthur, received at Shimonoseki.

During the war Hoffmann quickly ascended the ladder of outward military exaltation. But it was only vaguely and uncertainly that the people for whose future he was fighting, the great mass of the uninitiated, realized that this Lieutenant-Colonel who started as First General Staff Officer on the Staff of the 1st Army—G.S.O.,Ia, in fact—and became Chief of the General Staff to the Commander-in-Chief, Army of the East, was not merely a fine soldier but a very remarkable man.

When the unlucky General Prittwitz, the first Commander-in-Chief in the East, timidly decided to withdraw behind the Vistula, Hoffmann pointed out to him, coolly and soberly, that the retreat could not be carried out without a hard fight with Samsonoff's army; for the Russians were established nearer to the Vistula than the German General's troops. They would get there first, and bar the river passage. It was surely simple to advance upon the enemy and make every possible effort, by means of a surprise attack, to turn an inevitable battle into a possible victory.

General von Prittwitz began by protesting. Then
he saw the force of Hoffmann's proposal. He gave
up the idea of withdrawing his army behind the
river; he was now all for battle and attack. In
the great excitement of his momentous decision
the General had at once informed G.H.Q. of the
irrevocable withdrawal of his troops behind the
Vistula. He had not informed them that, in
the nervous agitation following upon the development of troop-movements and events, he had immediately reversed his own decision and determined
on the attack. Such a commander, who was far
too ready to retreat, and had been prepared to give
up German soil without a battle, was recalled by
the Emperor in disgrace; and with him his Chief
of Staff, Count Waldersee. A new Commander
hurried to the East, General von Hindenburg, accompanied by the new Chief of Staff, General von
Ludendorff. How emphatically fate immediately
turned in favour of the German troops in East
Prussia, and how disastrously against Samsonoff's
army, was generally known only a few days later.

But it was not generally known that the advance
which resulted in the battle of Tannenberg had
already begun while the special train carrying the
two generals was rolling eastwards; that the battle
resulting from the First General Staff Officer's
plans, and approved by General von Prittwitz, had
already been engaged, nor that, at the moment,
only two orders had been telegraphed by the
two generals on the way: the first being that the
8th Army should be granted a rest of twenty-four
hours — for twenty-four hours they were to do
completely as they liked—and, secondly, the Headquarters of the Army Command were to be moved
forward to a place specified. The twenty-four
hours' rest was regarded by the First General Staff

Officer as a grave tactical error, as it might delay the advance. He could not move Headquarters forward to the place appointed, as the troops had long since passed it. The entire Staff had to go back to report to Major-General Ludendorff in Marienburg. But when General von Hindenburg's Chief of Staff there went into the orders that were laid before him he found nothing to alter; the advance preceding the decisive battle was completed.

In subsequent years General Hoffmann never took much credit for the turn of events—at any rate for his share in the battle of Tannenberg. He was vain to some extent of his personal characteristics, and the prestige of his appearance—his Bismarckian skull, with its close-cropped white hair, the bushy eyebrows, bristling so powerfully forth from his forehead, which their possessor was not above training in the way they should grow, his unusually clear-cut features, so often lit up by his fine simple boyish smile, his small delicate hands, and even the creases on his trousers. But in his claims to the merits that were his due he was modest.

He often talked about the issue of the battle of Tannenberg.

" Nobody won the battle," he would say. " It developed entirely by itself. The Russians sent out their wireless ' in clear.' Grünert, the Quartermaster-General, again and again asked me anxiously if we should believe them. Why shouldn't we? At the worst something might happen, but nothing serious, if we were careful. I believed every word of it, on principle. And then the great question whether Rennenkampf would march to Samsonoff's assistance. I'm damned if he will, thought I. I had heard of the scene on the Mukden Railway Station. Samsonoff had then reproached Rennenkampf most bitterly for having left him in the lurch in the battle of Mukden.   The mutual explanations became rather heated, and both gentlemen boxed each other's ears.   They had been torn apart, and the Tsar had forbidden them to fight.   I made certain that Samsonoff would now be paid out. I don't know whether the scene at Mukden was at the bottom of it, but it did, in fact, not occur to Rennenkampf to march to Samsonoff's assistance."

Hoffmann never reckoned merely with the Army Corps.   He always weighed the *imponderabilia*, and tried to consider the enemy who confronted him, apart from the number of troops under his command, from the point of view of his psychology, his connections, his origin and previous history. As regards Tannenberg, General Hoffmann was always anxious to assign the honour much more to Lieutenant-General Ludendorff than to himself. The latter, he thought, deserved the highest credit for planning the thrust at and through Usdau.

He was disappointed when he first read in 1925 a passage from a letter that General von François wrote to him:

" The part played by Ludendorff at Tannenberg was not such, in my opinion, that he can claim any credit for the success.   It was on his responsibility that I was ordered to attack, at 10 A.M., on August 26th, the heights of Usdau, with insufficient forces.   That was a piece of tactical imprudence that would doubtless have led to complete disaster. The Seeben heights fortunately held up my advance on Usdau for so long that it was only on August 27th at 5 A.M. (by which time the whole Corps had arrived) that the attack on the Usdau heights could begin.

" Further, the order dated August 28th, 12.25, ordered a pursuit in the direction of Lahna.   As you know, I did not carry out this order, but pursued the enemy in the direction of Meidenburg. . . . Ludendorff's recollections have no historical value."

As a fact, the Lieutenant-General's attitude at Tannenberg was not that described later in his *Memoirs*. In the course of the battle there was a definite, decisive moment at which General Ludendorff's nerves completely gave way, and he wanted to cancel the orders he had given. At this point old Field-Marshal von Hindenburg, unshakeable in his calm and composure, achieved enduring fame by refusing to allow any over-hasty or muddled alteration of plans that had been carefully considered and adopted, and were now in process of being carried out.

Hoffmann's share in the Tannenberg victory remained obscure. It is almost symbolic that he suggested the name Tannenberg for the battle, originally christened " Frögenau," by General Ludendorff, in allusion to the Tannenberg battles of the old Teutonic knightly orders. In one place only was it known what the First Staff Officer Hoffmann had meant to the Engineering and Technical Services—the Headquarters of the Army of the East.

From that time forward all the important military events on the German Eastern Front are closely bound up with Hoffmann's military work. After the unsuccessful advance on Warsaw, and at the time of the retreat through Poland, he was able to inform General Ludendorff of the exact number of kilometres beyond which the enemy could not continue his counter-attack over the wrecked roads and railways. He then calculated with certainty, and made preparations for, the period of recuperation in which the retiring troops were able to re-form, carry out their brilliant move against Thorn and, subsequently, the tremendous flank drive on Lodz. But whether he was responsible for all this, and whether, later on, his was the decisive brain behind the battles of the Masurian Lakes, the fighting before Riga, or the Zborov offensive, which destroyed the last remnants of Russia's former military glory, so far as the German public was concerned he worked in entire anonymity. They knew far less of him than the Russians did of their enemy, "General Goffmann." He, however, remained unchanged in the midst of all these successes: since Tannenberg, the glory of which was entirely due to his foresight, though, as he always maintained, he had made no special efforts—since Tannenberg he grasped with a bold but pardonable sense of conviction that no enterprise which he undertook could end otherwise. He trusted in his luck: he basked in the inevitable prospect of success. Difficulties never stayed him, he took them in his giant stride: he saw them but he marched over them. And his luck was such that they really did give way before him.

To the Emperor, who spoke to him anxiously and doubtfully about some imminent enterprise, he once quoted the phrase:

" I had so many troubles in my life, and most of them never happened."

He was born under so lucky a star that fate never gave him the lie, and until the end he remained the undefeated German General. Of course the Commanders-in-Chief let him have his own way; occasionally he did not even consult them. What Marshal Conrad von Hötzendorf said of him—" He is the only man of ideas on the Eastern Front " —was equally well known to his chiefs. They experienced the truth of it every day. He might make gloomy or venomous entries in his diary, but all that was at once forgotten when the moment came for work and fighting. He thrived on work— it was pleasure, it was strength, it was the game his mind loved; and he thrived, too, on his success in circumstances that he had created and made to serve his ends. He could be so malicious and pitiless in his intellectual superiority that in many passages of his diaries the exact phrase has to be suppressed, or can only be hinted at. He could hate without mercy, and despise without pity, when he met with some impersonation of a strategist who could not so much as grasp the main idea of his operations. He had a horror of the army of commonplaces that led so many astray, of personal considerations in the conduct of a campaign, of the hunt for places, Imperial favour and popularity. In the field he spoke his mind fearlessly and unmistakably. After the tremendous successes at Lodz he was convinced that the provision of only two more Army Corps would have put the Russians out of the war. Hoffmann applied to General von Falkenhayn and asked that the two Corps might be sent:

" I begged for them on my knees."

The Chief of the General Staff refused. Hoffmann suspected that the Eastern Front was not to be allowed to be too successful. From that moment, and not merely after Verdun, he persisted in calling General von Falkenhayn " the criminal." He regarded him as responsible for the useless and bloody sacrifices in the West, for the mischief that came of the quarrel with Marshal Conrad—for, though he heartily despised " the Austrians," and was always cursing their troops, on a matter of military judgment he ungrudgingly regarded the Marshal as one of the greatest leaders in the war.

Although not much had hitherto been generally known of Hoffmann, as time went on, in circles where decisions were reached and knowledge counted, his influence became very great owing to his intimate understanding of the whole Eastern question and its ramifications. In practice he was the decisive authority in the East. Chancellors, generals, statesmen, politicians, members of Parliament, commercial magnates — all went to his Headquarters to see him and ask his advice. He was overwhelmed with memoranda and inquiries. Sharp as was his tongue, difficult as he found it to restrain his scathing wit, he was quick to recognize a head with something in it. In attack, in pursuit, and in the actual battle he kept, right to the end, something of the headlong daring of the young officer. But on the question of the U-boat war and Admiral von Tirpitz's adventures he was not for a moment deceived. The experiment was reasonable if there were enough boats to guarantee unconditional success. It was madness if—without any guarantee of success—it merely drove America to join the enemy. With bitter accuracy he reckoned up the number of Germany's enemies : there were so many to think of besides the Russians. The war must be really brought to an end some time : even if one is a soldier one must agree to that. A way to peace must at last be sought and found. Patriots run mad, land-hungry Imperialists with their Belgian, Polish and other aspirations, he repudiated with irony or contempt. He was moderate, cautious over every really complicated problem, practical and perfectly clear, averse from any vain imaginings. As were his statements, so were his demands. When the Emperor William, in the days when the Peace terms for Russia were being discussed at Brest-Litovsk, asked his opinion on the desirability of claiming Polish territory, though he had been ordered by the army chiefs not to speak too freely, he uttered an impressive warning. He said that more Polish territory than was indispensable for securing the frontier would be disastrous for Germany. This conviction, which he courageously defended to his Sovereign, meant a break with Ludendorff, who, apart from the matter in question, insisted that every officer was forbidden to speak to the Emperor without a preliminary interview with himself, even if the Emperor specifically ordered him to do so. General Hoffmann must henceforward learn elsewhere how to obey orders : and the G.Q.M.G. posted him to the command of a Division. But the Emperor vetoed this, and Hoffmann had to stay in Brest-Litovsk.

In Brest-Litovsk, again, he played a part quite different from that assigned him by public opinion. He figured as host to the Peace delegates. He was at once the representative and the interpreter of the views of the "Supreme Army Command." The G.Q.M.G. would not speak to him any more, since he had visited the Emperor, but gave his orders to the Chief of the General Staff on the Eastern Front through his own Staff Officer, until Hoffmann forbade such a proceeding. His position at Brest-Litovsk was difficult, and not merely on account of his open collisions with General Ludendorff. His personal convictions, much more than the views of G.H.Q., coincided with the conclusions of the Secretary of State, von Kühlmann, who represented the policy of the Government ; whenever he could see an opportunity he tried to get on with the negotiations for peace. While the Russian Commissary, Trotzky, much more intent upon the proclamation of new Russian gospels of humanity than upon peace itself, claimed an " open window " towards Europe and America, and while the Secretary of State reduced him to a hopeless technical and dialectical impasse, Hoffmann, who was in full accord with the Secretary of State, managed to separate the Ukrainians from the Russians. He disposed them to negotiate, and even induced them to sign the first treaty. Although, as subsequently appeared, the signatories were envoys of a collapsing and powerless Government, none the less the separation of the Ukraine was a great step forward. The self-confidence, the sense of power of an actually defeated enemy, but one who was consciously fighting with new weapons, was shattered by the realization of the possibility of a divided Peace. The General and the Secretary of State had long grown tired of the continual provocations of an adversary who daily repudiated what had been agreed the day before, and daily reintroduced what had been rejected. They had both at last set up a limit beyond which they would not allow him to go.

" You throw me the ball to-morrow," the General suggested to the statesman. " It can't go on like this! Just say : ' The word is now with General Hoffmann.' "

He wanted to take the responsibility of giving Trotzky a quiet warning.

At Trotzky's orders the Commissary Kameneff, after the opening of the meeting of the day in question, astonished the entire conference with a fresh oration, bristling with impertinences, the like of which can never have been so arrogantly delivered by the envoys of a defeated Power. By this time von Kühlmann had also had enough of it. However, he wished to preserve the unmoved superior

calm of the diplomatist; he must keep himself free
for future negotiations. But he threw the " ball "
to the General. Hoffmann remained calmly in
his seat, though he was boiling with indignation.
He made it clear in carefully chosen words that
he considered the Commissary's speech a piece
of insolence, and desired to stigmatize it as such.
He pointed out that they had "misunderstood the
situation. The German armies had advanced far
into Russian territory. . . . There is no object in
wasting time uselessly. It would be much better
to break off entirely than to go on like this."

From this prearranged reprimand, by no means
unduly severe, and justified by the continual
attempts at insult on the part of the Russian
Delegation, legend has created General Hoffmann's
historical blow of the fist on the table at Brest-
Litovsk. In point of fact there was no such blow.
General Hoffmann was accustomed to produce his
effects by looks and words rather than by martial
demeanour. He was never martial, though he was
perhaps impressive—quite a different thing. It is
entirely consonant with the idea of truth and history, current among the nations and their teachers,
that the General never won any fame from what
he actually did during the four years of war.
Something that he did not do first brought him a
questionable kind of glory: this quite imaginary
piece of bombast at Brest-Litovsk.

During the fourth year of war General Hoffmann
and the G.Q.M.G. lived in open estrangement.
They were not against each other, they worked
without each other: the Quartermaster-General,
with his vast powers of work, his unshakeable energy
in accomplishment, missed the " man of ideas "

who in previous times had not merely drawn up plans of campaign in actual collaboration with the Lieutenant-General but had taken the trouble to work out every situation, every plan, and every possibility up to the very end. At their last meeting in Berlin, at the beginning of the year 1918, the Major-General was disturbed to hear the Quartermaster-General observe that he did not know whether, in the coming great offensive, it would be better carefully to " probe " the Western Front by individual attacks or make a gigantic drive at a given point with concentrated forces.

" Exzellenz," the General had replied to his Commander-in-Chief, " any Second Lieutenant who tried to answer the question in that way would be hopelessly ploughed in his examination."

After that they never spoke at all. The G.Q.M.G. persevered in his probings of the Western Front. Hoffmann held the East with a thin veil of troops until the end. In the meantime, if the battle of the Marne possibly lost the Germans the victory, Quartermaster-General Ludendorff lost Germany the Peace.

When General Hoffmann came home from the war, after a most difficult time, that had daily and hourly subjected him to almost unceasing strain, he found it hard to come to terms with a state of affairs so changed by the Revolution and disaster. He felt himself still too young, too much the man of the moment by reason of his never-failing success, to remain idle. He had to leave the Old Army : it had ceased to hold together. In the New Army there was no place for one who would have been, in other circumstances, the next Chief of the General Staff. He would have nothing to do with the Peace of Versailles. He was one of the few who, having reflected a great deal during the war, never shouted and howled with the rest, but became more reflective than ever, and he changed his view of the origin of many things in the course of history. Now that he could no longer take an active part in affairs, all he could do was to try to give spiritual support to what he approved and contend against what he believed to be disastrous.

Accustomed, as he always had been, to considering and controlling vast situations, he could hardly see the politics of those days. Unprejudiced and unafraid as he was, he found it possible—to the painful surprise of many of his own rank, to whom he had always been suspect (" Intellectual paupers," he would say, " have never liked me ! ")—to get up suddenly among the audience at a workmen's meeting and confute the speaker by a few facts. His courageous bearing, which all could feel, inspired respect everywhere. But party politics did not attract him. He saw that the World War had created another Europe, which was really only in process of evolution. He abhorred senseless cries for revenge, though at bottom he cherished bitter feelings against France. He realized that France was situated next to Germany, that this could not be altered, that they must both at last come to terms, and that the Continent, and more, would collapse if they could not reach an understanding. If they could, then there would soon arise a great edifice of power, vast and indestructible by reason of common economic interests and exchange of goods, which would for all time put an end to this ruinous antagonism, and made immeasurably strong by two obedient and united instruments of power. Hoffmann was a European of the West. The French blood that flowed in the veins of his mother's ancestors brought him other gifts besides his wit at the dinner-table. He could not see any alliance with the half-savage or stupid barbarous destroyers who, if the Germans and the French quarrelled for much longer, would one day trample pitilessly to earth all that it had taken the two races a thousand years to build up for humanity. He knew the new Russia, and he knew the men who led it even better. He looked on them as the plague. He hated their subterfuges, their lies, their endless and inhuman cruelties, their corruption (to which he would swear), their readiness to destroy everything that man has inherited or created by his labour, their dangerous insolence in wanting to poison the world with new gospels—which were nothing of the kind. Russia was for him the great European nightmare. If the Bolshevist triumph were to continue, then the civilized world would be in continual peril of collapse. Even in August 1918 he had wanted to march to Petersburg. He attached no importance to the re-establishment of a Tsar. Whether there was a bourgeois regime, feudal institutions, a monarchy, or a republic in Russia was a matter of indifference to him, if the new Government could provide justice, and the rule of law, and allow the neighbouring states, Europe, and the world at large to go their way in peace. His proposal was not approved. Admiral von Hintze, to whom the General depicted the future in Russia, would not let him march.

" I know the Russians better than you," said he.

However, it seemed as though the General's knowledge and foresight were superior. Over and over again after the war, in countless casual conversations, in the frank interviews he gave to foreign correspondents—whether he were discussing the Russian attempts to stir up trouble on German

soil, the disaffection in the English colonies, in
London even, or the convulsions in China—he would
conclude his predictions, as punctual as clock-
work, with the words: "You'll find Moscow at
the bottom of it all." In the Imperial capital the
General kept open house for several years after the
war. Statesmen, men of learning, foreign generals
who wanted to meet the great soldier, Russian
spies skilfully disguised, came in and out. His
drawing-room often had something of the wild
atmosphere of a French revolutionary Convention
—of a soil volcanic and hot with passions, when
in times of excitement, amid a turmoil of strange
people, faces and dialects, some shabby Russian
general or marshal of the Court would crash his
stick down on the floor with a rather histrionic
emphasis and shout:

" Gentlemen, the place reeks of gunpowder ! "

However, the explosion never took place. The
General laughed when he, who was always watched
and spied upon by Russian agents, was warned of
imminent personal danger. In the days of collapse
in 1918, surrounded as he was by soldiers' councils
and retreating troops, he used to drive or walk un-
armed through the area under his command, and
no one ventured to molest him. And he smiled
when anyone nervously suggested that everything
that took place in his drawing-room would be
reported. What was never reported were his interviews with diplomats and generals of former enemy
nations, who went to see him and never smiled
when General Hoffmann spoke of Russia, and
foretold developments with their inevitable consequences and results. In truth, up to the last, he
hoped that one day yet an army of English, French
and Germans would march against the Bolsheviks.
He knew the secret history of the Denikin campaign.

He knew and shared the Western mistrust of the horde of Russian emigrants, who were sometimes inclined to accept the means to freedom and then forget their object. He saw that the road on which those warriors meant to march through the Ukraine and the Caucasus to Moscow was not paved with the bourgeois ideals of morality and liberty. He saw the oil trade of the world, the petroleum of Batoum, the naphtha wells, and he reckoned with the motive force of the continued deficits of " Royal Dutch," which were so alarming as to induce interested parties to finance an attempt to re-establish property rights in the naphtha area. Oil in itself was a matter of indifference to him. But he approved of any motive that tended to the extinction of Bolshevism.

It came to nothing. Many listened to Hoffmann in Germany, Holland, and England: Russian aristocrats, who were powerless, Frenchmen and Englishmen, who saw what was to come. Flatterers and fools, who forced themselves upon him, announced the imminent crusade against the Soviets as inevitable in the immediate future. Among them the General himself was the greatest sceptic. He certainly believed it to be inevitable: but only when England's colonies and Asia were ablaze—not till then.

He could no longer have taken command against Moscow. Beset as he had been for years by those who needed help and advice—a wise counsellor in need, and in anxious moments a pillar of strength and steadiness—he had slept but little, stretched for hours on his camp-bed, with half-open eyes and ears; and in those four years of war this giant had, unwittingly, destroyed his mighty frame. To sting his brain out of its lassitude he used to drink tumbler after tumbler of Cognac, and the strongest

Turkish coffee, day and night. If he ever stole out to get a moment's rest, one of his officers was bound to come in with some proposal, or plan for an advance, that he wanted to explain.

"Very well, fetch me the map," says Hoffmann.

The General then worked out the whole thing in outline on the spur of the moment. For a time he showed no signs of breaking: his faith in the mission he still had to fulfil, his hatred of the Bolsheviks, his rational impulse to contribute to the reorganization of Europe—all this kept him strong. In his last years he lived the life of a *grand seigneur*, with a melancholy longing for his long-dead subaltern days. He lunched, went about, and entertained like a great gentleman. Towards the end he realized that a supper—in the times of the general impoverishment, that touched him too— must not cost more than a ten-mark note. He resigned himself to this, but must needs lay an orchid, costing as much again, before the lady who was to share his table. At the end of his days he was the same as at the beginning—witty, amiable, lavish of his intellect and his possessions, irreproachable as a soldier and as a man, trusted by every friend. His word was a rock. He knew what he had accomplished. The last words he wrote, two hours before the death which he knew was near, were eloquent of his anxiety for Germany and Europe. In his last agony he rode once more at the head of marching troops: "Fire, fire . . . !" And then: "Artillery forward!"

That was the end. He died at noon on July 8th, 1927, in Berchtesgaden. On the face of the dead man was Lieutenant Hoffmann's gay and carefree smile.

KARL FRIEDRICH NOVAK.

GENERAL HOFFMANN

January 25th, 1869: born in Hamburg, Hesse-Nassau: son of the County Court Judge, Julius Hoffmann, and his wife, Frederike Charlotte Alwine, descended from the du Buisson family. At his baptism, in the Evangelical Church in Homburg, on February 21st, 1869, he received the names Carl Adolf Maximilian.

From Michaelmas 1879 to Easter 1887 young Max Hoffmann attended the Gymnasium in Nordhausen.

In the spring of 1887, after some delay in passing the leaving examination, Hoffmann entered the 4th Thuringian Infantry Regiment, 72, as a Gentleman Cadet[1] for three years' volunteer service.

From October 1st, 1887, to July 5th, 1888, he studied at the Royal Kriegsschule, in Neisse.

On August 16th, 1888, he received his commission as Second Lieutenant with Imperial "commendation."

From 1895 to 1898 Hoffmann, now a full Lieutenant, studied at the Kriegsakademie, in Berlin.

At the end of 1898 Hoffmann was sent to Russia to study for six months.

From 1899 to 1901 Hoffmann was seconded for service on the "Russian Section" of the Great General Staff.

---

[1] Musketier und Avantageur.

In 1901 he was promoted Captain, and in March of the same year he was finally transferred to the General Staff.

In 1904 and 1905 Captain Hoffmann was attached as military observer to the Headquarters of the 1st Japanese Army in the Russo-Japanese War.

In 1907 promoted Major.

In 1914 Lieutenant-Colonel Hoffmann joined the command of the 8th German Army in the field, as G.S.O.,I.

In 1916 Colonel Hoffmann, who was simultaneously promoted Major-General, was appointed " Chief of the General Staff to the Commander-in-Chief," Prince Leopold of Bavaria.

From 1919 to 1927 General Hoffmann lived in Berlin.

On July 8th, 1927, Major-General Max Hoffmann died at Berchtesgaden.

[The dates in the General's life, so far as they are ascertainable, are confirmed from Hoffmann's papers, and also by information received from his friend and comrade, Major-General Hans Kundt.]

WAR DIARIES, 1914-1919

The notes to these Diaries, so far as military affairs are concerned, have been contributed by Lieutenant-Colonel Alfred Niemann.

We have a hard task before us, harder, almost, than any in history. However, I am content, for I confidently hope that we shall be able to deal with it. The Commander-in-Chief is Prittwitz, the Chief of Staff, Count Waldersee, and I am G.S.O.,Ia.[1]

Our first idea, at any rate, comes from me. If it comes off, Prittwitz will be a great Commander, if it does not, we shall get into trouble. The responsibility is gigantic, and is more of a strain on the nerves than I suspected. If it is ever known later with how few men we have to hold the Eastern Front, it will be called the greatest piece of impudence in history. I am in complete agreement with the Quartermaster-General, General Grünert: he and I hold together, and until now we have forced our stronger wills on the Chief. Waldersee is rather weak—I hope he will not let us down at the last moment.[2]

[1] The High Command of the 8th Army was formed in Posen. Hoffmann was attached to it as First General Staff Officer—G.S.O.,Ia —whose specific duties consist in the working out of operations.
[2] In *The War of Lost Opportunities* he writes regarding the position at the beginning of the war: " The first considerations that occupied the attention of the Chief of the General Staff and myself regarding the task that awaited us were as follows. The great Russian cavalry raids which had been so much talked about gave us no anxiety: troops on the frontier would deal with them: on the contrary it was desirable that the Russians should, in fact, make such raids, and meet with a failure at the outset. For the rest, we had first of all to reckon with the advance of the armies based on Warsaw and Vilna, the existence of which was already known to us. . . .
" On entering German territory the Russian advance would be split by the obstacle of the Masurian Lakes. The Russians could only go forward with one army to the north and the other to the south of this chain of lakes. Our army had therefore to be prepared to attack one of these two Russian armies, while they were disunited by the Masurian Lakes, and defeat it. Which of the two would offer us the best opportunity could not immediately be foreseen. It might, however, be assumed that the Vilna Army would appear somewhat sooner on the scene than the

The successes in the West are magnificent, and promise well for the future. The capture of Liège was especially important. It had been long prepared for and the place had been thoroughly reconnoitred, so that it was very depressing to learn that the first attack had failed. We were weeks behindhand in the entire campaign,[1] and as everything depends on a speedy victory in the West, our joy over the success was doubly great. I do not doubt that things will go well and that this will soon lead to greater events in the West. The decision will of course be reached there, and, as a result, laurels grow more freely there than here. Still I must not be disappointed. Here we are thrown on our own resources and are independent.

BARTENSTEIN, *August* 21, 1914.

Yesterday was certainly the hardest in all my military experience [2]—retreat before the Russians.

one from Warsaw, which would have to work its way to our frontier through a wooded and boggy area, rather deficient in roads. . . .

" The mobilization and advance of our army was accomplished exactly as had been foreseen. The Army Staff moved to Marienburg on August 8th, and from that day took over the command. . . .

" Up to August 14th it was ascertained from the information available that the enemy was advancing with strong forces to the north and south of the Rominten Forest. . . . The Army Command concluded that, as had been already surmised, the Vilna Army had pushed somewhat more forward than the Warsaw Army, more especially as the airmen's reports still continued to show that the movements of troops could be observed in the roads from the south. The High Command decided to prepare the main body of the army for the attack on the Vilna Army."

In *The Truth about Tannenberg* Hoffmann remarks : " The 8th Army Command did not, as is well known, carry out Schlieffen's great plan of campaign—*i.e.* an immediate attack, with all forces, on the Vilna Army, and then, by a swing to the south-west, an attack on the right flank of the Warsaw Army. The XX. A.C. and the 70th Landwehr Brigade were left on the Southern Front. A suggestion of the Quartermaster-General, General Grünert, that the Landwehr Brigade at least should not be sent up north, met with no response from the Chief of the General Staff, General Count Waldersee.

[1] This refers to the fact that the movement of political events had given the Russians a considerable start in their war preparations for which the existing plans for the German advance had not provided.

[2] On August 20th the battle against the Vilna Army was opened at Gumbinnen. The battle progressed favourably throughout. Both wings

Strong forces are advancing from the Narev against our rear and threaten to cut us off from the Vistula. We are to break off the battle so successfully begun, and go back. It is shameful—poor East Prussia! I was against it, but I could not get my way. Grünert and I still saw a hope of victory—a slight one, as one of the Generals Commanding and his Corps had completely broken down—but it was there, and I would have seized it. So we must resign ourselves to defeat, although the I. Corps again made thousands of prisoners, captured many guns, and threw back the Russians.

The 33rd have fired on our own men, the Colonel having been treacherously shot by someone.[1] I am so terribly sad. It is true that our task was very difficult, and could hardly be undertaken with so few troops, but up till yesterday, middle day, I believed we should win a great victory.

MÜHLHAUSEN, EAST PRUSSIA,
August 22, 1914.

Our attack on the Russians at Gumbinnen was more successful than I thought. It is a pity that we could not carry it right through. I was almost convinced that the whole Russian Army could be destroyed. Our 1st Cavalry Division was magnificent.

---

were victorious. Only in the centre, where the XVII. A.C. was posted, was there anything in the nature of a retreat, and there only in so far as an attack with insufficient artillery support against the previously prepared Russian position had to be broken off owing to heavy losses.

In the afternoon the XX. A.C. announced that the Warsaw Army had reached the frontier on the line Chorzele—Friedrichshof, and that its total strength was estimated at 2-2$\frac{1}{2}$ Army Corps and 2 Light Infantry Brigades. General von Prittwitz then decided to break off the battle and withdraw the 8th Army behind the Vistula. Hoffmann and General Grünert urged without success that the battle should be fought out on August 21st.

[1] The 33rd Infantry Regiment, in the battle of Gumbinnen on the morning of the 20th, stormed the Russian positions on the heights of Ederkehmen from the north and west. In the process, the Colonel commanding the regiment was killed. As the attack was carried out from two sides there was probably a moment when German troops were firing at each other.

It made a series of attacks on the infantry (500 prisoners) and then routed both Russian Guard Cavalry Divisions.

MARIENBURG, *August 23*, 1914.

Great changes in the staff here. G.H.Q. are very indignant that we did not do what Grünert and I had proposed. Prittwitz and Count Waldersee are consequently superseded. The new Commander-in-Chief is General von Hindenburg, formerly in command of the IV. A.C., the new Chief of Staff is Ludendorff, who appeared to-day in all the glory of his honestly earned " Pour le Mérite " ribbon. When General von Wussow fell, he led the latter's storm-column against Liège, and was the only one who held his ground there, so he was really mainly responsible for taking the city.

There has never been such a war as this, and never will be again—waged with such bestial fury. The Russians are burning everything down.

OSTERODE, *August 30*, 1914.

Victory at Tannenberg — a fine revenge for Gumbinnen. To-day I thought would be a day of rest, but there is always something else to do. We have not been able to destroy quite the entire horde, and the rest are advancing on us.[1] Otherwise results are excellent — at least 20,000 prisoners,

---

[1] On the 30th, when the bottling up of the Warsaw Army was already nearly complete, an air report came in that the reinforced I. Russian Army Corps was marching from Mlava to Neidenburg, and, at the time the message was sent, had already reached a point 8 kilometres from Neidenburg.

The High Command ordered all available troops to march on Neidenburg to meet this menace. But this assistance could only become effective on August 31st. The crisis was overcome by the General-in-Command of the I. Corps, General v. François. He threw such troops as he could get together into the direct line of the enemy advance, without interrupting the encircling process to the north, and detached Mühlmann's force to attack the flank of the Russian column. By this means the Russian thrust was successfully averted.

including one Corps Commander, many colours, guns, etc. I could not write, I was busy day and night. Since the beginning of the campaign I have not yet had two successive hours of undisturbed sleep. I am always being consulted and called in. It is complimentary but exhausting. Otherwise I am in excellent form, except that I should like to get a good sleep. Drove yesterday afternoon over the battlefield—all the villages shot to pieces and burnt down, forests on fire, and chaos everywhere. The population are splendid—brave and cheerful.

OSTERODE, *August* 31, 1914.

The battle was a huge success—greater than we could have supposed. 4-5 Russian Corps destroyed, 50,000-60,000 prisoners, including two Corps Commanders, who have already been brought in here. One entire Russian army is disposed of: now for the other.

AKENSTEIN, *September* 4, 1914.

We have only gradually been able to realize how great was our success at Tannenberg. 92,000 prisoners have now been sent back—it is one of the greatest victories in history, and won by an inferior force. It is true that we had an ally that I can only talk about after it is all over—we knew all the enemy's plans.[1]

Now we are preparing for something new.[2] Ludendorff is a first-class fellow to work with. He is the right man for this business—ruthless and hard. We get on admirably, and I am proud that some of my ideas have been considered for his new plan of operations.

[1] The Russian wireless was picked up by the German stations, and was successfully deciphered.

[2] Even during the battle of Tannenberg preparations were in hand for a change of front against the Vilna Army.

I hope all will go as well as the other affair; the plans are all settled and in 10 or 12 days I hope we shall have another glorious time behind us.

ROSSEL, *September* 9, 1914.

I have been awarded the Iron Cross for my modest share in the battle of Tannenberg. I had never thought that this finest of all military decorations could be won by sitting at the end of a telephone line. However, I realize now that there must be someone there who keeps his nerve, and by brute determination and the will to victory overcomes difficulties, panics and suchlike nonsense.

INSTERBURG, *September* 15, 1914.

Our second great battle — called after the Masurian Lakes—is at an end.[1] Results are not yet fully ascertainable, but I should estimate about 35,000 prisoners, 180 guns. The Russians lost a great many killed. . . . It was a very fine piece of work, and we are ready for what may come next.

The Austrians are doing badly; they have asked for definite assistance, and we are going with a large part of our army to Silesia to help them: we are probably going to Oppeln in about six days.[2]

Well, well; until now, with our inferior numbers,

[1] During the days September 9th-14th the Vilna Army was defeated on the Masurian Lakes. There was no encirclement as at Tannenberg. Rennenkampf extricated himself, but was able to withdraw only the remnants of his army into the forest country to the west of the Niemen, on the line Olita—Kovno—Vileny.

[2] The offensive of the Austro-Hungarian Army in Galicia had completely broken down. The army had to retreat across the San to the farther bank of the Visloka, fighting a number of costly rearguard actions. To the support of our ally, 4 Army Corps and 1 Cavalry Division of the 8th Army were transferred to Upper Silesia, there to form the 9th Army with Woyrsch's Landwehr Corps.

On September 17th General von Hindenburg was given the command of the 9th Army, but at the same time he retained his command over the troops remaining in East Prussia, who, as the 8th Army, were placed under the orders of General v. Schubert.

we have defeated about 15 Russian Army Corps and 8 Cavalry Divisions, and we are not finished yet. " Now for it once again."

BEUTHEN, *September 23, 1914.*

Yesterday was our first row with the Austrians—they aren't out for business as we are. After some forcible explanations on our part they are ready for anything to-day. I am terribly on the stretch to see how the operation will work out. I think it will be all right.

BEUTHEN, *September 26, 1914.*

It looks bad for the Austrians: they have saved money over their army for twenty years, and now they are paying for it.

MIECHOFF, *September 29, 1914.*

In the earlier operations the object was clear—first, the Niemen Army, and then the Narev Army. But on this occasion nothing is clear.[1] We are on the point of a brilliant success: from the moment of our advance the Russian Army ceased to press the Austrians and is now in retreat behind the Vistula. The direction our attack will take cannot not yet be foreseen, and depends entirely on the news we get.

KIELCE, *October 2, 1914.*

We shall stay a few days here—how long depends on whether we are victorious or not. I do not believe we shall fail, but we might. In the

---

[1] On September 26th the 9th Army, accompanied on its right wing by the weak divisions of the Imperial and Royal Army, began a surprise advance against the Vistula, and found only slight enemy resistance; but the roads were almost impassable, and with great efforts they reached the Vistula between Josefov and Ivangorod.

The immediate strategic success was that the Russians hastily demolished their front on the Visloka, and raised the siege of the fortress of Przemysl. The Austro-Hungarian Army was able to march to the San without finding any noteworthy resistance.

first place we must reckon with the Austrians, and we have also left our best Corps and leaders in East Prussia.

I anticipate, however, that all will go well. It may develop into a very pretty piece of work, but there are various drawbacks. If all goes well we shall have thrown the fellows back on to the Vistula; but if it does not come off, then we must take to the defensive. We have already won a great success in so far as the Russians have ceased to press the Austrians and have retired. This, from both a military and political point of view, is a great thing. But in the last resort we can only get some air here in the East if we win a victory, in the sense in which we understand that word.

KIELCE, *October* 6, 1914.

No victory here, unfortunately. The Russians bolted behind the Vistula as we came up. Only about 3000 prisoners, etc. However, the strategic success is enormous, as the whole Russian Army on the Austrian front is in retreat.

KIELCE, *October* 6, 1914.

Our victories continue to grow smaller. The Russians are in such terror of coming to close quarters with us that they stopped the crossing of the Vistula, which they had just begun, and retired behind that river, so that we have been able to capture only comparatively few of them. Tangible result—only 3000-4000 prisoners, 15-20 guns and a large number of machine guns. On the other hand the strategic success is enormous. The Austrians are advancing at our side,[1] and the

---

[1] The Austro-Hungarian Army was to cross the San and attack the left flank of the Russian Vistula front. The attacking power of the Imperial and Royal Army proved so weak, however, that they did not succeed in forcing the crossing of the San.

Russian main army, which had forced its way deep into Galicia, is in full retreat. They had collected 9 Army Corps, with which they intended to fall upon us, but we were too quick for them, and by the 5th we were on the line of the Vistula, so that they had to fight to cross it. It is really marvellous how our men marched.

KIELCE, *October* 8, 1914.

Here everything is in excellent order, except for the Austrians! If only the brutes would move! They are letting the success we have given them slip through their fingers.

We are on the line of the Vistula and have the Russians opposite us on our entire front. A direct attack is impossible—the river is too wide (800 metres). The casual fighting has up till now brought us 4800 prisoners and 16-20 guns.

We are planning a very daring coup: let us hope it succeeds; otherwise we must wait.[1]

RADOM, *October* 12, 1914.

The Russians have launched four armies against us, so they mean business. By tremendous marches, taking risks that will go down to history, we got here before them, drove back their advance-guard and are now opposing their crossing of the Vistula.

[1] The Russians duly shifted their centre of gravity towards the north. General von Hindenburg had therefore to extend his front, by lateral and turning movements, northwards to Kalvarija. The XVII. A.C., reinforced by 4 Divisions, he sent against the Russian salient to the south of Warsaw. On October 12th, after victorious fighting, the Corps stood firmly established south of Warsaw, where it successfully repelled the Russian counter-attacks. In order to release further units for the support of the XVII. A.C. the front of the Austrian Army was extended to Ivangorod. The XVII. A.C. was withdrawn to a position between Rava and Lovicz, where it made connection with the lately brought-up Landwehr Corps under Woyrsch. South of the Pilica an attacking force, composed of the XX., XXI. and the Guard Reserve Corps, was to fall on the Russian flank when they moved against the XVII. Corps. At the decisive moment, on October 27th, the Austrian Army gave way. The position on the Vistula became consequently untenable.

Heavy fighting the last three days, many attempts to force a passage on a large scale—weak as we are. It was indeed the hardest time of the campaign in my experience: the strain goes on day and night—endless panics and alarms. And to-day a false report from an airman nearly destroyed us. Ludendorff and I stand by and support each other, and the Chief says: " God be with us, I can do no more! " I hope we may be out of the wood by to-morrow. One Corps is still heavily engaged and we cannot support it until to-morrow. If it has to retreat it will not be a very serious misfortune; we shall just have to straighten things out again. Then we shall stand on the Vistula and wait until the Austrians at last do something. Of course they attend to their own affairs first of all. The Russians have had to give up the siege of Przemysl—one of our successes.

RADOM, *October* 18, 1914.

Here we are in the midst of heavy fighting, and more to come: and what will be the end of it, God knows. We have done all that human wills and powers could do. We are not afraid, but it is possible that we may have to withdraw in the face of great superiority. We cannot place the smallest reliance on the Austrians, otherwise everything would be so simple. At any rate we have achieved much more than could be hoped. It was the best piece of work in our campaign hitherto. The Russian plan is upset, but 15 Army Corps against 6 is a little too much. I still count on victory; Ludendorff does so no longer. Nothing can go wrong. If we have to retreat, the Russians can follow us only for three days—after that they will be short of food. I have meantime had the Russian railways this side of the Vistula converted into roads. Without railways they cannot feed their troops.

RADOM, *October* 21, 1914.

Ludendorff has become frightfully nervous, and the chief burden lies on me. The main Russian forces are opposite us. I had hoped that perhaps we could still take Warsaw by an energetic thrust before the Russians got here, but, in spite of some incredible marches, we were too late. As, therefore, the Russians threatened to encircle us from the north, we have withdrawn our troops from before Warsaw. Our men carried out the retreat last night so admirably that the Russians did not notice it at all, but bombarded our deserted positions for hours yesterday morning with concentrated heavy artillery fire. On the right our faithful allies, the Austrians, moved up yesterday to reinforce us. To-morrow they are to attack. . . .

I should have thought it better to settle first either with France or Russia. If we had been given only 2 or 3 more Corps here I could have guaranteed a decision. As it is, we have to struggle on against this great superiority in numbers. If all our hopes fail, and we have to retreat, we have destroyed the entire railway and bridge system of the kingdom of Poland so completely that it will be weeks before the Russians can get forward. . . .

I am full of admirable schemes. There is already a shortage of food and coal in Warsaw—so we were informed by the men of a Russian company who shot their captain the day before yesterday and came over to us.

KONSKIE, *October* 24, 1914.

It seems mysterious to us that progress in the West is not quicker. If they had given us those fresh Corps I intended to have finished up our business here quick enough. They must have made some incredible mistakes. The worst of matters here is that Hindenburg simply cannot understand why we do not win another victory like that in East Prussia.

CZENSTOCHAU, *October* 29, 1914.

We were on the high road to a victory, greater than any until now, when the Austrians in our rear let themselves be defeated. . . . We have no fear of the Russians, even when, as at present, they outnumber us by three to one. Of course we shall not be able to avoid giving up a bit of German territory, so as to be able to strike a blow somewhere.

Apart from everything else I shall thank my Maker when we are out of this God-forsaken country. The roads, the filth and the vermin are beyond all belief. And with it all the land is rich and fertile—vast, picturesque, beautifully situated estates, like Konskie, where we were the last few days.

There will, of course, be tremendous excitement in the district when it is known that we must re-treat. Our attempt on Warsaw achieved great success, in so far as we have so thoroughly destroyed the railways for the Russians that for weeks they will not be able to bring supplies and munitions up to the frontier—but this will not be thought enough. Ludendorff and I get on excellently, in spite of a few differences of opinion, over which he finally gives way. Things go forward in the West, but very slowly. They cannot help us and are more anxious than we are. I had to telephone yesterday to tell them not to worry.

CZENSTOCHAU, *November* 1, 1914.

If only the Austrians had done what we told them! The position is now very serious, and we do not yet know how we can hold on. In any case we shall not stay here much longer. I fancy that we—*i.e.* Hindenburg, Ludendorff and I, with a small Staff—shall move to one of the frontier fortresses to reorganize the defence of the East. The idea is in this way to form a sort of small General Headquarters for the East. We get no troops from the West, and must depend on our own resources. Of course we cannot prevent the Russians crossing the frontier. We must send for certain sections of the 8th Army and see what we can do. In all, there are about 20 Russian Army Corps in movement against us from the line Ivangorod—Warsaw. We have beaten all the Russians we have met in open fighting, but we are being outflanked on our right and left . . . the ground was unfavourable.

Ludendorff was in Berlin the day before yesterday, to confer with Falkenhayn and Grünert.[1]

POSEN, *November* 11, 1914.

. . . However, our movements have hitherto been smoothly carried out, and I hope to be able to announce a great success in a few days.

[1] The retreat had been successful. On the line Czenstochau—Sieradz the 9th Army found safety and a breathing space. It was covered by Cavalry Divisions north of Sieradz and on the left was in touch with Landsturm formations on the line Kalisch—Warsaw—Thorn. Behind the cavalry was collected a strong attacking force based on Hohensalza and Thorn, for a proposed thrust in the direction Lodz—Lovicz, and an attack on the Grand Duke Nicolas' exposed left wing. General Ludendorff's attempts to get reinforcements from the West for these operations had been unsuccessful. G.H.Q. merely placed 2 Cavalry Divisions at his disposal. This important re-grouping had therefore to be carried out with the forces of the 8th and 9th Armies. The 9th Army, in the district north of Czenstochau, was relieved by Böhm-Ermolli's army.

On November 1st, Lieutenant-General von Hindenburg was appointed " Commander-in-Chief, East." His command included not merely the 8th and 9th Armies, but the districts of the I., XX., XVII., II., V. and VI. Army Corps, with all their Staffs, troops and fortresses.

On November 10th the re-grouping was complete, and the 9th Army was ready for attack.

POSEN, *November* 19, 1914.

The great battle, that we have opened, is now in progress. I hope it may be a great success. By all human calculations we must win, but waiting is nervous work.[1]

POSEN, *November* 22, 1914.

Our left wing is defeated. How we can get them out, and put things straight again, I don't yet know—but perhaps something will occur to me. We are on a razor-edge. It might have been a great victory, but the troops failed us; the poor fellows could do no more: their officers are dead and the enemy were too many for them. We have completely defeated 3-4 Corps in the last week— we have brought in about 50,000 prisoners; but now our strength is at an end. There is no ground for anxiety; the German frontier will hold. In particular, West Prussia need have no fear. We are standing firm on three fronts near Warsaw—but we have too few men. My nerves were worn out. Five nights' suspense is too much — one cannot keep it up. Now I feel steady as a rock and can look misfortune in the face.

I am only afraid that the Austrians are done for. I have made it clear to Ludendorff that he must go to see the Emperor at Mezières the day after to-morrow at the latest. We must know why, and for what objective, we are fighting. I can carry on

[1] On November 17th, after victorious fighting, the 9th Army stood before Lodz, and had already pushed forward a Corps through Brzeziny to the south. A force in echelon on the left wing covered the operation against counter-attacks by the Russians from the direction of Novo-georgievsk. Powerful attacks by the Russians from Skiernievicze produced a critical situation for the 9th Army on November 24th and 25th: it was successfully dealt with, but involved an important gain'in time for the Russians. The reinforcements now sent by G.H.Q. came in driblets and too late, so that the Russians succeeded in closing the gap between the Vistula and Lodz, withdrawing themselves from our encircling movement, and forming a closed front farther back.

for a long time, but in that case there must be a guarantee that there will be a victory in the West. Otherwise they had better give it up and bring the army over here.

POSEN, *December* 1, 1914.

The situation has worked out, from the military point of view, better than I could have dared to hope; especially after the idiotic way in which the 9th Army behaved. Morgen, especially, is splendid —his Corps made 36,000 prisoners in the last fortnight alone. So we hope to win a definite victory in the battle of Lodz. However, we cannot end the campaign here as I had at first thought. We should need some help for that. We have impressed on every section of the line engaged that they must do their utmost, but they can do no more. I am horrified at the way the war is being carried on in the West. Falkenhayn is the evil genius of our Fatherland, and, unfortunately, he has the Kaiser in his pocket. Now we must depend on ourselves.

INSTERBURG, *February* 9, 1915.

All in order here. We are even beating them again. I have only one anxiety, lest the Russians may get away, and we are not attacking hard enough. Up to date there are about 6000 prisoners, 15 guns, etc. I have strong hopes of 50,000. We shall not publish a figure until we get a respectable total. The snow is a nuisance. On our left wing, round Memel, it lies a metre and a half deep, and the attacking columns cannot get forward.[1]

[1] Russian Main Headquarters had planned a great offensive for the spring of 1915, in the north against East and West Prussia, in the south against the passes of the Carpathians.
The Austrian Command wanted to meet this offensive by an attack. For the support of this operation the German Southern Army was formed at Munkacz.
The Commander-in-Chief, East, also decided to anticipate the Russian

March 1, 1915.

The position yesterday was very unpleasant. The Russians had collected, on foot and by rail, about 12 Army Corps, and fell upon our whole line from the south up to this sector. We had to give up Prasznicz again, as a Landwehr Brigade under incompetent leadership gave way at this point. Now we are gradually getting things straight again.[1] If we had completely cleared the Augustovo forest— *i.e.* brought in our many hundred captured guns —then it would all be very simple: we should go back to the railway with our 10th Army and start a new scheme. But we must struggle on for a few days. We cannot leave our booty behind.

LÖTZEN, *March* 3, 1915.

Solf and Metternich here yesterday; to-day we sent them both, with Sven Hedin, who is also here, up to the front line. Mumm is coming to-day. The

offensive by an attack in East Prussia, and for this purpose asked for a reinforcement of 4 Corps lately formed in Germany. Three of these Corps were to constitute the 10th Army, and take up a position on the left wing of the 8th Army immediately south of the Memel, in order to outflank the exposed Russian northern wing. The IV. Corps, reinforced by an Infantry Division of the 8th Army, was to move forward south of the Masurian Lakes, crumple up the weak left wing of the Russian Army, and so effect a double outflanking of the Russian Army.

On February 7th the southern group advanced to attack Johannisburg and the Pissa sector: the 10th Army advanced one day later.

The ensuing battle, which was called the " Winter Battle in Masuren," led to the destruction of the 10th Russian Army, whose southern wing was encircled in the Augustovo forest. Strong counter-attacks of the Russians from Ostrolenka, Novgorod and Lomza continued through the whole of March.

[1] From the middle of February onwards, the Russians began to make another push in the direction of Mlava. General v. Gallwitz, who had been ordered to the southern front of East Prussia, decided to anticipate the Russian attack, and for this purpose was reinforced by divisions taken from the 9th Army front. The push that began on February 22nd led to the recovery of Prasznicz. But the enemy counter-attacked. The divisions had to be withdrawn and, in the face of savage Russian attacks, took refuge southwards behind the frontier position then being constructed. A further German push on March 8th came to a standstill on March 12th to the north of Prasznicz. Here, also, the fighting lasted until the end of March.

Imperial Chancellor is announced—we are having quite a gay time, in fact.

March 6, 1915.

I have just read Kapp's[1] article—it is a delightfully extravagant piece of work—anyone who thinks differently and is not prepared to hand the universe over to the victorious German people is no better than a scoundrel. With the railway system of to-day and modern facilities it is much easier for us than for Napoleon to march to Moscow, etc.

The man is quite right, but he proceeds from a false assumption. We have not yet won the victory and have no prospect of completely defeating all our enemies. In the West we are standing on the defensive, and without 8-10 additional new Army Corps have no chance of attacking anywhere with success. In the Eastern theatre of war we have, by our great victories, gradually reduced the enormous Russian superiority in numbers. We cannot utterly destroy the Russian Army—we could do that only if we were at war with Russia alone. In addition to this the Austrians are defeated. Galicia is hopelessly lost to them, and Przemysl will certainly fall by the end of the month, without any Russian attack—starved out.

I believe we can't be defeated, but equally that we can't so destroy our enemies as to be able to dictate conditions to them: I have said this to the Imperial Chancellor. We are *beati possidentes*; in other words, all our armies are standing on enemy territory. It is, accordingly, for us to ask them what they really want. I have spoken openly against an annexation of Belgium and Antwerp. Liège, perhaps. Antwerp would be an apple of discord

---

[1] *Generallandschaftsdirektor* Dr Kapp stood for an energetic war policy. Later on he made a sharp attack on the Imperial Chancellor, von Bethmann-Hollweg.

for a hundred years, and the additional population would be disagreeable, undisciplined and ultra-montane. Colonies are a different matter: we must have the Congo, etc. Here, too, in Russia I am against any considerable extension of territory. About the Baltic Provinces there can be no question—we have never conquered them and never can. Moreover, their population is not German and will have none of us—Balts, Finns, etc. Of the other Russian frontier provinces, with the exception of a few strips, I would take nothing: we have enough with Poland. That is my view. For the rest I find the Chancellor, with whom I had two long conversations, very reasonable. He takes some time to make up his mind, but he does not do so lightly. . . . Kapp is living in Utopia, and for that reason can only do harm. Someone must have a quiet talk to him.

LÖTZEN, *March* 9, 1915.

Really, the whole of Berlin seems to have gone mad. We are winning the greatest victory known to history, and three days later they all behave as if we had been defeated, because the pursuit comes to a stop after 200 kilometres. We stood, and part of the army still stands, before a strongly fortified Russian line. As we do not want to attack it we are retiring at certain points, to induce the Russians to come out . . . so that we may again attack them in the open. Our whole army stands on Russian soil. It is true that there was hard fighting at certain points, but all fighting is hard.

March 13, 1915.

We had prepared a nice little trap for the Russians to the north of the Augustovo forest, but they did not quite fall into it. They had so solemnly an-

nounced that they would chase us out of Grodno
that I counted on at least 20,000 prisoners. But
there were only 5000. As soon as they noticed we
were attacking them to the north of the forest they
ran like rabbits.[1] The bitter cold was bad for us
and caused us almost more losses than the enemy.
We are now waiting to see whether our Russian
friends will attack again. We have driven them
back through Prasznicz to the south, and are so
strong everywhere that we are ready for any
eventuality.

From the political point of view as well the position is not unfavourable. It is true that the Italians
are blackguards, but they would be stupid not to
make capital out of our embarrassments. Why on
earth was our policy so idiotic as not to force Italy
into the war on our side? Why did we declare war
on Italy instead of allowing her to declare it on us?
It was only that which gave them their *casus fœderis*.
The attack on the Dardanelles is, I think, all in
our favour, politically.[2] They are now quarrelling
over Constantinople, and the Balkan states are all
in a state of irritation. They none of them want
either England or Russia at the Dardanelles.

HEADQUARTERS, *April* 3, 1915.

When I have nothing to do I usually walk round
my little room and try to think how we can give
another twist to the military situation, but nothing
occurs to me. We are stuck fast on the whole Front.
Perhaps, now that our wire entanglements are

---

[1] The 10th Army had withdrawn its left wing to the Seiny area, so as
to be able to make another attack in case the Russians followed them up.
It was hoped to repeat the manœuvre of the winter battle. But the
Russians shirked the blow.

[2] On March 18th the combined Anglo-French Mediterranean fleet
attacked the Dardanelles. The attack failed. It was then decided to
make a landing operation on the Gallipoli peninsula. The first attack
at this point took place on April 25th.

electrified, we could release some troops at certain points and move them up to our flank, so as to make a further push, in case the enemy gives us a chance—but we have not the strength for an operation of any importance. I am convinced that we shall be able to prevent the Russians ever invading Germany; but that is all we can promise, unless we are given a new army. There is no prospect of that, though I do not see why they need so many new Divisions in the West. I trust they are not going to start another Ypres.

Kluck really has—and has had all his life—marvellous luck. Now he has actually been wounded.

From the military point of view our position is undoubtedly good, in so far as all our armies stand on enemy soil and we have obtained control over valuable properties, such as railways and coal-mines. But we are nowhere victorious, in the proper meaning of that word. Neither in the East nor in the West have we brought down the enemy: on the contrary, both the French and the Russians live in the certain hope of victory—thanks to the utterly mendacious news that reaches the armies. For instance, a short time ago Prince Hohenlohe received a letter from a Russian princess, in which she said how ridiculous it was of the Germans to publish these figures of prisoners taken—not a word of it was true—there had never been a Tannenberg nor any defeat of the 10th Army. Still, all our enemies at the Front have gradually been penetrated by the conviction that it will none the less not be so simple to bring us down by force of arms, but they all rely on England's guarantee that Germany will be starved out. Every day Russian airmen throw down proclamations on us: "Surrender, lay down your arms, your wives and children are starving!" In addition to this the Russians regard themselves as having beaten the Austrians, as, indeed, they have. We have again sent three Divisions to the Carpathians, and there is some hope that the line will hold—but no more. It is well known that there is deep depression in Austria.

We have constructed strong positions everywhere, which will enable us — with the Divisions (more than 7) lent to the Austrians and a few reinforcements from the West—to remain on the defensive and hold on.

A second question arises: was this stagnation on both fronts inevitable? This may be flatly denied; and the plain truth is that the responsibility is due to the failure of G.H.Q. The utter breakdown of every sort of initiative on the Marne was incredible, but this was only one of the many blunders. After the retreat it should have been possible to concentrate forces for a unified effort and get hold of the coast—the Belgians should not have been allowed to slip through our fingers after the capture of Antwerp, and we should never have committed the crime of those isolated, senseless attacks on Ypres. History will deliver judgment on us later.

Now, however, there is only one possibility of victory. The centre of gravity of the war must be shifted to the East. We begged and prayed that this might be done in November. We were treated like troublesome poor relations, and then got the bare minimum of help we needed in driblets and not as a whole.

The blunder lay in not allowing Headquarters to remain in Berlin, where it still ought to be—and for that reason France continues quite undeservedly to be regarded as the main seat of war, and the East as secondary. It was perfectly understandable that at the outset, before the Russian hordes got under way (especially before the Siberian troops

could arrive), we should have tried to defeat France
and possibly the English Expeditionary Force. But
after that both sides became of equal importance:
and they are still not considered so.

How can this war be brought to an end? The
simplest way would be to come to an understanding
with one of the parties. The most obvious would
be France, as I always said before the war: in
alliance with France we could rule the world. But
it is impossible. In France there is an epidemic of
utter madness. Moreover, Poincaré and Co. have
established nothing more nor less than a reign of
terror, and the voice of reason is not allowed a
hearing. They will be sorry for it later, but at the
moment the slightest overture on our part would be
published with scorn in Paris as a sign of complete
collapse.

Russia: with whom can we negotiate? The Tsar
might be willing, but Nicolas would simply have
him murdered. There is a disposition to peace in
Petersburg, but Nicolas has a marvellously energetic grip of the situation. For example, I am
quite convinced that the arrests for espionage in
Petersburg are no more than an intrigue against
the friends of peace. Besides, what could we offer
Russia? Galicia and Constantinople? But that
would mean beginning to betray our allies.

Last of all, England: the English hate us and
would like to destroy us, but they are gradually
realizing that this is not so easy. It is interesting to
follow the English newspapers. For some months
now there has been no more talk about the Kaiser
being arrested and taken to St Helena, nor is it
suggested that we are to scrape an existence as
charcoal burners and wretched peasants and fisher-
men. On the contrary, our newspapers are more
venomous than the English ones—and rightly, I

may add. Sir Edward Grey—God damn him!—
has recently stated under what conditions peace
can be obtained from him; the main point is the
restoration of Belgium, for England cannot allow
a German Antwerp—against that she must fight
to her last penny. Personally, I have no use for a
German Belgium; we do not want an increase of
Social Democratic and ultramontane agitators. We
cannot defeat England—at least, not yet. I shall
live to see it, but not in this war. Therefore, in
my opinion, we ought to try to make terms with
England. She will negotiate—she is hard hit at
many points: heavy losses, especially of officers,
domestic troubles (the effects of our U-boats have,
incidentally, been much over-estimated), Egypt,
the Sudan, India, the Dardanelles, and especially
Japan! We could make the following conditions:
the return of our Colonies, together with a few additional ones, the Congo in particular, a few Colonies
from France, and 25 milliards in money. Until the
payment of this sum we should occupy the mining
area of French Lorraine; from Russia a few slices of
frontier territory, and favourable terms for Austria.

England would then retain Calais and Boulogne,
and would have, of course, to keep in close relations
with us in order to protect herself against her
former Allies.

I should regard this as a possible basis for negotiations. It is, of course, possible that I am mistaken.
We may have a piece of luck, such as Turkish
successes against Egypt, or a revolt in India, or else
an earthquake, that may improve our situation.
It may, on the other hand, deteriorate, owing to
Italy, Rumania, the total collapse of Austria, or
something else.

The Field-Marshal wrote to the Chancellor a few
days ago more or less on these lines.

LÖTZEN, *May* 30, 1915.

H.M. is entirely under Falkenhayn's influence and does not love us. The military situation is such that we are gradually reaching a dead end. Of course we are intentionally rather thrust into the background. I already knew that a great many people did not like me. So long as I can remember only half my acquaintances have liked me. The less gifted have no use for me at all. However, I remain unmoved—I must bear it with resignation.

June 16, 1915.

In the military sense there is nothing fresh here. G.H.Q. goes on stripping us, so that we are glad if we can hold on and stick to what we have. Whether it is all necessary of course I cannot judge, but there is certainly some dirty work about it.[1]

---

[1] The position on the Austro-Hungarian Front had taken a very unfavourable turn. The advance to the relief of Przemysl had come to a standstill, and the Russian attacks on the Carpathians were being only feebly repulsed. In order to relieve the pressure on their allies German G.H.Q. decided to attack the Russian Front between the Carpathians and the Vistula and break through.

On May 2nd, General v. Mackensen, with the German 11th and the Austrian 4th Armies, took the Russian positions in the Gorlice-Tarnov sector, and by May 15th had already reached the San.

The Russians withdrew troops from all along their line opposite the Commander-in-Chief, East, to support their tottering left wing.

There were grave differences of opinion on the question as to how the C.-in-C., East, could best support General Mackensen's offensive, which was increasing to ever greater dimensions.

Hoffmann himself writes on the subject in *The War of Lost Opportunities*:

" I held the view that it was essential to bring into action on the left wing of the 10th Army all available forces from the area under the command of the C.-in-C., East, as well as all the troops that could be obtained from G.H.Q.: Kovno should be taken by a sudden attack, and the offensive movement driven through Vilna into the rear of the main Russian force. . . .

" Major v. Bockelberg, the G.S.O.,Ia, of our Staff, who as a result of many years' collaboration with General Ludendorff in the second section of the Great General Staff enjoyed his especial confidence, pleaded for an offensive across the Bobr to both sides of Osoviec. We had a pretty lively difference of opinion. I considered that an offensive across the swampy lowlands of the Bobr, where we should be quite unable to support our infantry attack with the mass of our artillery, was wrong, and that such an attempt would be doomed to failure from the very beginning.

LÖTZEN, *June* 18, 1915.

We sit here waiting to see whether G.H.Q. will also take from us the last 2 Divisions, that we have scraped together out of our entire Front, so as to be able to take the offensive again. If they need them in Galicia too we shall have to remain simply on the defensive: whether this is necessary, of course we are not in a position to judge. For the rest the position on the whole Eastern Front is good, and in Mackensen's command, excellent. Heavy fighting in the West; they cannot break through, but the losses are serious.

LÖTZEN, *June* 20, 1915.

Nothing new here. We have not men enough for any important undertaking, and G.H.Q. do not seem inclined to give us any. Whether they cannot, or whether they want to avoid the mischance of our again bringing ourselves to the notice of our worthy fellow-citizens at home by an important victory, I am not, of course, in a position to judge. They are, rightly, sending every available man to the Galician Front, but I am curious to know what they have in mind after the capture of Lemberg. With two Corps we could win another splendid victory.

His chief objection to my plan was that the capture of Kovno would take too much time.

" General Ludendorff decided for my view. . . .

" The preparations for the advance on Kovno and beyond were begun. The Orders, at least as regards the movement of troops within the area of the C.-in-C. on the Eastern Front, were already drafted when, on July 1st, Field-Marshal von Hindenburg and General Ludendorff were summoned by telegraph to report to H.M. the Kaiser at Posen.

" In the afternoon I received a telephone message to hold everything up: another plan was to be adopted. While in Posen H.M. the Kaiser had approved of General v. Falkenhayn's scheme, by which General v. Gallwitz was to break through the line opposite him, and take the offensive against the Narev. By this, in my opinion, the last possibility of carrying out a destructive operation against the Russian Army was lost. However successful the Gallwitz scheme might be, it could only result in the Russians having to leave Warsaw, and give up their salient positions in Poland."

June 29, 1915.

I am rather in a hurry, as I have to get off a longish telegram to Pless, giving our view of the progress of the campaign. It is rather a difficult business, as my opinion differs from that of Ludendorff and Bockelberg. I can do no more than state my own.

June 30, 1915.

Yesterday evening and early this morning I had to fight for my own ideas. Then the four Army Commanders had a meeting here; all agreed with me. Ludendorff now convinced. But G.H.Q. are trying to interfere. We are too weak to do what they want.

July 2, 1915.

Bockelberg, who went off with the Chief, has just telephoned what we are to do—of course not what we wanted. I am sorry; I thought our idea was better and more practicable. Well, well, so it must be; at least they are not taking any troops away from us. I had got so pleased over the other scheme, it would have been such a pretty bit of work. The Chief is coming back at eleven o'clock this evening; he will be furious.

Lötzen, *July* 5, 1915.

This evening I was able to make a hurried visit to Tilsit to dine with the Army Commander, General von Below. I regard him as one of the ablest and shrewdest of our commanders. In the evening we sat talking until twelve o'clock, both of us cursing G.H.Q. for interfering with our proposal and ordering us to do something which we all—Ludendorff especially — thought impracticable. G.H.Q. did not think our proposal would do. Ludendorff came back from Posen in a savage temper.

July 6, 1915.

Erni Hohenlohe, who has been so long with us here, is leaving this evening; he has been appointed ambassador in Constantinople. Whether Wangenheim is ill, as is reported, or superseded, I do not know. Less importance is attached to Hohenlohe's intellectual ability than to his connection with the King of Rumania (brother-in-law) and his friendship with the Bulgarians owing to the Coburg Regency.

July 7, 1915.

Meantime we are making the necessary troop movements so as to carry out the desired attack according to orders. Personally, I think the place and the objective wrong, but none the less we are taking every possible step to ensure a success. Moreover we, or rather G.H.Q., have had a piece of luck —the Russians are withdrawing considerable forces from our Front and sending them to Galicia.

July 9, 1915.

I'm sick of Headquarters. The fellow is not satisfied unless he can abuse us every day. Probably he hopes that some time he will get us out of patience and put us in the wrong. Well, we must bear this too.

July 10, 1915.

General Tappen, Head of the Operations Sections, arrived to-day in a special train from G.H.Q. to see whether we were carrying out our instructions properly. He gave another reason, but that was really what he came for. Hindenburg's and Ludendorff's fury can be imagined. I endured it with the utmost self-control, and even put forward my views again. So on the whole Eastern Front a great decisive battle will be opened on the 13th, 14th and 15th. I hope we shall have as much success as Linsingen and Mackensen.[1]

July 11, 1915.

To-morrow at noon we are going down to the Southern Front—viz. the Mlava-Prasznicz sector—and on the following day we are attacking at that point and on the day after in Kurland as well. And Mackensen's great attack starts again on the 14th. I hope the whole thing goes well. We have made such preparations as we could, and got together all available artillery and ammunition. I am fairly confident, but now, as before, of the opinion that it would have been better to concentrate on Kurland, and make an overwhelming attack there, capturing Kovno at the same time.

July 15, 1915.

The attack by Gallwitz's Army Group took the Russians completely by surprise, and in our first rush we took the first line, which comprised three fortified positions. Prasznicz, my child of sorrow, is again in our hands. Early yesterday morning we drove along the only traversable road through Mlava, and by 10 A.M. we had reached Prasznicz, which had been entirely destroyed, and abandoned by its inhabitants. Tremendous enthusiasm, of

[1] The 12th Army—the force hitherto under Gallwitz's command—stood ready on July 13th to break through the Russian positions on both sides of Prasznicz. Their forward movement forced the Russian Army Command to order a general retreat from Poland.

In the middle of July the army of the Niemen, on the left wing of the troops under the command of the C.-in-C., East, made a thrust in the direction of Kovno. The Eastern Command renewed its representations to G.H.Q., and requested that all available troops from those under Woyrsch's command, and from the 12th and 8th Armies, might be brought up in support of the 10th Army, so as to make a thrust beyond Kovno against Vilna.

G.H.Q. reinforced the 12th and 8th Armies by a Division each, but rejected the Eastern Command's proposal.

course, on the part of the troops at the sight of Hindenburg. We telegraphed to H.M. as soon as we got there. Good progress on the Niemen Front; and to-morrow, in the south, Mackensen and the newly formed Army of the Bug begin their offensive again.

July 16, 1915.

Gallwitz has broken through a further strongly fortified Russian position, south of Prasznicz, and the Russians are in retreat along the whole Front. Mackensen's advance, if successful, will be his decisive stroke. He is reopening his attack early to-day on the whole Front with a trifle of 40 Divisions: surely that must do the trick.

We are, of course, very much annoyed with G.H.Q. over the question of publicity. In the West every capture of 150 metres of trenches is a victory. Gallwitz has driven the Russians back on a Front of 120 kilometres, taken 12,000 prisoners, 13 guns, some 30 machine guns, and is fobbed off with two lines. Well, well, let us forget it. The main thing is that all goes well. If Mackensen wins a victory in the grand style, and that he cannot fail to do with his resources in troops and heavy artillery, it is to be hoped that Russia may collapse. [Here follows a brief but, at the date of publication, unreproducible criticism of his General-in-Command.—*Note by Editor*.]

LÖTZEN, *July* 18, 1915.

Things have gone well to-day too. The Russians have evacuated the whole position in front of the 9th Army, and have retired to the famous Blonje position before Warsaw. All is going well with Gallwitz, too, and to the north of the Niemen we have now taken more than 30,000 prisoners over the entire Front. This gives us food for thought.

The great question is whether we can succeed in crossing the Narev and getting at Warsaw from behind. And that depends on whether Mackensen is successful, as, in that case, the Russians will need their reinforcements down there, and cannot send them against us. Anyhow, we are in the thick of the greatest battle that history has ever known.

July 19, 1915.

All is in order here. Apparently the Russians are actually playing 1812 all over again, and are retiring along the entire Front. They are burning their own villages by the hundred, removing the inhabitants, etc. It is an appalling piece of lunacy, which will do milliards' worth of damage to the country, and is quite useless from a military point of view.

Gallwitz has reached the fortified positions on the Narev (Pultusk, Rozan, Ostrolenka), and is preparing an attack on them. His total of prisoners has mounted to about 30,000, so that since the 13th we have taken about 40,000.

July 20, 1915.

This time we are out for the big thing. If all goes well, we shall get Warsaw. In recognition of our good behaviour we have actually been promised two more Divisions.

July 22, 1915.

To-day Gallwitz launches his attack against the Narev. As we had anticipated, it moves very slowly, while in the area where we wanted to carry out the operation—in the neighbourhood of Kovno, and north of the Niemen—our attacks with the weak forces at our disposal have, of course, been marvellously successful. Well, we shall get across the Narev, and then Warsaw must fall this time.

July 23, 1915.

All is going well here. The great bridge-head position at Pultusk has just been stormed, and we are making good progress north of the Niemen, where the Russians are in full flight. The question of Warsaw is becoming acute, because to-morrow we are attacking the last position in front of that city.

On the West the position seems, unfortunately, a deadlock. We seem to have got a proper black eye at Arras. I heard to-day that our men would not have stood their ground if the French had attacked—*i.e.* with their infantry—but the French infantry in that part of the line can no longer be induced to attack. So the situation was saved.

H.M. is with Woyrsch to-day. Perhaps he, too, is to become a Field-Marshal. I wonder if he may chance to be a Field-Marshal who really does something himself. I doubt it.

July 24, 1915.

Notable successes yesterday and to-day. The Niemen Army has completely defeated and shattered[1] the Russian 5th Army, and Gallwitz has forced the passage of the Narev in strength. In the Wolff telegram little notice of course is taken of the victory of the Niemen Army in particular, as this was our idea and in conflict with the view of G.H.Q.

Well, we must bear it as well as we can—the main point is that we completely smashed our friends opposite.

[1] In June the Niemen Army had reached the line of the Dubissa at a point south of Schaulen, and the line of the Wenta and the Windau as far as the heights of Hasenpot. At the beginning of July they received the order to envelop and attack the enemy who had established themselves in the neighbourhood of Schaulen.

The Russians were completely taken by surprise and, after heavy fighting, the entire Russian 5th Army was flung back in the direction of Ponjewicz. On July 29th, Ponjewicz, and on August 1st Mitau, were taken.

July 25, 1915.

Of course we could not expect things to go on so smoothly as they have until now. The Russians facing Gallwitz have collected every man they could lay their hands on, and are putting up a desperate defence. It is quite natural, and we foresaw it—every frontal offensive comes to a stand some time and then goes no farther. And, unfortunately, that is what has happened to Mackensen. I hope G.H.Q. has now sense enough to bring an army up from Galicia and put it into the line where we wanted it at the beginning.

On Below's Front (the Niemen Army) we continue to do well. Unfortunately we are not strong enough there for the effect to be felt on the entire Front. I am curious to know how to-day's attack by the 9th Army, aimed direct at Warsaw, has developed.

July 29, 1915.

Not a word of truth in the news from Warsaw. We had tried to break through the Warsaw position, but had to give up the idea : it was too strong and we were too weak. However, Woyrsch has succeeded in crossing the Vistula, north of Ivangorod. For the time being, of course, this has had no great consequences, but it must make the Russians very anxious. The news from Mackensen to-day is also good. I hope I may be disappointed and that he is still advancing victoriously : I was afraid that he might get no farther. So much the better if I am wrong. It does not matter who wins the victories. To-morrow we shall start again also. Gallwitz, as well as Scholtz, had outrun their ammunition owing to the bad roads. To-day it has caught them up, and I hope we shall get forward. We must knock these fellows out while we are about it. The

American note is a piece of impudence, I hope we shall be able to get our revenge for it later on. H.M. may see from the American attitude what sort of thanks he gets for his affability to the Pork King and the Steel Magnates.

July 31, 1915.

Mackensen did very well yesterday, and Woyrsch's crossing of the Vistula is a very pretty piece of work; but it all takes a very long time and costs many lives: nor can we move any quicker here. The position is quite simple: we can get a quicker result only by turning the Russian flank. It is not such a glorious affair as the papers describe it, especially as there are no indications in Warsaw of any preparations for retirement. However, we are moving forward, and that is the main thing. And the situation in the West is quite satisfactory. The last attack on the Loretto heights cost the French so many lives that they cannot rely on their men for another great offensive. Their man-power is giving out. It has been calculated that, by February at the latest, the French will have lost so many men that from that date they will not be able to keep the effective strength of their armies up to the same point as formerly. Joffre has to reckon with this, so everything hangs on the English and the Neutrals. As regards the munitions question in the Dardanelles, opinions differ. Many take a pessimistic view, but there was a recent report that the Turks were much better off for munitions than had been thought.

August 3, 1915.

I might date this " The Eve of the Capture of Warsaw." It really looks as if the Russians intend

to evacuate the place.[1] On Gallwitz's left wing
the situation has improved, now that we have again
replaced one of the Corps Commanders. I have
been exchanging telegrams all the morning with
G.H.Q. It seems to be gradually dawning on them
that we were right after all. It is still not too late.
We cannot, of course, get back the 25,000 killed
and wounded that we lost so needlessly, but if they
give us the necessary heavy artillery, and then
allow us a free hand, we could have Kovno[2] in
10-14 days. In that way we should have a secure
base for our whole left wing, and the possibility of
an offensive against the unsupported Russian left
flank.

August 4, 1915.

The 9th Army is fighting in the Warsaw line of
forts. The Russians are evacuating the town. It is
undoubtedly a great triumph for the Falkenhayn
plan, but it is not a crushing defeat of the Russians.
This could only have been brought about by a
concentrated flank attack — *i.e.* with our 10th
Army. Apparently G.H.Q. are gradually beginning to realize this. At least they are no longer
vetoing the attack on Kovno, which is to begin on
the 8th.

We are still a long way from peace; the Tsar
will not have it. In the first place he is firmly
convinced that we, Germany, attacked him, and,
secondly, he is too honourable to withdraw from
his treaty with France and England. Unless it
comes to a Revolution—and of that there is at
present little prospect—the war will go on.

[1] At the beginning of August the Russians in front of the 9th Army
evacuated the outer works of Warsaw and the town itself. Warsaw was
occupied by the 9th Army on August 5th.
[2] On August 17th General Litzmann crossed the Niemen and took
the eastern forts of the Kovno fortress and Kovno itself. The Russians
began a hurried retreat to Vilna.

It would now be easiest to overthrow France.
All those who know the conditions assure us that
could we break through at one point France would
collapse. But I rather feel that we should first
think of the Balkans. We are now really well off
for munitions; but apart from this the Turks are
not, I fancy, entirely trustworthy. Our people
think that the Dardanelles is so important for us
that when that campaign is over we shall be forced
to clear up the situation in the Balkans—probably
we shall deal with Serbia next. However, all this is
still a long way off.

August 5, 1915.

In consideration of the fact that Warsaw, for
which we have been fighting since last autumn,
fell to-day, G.H.Q. were prepared to give us their
special attention.[1] They cancelled our orders for
the future disposition of the troops of the 9th Army
and placed it under their direct control. Apart
from the (deliberate) choice of the occasion for
such a change, we also considered the proposed
disposition was a blunder. We forced the Field-
Marshal to the point of threatening resignation—
he refused, until Ludendorff threatened to resign.
Such was our day of triumph!

August 6, 1915.

As a result of Hindenburg's threat of course we
had two slimy telegrams from G.H.Q. to the effect
that no one had meant to hurt his feelings, that a
Division from the West would be sent to us, etc.

Falkenhayn is so powerful with H.M. that no
other opinion has any weight. The great victory
that could have been won has not been won, and

---

[1] On August 5th Woyrsch's Force and his 9th Army were removed
from the control of the C.-in-C., East, and, as the Army Group of Prinz
Leopold von Bayern, placed under the direct orders of G.H.Q.

now it cannot be won. The Russians are getting troops together from all parts of their Front and moving them into the line against the Niemen Army. I don't really think that anything can go wrong, but we have not won the great victory that was easily possible. We must wait and see whether we have any further luck over Kovno. The worst of it is that Falkenhayn's frontal operation goes so slowly. And time presses: we must deal with Serbia somehow, so as to bring the Bulgarians to a decision and thus control the Dardanelles—the greatest problem of the war.

August 7, 1915.

All goes well here: the envelopment of Novo-georgievsk is almost completed; Gallwitz has apparently soundly defeated the enemy, and the bombardment and the attack on Kovno are to begin to-morrow. The Niemen Army makes me a little anxious, as the Russians are moving large forces in that direction. If only we had been able to handle the 9th Army as we wished I need not have felt any anxiety, for, in that case, an Army Corps would have been sent off yesterday to the north of Kovno. Well, we must hope for the best.

August 9, 1915.

Generally speaking, all goes well here. Novo-georgievsk is cut off; Gallwitz is making good progress. I count on the capture of Lomza to-morrow, and we are moving steadily towards Kovno. The quarrel between Falkenhayn and Hindenburg is developing. The Field-Marshal is at last telling him the truth. Nothing at all will come of it, and we shall all have to suffer for it, but he could not go on ignoring all these insults— petty and otherwise.

August 11, 1915.

All goes well. The situation is developing as we foretold—*i.e.* we are forcing the Russians back frontally—but, thanks to G.H.Q., there will be no crushing defeat. Of course we must not underestimate what we have achieved—the capture of the Vistula and Narev line, and the conquest of half Poland—but Russia is not smashed.

August 13, 1915.

Tirpitz is here to-day. If you listen to him you think he is right. According to him, the world is much more evil, weak and aimless than people have been accustomed to think. When one gets a close view of influential people—their bad relations with each other, their conflicting ambitions — all the slander and the hatred, one must always bear in mind that it is certainly much worse on the other side, among the French, English and Russians, or one might well be nervous. Of course he puts it on a bit—so as to make as good an impression as possible himself.

The race for power and personal position seems to destroy all men's characters. I believe that the only creature who can keep his honour is a man living on his own estate; he has no need to intrigue and struggle—for it is no good intriguing for fine weather.

August 14, 1915.

The frontal fighting in Gallwitz's sector is proceeding and we get no reinforcements for the left wing. We must see what we can do for ourselves. Interminable explanatory telegrams go daily backwards and forwards between Pless and here: in form very courteous, in content pretty forcible. I think it all rather pointless, but Hindenburg and Ludendorff insist on it for the historical records, which are a matter of more or less indifference to me.

For the first time in my life I have, during the whole war, seen "History" at close quarters, and I know that its actual process is very different from what is presented to posterity; in the final issue a few meannesses and misrepresentations make little or no difference.

August 15, 1915.

I am much more concerned by the fact that I hoped we should storm one of the Kovno forts to-day, and we have not succeeded. Otherwise our position here is excellent. If we could only put 3-4 Army Corps into the line on the left wing between the 10th and the Niemen Army then we might succeed in destroying the Russians. Unfortunately we have not got them and G.H.Q. will not let us have them.

August 16, 1915.

However, things are going better than G.H.Q. deserve. There will, indeed, be no smashing Russian defeat, but I believe the Russians will suffer pretty severely.

It is to be hoped that G.H.Q. will then make up their minds as soon as possible and send an army against Serbia, so as to clear up the Dardanelles situation at last. We cannot hope to wear the Russians down in the course of the winter unless we keep the Dardanelles firmly closed. We can only attack the English in conjunction with the Turks—via the Suez Canal.

August 18, 1915.

There is, of course, great rejoicing here—it will soon be all up with Novogeorgievsk. At any rate

we have intercepted a message from the wireless
officer, in which he said good-bye to his wife, in
view of his approaching departure to a German
war prison. H.M. has sent a gracious telegram to
Hindenburg: " Pour le Mérites " for Eichhorn
and Litzmann. If Novogeorgievsk falls, 3 Divisions
will be released, which we can put into the line
north of Kovno. Then we can proceed against
Vilna without reference to G.H.Q. Otherwise the
position is, in general, good. It is to be hoped that
G.H.Q. will be sensible and make up their minds
to go through with the scheme.

August 19, 1915.

Novogeorgievsk is still holding out. I had, in
fact, reckoned on its being taken to-day. How
right we were about Kovno is proved by the fact
that the Russians have abandoned their positions
on the whole front of the 10th Army and are in retreat behind the Niemen. With only 1-2 new Corps
—but we have not got them. We can only bring in
the troops that have been besieging Novogeorgievsk,
but they must take the place first.

August 20, 1915.

Yesterday evening the fall of Novogeorgievsk
could be seen to be imminent. As a result of this
a telegram came in at eight o'clock from Pless, to
the effect that H.M. would proceed there to-day.
No mention of Hindenburg. Ludendorff and I
were quite clear that this would never do. If
the Kaiser visited troops under Hindenburg's
command Hindenburg must be there, unless H.M.
expressly forbade it. So a special train was at once
put together and at 11 P.M. Hindenburg, Ludendorff, and Bockelberg as well, rumbled off to

Novogeorgievsk. I, of course, had to stay here. I am very curious to know what kind of faces H.M. and Falkenhayn made when they saw Hindenburg and Ludendorff.

The prisoners taken at Novogeorgievsk (85,000) are more than I had expected, and all goes well elsewhere. If only Gallwitz's persistent frontal attacks did not mean such heavy losses! Our conscience is clear—we set ourselves against any frontal advance.

August 21, 1915.

The others have come back from Novogeorgievsk. Meeting courteous but cool. Falkenhayn said to Ludendorff: " Now, are you at last convinced that my operation was right? " Answer: " On the contrary! " H.M. made a few non-committal remarks. Then decorations were distributed—to the wrong people, of course — troops reviewed, speeches delivered, and so home. And so it goes on. The futility of our (so-called) Great Headquarters is beyond description.

August 25, 1915.

From the tactical point of view we are going on well, and so is Mackensen farther south. The Russians don't seem in the least anxious to hold Brest-Litovsk, their last great fortress. Of course these are all notable successes, but we have not smashed them; and we could have done.

We are more and more annoyed with G.H.Q. As a memento, apparently, of the anniversary of Hindenburg's appointment in the East they have deliberately taken Poland from us and put it under a Governor-General at Warsaw (Beseler) directly responsible to H.M. So the Field-Marshal has asked to be allowed to alter his title of " C.-in-C.,

East," as this designation had been for some little time painfully ironical.

I hope Great (?) Headquarters will not be too late in deciding on the campaign against Serbia, the object of which is to hold out a hand to the Bulgarians.

August 28, 1915.

Nothing special to report here. On our right wing the Russians continue their retreat; on the left there is still heavy fighting in the direction of Vilna, but I hope we shall pull it off. We must do without Riga—unless the Russians abandon it to us. We are too weak up there. We are, of course, now sending reinforcements from Gallwitz up to the Kovno area, but it all takes time.

Another long series of instructions from G.H.Q. to-day. Good God, what an idea these people have of war! Of course we don't do anything they tell us, so there is no harm done.

August 30, 1915.

The answer to our telegram about " C.-in-C., East," was, as might have been expected, conciliatory. Since H.M. had been on the Eastern Front, the title was, of course, incorrect. But it had not been altered so as not to give the impression that Hindenburg's position was in any way diminished. There was even less cause to alter it at present, since the Eastern campaign would very soon have reached a defensive stage and the entire line would then be again handed over to Hindenburg, etc. Well, we have annoyed them, and that's the main thing.

As regards politics, the Rumanians appear to be strongly inclined to the Quadruple Alliance. It is high time that the Austrians made their offensive in Eastern Galicia. The Russians are cut off there owing to their retreat, so that an envelopment would be possible. If those fellows conducted the campaign with reasonable sense they might win a great success—free the rest of Galicia and drive some of the Russians on to Rumania. The latter would be especially desirable, as in that case the Rumanians would have to show their colours. The Serbian scheme, too, seems to be taking palpable shape. The attacking troops are to be the so-called Alpine Corps, hitherto stationed in Tyrol.

August 31, 1915.

The one thing that makes me anxious is the futility of G.H.Q. They are like a pack of Social Democrats—they can't make a decision and stick to it. The Turks are howling, the Bulgarians are ready, and the fellows — or rather the fellow — cannot make up his mind to send off these three Corps to Serbia. They have got them waiting ready behind the Front. Whether they are afraid the French in the West may make another great effort to break through, and they may need Reserves for that, of course I don't know. That would be the only excuse, but no real reason.

September 1, 1915.

As regards the situation in general, G.H.Q. seem to have come to a decision; whether a right one, it is too early to say. In any case we shall have to suffer for it, as the centre of gravity is to be shifted elsewhere. We shall probably be presented with what troops are left, and told to hold up what are left of the Russians. Well, we can do it. Falkenhayn probably hopes that something will go wrong somewhere and we shall let ourselves in for a minor reverse. He needn't worry ! . . .

September 2, 1915.

In the meantime we have at last got our way on one point against G.H.Q. They really wanted to hold up everything and carry off all the troops they could get. We simply could not allow it: we are still in the middle of an attack and—just as much as the 9th Army—must stick to it. After a lengthy dispute they gave in.

Vilna is a difficult business. The Russians are attacking there with greatly superior forces. Our men have held on up till now, and if they can hold till to-morrow then all will be well.[1]

September 3, 1915.

Here all goes well. At Grodno we have taken the fortifications this side of the Niemen and the city itself on the opposite bank—the latter by surprise. The Russians are now defending themselves desperately and trying to drive us back over the Niemen. All goes well in the Vilna direction: the Russians have had such enormous losses in their attacks that they have given them up and dug themselves in. Meantime the two Divisions we sent have arrived there, and all danger is over. But it will be four or five days before we can make the projected attack. It is tedious waiting, but the Russians have learned something, and so destroyed the railways

---

[1] It was not until the middle of August that G.H.Q. sanctioned the offensive towards Vilna. For this purpose the 10th Army was reinforced by the siege-troops from Novogeorgievsk, and by certain Divisions transferred from the 8th and 12th Armies. The reinforcements appeared so late that the decisive attack could not take place until September 9th.

The Niemen Army received orders to advance on Dünaburg. The Russians had to surrender Vilna, but the German advance then came to a standstill. The Russian retreat from Poland had already so far settled down into an orderly movement that the Russians could easily move Divisions to any threatened point.

The Niemen Army came to a stop, also, before it reached Dünaburg.

The counter-attacks of the Russians were everywhere repulsed with bitter fighting.

everywhere in their retreat that we have not yet finished repairing them.

September 9, 1915.

Bulgaria: so far as I know, the agreement with Turkey has been signed. 4-5 Austrian and 2 German Army Corps are now being transferred to deal with Serbia. I fancy the Serbians will be inclined to ask themselves whether they would not sooner make peace, and resign Macedonia to Bulgaria, taking Northern Albania instead; otherwise they will have to face a combined attack by Bulgaria and ourselves. I don't believe that Rumania will come in yet—I think the successes of Italy have frightened her off a little. But whether this is actually the scheme, and whether it will be actually carried out in this way, I don't know. Mackensen is to have the command of the expedition. Now that all available honours, titles and orders have been showered in so short a time on this one devoted head, after the capture of Belgrade there is nothing left for him but to be rechristened " Prinz Eugen." Large forces from the Eastern Front are being transferred to the West—let us hope it will lead to a success. We, too, shall have to give up a good many troops, but not until after the conclusion of the Vilna operation, which began early to-day, and of which I have great hopes.

The Tsar's decision to assume the Chief Command himself, and to supersede Nicolas, seems to me very significant. It is a *coup d'état* on the best model. Even if the Tsar does not want peace because he is convinced that we attacked him and made war inevitable, the removal of the Grand Duke, who kept the situation together with such iron energy, can only be to our advantage. I view the matter as the first step towards peace.

September 10, 1915.

The extract from *The Times* article has aroused general approval. It is exactly what we explained to G.H.Q. two months ago. Unfortunately there is no means of inducing General von Falkenhayn or H.M. to read the article. Hindenburg will send it to Lyncker, who will, of course, silently suppress it. It is poor comfort to reflect that we are guiltless of this folly. Yesterday I was told by Dürr (Adjutant-General of the Grand Duke of Baden, who did not leave until early this morning) that he had been officially informed that Bulgaria had come to an agreement with Turkey as well as with us and Austria. The treaties were signed three days ago. Mackensen has got the command against Serbia. I am sorry we did not get it. There is then to be an attack at one point in the West. I suspect that it will be conducted by Falkenhayn under his own orders and those of the Crown Prince, so as to put himself in an agreeable light in the latter's eyes.

September 13, 1915.

Yesterday I was in a bad humour. To-day things are better, although the Vilna business still fails to come off. They ought to be moving forward, but they seem to be hanging about doing nothing. The worst of such a situation is that one does not know where the cause lies. Probably there is some failure somewhere that the culprit will not confess and does not report. And so the whole line is held up. In the meantime the Russians have time to move up reinforcements by railway. However, it won't be another Brzeziny. Let us be content with a modest success — no more adventures. . . . I do not know when the campaign against Serbia is to begin; I assume at the end of the month. I hope

our people will come to a friendly agreement with
the Serbians and that Serbia will make peace,
receiving the whole of Albania and the coast now
claimed by the Italians, and giving Macedonia
to Bulgaria. Then a serious word or two will
be all that is needed to deal with Rumania. The
Austrians can use the forces thus set free against the
Italians and take Venice from those blackguards.
Here am I disposing of kingdoms!

On the 16th, H.M. is coming to Kovno for a few
hours. The Field-Marshal and Ludendorff must
of course be there to meet him. Ludendorff wants
me to go with him. He means it kindly, but it
would give me no pleasure. These people do not like
us, and what is the use of going there merely to be
treated offensively (as happened, for example, in
Novogeorgievsk, so Bockelberg told me)? However,
I shall have to eat the sour apple, I suppose.

September 14, 1915.

Nothing special to record—the operation against
Vilna is still in progress. It must be ended in three
days if it is to succeed. I have just had a row with
the G.O.C. 10th Army, who is inclined to be too
venturesome, and one with Ludendorff, who wants
to make a frontal attack. I want to strike a middle
course, content myself with 50,000-60,000 prisoners,
and take no serious risks. What they now decide
between the two of them is all one to me. I have
said my say to both of them, and wash my hands
with proverbial innocence. Tactics gradually get on
one's nerves rather, particularly when one always
has the worry of them, without being able to make
the decision.

September 15, 1915.

Our operation against Vilna is proceeding. To-
day things look a little better, as the 1st Cavalry

Division succeeded in destroying a railway some considerable distance in the rear of the Russians, but we have lost at least one day through the hesitation of the 10th Army. However they are now going to carry on according to my ideas.[1]

September 17, 1915.

. . . In the Royal train. H.M. had meantime reached Kovno. Dinner of ceremony. H.M. between Eichhorn and Ludendorff, and opposite Hindenburg. I next to Ludendorff, then Admiral von Müller, and opposite me Reischach, Treutler and also Valentini. Conversation not specially interesting. Treutler thought the Rumanian question quite simple. If the Austrians did not commit too many follies, he believed that he could keep the Rumanians out of it until our offensive against Serbia gets moving. As the Austrian railways are working so abominably, this will not be until October.

September 18, 1915.

All well here. Our offensive in the direction of Vilna prospers. The Russians are in retreat on their whole front as far as Galicia. . . . I was just now interrupted to be told we have got Vilna. Now G.H.Q. themselves must realize how right our view was.

As the Austrians have partly failed against Serbia, and we have to send more troops to that Front, our offensive in the West is held up for the present. I am glad of it, because that means we shall not have to give up any troops in the near future. Now

---

[1] The 1st Cavalry Division, far outstripping the infantry divisions, had reached the important railway Vilna—Molodeczno. They were heavily attacked by the Russians but decided to hold their ground until their own infantry came up. But the infantry advanced so slowly along the bad roads that the Division had finally to evacuate Smorgon with heavy losses.

we shall get at least as far as Minsk, and I can now see Riga in the distance.

Since yesterday we have had a Papal Prelate on a visit here. Apparently a German Jesuit. An unusually able fellow, a thorough diplomat, a friend of Erzberger. The object of his visit is to see what former possessions of the Catholic Church in Poland had been taken from them by the Russians, so that a claim might be made for their restitution. The Pope is, for that reason, rather disposed to be in favour of German annexation of Russian territory. On the other hand, the Pope is against the partition of Belgium. I liked what he had to say about Austria. The Pope thinks that after the war Germany must infallibly make a military convention with Austria. . . . There must be an exchange of officers. Great hopes are placed on Princess Zita, the wife of the Heir to the Throne. She is said to be clever and energetic; he is rather . . . , but "enough sense for a ruling sovereign." The most important thing was to break the power of the aristocracy in Vienna. Did we know any means of doing so? I said I knew of none, except strychnine.

September 20, 1915.

Nothing new here. Our Vilna offensive has still not produced the result I had hoped—*i.e.* a round figure of prisoners and guns. It is certainly a great strategical success, as the Russians are on the run along their whole line—quite like old times: they seem unimpressed by the fact that their Little Father the Tsar has taken over the supreme command, and has clearly stated that he now proposes to win the war. The citizen at home wants a victory, but he must have it expressed in figures, and so long as we have not got 50,000 prisoners it won't do.

September 24, 1915.

Heavy fighting last night. The Russians are attacking desperately where they are being out-flanked. Alas, we are always just an Army Corps short. The operation succeeded all right: we have got Vilna, the Russians are retreating along the entire Front, but we have not got the 50,000 prisoners I had hoped for. Our men are exhausted, added to which the railways are useless. Complete chaos, no telephone lines—a very difficult situation. In a few days we shall have reached the line that we were fighting for, and then we shall stop.

September 26, 1915.

Our offensive is slowly coming to a standstill. The Russians are defending themselves desperately. Moreover, we have to give up some troops. I wish we could have reached the Molodeczno defile; it would have shortened the line and by occupying it we should have some troops over. Then we could dig ourselves in, and the fighting in the East would be over.

September 27, 1915.

Heavy fighting over in the West.[1] On the 3rd Army Front our first line is lost: the second holds. Heavy losses: the French losses are, of course, heavier, but they are making the most desperate attempts to break right through. H.Q. has been on the Western Front for the last three days. It is difficult from here to realize what is going on, but I feel pretty sure that the new line will hold. Any troops we can spare are of course being sent towards the railheads, but it will be nearly three weeks before they can reach the West—we are 200 kilometres

[1] At the end of September the powerful Entente attacks started at Loos and in Champagne.

off the railway. It is at least fortunate that the Guard and the X. Army Corps had already been sent back from Galicia to the West.

We are now coming to a halt at last, and constructing a strong position which can then be held with as few troops as possible.[1]

September 28, 1915.

Yesterday went well for us in the West. It is to be hoped that the main storm is over. No troops from here can reach them in less than three days.

We have to-day withdrawn our left wing to the position intended for it. And with that the serious part of the operation is over. It will now take a fortnight or three weeks to get everything straight and then the war of positions will begin. It has been rather a disappointing affair. I had counted on 40,000-50,000 prisoners, but we actually made only about 30,000. I now know quite well why we did not do better. The infantry no longer attacks. The troops are without officers, especially without proper company commanders, and they are gradually deteriorating. The only comfort is that the other side is, of course, in the same case. We want a good long rest for our tired Divisions, then all will be well. We shall now have to put off the Riga affair.

September 30, 1915.

Heavy fighting in the night on the Western Front. But there is now a general conviction that the line will hold. To-morrow the I. Army Corps we sent from here will arrive at the most dangerous point. Three others will follow immediately and then three Divisions. It was very careless of G.H.Q. to send that Corps off to Serbia before the Corps had arrived from here to replace it.

[1] The Line Beresina—Kovno—Lake Narocz—Lake Drysviaty—Lake Novo-Alexandrovsk—Düna.

October 3, 1915.

In the West the affair seems to be over. Our losses are not so high as I had feared. The missing, excluding those taken prisoners, do not, as the French announce, amount to 23,000, but only 11,000. The total losses are only about 50,000, while those of the French and English must be enormous. So Falkenhayn has a little breathing space, which he employs in insulting us assiduously. Ludendorff will not stand it, so that on both sides there is much drafting of offensive telegrams.

It is important that the Serbian expedition should succeed quickly, so that we can get the way clear to Constantinople. If only we could send a few batteries of heavy howitzers, so as to prevent the English ships from landing provisions and water, the Gallipoli business would soon be over. When the Russians then saw that there was no means of exporting their wheat, or importing war material, there would be a gradual collapse in that country. And the English would be nervous about the Suez Canal.

In the West we must wait. French man-power is coming to an end. In the course of the winter France must reach the point when no more recruits will be forthcoming; in other words, it will no longer be possible to replace current losses. If, in addition, they become convinced that we can hold on, and mean to, they will gradually weaken. But this will take time and we must be patient.

October 4, 1915.

The danger in the West is apparently averted. There would have been none but for an idiotic piece of carelessness on the part of G.H.Q. A Brigade-Commander lately transferred to this

Front came through here the other day and told us an incredible story. The 3rd Army had foreseen the attacks in Champagne, and when, in spite of this, their last Reserves were taken from them, the Army Staff protested. Falkenhayn refused to listen, and the Chief of Staff (the Bavarian General von Höhn) asked to be relieved of his post, as he could no longer be responsible for the situation. He was relieved; a creature of Falkenhayn's took his place, and the French nearly got through. It is really unbelievable. Now they have got adequate Reserves which have been taken from us. As a result we are having a rough time, for the Russians have noticed the withdrawal of troops from our Front and are attacking in force. Well, we have had rough times before and got over them, and we shall do so again.

October 5, 1915.

All goes well in the West. At Souchez, as well as at Rouvroy, in Champagne, we have retaken the lost heights that served us as artillery observation posts. And the French and English seem to have had enough of their losses for the present.

Yesterday and early this morning there were no Russian attacks. Whether they are fed up, or are beginning to move off, we can't yet say. In any case we have now time to give our men a rest and dig ourselves in. In three or four days I expect everything will be straight here and we shall be able to face matters calmly. On the Serbian frontier our people are behaving very foolishly, in my opinion. Instead of getting on with it they are still hesitating over the first move. The main point was that the Serbians and the Bulgarians should fire the first shots. I don't really think that the Bulgarians could now draw back, but I would not trust these damned Balkan people an inch.

October 6, 1915.

Yesterday I had a long interview with the Under-Secretary of State, Wahnschaffe. The Imperial Chancellor sent him. There is no prospect whatever of peace: nor, in his opinion, can there be any in the immediate future, at least as long as we claim what the Jingo elements want—the whole of Belgium, French Lorraine, the whole of Poland, Kurland and Lithuania. I took the opportunity of expressing my view that a discussion of Peace terms could have any object only when one of the parties showed signs of wishing to negotiate. If Russia approached us separately we should have to treat with her, perhaps giving her back Warsaw. Warsaw is a distinctly troublesome point. We can't give it to Austria; it would be awkward for us; and Poland as an independent buffer State would be equally awkward. If England approached us separately we should have to give her concessions in Belgium. I am only afraid that neither of them will make any advance. In those circumstances— the worst possible for us—it will end in a war of exhaustion. In that case we must stick to what we have got and go on sticking to it. Our talk was really only a repetition of what we both knew, but again confirmed my view that the civilians, in general, do not know what they are talking about.

October 8, 1915.

Nothing special here: more trouble with G.H.Q. Ludendorff had sent an offensive telegram and to-day of course got an even more offensive reply. There is little point in the quarrel, as we are getting the worst of it.

We have visitors as usual every day here— Dernburg yesterday, and to-day Prince Henry is here again. Dernburg is certainly the most ill-mannered brute I have ever met in high places. He asked me what my exact position was here. I had a good mind to answer that I was on a visit, just as he was, but I stopped myself, for he certainly would not have understood. And the fact that I, like him, conducted the interview with my hands in my trouser-pockets did not make us any more disposed to be friendly. However, he had some interesting things to say about America.

Things were more quiet in the West yesterday and to-day. This afternoon they are proposing to attack Tahure, where the French broke through the day before yesterday. I hope they will succeed.

The King of Greece has plucked up courage to send Herr Venizelos packing. I shall be interested to see how long he is for this world. I believe the English Government pays good prices. If Greece remains absolutely neutral it would be a great advantage, for the enemy cannot march inland from Salonika with the mobile Greek army in their rear, not knowing what it may do.

October 10, 1915.

We are constructing our entrenched positions and quarrelling with G.H.Q. In the last dispute they were actually right. Ludendorff is getting nervy and loses his temper unnecessarily. On the 3rd Army Front the French are occupying our second line at Tahure and we can't get them out. However I don't think the position is critical. They have had so many reinforcements from us here in the interval that they must surely be able to hold on now.

To-day, for a change, we have had three Turkish Princes to visit us. It is rather a good move on the part of our Government; they have brought the three Princes next in succession to the Turkish Throne to Germany and are educating them here. All three of them make a very pleasant impression. Incidentally, I delivered a discourse to them.

In Serbia, Bulgaria and Greece everything seems satisfactory. The Serbs are defending themselves bravely and putting up a good fight. The Bulgarians are to launch their attack to-morrow. Whether the King of Greece can hold out remains to be seen. At any rate he is staking his head in our interest.

October 12, 1915.

Eisenhart[1] came back to-day from Berlin, where he had been for a conference, and brought with him much interesting news, some of which I may quote. The embezzlements in which Suchomlinoff was involved reached a total of 600 million roubles. The party mainly implicated was, however, the Grand Duke Nicolai Nicolaievich—hence his removal from the post of Commander-in-Chief. One must admit that the fellow does things on the grand scale. I can only suppose that the money was needed for distribution in many and various quarters in return for subsequent support of his claims to the Tsardom.

The most competent authority gives the following reasons for our withdrawal in the matter of the U-boat question: "We were on the verge of war with America. They could do us little damage by force of arms, but they could injure us financially and by political influence in the Balkan states. England would have pumped 20 milliards out of them, not merely 500 millions, as at present. America would have allowed the enrolment of recruits for the English Army, and all the Balkan

---

[1] General von Eisenhart-Rothe was Q.M.G. at Headquarters, East.

states would have been against us. Bulgaria had stated openly that if America was against us, then we could not win, and she would not play. For these reasons we had to give in." There is really nothing to be said on the other side, and our Foreign Office seems really to have handled the Balkans better than they used to do. . . .

It has been established that there is about twenty times as much German money invested abroad as there is foreign money in Germany. In England alone there is about 20 milliards of German money. This is a state of affairs that was scarcely realized before the war, especially in view of possible reprisals. There have been many complaints in the papers about the unjust decisions of the French War Tribunals. The French Government have offered that the documents should be examined by Neutrals. . . . Further, the French Government offered to exchange all documents affecting German prisoners of war against the documents of German War Tribunals affecting French and Belgian subjects. After careful examination our Government had to refuse the proposal: which speaks volumes.

October 17, 1915.

The Russians continue to attack at Dvinsk.[1] I do not feel at all anxious. The French show signs of being satisfied with their apparent achievements in the West. Yesterday also there was no attack. So that we have got past one of the worst crises of the campaign. It is to be hoped that G.H.Q. will now have the sense to return to Berlin or Potsdam. H.M. should then have a C.-in-C., East, and a C.-in-C., West. He can always move to the point where anything is going on.

[1] Russian name for Dünaburg.

October 18, 1915.

Ludendorff did not bring back much interesting news. Zimmermann was very pleased with his Balkan policy, and well he may be. Rumania has promised to remain neutral and to refuse any passage to the Russians. Greece, too, is still behaving irreproachably. In this connection, however, we can never be sure whether Venizelos may not again get the upper hand.

Yesterday was a critical day for us in the area south of Dünaburg. Very strong Russian attacks, but they were all beaten off.

Things are moving in Serbia. But the Serbs are stout fellows and are holding out magnificently. We have let it be known that if they soon make up their minds to give up the game, Serbia will be allowed to remain intact; otherwise it will be partitioned. At present they still seem to be relying on the Quadruple Alliance.

October 19, 1915.

To-morrow we are moving to Kovno. Exactly a year ago we changed our quarters from Radom to Konskie. It was the beginning of our retreat from Poland. Our position is now much better, but it was then far more interesting. At that time everything was still before us, we looked forward to mighty battles and mighty victories—now we are merely waiting for what may happen. It is a negative situation: we do nothing, we just prevent the other party doing anything to us.

October 31, 1915.

One of the most interesting of my experiences in Berlin was my visit to Zimmermann. He was very cheerful and optimistic. He hoped that Serbia would collapse very shortly and that Italy would then follow suit (perhaps at the end of December). The others have not expressed any very audible desires for peace. There was indeed one private inquiry from an influential personage in France (Paul Cambon) as to whether we should not soon be making overtures for peace; which was of course met with a flat denial. Zimmermann was, however, of the opinion that this was a good sign. In Russia the dislike of England was quickly increasing, and Isvolski, too, had entirely turned against England.

November 1, 1915.

We are making good progress in Serbia, and we may soon expect the end. On our Front the Russians are attacking persistently at Dünaburg and there is rather serious fighting there, though nothing that need make us nervous.

Yesterday B—— gave me some news from the West: very edifying. I believe the people there hate Falkenhayn more than we do.

November 2, 1915.

We are all in a state of disturbance and upset. Although there are no great tactical movements on hand, there is much to do. Ludendorff is getting bored and keeps everyone on the run from morning till night. This restlessness—work for work's sake —is extremely uncomfortable for everybody round here.

Yesterday there was the devil of a business in front of Dünaburg: the Russians attacked like men demented, and broke through one of our Divisions. Fortunately, we had another Division near by that we were able to throw into the line, so that all is straight again to-day. I think Morgen is breaking up. Whether it is nerves or his unpopularity I don't know. I shall go to Lauenstein early to-morrow morning and find out what is really the matter.

In Serbia the Bulgarians seem to be making a mess of things. They appear to be afraid that the French and English, who have lately landed, may take them in the rear, and are sending strong forces to form a southern Front, instead of going all out against the Serbians, and knocking them out before the Allies can come up. Not one of the operations is going forward as had been planned.

November 6, 1915.

Still heavy fighting in front of Dünaburg. The Russians are absolutely determined to break through and are squandering men and munitions. We have held on up till now and shall certainly go on doing so. In the West, also, all is well. We are prepared for the possibility that the French may make a last attempt. Now that we have plenty of Reserves in hand it could only be to our advantage. Good progress in Serbia. The Bulgarians have taken Nish. Consequently I do not attach much importance to the fall of the Zaimis Cabinet. It is clear that Venizelos is doing all he knows to get back to the helm.

November 13, 1915.

In Serbia a Bulgarian Division seems to have got into difficulties. A part of the Serbian forces is trying to break through to the south. Whether there has been some error in leadership it is impossible to say, but it would be regrettable if the break-through succeeded. From the news up to date it seems that 4 weak Serbian Divisions are involved, otherwise everything is going well in the West and in Serbia. I am very curious to know what plans our G.H.Q. is now making. In Serbia more than two of our Corps have been withdrawn as, owing to the concentric advance, there is no room for them. We have not the least idea of their destination—perhaps Salonika, via Sofia.

November 18, 1915.

G. had really nothing particular to tell us. He gave us a description of the disgusting state of affairs in Austria. Things are very likely worse there than we had hitherto supposed, and the worst of all is the old Emperor . . . with his old Habsburg hatred of the Hohenzollerns. Prices have doubled just as they have with us. The Government does nothing, because the highest aristocracy—in particular the Archduke Frederick—are doing very well out of it all.

November 19, 1915.

I have said fifty times before that we are fighting for our existence; that it is a hard fight and will grow harder; and that we shall never be in a position simply to impose our Peace conditions on the other side. However, I must keep on saying it.

The incompetence of the authorities and of G.H.Q. is greater on the other side than with us; and that is saying a good deal.

November 22, 1915.

The position here is unchanged, and will remain so for a time. The Russians seem to be very busy training new troops so as to attack us in the spring with their formations up to full strength. We shall do the same, so as to give them a suitable reception. There is no indication of an end anywhere. The hope that Serbia would weaken and make a separate Peace seems unlikely to be fulfilled. King Peter will probably act like Albert of Belgium. He has got a guarantee from England that his kingdom will be restored : he is satisfied with it, and reigns for the time being *in partibus infidelium*. According to all one hears, the war will last at least one year longer, and it is good to prepare one's mind for it, if only that one may not become impatient.

November 27, 1915.

The only interesting item is that negotiations between Austria and Montenegro are actually in progress; Nikita does not seem inclined to fall upon his kinsman Peter's rear and increase his territory at Serbia's expense.

November 28, 1915.

It is unfortunately true that we have not, and never have had, a definite political aim. The misfortune is that the Chancellor is actually a clever man, but he cannot bring himself to any decision; worst of all is Falkenhayn's ascendancy over H.M., so that the latter only hears what Falkenhayn thinks fit to tell him, and has a false idea, or no idea at all, of the real position.

December 2, 1915.

I am very curious to see the results of the Reichstag debates. Anxious as I am that our incompetent Administration, and in particular Herr Delbrück, should get a thorough dressing-down, I very much hope, all the same, that this process may not take place at a full sitting, but in committee, so as to avoid making a bad impression abroad. The only disadvantages will be that, in that case, there will be probably no change of ministers, and that idiot will go on ruining the Empire.

December 14, 1915.

We are all anxiously watching Salonika. The Greek is certainly in a painful position. If he throws over the English they will stop his imports, and produce a famine in a fortnight. On the other hand he would like to come in with the Central Powers, because he believes in a German victory. So he tacks laboriously backwards and forwards. Apart from this, the Greeks regard the Bulgarians as the hereditary enemy, which does not make matters easier. In order to avoid any Greek gun going off unintentionally, the Bulgarians have halted on the Greek frontier until the German and Austrian troops arrive. Then, and not till then, will Salonika be attacked, unless the English and the French prefer to clear out beforehand.

December 17, 1915.

The War Minister was here the day before yesterday. I sat next him at table and had a most interesting conversation. In particular he was able to remove certain of my anxieties regarding the possibility of our success. We have ample man-power to carry on the war for one more year. Naturally, we cannot commit any extravagances. I was amused to note that we were in complete agreement regarding the frontiers we should claim here in the East. He is the first man I have met who wants the same from the Russians as I do— namely, a line in front of Kalish, along the Warthe, then south of Vozlavek-Plotzk, south of Mlava, then straight ahead through Rozan to Bialystok, including Lithuania and Kurland. Poland and Warsaw he wants as little as I do.

December 17, 1915.

As a result of my last conversation with G.H.Q. we have again telegraphed to-day to ask for a

Division as reinforcement. I am curious to see whether we get it. They have enough in the West, and 3-4 Divisions have also been sent to the West from Serbia.

December 19, 1915.

Nothing fresh here from a military point of view. According to what the Austrian told me, Constantine of Greece still hopes that he may amicably induce the Entente to sail away from Salonika. I don't think he will manage it. If they do not withdraw voluntarily, the attack can begin at the end of the month. Until then Gallwitz will still be busy with his supplies and railway communications. There will also be a simultaneous Austrian expedition against Montenegro from the West.

The Bulgarians, incidentally, have not been content to remain on the Albanian frontier; they are pushing forward through North Albania to the West. To the great disgust of the Austrians they want to reach the sea, for which one cannot blame them. I shall be eager to see what happens when they come in contact with the Italians. I suspect that the latter will bolt without more ado.

December 21, 1915.

By way of celebrating the New Year, we have had an active row with G.H.Q. They want some heavy artillery from us, and we won't let them have it. Their tone is so insolent that I do no understand how Hindenburg stands it.

There was a slight mishap on the Austrian Front near Czernovitz yesterday,[1] but matters seem to have been put right again now. Here the position

[1] The Russians had made another attack on the extreme south wing of the German Army and the Austrian 7th Army. The latter were involved in heavy fighting in the Bukovina, which lasted into January. The Austrian positions were, for the most part, maintained.

is unchanged. Unimportant patrol fighting and artillery duels, but in general all is quiet. Our new Division is on its way, so that our minds are at rest for the future. According to news from Russia, they are suffering from a serious shortage of guns. It seems that foreign countries will deliver only against payment in gold. Moreover, the only way they can be got into the country is by the Siberian railway. Their position seems gradually deteriorating, while with us it is improving. When I read in the papers about the great new Russian Army of two million men I simply laugh.

January 3, 1916.

Nikita would like to, but he can't. He is threatened with famine if he does not negotiate. Besides, strange as it is, the Serbians and Montenegrins still believe in England's ultimate victory. They know all the bungling . . . that goes on in Austria and they cannot imagine that that country can come through. And yet the Austrians are doing better. Until now they have repulsed all the Russian attacks. The Russians apparently want to make an impression on Rumania.

Nothing fresh here. Young Hindenburg, who is G.S.O.,I, with the VII. Army Corps in the West, was here for a few days on a visit to his father, and told us some interesting news. God, what follies were committed over there in the early days of the war!

January 7, 1916.

Kapp would be a good catch, but I hardly think it likely. Solf has never had the slightest chance for the Chancellorship. I had not until now heard anything of the other things against him. My main objection to him was simply that he was a pessimist

and spread the most incredible rumours. As regards
Bulgaria, I never believed that they had joined us
for our *beaux yeux*. They are quite rightly pursuing
their own purely Bulgarian policy. The best of it
is that we can promise them at least as much as
the English, since we can divide up the whole of
Serbia, but if the Bulgarians were to get too near
Constantinople there would be objections on the
part of Russia.

The money question is naturally a difficulty,
since Rumania insists on payment in gold. However . . . even if the outlook for us is not very
favourable, it is much worse with the others, and
especially with Russia. The war will not end for
want of money.

The times when Hindenburg could get his way
against Falkenhayn are long past. Time has taken
the trumps out of his hand. The times have changed,
the times of our Great Deeds are long past, and
also the times of Falkenhayn's grosser blunders—
viz. Ypres, etc. I do not see how the situation can
possibly change under the present Emperor. It is
involved in the system. They all hold together and
support each other. His Majesty has no notion of
the position.

I don't much approve of an understanding between Ludendorff and the Crown Prince. There
would have been no object whatever in a visit from
Ludendorff, and it would only give the other side
ground for suspicion. In the first place, the Crown
Prince's entourage take an even more extraordinary
view of the state of affairs; further, the Crown Prince
is completely under the thumb of the Chief of his
General Staff, Knobelsdorff, who is on the worst
possible terms with Ludendorff. Besides, what is
worse, he has quarrelled with everybody, even from
the time he was in charge of a Staff Department.

Kovno, *January* 10, 1916.

The Austrian attack on Montenegro from the Cattaro direction is making good progress. General Gröner, who is in charge of field railways, was here yesterday and gave us some news of the general situation. The attack on Salonika is to come next. The difficulty is not so much a question of railways and supplies: it is a matter of politics. The railway up to the Greek frontier is ready. On the other hand the Austrians and the Bulgarians cannot agree. The Austrians, of course, began by being quite idiotic again, and actually claimed the Negotin district — *i.e.* the southern bank of the Danube south of the Iron Gates—for themselves, and intended to bestow on the Rumanians only a small strip of Macedonia. Now the Bulgarians are being difficult and claiming more and more. At present, not only the whole Negotin district, but the Morava Valley—*i.e.* the most fertile part of Serbia —has been assigned to them. Now the quarrel is over the Morava railway, which the Austrians will not let out of their hands.

We are trying to mediate, and Falkenhayn has been several times in Belgrade and Budapest about the matter. In my opinion the Bulgarians are right.

.

January 11, 1916.

Yesterday we had a crowd of guests at dinner. Our representatives on the governments of Lithuania and Kurland have been staying here for the last few days, and a few officials from Berlin have also arrived. It was very interesting to hear everyone's point of view. Yet I am actually none the wiser, for not one of them could contribute anything definite or new.

As to the question of supplies, it is only as regards

oats that the position is serious. Until the harvest we are short by more than 1,000,000 tons, and the communications with Rumania are so defective (railways are deficient and the Danube is not really navigable at the Iron Gates) that we import from there only 600,000 tons at the most in the next four months. We shall then be in for a real shortage, an experience we knew nothing of last year. However, we shall manage somehow. It is amazing how there is only one opinion of Delbrück's incompetence and disgraceful conduct, and yet it does not seem possible to get rid of the fellow.

The Austrian attack on Montenegro is moving slowly but surely forwards. It seems to be gradually dawning on the Montenegrins that they may go the same way as the Serbians.

January 16, 1916.

Even in our prison camps there is not one useless mouth. All the prisoners who are fit for work are working, and from all sides comes the cry: "Make prisoners; we want still more prisoner-battalions." But even with everyone digging and sowing we could not have got through. Apart from this, every possible acre has been cultivated in the German Empire and in the occupied territories. Most unfortunately the harvest of 1915 was the greatest failure that we have had for forty-four years. The yield was about 2,500,000 tons less than was expected. That is bad luck, and we must see how we can struggle through. This unfortunate fact is not very apparent from the newspapers.

January 24, 1916.

I have crawled through all the trenches and told the people in the dug-outs some news for which they were suitably grateful. The mud is terrible.

On the third day of my journey it began to thaw, the trenches were under water and everything was floating. The men were continually pumping the water out of the dug-outs, which are built on piles, but it was no use. And yet in spite of all this I was astonished at the extraordinarily cheerful spirit that I found everywhere. With the softening of the snow the car kept on breaking down, and we had to force our way forward with constant pushing and towing. One day I used six cars and eleven sledges to make my round; but in our billets in the evening they all wanted to be told what things looked like in the great world. I had nothing new to tell them, but the mere sight of a new face is a diversion to men who must move in a narrow daily round.

January 25, 1916.

The position in Greece is this: it would suit us best if they remained neutral; worst, if they joined us. In the latter event the English would instantly occupy all the Greek islands and thus create pledges which we should have to redeem with parts of Belgium and France. They are consequently using every dodge they can to drive Greece in on our side. Our Foreign Office has to do everything they can to prevent them joining us.

January 26, 1916.

Nothing special here. We have received a very interesting report from Russia. The majority of the population are war-weary, but the Tsar, however, is the soul of the war, and is by no means so insignificant as has been assumed. The disarming of Montenegro is proceeding according to plan. For the rest the Russians have apparently given up their attacks on the Bukovina frontier and are now collecting their forces in front of the Southern Army for an attack there. That is a mixed army of Austrians and Germans, and I feel no anxiety about the event.

January 27, 1916.

The situation in Montenegro is now clear. Nikita, in person, has withdrawn to the Entente, Mirko has taken refuge with the Austrian Army, and the army is capitulating. In this way nothing can go wrong. If the Entente wins, Nikita will come back to the throne; if the Central Powers win, Mirko will be King of a greater Montenegro.

January 29, 1916.

We thought something was going to happen, but we were mistaken. However, there was no quarrel —just nothing at all. No one knows why Exzellenz von Falkenhayn took the trouble to go to Lida and ordered Ludendorff to meet him there. He wanted information about the position, the morale and health of his army — and that was all. Either G.H.Q. has no important plans for the future, or, if so, they hardly think enough of them to tell us what they are. Ludendorff mentioned my idea of an offensive across the Düna, but this was rejected for the present. Otherwise all was amiable and pleasant.

January 30, 1916.

Nothing new on the East Front. The Russians seem to be collecting all the troops and heavy artillery that they can manage to move in front of the Southern Army (Linsingen), so as to try to make another decisive attack in that part. There are now 5-6 German and Austrian Divisions in reserve down there, and in all human calculation they cannot possibly be driven back. From the other Fronts we hear little or nothing. We have just got another gas regiment, and I find myself wondering how we can provide it with an opportunity to carry out its agreeable duties.

February 2, 1916.

I have been labouring all the morning over a mighty work which the Chief is to submit to G.H.Q. I should like to win another victory. For weeks past I have been trying to convince people that we can win a great success at Riga if G.H.Q. will give us the necessary troops. It is of course clear that there is no tactical necessity for an attack in that part. Moreover, it will probably not decide the war in our favour, but after all it will bring us in 100,000 prisoners and carry our left wing forward to the Peipus Lake. If, however, G.H.Q. is collecting all available forces for a blow in the West—the decisive point — or if they think they will bring Rumania in on our side by an attack in Galicia (which I doubt), then they will strike at one of those two points, and we shall get nothing. But if a decisive action in the West is impossible, etc., and if they want to go on waiting about doing nothing, and wasting time and men in useless small enterprises, then in the late spring, when the fodder shortage makes itself felt in Germany, the moment will come when the people will want another victory. I can provide it—if we can have another 7 or 8 Divisions. Whether the proposal succeeds—that is, whether Falkenhayn will sanction it — I don't know : at all events I have set my military conscience at rest by calling attention to the opportunity.

February 3, 1916.

Our Foreign Office is delighted with Rumania. The import of corn, as well as other questions, is satisfactorily settled. These alarmist rumours were nonsense. On the other hand there are further difficulties with the Americans. They really are shameless. Our people think that we must give way because the money-market could not stand a rupture with America. Partly in consequence of this, and partly as a reply to the *Baralong*, the U-boat war and the Zeppelin attacks are to be energetically pressed against England in March. I do not know why they were ever stopped. Probably some notion of H.M.'s. The latest news in high politics is that Tirpitz and Falkenhayn have met. Who will come to grief as a result of it is a pleasing speculation. The reference in the Speech from the Throne in the *Landstag* to a reorganization of the Prussian franchise is explained as an attempt on the part of the Imperial Chancellor to conciliate the parties of the Left so as to protect himself against the Tirpitz-Falkenhayn alliance.

February 4, 1916.

My discourse of yesterday in the presence of old Kessel and Kröcher was a complete success. I simply detailed all the occasions on which we made sensible proposals to G.H.Q. and were turned down. The Field-Marshal himself was unmistakably struck. . . . At the end I tried to interest the two of them, each of whom has a large and influential following, in my Düna offensive. In the meantime my scheme has gone up to Falkenhayn. For the moment he can't, of course, do anything for us, being actually engaged in an offensive against Verdun. I hope they may apply their minds to the matter a bit later—in May, perhaps —and gradually get used to the idea. In any case I feel at ease in my conscience.

February 6, 1916.

Incidentally, Keller, who has been to see his sick wife, brought the news that Falkenhayn is to be Chancellor. In my view this means that he is firmly convinced that all is going well, otherwise he would have let the others bear the odium.

February 11, 1916.

Knobelsdorff, at present Chief of Staff with the Crown Prince, will probably succeed Falkenhayn. I would prefer Ludendorff. However, it is better for us that he should stay here. Owing to considerations of age I could not succeed him (Eisenhart is older than I am), and I should then probably have to look out for another job, as I should not be able to work with a new chief. My position here with Ludendorff has been a far too independent one for that.

February 14, 1916.

Generally speaking, Staff officers may not be promoted out of turn. Falkenhayn has broken through this tradition in the case of three of his people—Pappen, Gröner and Seekt—mainly from a desire to emphasize how much more important and splendid were their services to the Fatherland than ours. At least it seems that Eichhorn, who asked that his Chief of Staff, Hell, might be promoted General out of his turn, gave some such explanation. Prince Oskar's wound was certainly a piece of carelessness. Eichhorn was visiting the positions of one of the Divisions of the XL. Corps. They were imprudent enough to walk along the fire trenches in a compact body. The Russians, of course, opened on them with artillery fire. As a result Lieutenant-Colonel Mengelbier, Chief of Staff of the XL. Corps, was unfortunately killed, and Hell and Prince Oskar slightly wounded. I saw them both on the following day. Mengelbier I knew very well — we were at the same time Divisional General Staff officers with the I. Corps —he was with the 37th Division. The Prince got a graze on the ear and a bruise on the hip, and Hell three scratches on the head.

I had a long interesting letter from Thiel. He favours an offensive against Livonia. He is working on Swedish propaganda. I shall write to him that if he can only get us a few Divisions and some heavy artillery he can have all Livonia.

February 15, 1916.

In the West it is apparently still raining, and nothing can happen as long as the bad weather goes on. They need dry weather for the new gas-artillery.[1]

February 16, 1916.

I have recently spoken to hundreds of men on the Fronts of three armies. I have sat with them in their dug-outs—alone, without their officers—and everywhere I have heard nothing but praise for the commissariat. I always say that Hindenburg has sent me to see how they are getting on and whether they are in need of anything : they all become confidential, but I have never heard a single complaint. Some did say they would like some leave, but that was all—not a word about ill-treatment either. Of course there is solid drill these days, and the men are better and more thoroughly trained than in the times of pressure; but it was high time too. There have also been deserters—Alsatians to a man. We had a number of unreliable Alsatian and Lorraine troops over

---

[1] The attack on Verdun had to be continuously postponed on account of bad weather. It began on February 21st.

here. But all that is months ago. It is quite untrue
that there were any deserters in the Dünaburg area.

February 17, 1916.

The Imperial Chancellor has again defeated the
conservative attack on him. He went to G.H.Q.
and returned with the assurance of H.M.'s fullest
confidence. That was what made him so truculent.
The suspension of the Economy Committee of the
House of Deputies was unquestionably his right,
and in itself correct: but the subsequent published
statement was a piece of folly — it was merely
flogging a dead horse.

February 28, 1916.

I have read a very interesting discussion of the
U-boat war by von Tirpitz. He guarantees that
England will be forced to make peace in six months
if everything is torpedoed without regard to America
and the Neutrals. If that is so, then he can go ahead,
but we shall have to reckon with America as well.

March 2, 1916.

Things are at a standstill at Verdun owing to
the powerful French counter-attack and the delay
in getting up our artillery. G.H.Q. is confident;
they are waiting for Verdun to fall. That would undoubtedly be a great success—calculated to destroy
the ineradicable French belief in victory. I hope
our people may prove to be right.

March 4, 1916.

There seems to be a high political crisis over the
question of America. Zimmermann is of the opinion
that we have had enough U-boats to carry the
thing through, and on that account he is unwilling
to depart from the position set forth in the last
Note—and on that hypothesis he is, in my opinion,

right. It seems that losses at Verdun have not
hitherto been great—indeed, from some points of
view, actually small — and the influential people
are full of hope for a successful issue.

March 6, 1916.

Deliveries from Rumania are at present punctual
and good. We owe it to the energy of our Inspector-
General of Field Railways, General Gröner, that
the carrying capacity of the Hungarian railways
and the Danube transport has been doubled, and
that in the month of February double the January
amount of maize, barley, etc., was imported from
Rumania—*i.e.* about 170,000 tons. Whether we
can still increase the amount, which would be very
desirable, I do not know. Rumania would gladly
send us more in spite of the English purchases.
They have two years' harvest to dispose of, and
could export about 5,000,000 truck-loads, while the
English order was only for 80,000 trucks.

It is certainly true that our Army Reports on
Verdun were not very inspired. The G.H.Q. view
is that hopes should not be raised too high, and the
papers should be prevented from publishing too
much nonsense. In spite of this the papers insist
on talking about a break-through, etc. What we
feel is that if we actually succeed in taking Verdun,
but don't break the line, the English and French
Press will turn our victory into a failure, as there
was no " break-through." Hence this careful and
restrained phraseology.

March 11, 1916.

Our G.H.Q. seems to have been rather to blame
over Fort Vaux.[1] It seems that it was never in our

[1] The attack on Fort Vaux on March 6th was pushed right up to the
fortifications, but at the last moment was brought to a standstill by French
flanking-fire from Danloup and the Vaux ravine. The hasty report of
the capture of the fort proved incorrect.

hands—at least so the French persist in maintaining. Whether the troops were mistaken and, having occupied some other fortified position, reported in good faith that they had captured Fort Vaux, or whether G.H.Q. was too optimistic and anticipated the event, is not quite clear. In any case, it is an unfortunate affair. The only advantage is that, if we were never inside it, we could not have been driven out of it, and cannot have had heavy losses. G.H.Q. continues cheerful and confident. No further news.

March 12, 1916.

I am doubtful about these rumours of peace by September. There is, I do not doubt, a desire and intention to come to terms with the French, but I don't see how anyone can speak of it to-day, and fix a date.

As to the officers in Wiesbaden, I take rather a different point of view. The Bulgarians behave so discourteously to our officers in Bulgaria that it does our Bulgarian comrades in Wiesbaden a great deal of good to be shown their proper place. As regards the Austrians, no one can expect a German officer who has to fight in their company to love them. One of these days, the next time a man from the War Ministry is here, I will make inquiries on the subject.

The Kaiser is, of course, in the West. The Imperial Chancellor is still at G.H.Q. and seems to have got his way over the U-boat question. He wants the U-boat campaign carried on as it was in the year 1915—*i.e.* that the enemy ships should be hailed and their crews given the chance of getting off in the boats; neutral ships to be sunk only if carrying contraband. Tirpitz would sink every ship approaching the English coast, without challenge or warning. The latter course, if he had enough U-boats, would of course force England to make peace in a few months. As he has not, he must inevitably involve us in war with all the Neutrals, and that would be too much even for me. So I hope they will be reasonable.

March 14, 1916.

It seems that the Russians have been planning an attack against us, and I am wondering whether we should bring up our Reserves by railway or not. As the Chief is away, the decision rests with me alone. On the one hand, I don't want to show too much anxiety, if I move the troops too soon; on the other, I am responsible for seeing that they arrive at the right time. I have all in readiness, but I shall certainly take no steps to-day. We have got so unused to the idea of responsible decisions that I am almost a little excited. What suggests a Russian attack is the fact that the French will, of course, urge that something should be done. The Italians also began a fresh attack on the Isonzo Front—of course with no success. The Chancellor has apparently won a complete victory over the U-boat question: Tirpitz departs. I cannot weep over him. If he had built more U-boats and fast cruisers, and fewer battleships for Naval Reviews, we should have been in a better position to-day.

March 16, 1916.

The report about Vaux was an error—we never got into the place and, consequently, were never turned out of it. As G.H.Q. had announced the storming of the fort with so much jubilation they would not contradict themselves, and lied about it. I should have thought it better and more practical to admit the mistake without more ado. The result is that everyone thinks our losses in the affair were enormous.

March 17, 1916.

There is a violent conflict of opinion over the question of the U-boat campaign. Tirpitz seems to have used every possible means to get his way, and incidentally to have made terms with the Bavarian, Hertling. He is to be Imperial Chancellor, and in return the King of Bavaria is to support Tirpitz. Whether all this is true remains to be seen, but these are the stories going about Berlin. It seems that Falkenhayn has allied himself rather closely with Tirpitz, and as a result of the Chancellor's victory, and sundry other matters, his position with H.M. is somewhat shaken.

March 19, 1916.

The Russians have attacked very strongly at more than one point, and until now have been beaten off everywhere with heavy losses.[1] In front of the XXI. Corps alone 9270 Russians dead, lying in front of their own lines, were counted from our positions. We have not yet needed to bring up any of our Reserves, and our own losses are amazingly slight—about 560 men, up till now. So we await developments with equanimity.

[1] The German attack at Verdun produced attacks on the other Entente Fronts, designed to relieve the strain.
The Russians began to attack in March. The main attack came off between the Visnieff and Narocz lakes, and in the neighbourhood of Postavy. The object of it apparently was to envelop and drive in with flanks of the German XXI. Army Corps and so make an opening for a break-through on a larger scale towards Vilna and Kovno. Other attacks, by way of diversions, took place in the Vidzy area (south of Dünaburg), at Dünaburg and Jakobstadt. After heavy drum fire, mass attacks by the Russian infantry were launched on March 15th, March 18th-21st, and on March 26th there was danger for a time between the two lakes and near Postavy, but this was happily averted.

The news from the West sounds good. There is progress at Verdun, though it is slow. We have no details, but I was informed to-day that the army in the West is in magnificent form.

We happen to have a naval officer at Headquarters who is here on duty. He gave us some very interesting information about the U-boat campaign, and gave me the numbers of the boats now on service, and those that have been lost; and I am only confirmed in my opinion that the Chancellor is right and Tirpitz wrong. However, that does not prevent Tirpitz making propaganda for himself and his U-boat campaign, and getting questions asked in the Reichstag, in a way that almost amounts to high treason.

March 20, 1916.

Tirpitz wants all ships that approach the English coast to be torpedoed without warning, whatever they are, enemy or neutral vessels. That would unquestionably be the best method of bringing England down, and the Foreign Office agrees, but we have not enough boats to manage it. Moreover, as a result, we should unquestionably have to declare war on all Neutrals—America, Holland, Denmark and Rumania. Added to which, the Turks and the Bulgarians would probably break away. This would be too much for us, and we must consequently impose limitations on the U-boat campaign such as we announce in our Note to America. However regrettable the matter may be —presupposing that we have, in fact, too few boats I believe that the standpoint of the Foreign Office is correct. The essential point is the number of U-boats, and that I do not know.

Yesterday and the night before there was heavy fighting at several points on the XXI. Corps Front.

The Russians, with their usual indifference to losses, kept on hurling masses of men against our positions. I estimate their losses at 50,000-60,000 at least. We have hitherto had to bring up one regiment only from our very strong Reserves.

March 22, 1916.

Yesterday the Russians made another furious attack. Unfortunately one of our Divisions was driven back. Two regiments broke and, of course, suffered severely. As might have been supposed, it was one of the Western Divisions — a Baden Reserve Division. The Russians will, of course, hurl themselves with redoubled force at the point where they have scored a success. We at once sent one of our good Divisions into the gap. Another good Division is arriving by rail to-day—at least, the first part of it. Personally I feel no anxiety whatever about the battle. Still, it is little failures of this kind that particularly get on one's nerves.

March 23, 1916.

The Foreign Office and Bethmann say that we have not enough U-boats to go through with it, that we should foolishly and to no purpose bring the Neutrals about our ears, and that this would be more than we could cope with. One could only decide which side was right if one knew the number and the capacity of the U-boats. According to the information put before me we have not enough. I am, consequently, on Bethmann's side in this matter, and I consider Tirpitz's conduct is a public danger, and the attacks of the parties in the Reichstag are, in my opinion, something like high treason. It is true that Bethmann is not suited to the position of Chancellor. If it is thought best to supersede him, let it be done, but the people should not be allowed to get in such a state of irritation over a question of national defence. They, of course, believe that we had 200 U-boats, and that refusal to go on with the campaign was simply Government imbecility, or, as someone wrote to me yesterday: " International High Finance has won, we are not to be allowed to destroy England." People are really too idiotic—nothing can be done with them. Bethmann will carry on the U-boat campaign on the same lines as before. It was incredibly stupid of our Government to allow the newspapers to start all this business about the " U-boat war of annihilation."

May 4, 1916.

There seems to be a deadlock before Verdun, which is, of course, not pleasant. It is mainly due to the bad planning of the operation and poor leadership.

May 7, 1916.

The Austrian offensive against the Italians seems to have petered out. Fleischmann is beside himself over the incompetence of the leadership on that Front. They were all ready a month ago and waiting only for good weather. Then the Italians attacked at the Col di Lana, and various other points — nothing of any importance — but the Austrian Government got nervous, and actually brought up strong reinforcements to the points in question. As a result of this idiotic marching to and fro, the Divisions involved really suffered as much damage by their exertions in the mountains as if they had been through a bigger campaign than the one they were about to start.

May 10, 1916.

The American reply seems—at least, as reported in the Reuter telegram—a gross piece of impertinence. The fellow would probably treat Mexico with greater courtesy.

May 12, 1916.

From the West we hear of various changes in the commands. Among others, some Chiefs of Staff are to be superseded. Falkenhayn is apparently looking for scapegoats for his own and Tappen's failures.

May 22, 1916.

The situation here is unchanged. I see it stated that as a result of the creation of special authorities for the distribution of food in Germany there is a general belief abroad that Germany will be done for by the autumn at the latest. The Russians think, consequently, they need attack no more, as starvation will settle our business for them. Well, that is all to the good. The Austrian offensive progresses favourably. I think it by no means unlikely that the Italians will squeal so loudly that the Russians will find themselves compelled to start an offensive in Galicia to relieve them. In that case they will probably move some of the troops accumulated on our Front down farther south. Then perhaps we shall be able to get something done, even without G.H.Q.

May 23, 1916.

I have not yet read anything about the change of feeling in America, but I do not place much reliance on it. The most important event of the moment is the excellent progress of the Austrian offensive in Italy. In my opinion, it will inevitably have the effect of making the Russians attack either us or in Galicia. For the latter purpose they will have to move troops down from here. In either event we shall have something to do, and get rid of our boredom.

Whether the choice of Batocki was a good one remains to be seen. He is certainly a clever man, but quite unpractical in many respects. Besides, I have the impression that there are too many heads in the Food Ministry to allow of exact and smooth administration.

May 24, 1916.

I have a distinct feeling that the Russians are moving troops away from our Front, probably to the south against the Austrians, but I cannot yet prove it. Perhaps they will so redistribute their strength that we shall be able to start another show.[1] I hope that in any case the Austrians will not allow themselves to be influenced. The Italian operation is progressing excellently at present. The Italians seem to be simply fading away. Otherwise the capture of such enormous numbers of guns compared with so small a number of prisoners can hardly be explained. The moment Cadorna evacuates the Isonzo, so as to avoid being cut off, that will mean a decisive Italian defeat.

May 26, 1916.

In Italy the offensive has come to a temporary standstill in consequence of the snow, at least on

---

[1] In dealing with this point in *The War of Lost Opportunities* Hoffmann writes : " The most desirable point of attack for us would have been Riga. But we could not have managed this with our own forces. . . . If G.H.Q. had been in the position to place six more Divisions at our disposal it would have been possible to carry this plan into effect. It offered the prospect not only of destroying the Riga bridge-head, but of developing into a notable blow against the Russian Army. . . .''

General von Falkenhayn refused the request for the transference of the Divisions.

one of the Austrian wings. However, I think this rather fortunate, as it gives time for the rear formations, more especially ammunition and supplies, to come up. On our Front it certainly looks as if our Russian friends contemplated an attack, at one point only, but in great force. Well, I don't mind, we are prepared for everything.

May 27, 1916.

He will arrive on Monday evening.[1] His arrival will be followed by an address of welcome, a dinner, and then he will depart. I don't think the pronouncement that will doubtless follow is likely to prelude any radical changes — *i.e.* any fresh appointments to responsible positions—or at least I venture to hope not. I doubt if the idea for an offensive that was originally put forward by me will go through without objection. It depends on whether the West can help us. It will not be possible to break off the operation at Verdun, nor indeed could we advise it, and whether they have something else in mind I do not at present know. In any case I am all on the stretch. I am up to the eyes in work, as all the arrangements for H.M.'s safety and reception fall on me, apart from the fact that I am working out the speech that the Field-Marshal is to make.

May 29, 1916.

I share Kapp's views about Batocki: I consider his selection was a mistake. Gröner is very able— it is possible he will get the control into his own hands.

Here we are all in a state of feverish activity for this evening. The hope that Falkenhayn would

[1] H.M. the Kaiser was expected in Kovno to visit the district under the command of the C.-in-C., East.

not come with him has failed—he is coming. Only
Tappen is staying in the West. After what has
happened at Verdun they cannot all travel about
the country. I don't anticipate much from the
visit. It looks more like an attempt to get a little
change and distraction. Besides us, it is proposed
to visit all the Army Commanders, and they will
all of them have to make speeches. So as to avoid
any nonsense, I sent for all four G.S.O.,Ia's, of
the armies yesterday, explained to them what will
be said here, and got them to tell me what their
Commanders wanted to talk about. I'm against
any surprises. So far all seems correct. We shall
be rather short of food in our villa, as the Royal
train alone is bringing sixteen visitors.

May 30, 1916.

A very pleasant visit, which went off excellently,
but from a military and political point of view
quite futile. There was a great reception at the
railway station, then we drove through the prettily
decorated streets to our quarters. Speech by the
Field-Marshal. Present: H.M., the Field-Marshal,
Ludendorff, I, Falkenhayn, General von Lyncker,
and Chelius — representing Plessen. Everything
possible was said in support of an advance on our
Front. Whereupon Falkenhayn replied before
H.M. spoke, and explained that, though our idea
was certainly good, the operation on the West must
be fought out first. If all that H.M. and Falkenhayn
said is a correct statement of the present situation
then they are right, and we must acquiesce. How
far it is so, it is of course impossible to judge. I
spoke to the officers of the Operations Section who
were there, but unfortunately too briefly to get any
insight into the position. However, they assured
me that the situation in the West was good. Our

losses before Verdun are heavy, but those of the French are much heavier. The English are continually growing stronger, but do not show any inclination to attack. In any case we must have strong Reserves there to cope with an English attack.

June 2, 1916.

Here the position is still unchanged. South of Smorgon the Russians are pushing forward, but they have not yet attacked. The suspense makes one a little nervous—will they or won't they?

There is of course great enthusiasm over the naval battle.[1] According to the German report the English have lost more than 100,000 tons, and we about 20,000. I am of course very excited to see the English report. Probably they will deny everything as usual.

June 3, 1916.

Well, the English admit their heavy losses in the naval battle, with the exception of the *Warspite*. The latter point is so far interesting in that the *Warspite* is one of the larger modern battleships, and they want so to distort the story of the battle as to make it appear that we came into action only with their cruisers, and when their heavy ships appeared we broke off the fight. In this way the confidence of the English people in the superiority of their ships of the line may remain unshaken. I hope our Admiralty may be able to produce definite proof of the loss of this vessel.

If it were feasible, an early attack by our fleet would be an excellent thing, so as to show the world that we were not much damaged.

Yesterday we had news from the Western Front

---

[1] The battle of the Skager-Rack was fought on May 31st.

that Fort Vaux had been taken.[1] I am anxious to
know whether this is all right—*i.e.* whether they have
really got it—for my information comes from the
Operations Section; the question is merely whether
the French have surrendered it to us. This would
of course make a great moral impression.

The Italians are wringing their hands and crying for help—they do appear to be in a bad way.
Now of course it will be for the Russians to effect
a diversion. The simplest way of doing so would
be a strong Russian attack on the Rumanian
frontier. They would perhaps be prepared for this
—only they have all their Reserves, or, comparatively speaking, the main part of them, here on
our Front. The difficult question for them now is
—shall they entrain part of them again and send
them south against the Austrians or shall they attack
us? In any case, the question is urgent and must
soon be decided.

June 6, 1916.

We had a damper to-day again, after all the
recent encouraging military successes. The Austrians have got another thrashing from the Russians
in the neighbourhood of Rovno. Linsingen, in
whose Army Group the affair happened, has sent
a furious report. . . . It seems that the entire
Russian Reserves are on our Front, and in Galicia
the Austrians have the superiority in numbers. . . .
It is a raging scandal. Wails for help, of course,
from Teschen to Mézières, and an inquiry from
them: " What can you let us have ? " We can't
let them have anything with a good conscience, all
we can do is to help them out for the time being.
And, even so, we shall have to apply to the West

[1] Fort Vaux was stormed on June 2nd; the fighting in and about
the fort lasted till June 7th, when the garrison, which had been buried
underground, capitulated.

to fill up our gaps. . . . Well, once more we shall
have to manage somehow.[1]

June 7, 1916.

It is always the same story: the 4th Austrian
Army retires as soon as it is attacked. As it is
under the command of an Archduke nothing can
be done. The disaster is of course merely local.
Meantime the necessary Reserves are on their way
to repair the damage.

Kapp has just sent me his Memorandum against
the Imperial Chancellor. It contains a great deal
that is right, especially as regards the food question,
but is so aggressive that one cannot be surprised that
the Chancellor has defended himself pretty savagely.
The other pamphlet which the Chancellor inveighs
against is an anonymous and destructive attack on
our entire foreign policy for the last twenty years.
It is nominally directed against the Chancellor, but
it is indirectly intended for H.M.

June 9, 1916.

The Russians are themselves so astounded at
their victory that they came to a halt yesterday, and

[1] The general Entente attack on the Germans was timed to begin on
July 6th, in the West on the Somme, and in the East on the Baranowiczi—
Smorgon sector. The main Russian attack there was to be supported by
subsidiary attacks at Riga, Luck, Tarnopol, and on the Dniester.
    The effect of the situation in Italy was that the intended Russian
subsidiary attacks on the Russo-Hungarian were launched prematurely.
When, on June 4th, the Russians attacked the 4th Austrian Army at
Luck and the 7th Austrian Army in the Bukovina, both gave way without
putting up any serious resistance. Luck had been already taken by the
Russians on June 7th. On the 13th their advance-guards reached the
Stochod, S.E. of Kovel. In the Bukovina, after the capture of Czernovitz,
their advance reached the line Dniester—Kolomea—Kimpolung. This
success led to the alteration of the Russian plan of operations. In order
to exploit their success, the Russians moved strong Reserves to the south,
but in spite of that they remained strong enough to attack on their other
Fronts. On June 13th a heavy attack was launched against Woyrsch's
Army Group at Baranowiczi: and secondary attacks took place at the
Narocz Lake, Smorgon, Dünaburg, and the Riga bridge-head.
    G.H.Q. had to make up their minds to withdraw strong forces from
the West so as to re-establish the position in the East. This was all the
more difficult as the Entente attack on the Somme was then awaited.

have done nothing since. In the interval the troops we sent have had time to come up. I think the situation will soon be put right again.

June 11, 1916.

Hard at work to-day again over the affairs of our honoured allies. We are, of course, sending all the help we possibly can. The amusing thing is that probably no one could be more astonished at the victory than the Russians themselves. As before, they were preparing their main attack against us up here in the north. In the south, on the Austrian Front, it was considered only as a demonstration on a large scale. Unfortunately the Austrians misunderstood the affair. Our own G.H.Q. must bear part of the blame. They should never have withdrawn all the German troops from the Austrian Front. We were needed to keep them steady. The chief disaster is the break-through at Luck: and this, I hope, will be put straight again in a few days. The chief culprit, the Archduke, who was in command, has at last been superseded. His successor is a Hungarian general with an unintelligible name.[1]

June 12, 1916.

The position here is still unchanged and the great Austrian *débâcle* at Luck shows signs of improvement. There are so many German troops there by this time, and others on the way, that there seems no more need for anxiety at that point. This is of importance to us in so far as any further retirement on the part of Linsingen's Army Group would have affected the position of Woyrsch and the 9th Army, and then we should have been in the soup. This danger is now over. . . . What is tragic, or rather

[1] General von Tertszczanski.

tragi-comic, is that our G.H.Q. is cheerfully releasing more troops to help the Austrians than we needed for our offensive.

June 14, 1916.

The reinforcements are on their way to the Austrians: part of them are already there, and then we shall gradually have everything in order again. The Rumanians have now loyally announced that they will disarm the Russians that cross the frontier, but I rather think that if the Russians cross the Rumanian border with strong forces Bratianu will content himself with a protest on paper.

June 16, 1916.

G.H.Q. wants a long statement of the Field-Marshal's opinion on the situation, so I had to set to and write it and leave everything else aside. . . . The position here unchanged. As regards the Austrians the counter-measures we have arranged take time and we must accordingly have patience. The Austrian defeat is not, of course, agreeable, but we must not pull all our hair out at once.

June 19, 1916.

As the situation stands at present, the Austrians could not hold Czernovitz, so they had much better give it up instead of losing 100,000 more men over it. For we could not help them there. There are no railways to those parts, or rather only one little single-track line, on which reinforcements could not be brought up quickly.

The whole situation on the Eastern Front is as follows. The Russians have planned a great offensive, probably in conjunction with the French and English—and certainly against us. On the French

Front, Verdun has intervened, where the French Army is gradually being destroyed. Whether the English are still for it, or whether they will not venture after the recent battles at Ypres, still remains to be seen. In any case the Russians had collected their main forces, about 76 Divisions, on our Front. The Austrians, suspecting nothing, had over-confidently withdrawn too many troops from their line and sent them to Italy. Our G.H.Q. made the same mistake, and likewise withdrew the majority of the German troops that were on the Austrian Front and sent them to the West.

Why the Russians did not carry out their plan I do not know. However, it is very flattering to us that, in spite of a three- and fourfold superiority, they did not venture to attack us. What they did do was—urged by Italy, they collected such forces as they could on the Austrian Front and made a purely local attack. . . . The Russian success was so great that they said to themselves: " We don't want to take any risk with those damned Germans : we had much better bring our Reserves down south and make the most of our victory." This is what they must have thought, for they have been marching off from our Front as fast as they could go for the last forty-eight hours.

The Austrian Front is now supported on all sides —the Austrians themselves, by our G.H.Q. and by us. At Luck we succeeded in getting them to hold on and, at certain points, to counter-attack: farther south, especially in the Czernovitz district, nothing could be done, as I have said before, simply owing to the nature of the railways. We can only help them considerably farther back. Naturally, this is a great moral encouragement to our enemies, but it is not without its advantages. The Austrians had become so conceited that there was no speaking to them. So we must wait patiently; it will all come right in the end.

June 20, 1916.

In the Kapp Memorandum the main line of attack is, as before, the U-boat policy. People are stupid about this—we have not got the boats, unfortunately, and without them the desired results cannot follow.

June 21, 1916.

On many points I am in entire agreement with Kapp, but not on the U-boat question. On the latter point the general conclusions are wrong. If, at the beginning of the war, we had had our present number of U-boats, and if, before the English had organized their defensive measures, we had declared an energetic U-boat blockade of England, and had carried it through, then it was feasible. Now, what with mines and net barricades, the arming of thousands of fishing-boats and patrol-vessels, the organization of flotillas with drag-nets, the situation has become much more difficult for the U-boats. No boat can come up in the neighbourhood of the English coast without being at once attacked on all sides. The U-boat campaign must, consequently, be transferred to the high seas, and for that purpose we want many more boats than the trifling number that Kapp and the conservatives assume to be necessary.

We knew that the English Fleet, or at any rate part of it, was at sea. Our entire fleet does not go out to catch a few merchant ships. As a result of bad leadership the English suffered very heavy losses in the first engagement, so that the decision of our Admiral to break off the battle after he had received a report that another English squadron was coming up, which threatened to cut off our retreat, is open to question. The English, in fact, did nothing, and we could perhaps have fallen upon this fresh squadron with all our strength. However, criticism after the event is easy, and there are no precedents for naval battles. It was a German success, and a great success—this is un-questionable, even if it is not quite the victory that it was first made out to be. Only those ships whose names have now been published were lost. Of course there is also a great deal of damage, part of which will take months to repair. However, we have certain information that the number of English ships needing repair is very much greater. There is only one point in the whole sea-fight that I do not understand: what was the entire English fleet doing in that neighbourhood? In any case, they must have been intending some great coup, which beyond question failed.

June 22, 1916.

We are still to send troops to the south, and I had to get them on the move. The Russians seem, in fact, to have given up any idea of an offensive against us, and are sending all the troops they can down south. We are making progress at Luck, but slowly, as our people have to do all the work. We are quite strong enough there now. We must get the position straight at Luck first before we begin to think of Czernovitz. In the West we are wait-ing in complete confidence for the English attack. Whether the French are going to make a simul-taneous offensive at some other point remains to be seen, but I do not think so.

June 29, 1916.

Willi Solf rang me up yesterday. He wants to come here and deliver his speech about our future

Colonial policy. It seems no one wants him, and I am sure we don't want to listen to some pessimistic lucubration. He is still dreaming of an understanding with England, and wants colonies without a big fleet—that is, more or less by England's favour.

June 30, 1916.

Well, I got the Field-Marshal to sanction Solf's visit. He is to appear next Wednesday. Helfferich also had previously proposed himself. What all these people want I don't know—mainly, I suppose, the Field-Marshal's support for their policy.

July 2, 1916.

The Anglo-French offensive has begun. They have been accumulating such masses of artillery and ammunition that our line cannot help being driven in, and we cannot help losing prisoners— we must make up our minds to that.[1]

July 2, 1916.

It seems that the Chancellor has made a fresh attack on Falkenhayn. Whether he will pull it off seems to me, however, still doubtful. H.M. will surely realize that the present difficult military situation is to be ascribed to the mistakes of G.H.Q., but I hardly think he will draw the necessary conclusions and dismiss Falkenhayn. And the Chancellor is certainly not energetic enough to handle so vital a question successfully. If he does so, then Falkenhayn will fall, but Bethmann will sit firmer in the saddle than ever. For the time being, therefore, I think it would be more practical for

---

[1] On July 1st the Somme battle began with a powerful attempt at break-through.

Kapp to do nothing at present, because no good can result. At the moment we have, unfortunately, no other Chancellor in prospect.

It is all rather exciting. Ludendorff, of course, is very much up in the air. The only person who truly preserves an Olympian calm is the Field-Marshal.

July 4, 1916.

We're in for a devil of a business here—it would be a pleasure to be a soldier if our G.H.Q. and the Austrians were a little better. All the Russian attacks upon us were driven back without effort. Now we are scratching troops together from all possible holes and corners to send down south, where there is danger. I went home at 2 A.M. this morning and have been at the telephone again since 6.30. In the West they are well content—the English are not advancing at all, and the French gains on the Somme are not so important that they need cause any anxiety. Of course there will be heavy fighting on all Fronts in the near future—but personally I am entirely confident of the result.[1]

July 5, 1916.

With us all is in perfect order; on the other hand there is heavy fighting on our right. We are sending them everything we can spare. The idiocy of the thing is that we are not in supreme command. The Austrians were quite willing, but Falkenhayn will not allow it. Ludendorff and I have explained

[1] In the second half of June the German and Austro-Hungarian reinforcements arrived in the Luck salient, on the Dniester and in the Carpathians, and began a counter-attack, which, however, soon came to a standstill in the face of the Russian superiority in numbers.

The hard-won gains in the Luck salient had to be given up. On the Styr, to the south of the Dniester, and in the Carpathians, the Russians gained ground in the middle of July: and a serious crisis arose on the Eastern Front.

to the Field-Marshal that he must again write to H.M., or, in other words, to the Adjutant-General on duty, for him to report to H.M.—it can't go on like this. I am just composing the letter. There was an amusing incident yesterday at breakfast. Helfferich and Lewaldt sat drivelling away about England, etc. At last I really could not bear it any longer and said: "We can't go on much longer with a damned slack Government like ours; it is beginning to stink to heaven, etc." Their faces! Lewaldt said he supposed I had read the Kapp Memorandum. I said I didn't need any memorandum; my own understanding was enough.

July 6, 1916.

Solf was here yesterday and to-day. However, he had nothing much new to tell us. Food would hold out. There were difficulties, but they could be overcome. Very thick with Bethmann. Still in hopes of an understanding with England. They're all a band of brothers when it comes to hating Falkenhayn; but so long as it's only platonic, and no one will take a risk, I see no possibility of success. The Field-Marshal has actually cut out a few passages from my very mild and courteously expressed letter. Whether it will be allowed to go remains to be seen.

All is in perfect order here. The Russians are attacking at a few points and senselessly wasting their ammunition: very slight results and a futile loss of life. Our positions are very well constructed and nothing has any effect on them. For example, yesterday 4600 shells fell on one Divisional Front. Result: one man wounded.

Our child of sorrow of the last few days— Woyrsch's Force to the south of us—is apparently out of its worst difficulties, thanks to the reinforcements we have sent there.

In Volhynia and Galicia prospects are not very bright in one or two places, the cause being the unreliability of the Austrians and bad leadership on the part of the Germans. There's really nothing more we can do. As long as the position down there is not really critical they won't give us the supreme command.

July 7, 1916.

As I had anticipated, the letter — after much polishing and many corrections—was not sent off; the plan was to send the letter at the same time as a demonstration by the Chancellor was to take place. Eisenhart, whom we sent to the Chancellor, has now telephoned that he—the Chancellor—has, for some reason or another, decided to do nothing for the time being, so that the whole affair is hung up.

In spite of furious Russian attacks our whole Front is in the best of good order, but the Austrians, on the other hand, are still in a mess. The proper thing would be for us to be given the supreme command on the East Front, so that we could put things straight for them. After a long conference this morning Hindenburg did at least send a short telegram in this sense to G.H.Q. It will probably be no use, but we have relieved our consciences.

July 8, 1916.

Our wire of yesterday to Lyncker actually produced some effect. The area of our command is to be probably somewhat extended, and we are to take over part of the Southern Front. Under that arrangement we shall change our quarters—perhaps to Warsaw: an idiotic thing to do,

July 11, 1916.

General Grünert was here yesterday — he was
Q.M.G. with us at the beginning of the war, then
Chief of Staff with the 8th and 9th Armies here in
the East, and then with the 2nd Army in the West.
The 2nd Army was the one involved by the Anglo-
French attack. Although he had predicted the date
of the coming attack, and asked for reinforcements,
none—as usual—were given him. Hence the first
successes of the French. He was made a scapegoat
and superseded, and was given a Division here on
the Eastern Front. He is pretty savage with G.H.Q.

July 14, 1916.

G.H.Q. has not actually put Linsingen and
Woyrsch under our command, but something at
any rate has been accomplished. Every two or
three days Herr von Falkenhayn asks what we think
of the position there and what arrangements we
propose to make. So something is happening. It
has been a truly complicated business, but we are
getting there.

July 18, 1916.

There can be no sort of doubt but that the general
position is serious at the moment. For the first time
they are making a simultaneous attack upon us and
are consequently preventing us from moving our
Reserves between the two Fronts, because they are
being shouted for everywhere at the same time.
Still I don't think the situation is one for real
anxiety. We must just hold on. Even if we lose
this or that position, or have to retire a few kilometres, there is no great harm. The main thing is
to keep one's head calm and clear.

On our Front the Russians began an attack

yesterday in the neighbourhood of Mitau. Up till now we have beaten off all their attacks. Early this morning I pushed up a few Reserves, and I await the outcome with confidence.

July 19, 1916.

The prevailing depression is very natural. Most people do not realize that we have not won such an unconditional victory as the Pan-German papers make out, and that we shall still have to fight hard to hold what we have won.

July 20, 1916.

The Chief's journey to Berlin was entirely superfluous. The question of the supreme command was not touched upon, and only such matters were discussed as could have been perfectly well dealt with in writing. Probably Falkenhayn wanted to give H.M. the impression that he took Hindenburg into his confidence over all operations. As a result of it all, Ludendorff came back in a pretty savage temper. He had also talked to the Chancellor, but there is nothing doing there. Falkenhayn is confident that we can hold on in the West. Our Austrian comrades are the difficulty. We shall perhaps bring a few Austrian Divisions up here and so release a few German ones.

By the middle of August our fleet will be ready for sea again; the English fleet will not be ready for some time.

July 22, 1916.

A savage amount of work here. More discussions as to the extension of the supreme command over the Austrians, or at least a part of them: but, as usual, it was all brought to nothing by some idiotic scruples.

July 23, 1916.

I have not yet had a serious conversation with the Field-Marshal about Kapp. He cares absolutely nothing about Kapp's proposals. Ludendorff agrees, as I do, with a part only of his Memorandum. What Kapp wants is to get the Field-Marshal and Ludendorff to bolster up his U-boat theory, and there I can't help him. At present, none of us here have changed our point of view on this subject: " If we have enough U-boats, well and good." If we shall have enough by the autumn I don't know. The Chancellor's inclination to treat Kapp's Memorandum with contempt, like the anonymous one, is generally disapproved. Tirpitz I don't trust an inch. His own subordinates call him " The Father of Lies," and at present there is much contention as to who has told the most lies in all the negotiations over the U-boat question—Tirpitz or Falkenhayn.

Yesterday's exchange of letters and telegrams about the extension of the supreme command was simply comic. . . . However, we gave thanks for small mercies.

July 27, 1916.

I spoke with Bockelberg, who had travelled with the Field-Marshal and Ludendorff, immediately after Kattowitz. They reached Pless about eleven o'clock, and before their reception by H.M. they had a talk with the Chancellor, who had also betaken himself to Pless. Falkenhayn visited the Austrian Headquarters at Teschen yesterday — I assume to organize the opposition to the Field-Marshal's taking over the supreme command.

The fact that the arrival of the Turks in Galicia, even before they have got here, has been so loudly proclaimed is surely rather humiliating for the Austrians. A Division is actually on the way. Enver has long wanted to increase his prestige by taking a share in the war in Europe.

It would be very desirable, if it were practicable, to stimulate the Bulgarians to greater activity, especially against the Rumanians. The King of Rumania is determined to remain absolutely neutral, Bratianu has given the strongest assurances to our Foreign Office to that effect, and the Rumanian banks have been warned, for the present at least, to reckon in their operations and speculations on the continuance of neutrality for the next six weeks. However, one would like to make sure, and if the Bulgarians appeared on the Rumanian frontier with 4 or 5 Divisions the enthusiasm of the Rumanian hooligans would be sensibly damped.

July 26, 1916.

The position as regards the Austrians is still far from satisfactory. As a result, it is not impossible that the supreme command may be transferred to us, at least as far as, and including, Linsingen's army. I only hope the Field-Marshal will not let himself in for half-compromises. In this connection I have been feeling considerable anxiety, for he has been repeating since yesterday: " Yes, what my King commands, that I must do! "

July 30, 1916.

Falkenhayn's position much shaken, ours much strengthened.

July 31, 1916.

Yesterday we took over the command of Prince Leopold's Army Group,[1] and this evening we are

[1] Hoffmann writes on this point in *The War of Lost Opportunities* : " At the end of July, Field-Marshal von Hindenburg and General Ludendorff were again ordered to General Headquarters. The difficult position on the Eastern Front called for energetic measures. In particular the fall of Brody, news of which had just arrived, silenced such trifling scruples as

going to Brest-Litovsk, there to take over Linsingen's and the 2nd Austrian Army (Lemberg). Thus we have achieved what we could. As I wrote yesterday, the Field-Marshal and Ludendorff came back very well satisfied from Pless. Falkenhayn's star is sensibly on the wane. In the conflict, which at times became rather acrimonious, between Hindenburg and Ludendorff on the one side and Falkenhayn on the other, H.M. decided throughout in favour of the former. Falkenhayn did not subsequently appear at the Imperial dinner-table, which gave rise to a general hope that he was possibly so offended that he might take his departure. Unfortunately not; but in any case our position is now very much more secure. The task of putting all that mess straight in the south is of course naturally not an easy one, but I have no doubt that we can manage it.

BREST-LITOVSK, *August* 2, 1916.

Early yesterday morning, I am glad to say, we disembarked here. It was, I think, high time. The moment we arrived we took over the command of Linsingen's Army Group and, on the following day, of the 2nd Austrian Army as well. So our command extends from south of Lemberg to the Baltic. It is fortunate that in these days one does not lead armies on horseback.

August 4, 1916.

At 3 A.M. this morning we returned from our journey to Kovel and Lemberg. Our worthy allies'

there were." They could not yet decide to make a complete job of it and extend the Front of the C.-in-C., East, as far as the Carpathians: but they did at least decide to place under his command the whole front as far as the area to the south of Brody, including Böhm-Ermolli's Army Group.

Pflanzer-Baltin's army, the Austrian 3rd Army, and the Southern Army were formed into a new Army Group, under the Archduke and Heir-Apparent Karl. The German General von Seekt was assigned to him as Chief of Staff.

prospects do not look too good. We shall have to spit on our fingers pretty smartly, but I don't doubt that we shall pull it off.

Princely receptions, of course, everywhere, with guards of honour, and all manner of flummery and banquets, etc.

August 5, 1916.

On our Front, as far as the German troops reach, all is well. Only the Austrian 2nd Army in front of Lemberg makes me anxious. I shall not be easy in my mind until we have moved German troops down there.

August 6, 1916.

The command of this gigantic Front may be a very honourable position: but I should like it better if it involved less work. And the whole thing is continually on my nerves. Added to which there is eternal friction with G.H.Q.

August 7, 1916.

Surprises are never at an end here.[1] Yesterday at midday all was in excellent order on the Front of the 2nd Austrian Army: at 2 P.M. it was reported that the Russians had attacked with superior numbers; the whole army was in retreat, position very serious, etc. We took all possible steps to help them. Report from the Austrians in the evening: position not so bad as had been thought, on no account to move from where we were that morning. Report early to-day to the effect that the Russians

[1] From 8th-10th August, Linsingen's Army Group and the left wing of Gronau's army was again attacked. There were simultaneously attacks on the Austrian 2nd Army and the Archduke Karl's Army Group. The 2nd Austrian Army was broken through. Two German Divisions just placed at the disposal of the Eastern Command by G.H.Q. had to be moved down to stop the retreat of the Austrian troops.

had broken through at so-and-so and so-and-so, situation serious, etc. The fellows lose their heads at once. If we had a German Staff and a few German Divisions down there then peace would come upon the land. However, the last few days have been rather exciting.

I had a talk yesterday with the Director-General of Railways, General Gröner, a very clever man. He has lately come from the West, and he thinks the position there is now quite secure. The heavy fighting will go on for a time, but the crisis is over. The Entente is still making the most colossal efforts to knock us out by the spring. No one is very keen on a third winter campaign. Nor—speaking frankly—am I.

The situation looks rather ominous in Rumania. The King certainly is a man of good will, but English and French gold have been assiduously working on public opinion, which makes it more essential that the Austrians shall be made to stand their ground. It is a pity that G.H.Q. does not lighten our task. Personally I am absolutely confident. If Rumania is so stupid, then the Turks and the Bulgarians must be let loose upon the land. The Rumanian Army is bad and has no ammunition. The Entente's Salonika Army is bluff.

August 8, 1916.

Not a day without some special attraction. We had our Front in tolerable order. On the Sereth, where the Russians had driven back the Imperial Army in front of Lemberg, we were going to put so many German troops into the line to-day that we should have been able to attack to-morrow: then, farther south, there was an attack on the Archduke Heir-Apparent's troops who are not under our command. Seekt, who is Chief of Staff there, sent up a wail for help. So we had once more to entrain a part of our Reserves and send them southwards.

August 10, 1916.

. . . If, after the war, anyone comes near me with a Nibelung's oath of fidelity and an offer to die at my side in battle, I shall certainly knock his head off. . . . In the army group of our right-hand neighbour, the Archduke Karl, there was the devil and all to pay, and we exchanged friendly telegrams. We are still sitting in a train, as the furniture from Warsaw has not arrived.

August 14, 1916.

Continual friction with the Austrians, and almost more with G.H.Q. The day before yesterday the Field-Marshal telegraphed to H.M. at our urgent request, in reply to which he received the all-gracious instructions to mind our own business. I have said to Ludendorff and Hindenburg that in my view Hindenburg must at last take the matter in hand seriously and offer the alternative: Falken-hayn or himself. But he will not. And one can do nothing but worry. The comical thing about the whole business is: G.H.Q. do everything that we telegraph them to do, but it must look as if they had done it on their own. One needs nerves like ropes. The other day I was so sick of the whole thing that I asked Ludendorff to let me go as Chief of Staff to a Corps. He over-persuaded me kindly, and I am still here.

August 15, 1916.

The position is unchanged here. The Russians are apparently still shifting troops to the south so as to make the most of their success against the

Archduke Karl. In the meantime our Staff has investigated the mistakes that were made, and has so strongly reinforced the Archduke that from to-morrow he should be able to hold his ground. Thus we are gradually getting things straight again —and the whole affair was so unnecessary. Everyone could have foreseen it weeks ago, except Herr von Falkenhayn.[1]

August 16, 1916.

Our cry of despair that something must be done has had some effect—in any case G.H.Q. came to Pless this evening. Whether enough troops can be transferred to the East in any reasonable time to drive the Russians out of the Bukovina again seems to me very doubtful. Ludendorff and I have, in fact, an idea as to how it might be done.

August 17, 1916.

Nothing new here, for continual rows and disputes with Falkenhayn are nothing new. He wants to take reinforcements from a part of our line where they cannot be spared.

The visit we projected yesterday has come to nothing, though H.M. sent his most all-gracious thanks; he does not much value our visits. When Hindenburg and Ludendorff went to Pless they carried all before them. Falkenhayn did not appear at dinner and all the world thought that he would send in his resignation. He did nothing of the kind —he let the two of them depart and then got hold of H.M. again. I can only explain it by the fact that he gave him false information about the state of affairs, and about his and our proposals. Anyhow, H.M. twice decided against us—*i.e.* he first had a

---

[1] Hoffmann overlooks the difficulties connected with the distribution of forces in the face of the threatened attack on the Somme.

telegram sent to the effect that we should confine our attention to our own Front, and now he has rejected our protest against Falkenhayn's decision to take a Division away from us. Ludendorff had already sent off an orderly with a request to be allowed to resign, as Hindenburg wanted to pass the thing over. It was only Ludendorff's threat of departure that moved him to ask H.M. for an interview. H.M. refused, so a long dispatch went off to him to-day. What will be done depends on the answer.

We cannot at present get Hindenburg to ask to be allowed to resign—not even by Ludendorff threatening to depart. I have had to persuade him personally that he must not, in fact, let Ludendorff go—he must, for the time being, await the answer to the letter that is to be sent off to-day.

August 21, 1916.

Heavy fighting now in progress at one point of our Front on the Stochod. For two whole days I was rather anxious, but we have now been able to bring up enough Reserves there. The Austrian Front is like a mouth full of sensitive teeth. So soon as a breeze gets up there is toothache somewhere. Otherwise, nothing special. We are trying to scratch up some troops from anywhere we can, so as to get together some new Reserves, as one never knows what the next hour may bring. The letter to H.M. went off yesterday. It will not make very much impression. It could deal only with the purely local conditions on our Front.

The vast mistakes that G.H.Q. have made, and continue to make, cannot be spoken of openly. What is done cannot be undone; to talk of them would only make the nation discontented, and no power on earth will convince H.M., when he has once agreed to an operation, that it is wrong.

Verdun, for instance. The attack on Verdun was right if it was successful. But when it became obvious that the French were staking everything on holding it, and when it began to call for such sacrifices, not merely in men but in ammunition, it should have been given up. Everyone knew about the great French attacks on the Somme a month before the time, only G.H.Q. did not believe in them and took no precautions. When the Austrian disasters began 6 Divisions should have been put on the railway and sent across at once. Falkenhayn got on his hind legs and said he had none to spare. So things go from bad to worse, and now he has sent 12 Divisions—*i.e.* he has now had to send twice as many to repair the damage. That is the kind of thing that makes one so angry, and there are dozens of instances.

August 23, 1916.

H.M. has not yet answered our dispatch, and the Field-Marshal is in a state of great excitement. Two years ago this day he appeared with Ludendorff in Marienburg. God, what has happened since then! So much, that in Hindenburg's place I should act and speak very differently.

August 24, 1916.

H.M.'s answer to our dispatch came yesterday. It consists of a very gracious autograph letter to the Field-Marshal; no grasp of our difficulties and a number of observations that no one has ever disputed. So that's the end of that, and we might again have saved ourselves the trouble.

August 27, 1916.

. . . In addition to this we are anxious about the Austrians, who always come to grief: they can't seem to take the war seriously. . . . The officers on the active list occupy comfortable chairs in the higher Staff appointments—on the Lines of Communication or somewhere of the sort—and the clerks, actors and small officials, who figure as officers in the front line, know nothing and can do nothing. And if they are any use, and try their best, they have no sort of authority among the men. Besides, there are all these different races mixed up together — no less than twenty-three distinct languages. No one understands anyone else.

On the Polish question I have just heard that there has been an agreement with Austria-Hungary.[1] A Kingdom of Poland is to be established—in the main the old Congress-Poland with an Austrian Archduke as King. The new kingdom will, however, not be connected with Galicia, but is to maintain a military convention with Germany; in other words, we are to take their army in hand as well as their diplomatic representation. The settlement would have been published already, chiefly to enable Polish legions to be raised, but H.M. has still a strange hope of coming to a separate understanding with Russia, so that it is not thought wise to offend the Tsar over Poland. I have not much faith in a separate understanding with Russia, though it is true that there have of late been voices heard in Russia pointing out the futility of continuing the war.

August 30, 1916.

After our latest disputes with G.H.Q. we have confined our activities to the Ober-Ost[2] area, and

---

[1] On August 11th the Chancellor, von Bethmann-Hollweg, reached an agreement with the Foreign Minister of the Dual Monarchy, Baron von Burian, providing for the establishment of an independent Kingdom of Poland.

[2] "Upper East." The usual term for the Eastern War area and, being brief and convenient, here retained.—*Translator.*

have abandoned all further attempts to stiffen up
the Archduke Karl's Army Group, etc. After the
entirely unexpected entry of Rumania into the war [1]
they all seem to have got into a state of nerves.
The day before yesterday, after noon, Lyncker
telephoned to Ludendorff asking the Field-Marshal
and him to come at once to Pless: Falkenhayn, he
said, knew nothing about it, and would be informed
only after they had arrived. I at once said to
Ludendorff that the time for the discussion of trifles
was over, and that the Field-Marshal must go all
out: he must say quite definitely to H.M.: "After
the way Falkenhayn has behaved I can no longer
merely offer advice. I am ready to pledge my
reputation and popularity and to take over the
difficult post of Chief of the General Staff of the
Army in the Field. If Your Majesty agrees, then
let Falkenhayn depart to-day—or else let me go
back peacefully to Brest-Litovsk." He seems to
have said something of the kind, for the telegram
came yesterday. . . . It is a big jump for me: all
the Army Group and Army Commanders are, of
course, considerably my seniors (I shall actually
become an Excellenz!), so I must be rather particularly careful.[2]

August 31, 1916.

I have no Commander-in-Chief, no G.S.O.,Ia
(he is not yet appointed), and no Ib, as Ludendorff
has taken Bockelberg with him, whom I can very
ill spare. He is quite unsympathetic to me, but an
uncommonly able man. So I am all alone in the

[1] On August 27th Rumania declared war on Austria-Hungary.
[2] On August 29th, Field-Marshal von Hindenburg was appointed
Chief of the General Staff to the Army in the Field, and Ludendorff the
First Quartermaster-General. Field-Marshal Prince Leopold of Bavaria
succeeded Field-Marshal von Hindenburg as C.-in-C., East. Lieutenant-
Colonel Hoffmann was appointed Chief of the General Staff to the
Commander-in-Chief, with Lieutenant-Colonel Keller as G.S.O.,I, later
replaced by Major Brinckmann.

world, and in addition to my official papers my writing-table is piled with congratulations and petitions.

September 3, 1916.

I cannot do more than hold on to what we have, and, for the rest, try to spare as many men as possible to help at other points. Then I shall have carried out my task. At present it is not easy. The Russians are violently attacking the army on our right and Linsingen's Group as well. We have beaten them off up till now, and I am quite confident of the issue as a whole. If things look rather bad at a particular point—well, we must just spit on our hands.

Yesterday I had my first quarrel with Seekt. He is Chief of Staff to the Archduke Karl and therefore not under my control. . . .

Well, I applied to Ludendorff and got my way, and all was peace in the land.

September 5, 1916.

All is in excellent order here, and on our right the position seems to be slowly improving. Mackensen's march into the Dobrudja with a few Bulgarian Divisions and a German force has made a paralysing impression on the Rumanians: they have not stirred for the last three days in Transylvania.[1]

In the West there is heavy fighting on the Somme.

[1] On August 27th Rumania declared war on Austria-Hungary, and Russian and Rumanian troops pushed forward over the borders of Moldavia and Wallachia as far down as the Danube, and into Transylvania and Hungary.

G.H.Q. was then confronted with the task of strengthening the Army Group of the Archduke Karl, and providing for a stroke against Rumania that would secure that part of the Front. As no troops could be spared from the Western Front, the C.-in-C., East, was instructed to withdraw troops from various points in his line.

South of the Danube, Field-Marshal von Mackensen received an order on August 28th to take over the German, Austro-Hungarian and

September 6, 1916.

The situation on our Front is, of course, perfectly satisfactory, but the Austrians on our right are still very shaky. I am continually taking troops out of the line and sending them south in support. I am in constant telephonic communication with Ludendorff, as I hope to get sanction for my proposals regarding the command farther south. I continue on excellent terms with my C.-in-C.

September 7, 1916.

The Duke of Brunswick was here at midday. I did the honours as Chief for the first time. He was very charming and agreeable. This afternoon Prince Leopold went off for a three days' visit to the Austrian 2nd Army, which forms our right wing. On our immediate right the Army Group of the Archduke Karl is under the orders of the Army H.Q. at Teschen. We—*i.e.* Seekt and I—exchange views. I have already complained of him twice at Pless. In Bulgaria—*i.e.* for the Dobrudja offensive—Mackensen is in command.

September 10, 1916.

Hindenburg and Ludendorff have been on the Western Front for a few days. Ludendorff rang up just now and said that there was severe fighting

Bulgarian troops then posted on the line of the Danube and the Dobrudja frontier. There were also at his disposal: the Austrian Danube flotilla to the west of Orsova, some Bulgarian Landsturm in Donauschutz, a mixed German force at Rustchuk, a Bulgarian Division in the same place, and further unimportant Bulgarian forces as far as to the east of the railway line from Bulgaria into the Dobrudja. And a few German heavy batteries and a Turkish Division were on the way.

Field-Marshal von Mackensen was instructed to invade the Dobrudja with these forces. He began to march at the beginning of September: by September 6th Tutrakan was taken, and by the 9th, Silistria.

In the meantime the 9th Army was concentrated at Mühlbach, in Transylvania, and the Austrian 1st Army on the Maros.

in the West, but no cause for anxiety. Dreadful mistakes have been made and it is high time that matters were put straight.

September 10, 1916.

The programme of the very successful journey with H.M. was as follows: at 7 P.M. a guard of honour met H.M. in Kovel; reception, etc.; march past; after which H.M. distributed decorations, the first being a " Pour le Mérite " for me. Everybody—Lyncker in particular—congratulated me most kindly. Then dinner at Linsingen's Headquarters, where I sat between Lyncker and Gontard. On the next day a review of the 42nd Regiment near Vladimir Volynsk, followed by a speech by General Litzmann in the Royal train at Sokal. After this, breakfast in the train, at which I sat by H.M., and he very graciously drank my health. We then crossed over into our own Royal train and went on to Krasne to Böhm-Ermolli, where we were to meet H.M. the next morning (7.10). Another full-dress reception at the station and then on to Zloczov to Eben's Corps. From Zloczov we went by car to the Front, with soldiers lining the way on either side, cheering and looking fine. On a bit of rising ground, from where we could see the Russian positions, Eben made a speech, and then a review was held of all the troops in reserve, against the background of a wood with all its autumn foliage. Great enthusiasm. Address by His Majesty. Our men are really splendid. They had just been through weeks of heavy fighting and looked as though they had come out of a band-box. . . . Then back to Zloczov, where we again had breakfast in the Royal train. Then we parted. H.M. very gracious and in the best of spirits—as he had had nothing but good news during the entire trip (from the West, from Transylvania, and about the Imperial Loan). At parting he shook me very heartily by the hand and said: " Well, I hope you will carry on like this! " H.R.H. and I then went on in a car to visit the Southern Army, where my impressions were not very encouraging. At night I took a special train back to Brest-Litovsk, got through a part of the pile of work that had accumulated on my table, and the same evening took another special train back to Kovel, met H.R.H. there early yesterday morning, and then we both went to meet the Archduke Frederick. After exchanging a few resounding orations in H.R.H.'s saloon we got back here at midday yesterday.

September 13, 1916.

There is heavy fighting in the West. I am accordingly afraid that it may not be possible to withdraw the new formations from that Front, and that we on the Eastern Front shall have to supply the further Divisions needed for the Transylvania campaign. However, we shall manage it.

September 14, 1916.

We have now so many German and Austrian troops in Transylvania that there can be no question of any further Rumanian advance. I hope that the troops now arriving may be collected for a combined attack on one Rumanian Corps and destroy that: then proceed to the next, and so on.

England is, of course, skilfully working on the feelings of the Neutrals, more especially Spain and Denmark: but I have great hopes it will all come to nothing. For this reason it is most important that the campaign in Transylvania should be well conducted, so that we may finish off these Rumanian swine as quickly as possible. Good progress in the

Dobrudja. Our stroke there took the Entente by surprise, and there are only one Rumanian, one Russian, and one or, at most, two Serbian Divisions in that part, the latter being composed of Austrian deserters of Serbian nationality. It is important to reach the Bukarest-Costanza railway as soon as possible and prevent the Rumanians from using it. It is the shortest route between the Danube and the sea. Then, even if the enemy succeeds in bringing reinforcements up as far as that, we can still hold this short stretch of line with comparatively weak forces.

September 17, 1916.

I do not know what has happened to the Polish question. Civil authorities, like the Chancellor and the Foreign Office, do not make decisions as quickly as all that. Two days ago I had a long conference with Prince Lubomirski (from Lemberg), who wanted to see Prince Leopold and put the Polish case before him. The fellows are completely mad. I let the man talk and then told him to put it on paper and send it all to me in writing.

Yesterday the Russians began another attack, like men demented, on our extreme right wing, and on Linsingen's Front. We have repulsed them all here: but they have driven Seekt back in a few places, and we had a pathetic appeal from him early this morning. After a talk with Ludendorff on the telephone I sent one regiment and three batteries. The U-boat question is still in suspense. The opinion that it has no great prospect of success is becoming more and more general.

September 19, 1916.

I have just reported to Ludendorff, who calls up nearly every day, that all is in order here.

To-day he was badly in need of some more troops for another purpose, and I was able to say: "They can start this very evening." Even he was taken aback. It is, however, very interesting to manage with so few troops on such a gigantic Front and still be able to spare some for elsewhere. On the other hand, it is rather a self-sacrificing sort of affair. I would rather be the one who received the troops and was able to do something with them. Still, one cannot have everything, and must be patient.

September 22, 1916.

As far as the Danish question is concerned the English and a certain Germanophobe party in Denmark have very cleverly worked on the Danish Press to force Denmark gradually into an attitude of unfriendliness to Germany. However, the counter - measures taken by us — the transfer of troops to the Danish frontier, the construction of a fortified position there, the demand for repayment from Danish customers, etc.—have had a very cooling effect. The majority of the Danes are neutral. As long as the present Ministry remains at the helm Denmark will certainly remain unconditionally neutral.

September 24, 1916.

According to all reports the Russians appear to contemplate another determined attack upon us here. I am confident of the result, but the burden of responsibility is very great.

September 29, 1916.

Our Front extends from Zborov, on the railway from Lemberg to Tarnopol, to the Baltic, and consists of the 2nd Austrian Army (Colonel-General Böhm-Ermolli) and the three Army Groups of

Linsingen, Woyrsch and Eichhorn. Every Army Group is composed of several armies. In addition to which we control the administrative district called Ober-Ost, consisting of the provinces of Bialystok, Grodno, Vilna, Lithuania and Kurland. The entire area is as large as East and West Prussia, Posen and Silesia all together, or as large again as the territory under the Governor-General of Warsaw, which is not administered by us. At the head of it all is Ober-Ost, with a Central Administration in Kovno, and at the head of the individual administrative areas are Provincial Governors, with the necessary sub-Centres, civil officials and so forth. As Ober-Ost is at present established in Brest-Litovsk the Quartermaster-General, von Eisenhart, who remains at Kovno, carries on current business there. More important matters he comes to discuss here, or he sends the Departmental Minister concerned (Finance, Religion, Forests, Agriculture, etc.).

September 30, 1916.

I don't believe in this indecisive Peace by Christmas; not so much because I would not trust Bethmann to negotiate such a Peace, but because England would not at present agree to any sort of Peace we could accept.

Much liveliness here. The Russians seem at last to be making a determined attack on the 2nd Austrian Army and Linsingen.[1]

October 2, 1916.

That was a pretty bit of work in Transylvania. Our Rumanian friends must be feeling rather poorly to-day. I should like to see a few more of

---

[1] The Russians made persistent and furious attacks to the west of Luck, at Brody and Zborov, at Brzeczany and on the Narajovka, as well as in the Carpathians.

their Divisions destroyed and then offer them peace —that would be the best end to the business.

Ludendorff is going slow and concentrating on training troops, so as to be able to dispose of a large body of trained men in the spring.

October 3, 1916.

The Russians made further attacks yesterday: the I. Russian Guard Corps attacked seventeen times—all repulsed and our line intact. But I must see if I cannot scrape together some more Reserves from somewhere.

Item: H.M. is to appear within the next few days to thank the troops under Böhm-Ermolli and Linsingen.

Item: The Archduke Frederick then visits us, and not long after the King of Bavaria. I seem to be becoming a sort of Court Chamberlain. Ludendorff has just rang up to say that he would like to extend the area of our command still farther to the south, as our friends down there are playing the fool. I am honoured by his confidence, but it is getting rather much for me.

October 4, 1916.

So H.M. comes to-morrow. I shall go with the C.-in-C. to Linsingen's H.Q. at Kovel, so as to be there to receive him. We shall spend the night in the train at Kovel. On the 6th he will visit General von Eben, on what has hitherto been our extreme right wing, stopping at the various Headquarters on the way. On the 7th he will travel back to Pless; H.R.H.—my C.-in-C.—and I, after a few stops at intermediate points, will proceed to the Southern Army, commanded by Count Bothmer, which, as from to-morrow, is also under our command. This will make something like a Front. I shall have to spit on my hands, I can see.

October 5, 1916.

On the afternoon of the 7th, H.M. goes home again. H.R.H. and I will proceed by car to visit the Southern Army that we have just taken over. I shall put matters straight there and come back here the following night by special train. H.R.H. will stay over another day and show himself to the delighted populace.

October 12, 1916.

We all know that the Imperial Chancellor is a weak personality and should long ago have been superseded. Odd as it may sound, we have no one better at the moment. At least I know of no one. A soldier would be continually bothered by not knowing the ropes: Tirpitz, Helfferich—no, I know of nobody. It is just the same with the Foreign Office. There is no use in turning Jagow out unless the whole system is changed, and a change in the system would mean a complete change in our whole social organization. . . . I spoke to Plessen and Lyncker about Jagow and the Foreign Office. Both told me that they had several times talked to H.M. and the Chancellor about getting rid of Jagow; but they could not get away from the fact that he is cleverer than the others, and we have no more suitable man.

Prince Leopold is certainly much cleverer than —— but he is scarcely the star performer of the German political stage.

October 14, 1916.

As we have lost a part of our prepared positions, it is obvious that bad mistakes have been made. In the first place, further strong positions should have been constructed. Several fortified lines should have been constructed in the West, one behind the other, and more ammunition, etc., should have been available. These are our blunders, but they are now recognized, and Ludendorff is doing what is humanly possible to put matters right. More cannot be expected for the time being. H.M. has also been informed of all this. Hindenburg and Ludendorff see him every day, so that there is no longer any question of not being able to penetrate the ring surrounding him. The person responsible for the ammunition shortage has also been superseded, so at the moment I know of nothing more that could or ought to be said to H.M. about the Somme battle.

October 15, 1916.

It is clear that the only possibility of an agreement with Russia lies in a satisfactory solution of the Dardanelles question.

There is a mass of tactical work on hand, as in the next few days we are extending our area of command over the 3rd Austrian Army as well. Thus we shall be in control from the Baltic to the Carpathians. The Archduke Heir-Apparent, with Seekt, commands in Hungary and Transylvania, which makes a convenient break in the line.

October 17, 1916.

From the Carpathians to the Gulf of Riga I have my own saloon railway carriage, and more often than not a special train, automobiles, full-dress receptions wherever I arrive, and everyone in helmets on the platform when I depart, etc. I shall feel very strange when I take over my infantry regiment after the war. And yet I would not be sorry to do it to-day. The anxiety and responsibility are very great, and they make one so old.

October 20, 1916.

I am watching with curiosity how the Russians are going to help their threatened Rumanian allies. They are withdrawing troops along the whole Front, and will probably transfer them to the Carpathians, on the Transylvanian frontier, where they are making a thrust against the Austrians. Then we shall have to reply by taking troops out of the line and sending them down to the Carpathians in support of the Austrians, so that the Russians will then have Germans to deal with. The essential point in the whole business is to find out as early as possible at what parts of the line any troops can be spared, so as to be able to move them down by rail before the enemy can move theirs. We, of course, can move ours quicker, but one must always reckon to lose time on those meandering Austrian railways, with their infamous staff. Hence the delays in the campaign against the Rumanians : the German troops can never be got up in time.

October 25, 1916.

Generally speaking, our Front is quiet; we are going forward well in Transylvania and in the Dobrudja ; only in the West our people seem to have gone to sleep again. The recapture of Douaumont, reported to-day, I can only ascribe to the fact that we have once again been taken by surprise.[1] There are no details.

November 3, 1916.

Nothing special here from a military point of view. We are regrouping some of the troops; the Austrians are howling for reinforcements on the Italian Front, and I am sending some.

[1] After the Somme battle had burnt itself out, the French attacked on October 24th on a Front north-east of Verdun. Fort Douaumont was lost. And on November 1st Fort Vaux had also to be evacuated.

November 4, 1916.

Ludendorff has just rung me up. To-morrow the proclamation providing for a Kingdom of Poland is to be issued, and in eight or ten days the formation of a Polish Army is to begin. The difficulty over the formula of the oath of allegiance has been solved. The Poles are to take the oath to the German Emperor as the Head of their Army during the war, and to the Emperor of Austria as Guarantor for the establishment of the Kingdom of Poland.

November 5, 1916.

I am, of course, much intrigued to know what impression the Polish Manifesto will make, and whether we shall really get any appreciable number of Polish recruits. The Operations Section at G.H.Q. has just rung up again to say that Ludendorff wants yet another Division from us — this time for the West, where, apparently, things are rather serious. Ober-Ost is like the widow's cruse of oil. It will be gradually emptied, though this time we can perhaps manage it.

November 7, 1916.

The supply of horses is causing extreme difficulty. We get no more from abroad and the losses can no longer be made good from home. We must consider every possible source from which horses can be spared. A few days ago one of the Army Groups sent in a request for 23,000 horses.

I have seen no foreign newspaper comments on the Kingdom of Poland—only the French wireless; they are incredibly abusive, so obviously they do not like it.

November 11, 1916.

My visit to Pless went off very well. Ludendorff himself met me at the station (I arrived at 3.36 in the afternoon) and we drank tea at his quarters. Of course we at once began to talk about Service matters. I explained just exactly how many more troops I could let him have, and he seemed very pleased. As we were going to his office, Ludendorff told me about his work and what he had achieved. After all it was high time that Falkenhayn, Wandel and Wild were got rid of, or everything would have burst up in the autumn. But by taking the situation in hand energetically he had pulled things round, and we were now on the up-grade. One of Ludendorff's measures will soon be generally known. A law regarding compulsory labour will be put before the Reichstag. " Every German must work." In that way we shall be able to deal with the shortage of munition-workers, and the munition question is still the decisive one. A law providing for the rationing of the population of Germany on the military scale is now being worked out. Ludendorff is in conflict with the Chancellor and the Admiralty— with the former because he will not turn Jagow out, and the latter because they have no sense of realities. Ludendorff was the moving spirit of the U-boat campaign in the Polar Sea, which has been so successful—not the Admiralty at all.

Position in the West: heavy fighting, but no need for anxiety. As the nerves of the troops in the West are more badly shaken than in the East, we must arrange for some exchanges; there will be no difficulty about this.

Then General von Cramon, German Intelligence Officer in Teschen, came in, and we had a talk about the Polish Legion and Polish Army. Ludendorff, of course, fully realizes the disadvantages in which a Kingdom of Poland may involve us, but we need reinforcements and must take the disadvantages as well. The question as to who is to be King is still undecided, and there is no hurry. Anyhow, a King cannot be chosen before there is an Army and a Government to support him.

Then appeared Conrad von Hötzendorf, with a few officers of his Operations Section. We discussed the progress of the operations in Transylvania and whether I could spare any more troops for them.

H.M. was in Pless, but he was ill. Ludendorff did not believe in the illness, and was of the opinion that he had frightened him with his Labour Law, etc., and that H.M. had evaded any further proposals on a plea of illness. Everyone here is amazed that Ludendorff tells H.M. everything and puts the true situation before him, extenuating nothing.

November 19, 1916.

There has been a devil of a rush here to-day again—one incessant stream of visitors since 7.30 this morning: and Pless calling up every five minutes and demanding troops for the Salonika Front. The Bulgarians are howling for help. However, I have refused : I can't do any more. Ludendorff can scrape together some troops from the West Front.

November 20, 1916.

Ludendorff wanted a few more troops—I am now stripped to the bone—all for Rumania, where things are going well. It is to be hoped that Mackensen will cross the Danube to-day or to-morrow.[1]

---

[1] Field-Marshal von Mackensen's operations in the Dobrudja had led to a complete success. The Rumanian Army in those parts was completely defeated, and Costanza was taken on October 23rd. The advance was then stopped. Mackensen received instructions to re-group his forces, and in the second half of November to cross the Danube south of Bukarest, and thus combine operations with the 9th Army, which, after its victories in Transylvania, was drawn up in the Szurdak Pass ready to invade Wallachia.

November 25, 1916.

There is much liveliness opposite our Front, and the Russians are possibly going to attack at some point in order to relieve the Rumanians. The beloved Entente has left these Rumanian ruffians completely in the lurch, and quite right too. I have great hopes that we shall get to Bukarest.

I have long known that Ludendorff was a possible candidate for the post of Chancellor. I discussed it with him in Pless also, and I told him that I knew no one but himself who was fit for it.

November 26, 1916.

I have invited the Commander of the Polish Legion and his Staff to dinner the day after to-morrow. The Legion will be withdrawn from Baranovici to Warsaw and the neighbourhood. The New Polish Army will be formed out of the Legion.

H.R.H. brought very little news back from Vienna: however, perhaps he did not want to tell me any. He has got no further with the Polish question. The Austrians have too much regard for their prestige to be willing to give up the Governor-Generalship of Lublin: on which account I see trouble brewing over the Polish Legion.

December 13, 1916.

The Peace question [1] has, of course, caused great excitement here. England will move heaven and earth to suppress the whole thing. It is certainly noteworthy that, although the Italians' preparations for an attack on the Isonzo have been ready

[1] On December 12th the Peace offer of the Quadruple Alliance took place.

for the last fortnight, in spite of the fine weather
they have made no move. Moreover, a somewhat
strange decree has been issued by the Austrian
Emperor, so that for some days past I have had the
impression that Austria and Italy are negotiating.

Russia and England are having differences about
the delivery of war material. It is not beyond
the bounds of possibility that some negotiations
may take place, but I don't believe that England is
ready to make peace now. However, perhaps our
broaching the question of peace will have the effect
in America (if the proposal is rejected by England's
influence) of making people more reasonable over
the U-boat question.

December 14, 1916.

I have some heavy work on hand, and I am
shortly sending an officer to Pless to put before
Ludendorff a proposal for the development of the
operations against Russia.[1] I have an idea and I
am anxious that Ludendorff should know about
it. Whether it is feasible is, of course, impossible to
say from here.

[1] In this connection Hoffmann writes in *The War of Lost Opportunities* :
" About Christmas I wrote a letter to General Ludendorff in which I
explained that in my opinion the offensive in Rumania, that had now
become a purely frontal advance, would come to a standstill on the Sereth
in the New Year. If it was desired to continue the campaign and finally
put Rumania out of the war, in that case, in my opinion, there was only
one thing to be done, and that was to give up the attack in the south
and make a thrust from the north. If G.H.Q. was in a position to send
4-6 Divisions to the C.-in-C., East—it would be simplest to send some of
those now fighting in Rumania—I thought we could carry the movement
through. I proposed that the reinforcements and all the troops that could
be collected from C.-in-C., East, should be concentrated in the neighbourhood of Zloczov; the Russian position to be broken through at that
point and the offensive to be carried through Tarnopol along the main
line to Odessa. The bulk of the Russian Army in the Carpathians would
thus be brought into an untenable position, and I believed that the
operation would lead to a great success.

" General Ludendorff did not feel in a position to promise reinforcements.
" For the moment no troops could be spared from the West, and in the
present state of the Rumanian and Hungarian railways it was impossible
to transfer troops quickly from Rumania."

December 16, 1916.

Before the New Year I shall move the administration from Kovno to Bialystok, so as to have it nearer. In the dispute over the control of the administration I have won all along the line. The administration remains not merely under our authority, but is to be extended over the whole Ober-Ost area.[1]

December 21, 1916.

It is clear that matters are not going as well as might be wished; but the Conservatives are making all this fuss, not because they are afraid that anything may go wrong with the Fatherland, but much more from fear that their political predominance may suffer. We cannot dictate a German Peace. To do that we should have had to win the battle on the Marne, or at least, after it, to have put Ludendorff, not Falkenhayn, in control. So we must cut down our demands on one side or another, however regrettable that may be. It is no use banging on the table or playing the strong man.

December 27, 1916.

I have a great deal to do. By the 1st, Ludendorff wants to have before him schemes for all manner of different possibilities. Personal reports on officers come in at the same time. In addition, the extension of the administrative area involves much work. The Peace offer is, as was to be expected, rejected by everyone. More especially the Russians emphasize the fact that there can be no talk of peace until they get Constantinople.

[1] There were movements on foot to withdraw the control of the administration from the C.-in-C., East, and place it immediately under the Quartermaster-General. General Ludendorff decided that matters should remain as they were. The Administrative Departments were moved from Kovno to Bialystok so as to be nearer Headquarters at Brest-Litovsk.

The Italians, however, I can't understand. Why on earth don't they attack on the Isonzo? They have been ready for weeks, and remain inactive in spite of the fine weather.

December 30, 1916.

The Chancellor's Peace terms are, so far as I have been able to ascertain them, better than I should have given him credit for.[1] He certainly should not accept anything less. They are more or less my own. Of course I cannot tell whether we could get better terms, or whether the U-boat war may reduce England to such extremity that she may be forced to be more accommodating. On the other side the military situation in the West is certainly secure, but not brilliant. Everybody, including the Generals, have been asleep for so long over there, and there was, and is, so much leeway to make up — infantry training, heavy artillery, airmen, etc. However, it is to be hoped that we are now out of the wood.

January 6, 1917.

I have had the most troublesome time of late. And, in addition, a horde of visitors—the Q.M.G., Generals, Chaplain-General of the Dutch Army inquiring into " spiritual welfare " arrangements, Turkish princes, Generals on their way through— my head is positively swimming.

January 9, 1917.

I had a letter from Ludendorff yesterday. He complains of the Chancellor and the Foreign Office; neither of them know what they want.

My view of what we want has not altered for the last two years. I do not want Belgium, more

---

[1] Following upon the Peace move there had been an exchange of views on Peace terms, to form the basis of instructions to the German Ambassador in Washington, Count von Bernstorff.

especially because of the unpleasant addition to our Central and Social Democratic parties that it would involve. I want only so much of France . . . as they will redeem for 25 milliards. Belgium, too, must pay a war indemnity. Until it was paid we could keep control over the Belgian railways. Only Liège we must keep as a matter of prestige.

As against this, we want Lithuania and Kurland in the East. Our frontiers against Poland must be improved from a military standpoint — for which purpose Ossowiec is absolutely essential to us.

Vilna we do not want — that may be left to Poland, who can push her frontier as far to the East as she likes.

Bulgaria should get Macedonia and the Dobrudja. Austria to have a good slice of Serbia, but she *wants* a further division of Poland, if we do not agree to the whole of Poland coming under Habsburg sovereignty. Rumania must pay.

The question is how we are to secure these terms. My view is that it is possible to bring Russia to her knees, if the necessary troops can be placed at our disposal on the Eastern Front. In the West we can only remain on the defensive, and, if we have the necessary number of U-boats, there is always the intensified U-boat campaign: that point is beyond my judgment. In any case, it is the only means of putting pressure on England, though we should have America to reckon with. If there are not enough U-boats, then we must just hold on until the distress is so great in England, and more especially in France, that they are ready to negotiate. At present we must get enough troops and ammunition in hand to be able to resist the great offensive in the spring. It will certainly come, but we have enough Reserves to be able to face it with equanimity.

January 11, 1917.

Nothing special here.   The Russians are very lively on their entire front; they naturally want to prevent us bringing up troops and sending them to Mitau, where a few days ago, as the result of the failure of a Landsturm battalion, they took a few of our trenches.   They know us well enough to be afraid that we shall bring up Reserves and turn them out again.

January 15, 1917.

I am all against Bethmann-Hollweg — mainly, indeed, on account of his want of decision.   He must do something; what he does is less important than that something should be done, but nothing *is* done.   Neither he nor the Foreign Office know what they really want—that is what is the matter. If he wants Belgium he should say so; if not . . . he should say so too.   But in either case he is afraid of one party or the other, so he will not speak out either way.

January 16, 1917.

Kapp was here yesterday.   He explained the whole miserable incompetence of our Government. This time we were in pretty general agreement: an intensified U-boat campaign, and, as the Chancellor does not seem to know what he is about —as witness his futile vacillation in always postponing it—he should be superseded.   That is what the large majority of the people wants.   However, Kapp overestimates my influence in the matter.   I gladly promised I would write.   The question of a successor is a difficult one.   His candidate is Tirpitz. The worst of it is that I do not know another at the moment.   Ludendorff cannot yet be dispensed with, and he has not yet sufficient grasp of the political interrelations of the various States. Moreover he has hitherto had too little to do with policy. It would therefore be desirable that Tirpitz should merely keep the place warm, and that Ludendorff should succeed him later. These were the main points of our conversation.

H.R.H. Prince Henry is coming to-morrow. I can't guess what he wants, but I assume that he wants to become Duke of Lithuania and Kurland —perhaps also King of Poland. Everyone who has been here until now has wanted something or other.

January 17, 1917.

I laughed heartily over Witting's lucubrations. Who was it that was always shouting that we should have to go to war at last, that we could not go on standing this sort of thing, etc.? Why, Herr Witting! Of course we could have knuckled under again in the summer of 1914; in which case the Entente would have certainly struck in 1917, that being the earliest date by which they could have been ready. To that extent, I agree, we began the war. The unfortunate thing was simply that our military leaders failed. The difference between Witting and me now is that I will have nothing to do with a Peace patched together by international banking interests. I want a victory. It is still possible—not of course in the sense in which we understood the word earlier—*i.e.* the entire capture or destruction of the enemy armies—but we could, for example, take Petersburg, and so force the Russians to make peace, or bring England to her knees through the submarine campaign.

Undated.

This was my trip in brief: went with Seekt and Hell to Pless; usual kindly and cordial welcome from Ludendorff and Hindenburg. Ludendorff then explained the general situation and his own views. Of course the position could not be rightly estimated until the U-boat war had begun. Our —very modest—requests for the Eastern Front were, in general, granted.

I then had a private talk with Ludendorff about Bethmann-Hollweg and the Foreign Office. Hindenburg and Ludendorff are at considerable loggerheads with the civil power. Bethmann-Hollweg, Helfferich and Zimmermann recently came to Pless for a conference and Hindenburg did not invite them to dine. At Ludendorff's request I then had a further half-hour's private talk with Hindenburg about politics. At the end of it he was prepared to speak to H.M. provided I would put all I had said to him in writing. For the moment it is not practicable to replace Bethmann-Hollweg just because the U-boat campaign began to-day. We must wait a few weeks more and then he must go.

February 5, 1917.

America's prompt answer points to the fact that there is, in fact, a secret understanding between Wilson and England. America would, therefore, certainly have come in, according as events turned in any way to our advantage. Well, it's a good thing to have the situation cleared up at last.

February 8, 1917.

In the next few weeks we are combining the administrations of Lithuania and Vilna-Suvalki (up till now two separate large administrative areas) into a Greater Lithuania, with a capital at Suvalki. This arrangement will probably cause a political sensation, as the Poles must regard it as directed against themselves, which, in point of fact, it is. We shall produce clear evidence to show that the ancient government of Suvalki, which Napoleon in his time turned over to Congress-Poland, should not be allowed to fall to Poland, but remain independent.

The attitude of the European neutral States towards us over the U-boat question is unexpectedly favourable. I have had excellent and reliable news on the point, that will also damp Herr Wilson's fervour a little.

February 11, 1917.

That there is a movement in various circles against Ludendorff — military circles as well — is known to him and to me. At the moment Ludendorff cannot be superseded—that is quite impossible, as Hindenburg would go too, and the consequences of such a step would mean the End. So we are unperturbed.

February 14, 1917.

How far the Rittmeister is correct in his observations on France and French politics I cannot, of course, judge. I do not greatly believe in the possibility of overtures to France and a separate Peace. Besides, at the moment, the French are too much strung up by the hope that they may yet win the war.

As regards N. and D., I have never much trusted either of them during the war, especially not D. I fancy S. too is a member of the gang. For the moment it is not possible to get rid of D., but Ludendorff is arranging to get N. removed.

It is very odd to think that a fortnight ago I asked Prince Isenburg to induce Erzberger to come here again. Erzberger is complaining about our administration in Lithuania, and I want to show him that his information is false. In any case I am curious about future developments. If he could come here I should, of course, talk to him about political questions, Ludendorff, etc.

February 16, 1917.

Nothing special here. A few days more and my troubles are over. It is not a pleasant feeling to be so entirely without Reserves. In the West things are slowly getting livelier; but I do not expect the great attack until the middle of March. Whether our Russian friends will be far enough advanced by then remains to be seen; but in any case I am ready for them.

From the reports in the newspapers the U-boats seem to be doing well. In order to produce an effect we must sink 800,000 to 1,000,000 tons of shipping in the next three months. I think that will be enough. This will produce such a state of nervousness that a great many ships will not put to sea at all.

There is very encouraging news from the interior of Russia. It would seem that she cannot hold out longer than the autumn.

February 22, 1917.

In the West they are all complaining of the cold. There are no dug-outs and they are lying in shell-holes. It would be more sensible to give up the present fighting area on the Somme and the Aisne and retire a few kilometres to the next well-prepared position. We should thus transfer to the other side the privilege of lying in the mud without proper shelter. Whether Ludendorff will do this I don't know, but I hope he will.[1]

---

[1] On March 16th, in the West, the so-called Alberich movement began. The entire salient of the German position between Arras and Soissons was evacuated, and, along the chord of this arc, the so-called Siegfried position was occupied.

February 23, 1917.

It is natural that the Poles should carry on a strong propaganda for the inclusion of Lithuania and Kurland in the Kingdom of Poland. I am at the moment engaged in an extremely acrimonious correspondence with Warsaw, the Foreign Office, and the Imperial Chancellor, to get them to put a stopper on this Polish propaganda.

February 28, 1917.

There are four conflicting elements in this area —German, Polish, Lithuanian and Lettish—and no politician in the world can bring them together. All we can do—while the war is on—is to say: " The Germans must come first, and the others will be treated with absolute impartiality." All three of them hate us because each of them wants to pre-dominate: nothing will alter that. My conscience is clear in the whole business, as is obvious from the fact that I have invited the various representa-tives to come here and look into the circumstances for themselves.

We all know that Ludendorff is no politician, he is too impulsive. He always wants something to happen at once, while the politician must know how to wait.

March 2, 1917.

There is nothing in the French newspaper-cuttings that I did not know before. Every sensible soldier knows that Ypres and Verdun were Falkenhayn's greatest crimes.

March 4, 1917.

Our small affair on the Stochod yesterday went off well — 9000 prisoners, including 4 regimental commanders, 15 guns, 200 machine guns and trench mortars, are a very pretty result. I had reckoned on 3000 at the outside. The Russian Army is deteriorating.

The Russian Revolution is, from the military point of view, a great piece of luck for us, and our withdrawal in the West is extraordinarily unpleasant for the Entente; they wanted a speedy success and hoped to obtain it after their colossal concentration of men and material on the Somme. For the moment time is on our side.

I have just arranged for Erzberger's and Richthofen's travelling permits to be sent to them from here. I have heard no more of Zimmermann's blunder over Mexico; in point of fact, the blunder consisted in being found out: in itself, his action was, of course, perfectly right.

March 5, 1917.

For the rest, a state of violent activity continues on the whole Russian Front. The Russians are constructing a large number of new positions and they certainly will not attack until these are ready. Generally speaking, this is to our advantage. I am gradually disengaging so many Reserves that I can look forward to further developments with equanimity. It was extremely fortunate for us that the Russians left us entirely at peace during the last few weeks. If they had attacked at certain points during the last three weeks I should have been in a damnable mess. And this feeling tends to get on one's nerves in the long run — which partly explains my bad temper these last weeks. In addition to which I had a passage of arms with the authorities at Warsaw. They go on with their Polish propaganda—and what our Lithuanians say is all one to them.

March 10, 1917.

I had a letter from Frau Ludendorff about my influence over her husband, and asking me to use it. Now the trouble is that in trying to influence anyone by letter one cannot meet his objections. One can influence a man in political questions only by talking to him. . . .

I can see from the papers and the debates in Parliament that the outlook at home is bad.

All reasonable people are agreed that we cannot starve England out by the day after to-morrow; on the other hand, the shortage of raw material (ore, pit-props, etc.) in England, and of coal in France and Italy, is likely to be so great in the course of the next three or four months that the various Governments will have to consider whether it would not be more sensible to negotiate. We must take care that the Entente does not win any considerable success in the field during this period —such as Verdun, or the first few days' fighting on the Somme.

March 12, 1917.

I have just written a letter of some length to Frau Ludendorff (she had applied to me to work for Nicolai's dismissal), so my spare time is all used up.

March 14, 1917.

The situation here is unchanged.

There seems to be serious disorder in Petersburg. I think it will probably end in an open conflict between the Duma and the Government, which might easily bring down the Tsar. Whether it will have any effect on the conduct of the war cannot, of course, yet be seen, but it is by no means out of the question.

March 15, 1917.

Our 1st Adjutant, Captain von Trotha, said to me just now before he left me: " Well, sir, your work's up to full strength, anyway "; and he was right. Such time in the morning as H.R.H. has left me is completely taken up by appointments with General Staff Officers and Adjutants. Erzberger and Richthofen are coming to lunch. In the afternoon I am expecting the A.Q.M.G. with seven officers to discuss various important questions of administration. General Riemann is coming before dinner with various requests regarding personnel and tactics. In addition to the above-mentioned, General von Bernhardi, who has been visiting one of the Divisions here, and Prince George of Bavaria are coming to dine. After dinner I shall receive the two Deputies—I have had no time for them before: and I fancy that interview will last until midnight. Then I have to look through the evening mail, and all the incoming reports. There are many days when twenty-four hours are not enough. To-morrow Erzberger and von Richthofen are to lunch with the Prince at Szkoki, and in the afternoon I shall send them in my private saloon, with an orderly officer in attendance, to Escherich at Bialovicz.

There is actually serious disorder, and street-fighting, in Petersburg. I don't know the facts yet, but I suspect that the Government wanted to send the Duma home, and that they would not go. We have no further news yet. What repercussions, if any, this will have on the Russian Army cannot yet be foreseen. I am far from being an optimist, but the cutting of railway lines, strikes, burning of factories, etc., must at least gravely endanger the output of munitions, and thus weaken the Russian Army. We must wait and see. In the meantime I am having a leaflet printed to explain the cause of the troubles to the Russian soldiers in the trenches. Otherwise the poor fellows would know nothing about it, which would be a pity.

March 17, 1917.

Erzberger and Richthofen sat with me the day before yesterday from 10 P.M. until 1.45 A.M., yesterday morning from 8 to 10 and yesterday afternoon from 3.30 to 5 o'clock. They then left for Berlin, travelling straight through, via Warsaw. My proposed journey to the Front and to the occupied territories had to be put off owing to lack of time. It was all very interesting, especially to hear Erzberger's views and expositions. He is a very clever man, with an amazing fund of varied information. Yet, in spite of it all, I was rather disappointed with the visit, for they neither of them threw a really fresh light on anything. It was just a succession of opinions and wishes, of course deserving of respect—but no more. I promised—this was the main object of the visit—to pass it all on to Ludendorff, and this I will do to-morrow; I cannot deal with it to-day, there are too many arrears of work. Of course we also talked about Kurland and Lithuania, and I was astonished to find that Erzberger shared all my views on this point; so I asked him to inform me direct of any complaints that looked like being more than usually vocal, so that I can investigate each one thoroughly.

March 18, 1917.

It is not advisable to be too optimistic about the Russian Revolution at present. There has been no trouble with the army as yet. The Grand Duke Nicolai Nicolaievich has once more become Commander-in-Chief of the entire army. His aim will be a victory, and then a march to Petersburg with the victorious troops to hang the revolutionaries and make himself Tsar. On that account he will very soon make a great effort to win a victory. Things may, of course, work out differently. The whole business is naturally very encouraging for us, as a domestic convulsion of this kind is never a very practical proceeding for a State at war.

March 19, 1917.

In the West the withdrawal has now been carried out. I consider it an excellent piece of work. The French and English have to start their preparations for the great Spring Offensive all over again; they are lying in the open, unprotected from our artillery fire and from the weather, and in front of a fresh line of defence which we constructed months ago. And as it is considerably shorter, we shall save a good many Divisions, as well as artillery.

March 21, 1917.

I think Erzberger is wrong in arranging a meeting with Ludendorff for the end of the month in Berlin. I told the two of them repeatedly that I was perfectly willing to pass on a number of ideas and hints to Ludendorff (as in fact I did yesterday in a letter of several sheets which I sent off by old Israel), but that I must point out to them it was naturally very difficult to exercise any influence on a third party by means of the written word. A personal interview was better. I would therefore ask Ludendorff to let me know when he was next coming to Berlin, and I would try to meet him there. I could not fix a date, as I did not know when Ludendorff would be next in Berlin. I probably cannot manage the end of the month, as the C.-in-C. is going to Munich on a fortnight's leave.

It goes without saying that there will be an attempt to negotiate with Russia. It will be difficult, because at present no one knows who holds the sovereign power in Russia, and the whole affair might be wrecked by too much precipitation. However, that is no reason for me to hurry to Berlin, as the establishment of any such relations is not my business, and it will not take place in Berlin. So far as I know, the steps to be taken in the matter will be discussed upon the occasion of the Chancellor's visit to Vienna.

March 23, 1917.

There is always something up somewhere, and yet we live in perpetual boredom here. We sit and wait while things happen to other people, instead of being able to do something ourselves.

March 26, 1917.

Israel, whom I had sent to Kreuznach, brought me back a long screed from Ludendorff. He, of course, disagrees with Erzberger's and Richthofen's views on various points, especially over the Chancellor and the Foreign Office. He writes very pointedly on both subjects. The Nicolai business cannot be dealt with yet, although he does not trust the man either, but he will not be able to do anything until later on.

March 28, 1917.

There are four problems at the moment which are giving me endless trouble and driving me nearly crazy. But the stupid thing is that all our affairs and decisions go straight up to H.M., as there is no one else over us, and in all such matters the Cabinet is incredibly petty, and irritating beyond measure.

April 2, 1917.

Yesterday evening Erzberger sent me a very interesting memorandum on Russian and Italian relations: from which I observe that I was, generally speaking, right.

April 6, 1917.

Wilson's message is very interesting. England's expressed attitude now is: " We are not making war against Germany or the German people, but only against the House of Hohenzollern and their Prussian adherents." Very astute in itself, but also a promising sign for us. The idea that Germany must be crushed and destroyed has been gradually given up. It is astute in so far as they are speculating on the assistance of the Social Democrats. In point of fact, I think I can see the Internationale hard at work in all this.

April 12, 1917.

The loss of positions in the West is of course very unpleasant. But these are inevitable mishaps for which we must be prepared. Two Divisions, as I have just gathered, went to sleep, did not expect the attack until later and allowed themselves to be taken by surprise. Yesterday's news from Ludendorff suggests that he hopes that the affair may be localized. We must keep calm and just hold on, and whether we do so a few kilometres to the east or west is of no importance.[1]

April 28, 1917.

I had a heart-to-heart talk yesterday with the Burgomaster of Bremen, Dr Buff. He shares the

---

[1] On April 9th the English attacked at Arras on both sides of the Scarpe and overran the German front lines. It was the opening bar of the great battle of Arras.
The battle was still at its height when, on the 16th April, the French began their attack on the Aisne and in Champagne.

view of all sensible men that the Chancellor must go, only he knows of no successor. Buff made a most excellent impression on me.

April 30, 1917.

Nothing to report here. We are showering newspapers and leaflets on the Russians and trying to get at them in various other ways. Whether anything will come of it remains to be seen. In any case, for the time being we need no munitions, and they can all go to the Western Front; which is very fortunate, as the consumption there is enormous. All seems to be going well at Arras: at Rheims the French will certainly attack again. In any case, the Russian Revolution is a godsend to us, for if there had been heavy fighting in the East at the same time we should have been up against it.

May 2, 1917.

Richthofen's estimates are greatly exaggerated, the French cannot hold out for three years more, nor can the English, for by that time they would not have a single vessel left. So, as the saying goes: " Do not drive young horses over-hard." I think it quite out of the question for Ludendorff to take any part in a matter of politics. Nor, indeed, is it necessary, for if left to themselves these people may have some views of their own.

May 12, 1917.

Nothing special here. We are giving the Russians much good advice, telling them to behave sensibly at last and make peace, but they don't yet seem very anxious to do so. Yesterday, for the first time, there was a rather more important interview, for which some of our officers proceeded to Dünaburg, to the Russian Headquarters there. But nothing much came of this either.

May 19, 1917.

I had a visit from two Reichstag Deputies, the Conservative von Winterfeldt and the Social Democrat David—the latter of the two was by far the abler and more interesting man. We all enjoyed talking to him. They are now to see something of our Ober-Ost Command and its administration.

There is nothing to be said against the Chancellor's speech. The questions of the Conservatives, having regard to the present state of affairs, showed once again incredible political crassness, and the Chancellor extricated himself from the affair pretty well.

May 20, 1917.

In the West the great offensive seems to be at an end. During the last few days the French and English have made only partial attacks, and the French newspapers are openly expressing their indignation that the great offensive has been broken. Of course it is not beyond possibility that they will have a try at another point. The new Generalissimo Pétain must show what he is made of. However, perhaps he thinks it better to leave well alone and puts his hope in the spring of 1918.

May 24, 1917.

I have not much use for my suggested rôle as scapegoat between the Chancellor, G.H.Q. and Parliament. Such a position is neither one thing nor the other, and leads to no result. Stein's manœuvre was unfortunate, though the outcry over him was excessive. He certainly intended nothing by his phrase " Greek gifts," least of all to provoke the Reichstag.

May 26, 1917.

The Russians are making violent counter-propaganda against our efforts to paralyse their army by suggestions of peace. It seems that Kerenski has gone to the Front, and he is perhaps trying to get them to attack again. Well, they may, for all I care. The Italians are attacking with great energy on the Isonzo and the Austrians have lost a few positions. I do not consider the situation serious at present—of course we shall have to help them again.

May 29, 1917.

Yesterday Erzberger sent me a report from Russia according to which the situation there is growing more and more unmanageable. He takes a very optimistic view of the future. Well, people say he was always too optimistic, but in any case I prefer him a thousand times to Witting and his friends. After a general review of the earlier policy of the Government one can only say: " The Russian Revolution was a surprising piece of luck, which you did not deserve! " Still, there it is, and Russia is collapsing. The great question now is, which will come first—the breach with America or the Russian collapse. The latter, I think. I am very curious to know how England will answer the Russian request for a restatement of war aims. If she refuses, that will be a proof that our U-boat war is not so effective as we hope, but if she shows signs of reconsidering the point, then we shall know that the U-boat war is producing results. It is an excellent opportunity of finding out.

Still nothing fresh here. A few days ago, as a result of our propaganda at the Front, we got an opportunity of getting into direct touch with an Army Staff. General Dragomiroff, the Commander-in-Chief on the Russian Northern Front, sent a request for a few German officers to come to see him. He went on to explain that this was not his own wish, but that the soldiers had compelled him to write. In any case I did not want to let the opportunity slip and I induced H.R.H. to write a letter to Dragomiroff, which was, of course, very galling to the Russians. He acknowledged the letter, but did not answer. To-day we have printed the letter, with an explanation of its object — a request for an armistice with a view to peace—in a leaflet, and scattered it over the entire Russian Front.

June 1, 1917.

An armistice is, in fact, in being at many points on the Russian Front: at other points firing is going on—it is indeed a strange war.

I am very curious to know what is going to happen in the West. I cannot suppose that the English are going to give up their great offensive without a word or an effort. I think they are going to collect their forces again somewhere else, perhaps in conjunction with a landing. The West is strong enough in Reserves to face such an event with equanimity—thanks to the Russian Revolution.

June 7, 1917.

The Russians are becoming more energetic in their counter-propaganda. Alexieff had promised to attack, but in the meantime he has been superseded and Brussiloff put in his place. Whether he will manage it remains to be seen. In any case we have made all necessary preparations. I regard the thing as a piece of folly : they can't possibly break through, so it is simply a senseless waste of life in England's honour.

It was apparently Hertling that backed up the Chancellor last time. We shall make another attempt very shortly. Hertling has the King of Bavaria entirely in his pocket. Zimmermann does not want to stick to his office. On the contrary, I think he would be only too glad to go, as soon as he was told that it was essential in the interests of peace. There is no point in my going to Berlin to talk to a dozen people. There is no point in talking. These fellows must do something. I myself am a soldier, so I can't go and say: "Your Majesty, please dismiss the Chancellor." The politicians in Berlin can, but they don't do it.

June 8, 1917.

I have read Braun's articles. They are in general agreement with the views of reasonable people— viz. that after the war we must come to an understanding with Russia and Japan. That is just as much in the interests of the other two as in our own, so as to provide a counterpoise to the enormous commercial predominance of the Anglo-American alliance.

June 9, 1917.

Administrative questions that have to be disposed of quickly, letters to Erzberger (who wants money from Ober-Ost to distribute in Lithuania), to Witting, who wants me to mediate for him in certain railway matters, etc., and, in addition, a mass of purely military business. It is not beyond the bounds of possibility that the Russians will attack at one point or another; what Reserves and war material we have must, consequently, be shifted to where the enemy is making preparations for an attempt. No sooner are we settled than the West comes along, takes our men away, and gives us in exchange troops that are sorely in need of a rest after their experiences there—and so the whole business begins again.

June 11, 1917.

I am not furious about St., I shall receive him quite affably. Letter from Erzberger, this time less optimistic about Russia. The English are doing all they know to keep Russia steady and induce her to attack. Apparently they are successful; at any rate, at certain points in the line it looks as though their friends were going to try their luck again. We are quite on the spot with everything needed to deal with them.

June 12, 1917.

There is still much liveliness opposite us. Kerenski has pledged himself completely to the English, and, I imagine, undertaken to attack again in the next few weeks.

June 13, 1917.

I had a very interesting letter from Erzberger about our awkward foreign relations. Very sensible, and not so wildly optimistic as he usually is. His information comes from the General of the Jesuits and the new Nuncio in Munich—two unexceptionable sources. Still, I fancy that both of them—Italians in the last resort—want to create a depressing effect, so that Germany's demands may be as moderate as possible.

June 15, 1917.

I have now taken the river-fishing energetically in hand, and we are daily getting supplies of the most excellent pike, etc., by the hundredweight. It is a pity that we are too far from where it could be packed and sent home. If the catch increases I shall start a fish-smoking establishment.

June 16, 1917.

A brief anecdote, tending to show the good sense and acuteness of our Foreign Office. A certain von Maltzahn, Counsellor of Legation, is to be appointed to Ober-Ost and is due to arrive here any day. I received the following telegram to-day: "Counsellor von Maltzahn arrives Warsaw 18th at 6 P.M. Please make arrangements for his journey to Brest-Litovsk: sgd. Stumm." I really wanted to reply: " Please instruct von Maltzahn not to make a mistake and get out at Warsaw, but to stay in his compartment: will then unavoidably arrive destination Brest-Litovsk." These people are really too . . .

June 19, 1917.

Apparently the Russians are really going to attack us in Galicia. Well, let them. Ludendorff has put a little more artillery at our disposal, and I can face any further developments with equanimity.

June 25, 1917.

The Russians are keeping absolutely quiet. I have not heard a single gun, nor, in spite of the fine weather, seen a single airman. I don't think they will attack again there in the near future. Whether it will come off in Galicia I do not know. I think it possible, but I still have my doubts. In any case all my preparations are made: " Let them come and we'll give them a welcome! "

June 26, 1917.

As regards the removal of " certain people," Erzberger told me yesterday on the telephone that his patience too was at an end, and that he was for a change. He will give me his reasons in writing.

June 29, 1917.

I had a frank discussion with the Minister Lentze, Drews, and three Privy Councillors, which lasted until shortly before one o'clock: by that time we had reached an agreement on all points. It was half-past two before I had looked over the correspondence, etc., that was waiting for me. The work does not diminish unfortunately, it increases.

I just sit and wait to see whether Brussiloff will attack in Galicia or not. It is to be hoped he will —and I hope I shall be able to provide him with a pleasant surprise. But at present we cannot tell whether he can get his Comrades out of the trenches or not.

According to what Drews, the Under-Secretary, told me, another crisis with the Imperial Chancellor is imminent — I hope it may hasten his fate. Ludendorff is going to a conference at Vienna in a day or two.

June 30, 1917.

I sit and wait (like children waiting for Father Christmas), wondering whether the Russians will attack at last. But we have no luck. They make half-hearted attempts at a sort of attack, but until now they have not really brought one off. It is a pity—it would have been a good show. We had provided such a delightful surprise for Herr Brussiloff.

July 1, 1917.

The Russians are attacking us in Galicia. I hope they will keep it up for eight or ten days, so that we can give them a proper dressing-down.[1]

[1] The C.-in-C., East, planned for the second half of July an attack on a large scale along the Lemberg—Tarnopol railway. G.H.Q. had placed 6 Divisions at his disposal for this attack.
On July 1st the Russians broke into the Austrian positions between

July 2, 1917.

The Russians are really remarkable people. At the bottom of my heart my only anxiety was lest they might not be induced to attack in Galicia, and so prevent us carrying out a very neat counter-operation. Instead of which they have been attacking for the last few days with such fury and with such a concentration of troops as we have never seen in the East : 7-8 Russian Divisions against one of ours. Which is rather more than I like. . . . In any case the position here is, at the moment, very interesting. I am not anxious in the least, but we must be very careful, because even a trifling Russian victory would, of course, influence public opinion among all classes in favour of the war.

July 6, 1917.

We shall have to wait ten days or a fortnight before my " surprise " can come off. Meanwhile I hope the Russians will press their attacks.

July 7, 1917.

All in perfect order here. Heavy fighting yesterday. The Russians attacked in positive hordes—all beaten off. My preparations for the " surprise " are proceeding according to plan.

Zborov and Brzeczany. The situation was restored by the German Divisions which had just come up.

After a powerful attack on July 4th against the Southern Army, which was repulsed, on the 6th and 7th powerful Russian attacks were launched against the Austrian 3rd Army south of the Dniester. The 3rd Army retired behind the Lomnitza and Kalusz fell into Russians hands.

The German troops intended for the break-through at Zloczov had to be diverted to the 3rd Army : and by these means the Russian advance was brought to a standstill.

The German attack near Zloczov began on July 19th and led to a complete success. Tarnopol was taken on the 25th, and the whole Russian Front was shaken. In the first days of August, Galicia and the Bukovina were cleared of Russians.

While this operation was still proceeding, preparations were started at Mitau for an attack on Riga.

July 11, 1917.

Much work and much trouble over our worthy allies. Heavy fighting in Galicia, but no cause for anxiety.

July 17, 1917.

Yesterday's news has quite relieved my mind. Litzmann has retaken Kalusz, and there are now such strong German reinforcements in those parts that nothing need worry us.

The weather has also improved, so that I hope to take rather more vigorous action in the next two or three days. The Austrians have grown more and more . . . dear to me in the last fortnight. They are really impossible. . . . Not content with running away, they lie and send false reports, and with it all they are quite unashamed, and make difficulties wherever they can. I should like to go to war with *them*.

July 18, 1917.

If the weather holds, I shall proceed to the offensive at a certain point. It won't be so big an affair as I had hoped, because I had to use too many troops to stop the Austrian retreat in the neighbourhood of Kalusz.

July 19, 1917.

Our little surprise at Zloczov made a good beginning yesterday. We broke through the Russian positions on a twenty-kilometre Front, and I hope we shall make good progress in the next few days.

July 21, 1917.

The affair is developing according to plan. I should like a few more prisoners. The fellows ran away so frantically that we could not catch any of them. Only 6000 up to date, and only 70 guns.

I can't of course predict how things will go, but I hope all right.

We are still sitting in the train at Zloczov, and shall stay here till the end of the month. I don't want to let the operation get out of hand.

July 23, 1917.

We are succeeding beyond expectation down here. Unfortunately we have made only a few prisoners — they ran away too fast — and only 50 guns.

On the other hand, I am worried about Eichhorn's position up in the north. The Russians are attacking heavily at Smorgon and Dünaburg, and yesterday they broke through our line at one point. Steps have been taken to deal with the situation.

Well, once more I am glad to be a soldier: politics leave me cold.

The Emperor of Austria was here yesterday, and he behaved himself in the sort of way that falls just short of direct discourtesy. There was of course no question of any thanks for the reconquest of a province for him.

July 25, 1917.

H.M. came early yesterday morning and pressed the " Pour le Mérite," with oak leaves, into H.R.H.'s hand and into mine. I then gave him an account of the situation. Next we went in a car towards Tarnopol to see Prince Eitel Friedrich, who took Tarnopol this evening with the 1st Guard Division. In H.M.'s car were His Royal Highness, Prince Fürtensberg, and My Insignificance. In the evening, at dinner in the Royal train, I sat on H.M.'s left. He was of course in a brilliant humour.

To-day he visited the Southern Army. I had work to do and let H.R.H. go with him alone.

Ludendorff has sent me a number of very good Divisions, which helped us to win the battle in a style I could have scarcely dreamed of. We are going forward well, and the Russians are on the run as far south as the Carpathian Front.

There is now no decoration left that I should care for.

July 26, 1917.

All proceeds according to plan; we reconquer Galicia and the Bukovina for the Emperor Karl and he has not yet once said " Thank you."

Our Emperor was about all day yesterday, and to-day he has gone to Tarnopol. Yesterday I was again invited to dine with H.R.H. H.M. was again extraordinarily gracious and friendly, shook hands with me three times when I took leave of him, etc. An invitation has just come for me to dine again this evening. The day after to-morrow we shall go home again (H.M. is going on to Vilna to-morrow).

July 28, 1917.

Yesterday we dined with H.M. for the fourth time. I sat on his right, and he was as gracious and friendly as he had been all day. He left for Vilna at ten o'clock. They were very good days, but I am glad they are over. I am not much of a courtier.

We are leaving this afternoon, and shall be home again on the morning of the 29th. Our work down here is practically over. I should not have dared to hope that the operation would be so successful. I certainly believe that in the next few days we shall succeed in throwing the Russians and Galicians over the Galician and Bukovina border. Then we shall necessarily come to a stop, because we shall be so far from the railways that are still intact that

we shall not be able to bring up supplies and reinforcements. Then we must try something else—if
Ludendorff will let me have the troops. I have just
had another admirable idea.

July 30, 1917.

Our operation progresses: on the Galician
Front we shall reach the frontier at every point
to-day. It will be another two days before we take
Czernovitz. . . .

July 31, 1917.

Much work, and a great deal of worry. The
Russians are defending themselves very obstinately
in the Bukovina and progress becomes daily more
difficult. Still, I hope we shall take Czernovitz all
the same.

August 1, 1917.

Ludendorff has just rung up. He is satisfied with
yesterday's great Entente offensive in the West.[1] The
losses are of course considerable, and we have lost
a certain amount of ground, but—and this is what
I care about—he needs no troops for the West.

Our operation here is coming to an end. I still
wish we could get Czernovitz.

August 2, 1917.

I could really do with a few days' leave—I am
gradually beginning to feel the strain and anxiety
of three years of war—but it can't be done. I have
to carry the entire responsibility for the Eastern
Front—no one regards the Prince as responsible—
so I can't get away for the time being. H.R.H. is
going to Bialovicz to-morrow—the shooting season
has begun.

[1] The great Flanders battle began on July 31st in the West.

Something very pleasant happened yesterday evening. H.R.H. ordered champagne at dinner, stood up and announced in a neat speech that H.M. the King of Bavaria had conferred on me the Cross of a Knight of the Military Order of Max Joseph. He made some very nice remarks about me, and concluded by calling on the company to drink my health. The Military Order of Max Joseph is the Bavarian " Pour le Mérite," and they very rarely, and reluctantly, give it to non-Bavarians. H.R.H. proposed me for it, without saying anything, and the whole manner and method of the announcement was very charming.

A report has just come in that detachments of our troops have entered Czernovitz. I hope the Russians have not too utterly destroyed the place. As far as our Command is concerned, the affair is practically at an end—we are now on the frontier of the Bukovina and Galicia, both of which provinces we have reconquered for the Emperor of Austria. Whether the Russians will make any serious counter-attacks I cannot yet say; it is not probable, but it is always possible. In any case, I hope that the situation is clear until the middle of August, and that we can turn our attention to something fresh. We ought not to leave the Russians any peace until they collapse. Propaganda and guns must work together.

August 4, 1917.

Nothing special here. Czernovitz was taken yesterday, and with that my interest in the operation comes to an end. Now the Archduke and Mackensen can take on the business.

August 5, 1917.

Our operation is practically at an end and I am devising something new.

August 9, 1917.

According to a newspaper report the Emperor of Austria has conferred on me the Iron Cross (Class II.)—a distinction that I can hardly regard as adequate to the services rendered.

The Emperor of Austria has made General von Kövess a Field-Marshal for the taking of Czernovitz —I have already said to Fleischmann, and will say it again in writing: "The idea of the Galician battle was mine and mine alone, and was carried out entirely in accordance with my instructions."

August 10, 1917.

There are some troop movements going on, and as they all come through Brest, if they can, every-one wants to know where he is to be sent. I hope the information I give them is correct and that no one will make me look a fool. There ought to be some sort of insurance against the loss of military reputation in such circumstances.

August 11, 1917.

Our nerves were rather on the stretch yesterday. Seekt, Chief of Staff to the Archduke Joseph, had started an offensive in continuation of our victory. Now we are being overwhelmed with appeals for help. I am against this, as a campaign in the Carpathians in support, or *ad majoram gloriam*, of the Austrians is futile. The railways are so bad that we could not get the troops down south, and, what is worse, we could never get them away again. The negotiations are going on at this moment. I do not want to give up my new plan—I want to carry it through in any circumstances, supposing the situation in the West makes it in any way possible. Ludendorff never leaves me in the lurch and has not done so this time: he shares my view. If all goes smoothly we may see a very pretty bit of work about the middle of September.

August 13, 1917.

The position is unchanged. All depends on whether we can hold on to our troops or not. Mackensen is calling for help, so is the Archduke Joseph, likewise the Chief of the Operations Section, who wants more troops for the West, but until now Ludendorff has been obdurate and refused them all. Unfortunately it is still some time until the beginning of September, and anything may happen. This waiting gets on a man's nerves.

August 14, 1917.

My military heaven is rather clouded over. I am afraid I shall have to give up some troops to the West. The English and French are apparently launching big attacks in Flanders, on the Aisne, and at Verdun, on both banks of the Meuse. I shall be very sorry if, as a result of this, nothing comes of our scheme, but I am afraid the prospect is poor. Insurance against loss of military reputation is becoming an absolute necessity.

August 15, 1917.

After a long silence I had another letter from Erzberger yesterday. The man is gradually becoming a public danger. He writes that he has been in Switzerland, where he has been negotiating with the Lithuanian leaders. He has apparently made promises to these people which are quite inconsistent with our views, and some of which could not possibly be made good: for example, he has promised them an independent kingdom. The Lithuanian is just about as capable of governing

himself as my daughter Ilse is of educating herself.
I have just rung him up to tell him so very politely.
I have no intention of quarrelling with him, though
his ridiculous Peace resolution is enough to make
one do so.

August 18, 1917.

Ludendorff has just rung up to say that the need
in the West is very urgent. Everyone is asking for
troops. For the present he will not take any away
from me. The question is what will be the outcome
of the French attack at Verdun. If the need becomes very great there, then there is no help for it:
we shall have to give up troops. I see that clearly
—it can't be helped.

August 21, 1917.

Ludendorff rang up early yesterday morning:
" I'm very sorry, I must have some troops." Very
well: I sent out all the orders. In the afternoon
he rang up again: " Perhaps I can manage ": so
I cancelled all the orders. To-day we shall probably get counter-orders again. I cannot blame
Ludendorff: he would be only too glad for me to
carry out my plan, and would like to leave me the
troops. But it is, of course, more important that
the Western Front should stand firm. The great
French Verdun attack is, so far as the main objectives
are concerned, a failure—only the " Mort-Homme "
has been lost.

August 26, 1917.

Yesterday and to-day we had a crowd of guests.
Turkish officers, high Staff officers passing through,
Duke Johann Albrecht of Mecklenburg (who would
like to be Duke of Kurland as well), all swarming
around here. Dryander is coming shortly to hold

Divine Service on the Eastern Front. In the meantime there will be visits from Deputies of the Reichstag and Press representatives. I often hardly know how to manage them all.

September 10, 1917.

We got back yesterday afternoon. The first part of the Mitau offensive went according to plan.[1]

The Russians expected our attack farther to the West: they appear to have been convinced that they could not stand their ground on this side of the Düna, and had consequently made all preparations for a retreat to Riga. Our thrust was delivered near Uexküll and took them utterly by surprise: they immediately realized that they could no longer hold Riga and prepared to retreat beyond that city. We changed their retreat into something like a rout. Guns, boats, field-kitchens, and material of all sorts, were left standing and lying about everywhere. Unfortunately we made fewer prisoners than I had hoped, as the great majority of their troops, whom I had hoped to cut off, had just been evacuated from the bridge-head.

We should of course have liked to continue our advance in the direction of Petersburg, but unfortunately we had to stop, as Ludendorff, with the best will in the world, could not let us keep the necessary Divisions. He needs them, and Austria needs them,[2] so we must resign ourselves. H.M. has been here for three days, as gracious and kind to me as ever. As there are no more Prussian war decorations that could be conferred on me he has

[1] On September 1st the passage of the Düna was forced and Riga taken. After this preparations were made for the capture of the bridge-head of Jacobstadt and the occupation of the islands of Ösel, Moon and Dagö. The first operation took place on September 21st, and the second from 11th to 18th October: both were successful.

[2] In the meantime, on the Italian Front, the 11th battle of the Isonzo had started. The Italians had some success north and south of Gorizia.

given me his signed photograph in a gun-metal frame. H.R.H. applied for me to be promoted General: but Lyncker would not hear of it. It was no more than I had expected, so I was not disappointed. I greatly enjoyed my visits to Riga. Both on the first occasion, when I went alone with H.R.H., and especially when the Kaiser made his entry, the enthusiasm of the German population was most moving. We did not feel as though we were entering a conquered city, but a German city just set free. The marvellous weather and the magnificent panorama of Riga added to the effect.

September 11, 1917.

Russia seems to be all upside down again—the two Commanders-in-Chief, Korniloff and Kerenski, are actually fighting for the Dictatorship. I don't believe any other nation in the world has suffered such a state of affairs during a war.

We have more visitors: the Burgomaster of Lübeck, in addition to eight Reichstag Deputies. I am more excited about the last than the first.

Friend Erzberger has had a bad Press lately. Personally I think he has made a fool of himself. I have the impression that the Emperor Charles and, more especially, the Empress Zita have been making use of him against us, and to the advantage of Austria.

September 13, 1917.

Russia seems to be in a dreadful mess. Korniloff and Kerenski are fighting for the Dictatorship. It is such a pity we could not carry our offensive any farther. A German advance on Petersburg now would bring about the complete collapse of Russia.

September 14, 1917.

Colonel von Wrisberg, the most important man we have in the War Office, was very interesting on the subject of the situation in the Reichstag, and the Chancellor's incompetence to manage it. He had not a good word for Erzberger—no one has at present—who had, he said, allowed himself to be hopelessly entangled by the Emperor Charles and the Empress. The news of the domestic situation in France sounds excellent. The country is sick of the war, and the accounts we get from responsible and impartial persons in Switzerland are most encouraging, from our point of view.

September 29, 1917.

I do not share the anxiety that Ludendorff's position may be shaken. I know that Nicolai does not like me. I duly got him his job on the General Staff, and there is always something burdensome about a feeling of gratitude—it easily changes into dislike.

October 6, 1917.

A good half of the German people is convinced that if we hold on firmly we shall win an easy victory. I take a middle view : I am convinced that we cannot be conquered, but, on the other hand, that we are not in a position to win a complete victory over the English. On these grounds I am for a Peace by compromise, but not for one that means annexation.

October 10, 1917.

News came in the day before yesterday that the Emperor of Austria wanted to visit the Linsingen Army Group, and would like to take the opportunity of seeing H.R.H. Prince Leopold. As the

Prince does not come back from leave until to-day I decided to go to Kovel and meet the Emperor. After my experiences at Zloczov I did not look forward to doing so, but I was completely surprised. The Emperor was uncommonly friendly, invited Linsingen and myself, after he had reviewed the troops in Kovel, to go with him to Vladimir Volynsk and join him at lunch. I sat opposite him and we had a good talk. He is not exactly a shining light, but much cleverer than a Monarch needs to be.

Nothing special here. The Reichstag debates are a regrettable storm in a teacup. The excitement over the propaganda in the army is ridiculous. The Lecture Organization — combined with legal and other advice for the men—is not political, and of course will be conducted just as before. The Parties seem to have come to terms again with Helfferich. I can only laugh at the whole business.

October 12, 1917.

Our friend the Chancellor has postponed his visit here for forty-eight hours. I thought his attack on the Independent Socialists was foolish.[1] Either the three Comrades were so deeply involved in the Navy Treason case that they could be imprisoned, or he should have kept his mouth shut. On the other hand, the Reichstag impressed me less than ever throughout the whole affair. The attack on Helfferich reminded me irresistibly of the shootings at Hornberg.[2] Either refuse a man his pay, so that he has to go, or don't raise the subject at all.

[1] The Chancellor, Dr Michaelis, had made a sharp attack on the Independent Social Democratic Party in the Reichstag. The question raised was the connection of the Party with insubordinate elements in the High Seas Fleet. The Majority Parties in the Reichstag supported the I.S.D.P. against the Chancellor.

[2] A German proverbial phrase for invariably missing the mark.— *Translator.*

October 13, 1917.

A few days ago there was an attack by certain Deputies against the administration of the C.-in-C., East. Colonel von Brandenstein, who came to report on the debates, tells me that, besides the Social Democrat Ledebour, friend Erzberger has been incredibly abusive. These gentlemen take the view that all products of the occupied area belong to the inhabitants, and that it is an incredible piece of brutality on our part to send foodstuffs home from the occupied area. Only what is freely offered by the inhabitants should be taken for the use of the army and the population at home. We cannot of course accept this point of view. In Erzberger's case this is not a matter of conviction but a party move.

October 14, 1917.

It is very inconvenient that H.M. is not in Berlin at the moment, but on a visit to our Eastern Allies in Sofia and Constantinople. His visit to the Sultan is however essential, I believe, as our popularity in Turkey has considerably fallen off owing to lavish expenditure of American money.

October 18, 1917.

A report has just come in that we have successfully occupied the island of Moon. The Naval people were much more use, and more intelligent, than I had expected. They gave us more help than their officers thought they could promise when the affair was being discussed.

Now we have to take Dagö, and then we shall come to a stop once more. Anyhow we took about 10,000 prisoners at Ösel and about 50 guns. At the beginning of the war it would have been a great victory.

I met the Chancellor in Vilna and found him,

as I have said, better than I should have expected after his late performances in the Reichstag. He is not imposing, he makes no great impression upon further acquaintance, and he looks at all political questions rather from the point of view of a Finance Minister than a Statesman — still, compared with Bethmann, he has the advantage of at least speaking his mind clearly and calmly. We were in general agreement in all our political views, and in particular as regards the extent of the future Eastern Province. The question is whether he will stick to what he alleged to be his views.

October 19, 1917.

The propaganda for Falkenhayn is very amusing, but too late. At the time it must have been very difficult for him to find anyone to write this sort of stuff for him. The operations against Ösel, Moon and Dagö are making good progress. We have provisionally appointed a Governor for all three islands, although we have not yet got Dagö. On Moon we have captured a General with 5000 men. The Russian Army is in a bad state—what a pity we can't take advantage of it. If I hadn't had to give up those Divisions we should have got to Lake Peipus.

October 26, 1917.

One of the armies in the West was again too optimistic and helped the French to success, which will greatly encourage them to enter upon another winter of war. It is too bad! Every time there is a great success in the East, or one of the other theatres of war (*e.g.* Ösel and Italy), the West puts an extinguisher on it.[1]

---

[1] Since September 20th the third Flanders battle had been raging in the West, and in the course of it there were several serious crises. On October 22nd the French stormed the Laffaux salient—south-west of Laon—and completely shattered some German Divisions.

October 28, 1917.

There is heavy fighting in the West, the English mean to win a victory at all costs: which is a good sign. Good progress in Italy.[1] Many more than 60,000 prisoners, and more than 500 guns. We cannot yet foresee developments. I fancy that the Italians will very soon evacuate Gorizia, and go back behind the Tagliamento.

Yesterday I had a very interesting political interview with three gentlemen from Riga. The Livonians are more imposing than the Kurland Barons—they made a most excellent impression on me.

A report has just come in that the Austrians are already west of Gorizia, so the Italians must certainly have evacuated Gorizia yesterday. That city was the sole achievement of their eleven Isonzo battles.

October 30, 1917.

A telegram came in yesterday that H.M. had promoted me Major-General. I had ceased to count on it. H.R.H., upon the occasion of the capture of Ösel, Moon and Dagö, had telegraphed to Hindenburg and again asked for me to be promoted. Hindenburg and especially Ludendorff brought very strong pressure to bear and overcame the Cabinet's resistance. I gain two years and four months' seniority by this; the Colonels of April 1914 are now due for promotion, while my Colonelcy dates from August 1916. I am of course delighted with such an acknowledgment of the fact that we on the Eastern Front have really done our bit during the last year. Michaelis has gone. I hope Hertling will succeed him. I know of no other.

---

[1] The attack on Italy at Tolmino had begun on October 24th.

November 13, 1917.

I have a great deal to do. A long interview yesterday with Waldersee and Falkenhausen, neither of whom will take orders from the other, etc.[1]

November 20, 1917.

I have much to do, both over the scrapping of the whole administration, and also the complete *détente* on our Front has meant a great deal of work on the military side. We can take troops out of the line, drill and train them, etc., for I don't believe the Russians will ever pull themselves together for another attack on us.

November 21, 1917.

We cannot get a clear view of the Russian situation as yet. I have requested that the Imperial Chancellor should answer the Bolshevik peace-offer in his speech on the 29th. He can quite safely say: " Certain persons in Petersburg have sent out a wireless inquiry about peace. The German Government cannot tell whether the inquiries emanate from those who do in fact represent a Russian Government possessing the power to conclude a Peace. If they do, then the offer should be conveyed to us in the proper manner through the ambassador at Stockholm. We are ready to enter into negotiations." In this way we should deprive the Entente of their opportunity for counter-propaganda. At the moment they are of course saying to the Russian soldiers : " Now you see what the Germans are like, you offer them peace and they do not even answer you." Whether the Chancellor will do this, I cannot of course say.

[1] There had been a change in the administration of the area under the control of the C.-in-C., East. At the head of it were now a specially appointed Governor-General, General Count von Waldersee, and a high civil official, the Under-Secretary of State, Freiherr von Falkenhausen.

I had a long interview with Waldersee and Falkenhausen yesterday and drew up a scheme for the new government of the occupied territory.

November 26, 1917.

Here I sit advising the Russians to declare an Armistice. Whether they will I cannot yet say, and we have no clear picture of what is likely to happen in the interior of Russia in the immediate future.[1] Anyhow I have collected here during the last three days all the people I could who may be able to help me: Rosenburg of the Foreign Office (the most agreeable and sensible fellow they have got), a representative of the Naval Staff, a few Austrians, etc. At the moment they have nothing to do; they just sit around and make work.

November 27, 1917.

I hope we shall manage to finish off this business. Negotiations are going forward over the entire Front. Fighting has stopped at many points, and I hope we may establish a proper Armistice on the entire Front. I am expecting representatives of the Austrian G.H.Q. and the Austrian Foreign Office.

February 17, 1918.

To-morrow we are going to start hostilities again against the Bolsheviks.[2] No other way out

[1] In November the Bolsheviks had seized power; on November 26th the Government sent out an inquiry by wireless as to whether the German G.H.Q. were ready to conclude an armistice. G.H.Q. answered that they were. On December 2nd the Russian Armistice Commission crossed the German line at Dünaburg and went on to Brest-Litovsk. The C.-in-C., East, was authorized to conclude an Armistice, and on December 15th the Armistice was signed. It was to last until 12 noon, on January 14th, 1918.

[2] The Peace negotiations at Brest-Litovsk dragged on until February 10th, without any agreement having been reached. A separate Peace had been concluded with the Ukraine. On February 10th, Trotzky

is possible, otherwise these brutes will wipe up the Ukrainians, the Finns and the Balts, and then quietly get together a new revolutionary army and turn the whole of Europe into a pigsty. Of course, with the forces at present at our disposal here, I can't run a victorious express train to Petersburg, but I hope to achieve something all the same. I am very curious to see whether the Russians will defend themselves at all, or whether they will clear out without a fight. The situation in the Ukraine is not encouraging. The Ukrainian troops are, like the Russians, totally disorganized by revolutionary ideas, and they, too, simply want to " go home." The whole of Russia is no more than a vast heap of maggots—a squalid, swarming mess.

February 18, 1918.

To start hostilities again was certainly the right thing to do. The Foreign Office was against it, mainly from anxiety as to its possible effect at home. Whether we shall succeed in overthrowing the Bolsheviks sooner, we must wait and see. The situation in Russia must, indeed, be appalling—the most patient race in the world could scarcely stand such a state of affairs for long.

The Poles have apparently gone quite mad over the question of the Cholm district. There are strikes and all sorts of troubles in Warsaw. They let their political imagination run away with them. They have not moved a finger for their Kingdom, and yet, like children, they want everything.

stated that he would make no definite Peace, but that Russia regarded the war as at an end. As a result, a week later, the German Eastern Army began a general advance; the consequence of this advance was that the Russians expressed themselves as ready to continue the negotiations and conclude a Peace. Peace was made on March 3rd, and was followed on March 5th by the conclusion of a preliminary Peace with Rumania.

February 19, 1918.

We started our advance yesterday: took Dünaburg in the north, Luck in the south; and Trotzky
and company immediately wirelessed from Petersburg that they were willing to sign a Peace.

February 20, 1918.

Events are moving here. The Russian Army
is more rotten than I had supposed. There is
no fight left in them. Yesterday one lieutenant
with six men took six hundred Cossacks prisoner.
Hundreds of guns, motor-cars, locomotives, trucks,
and several thousand prisoners, were brought in
without any sort of fighting at all.

Yesterday, in accordance with my instructions, I
sent a wireless message to Herr Trotzky to the effect
that his offer had been received, but that he must
confirm it in writing to the " German Commandant
at Dünaburg." Last night a reply came in at once
that a courier was on the way with the document.
He seems to be in a devil of a hurry—we are not.
Unfortunately, our advance is very slow; we are
short of horses for transport and the roads are
bad; it will be some time before we can get to
Lake Peipus.

February 21, 1918.

Our advance proceeds. Yesterday we marched
across the ice from the islands into Esthonia.
The Bolsheviks ran before we reached them. Up
to yesterday evening we had captured more than
1500 guns, which were standing about all over the
place on railway stations ready to be sent back.

Trotzky's written offer to sign a Peace has now
come in. For the time being I have no notion how
the Chancellor will handle the business. Anyhow,
every day's delay is in our favour.

There is also a hitch in the negotiations for peace with Rumania: this is not so much due to the Rumanians as to the fact that we and the Austrians cannot agree over the spoils. We of course want considerable commercial privileges in connection with the petroleum wells, etc., and the Austrians are crying aloud to Heaven that they are getting nothing.

It seems that Kühlmann is going to Vienna to-day to join Czernin, and then they are both going on to Bukarest. At least that is what I hear—I can't guarantee its truth.

February 22, 1918.

Early this morning the ultimatum was sent off to Trotzky. It must be admitted that the Foreign Office and G.H.Q. have worked well together. It contains everything we ought to insist on. Whether Trotzky will accept it seems to me more than doubtful. But the position of the Bolshevik regime is probably so shaken that he will have to snatch at it. Our movements are proceeding according to plan. It is the most comical war I have ever known— it is almost entirely carried on by rail and motor-car. We put a handful of infantrymen with machine guns and one gun on to a train and push them off to the next station; they take it, make prisoners of the Bolsheviks, pick up a few more troops and go on. This proceeding has, at any rate, the charm of novelty.

February 25, 1918.

I am expecting the Peace Delegations to come in one by one to-day and to-morrow. Whether Trotzky will take the road to Canossa in person, or will send someone else, is not yet certain. The negotiations here will last three to four days at the most, as this time the Comrades must simply swallow what we put before them.

March 1, 1918.

The first meeting is to be at eleven o'clock to-day. According to my information the Russians will protest, but will agree to all the demands contained in the ultimatum. Any additional demand they will certainly refuse.

I have endless work to do. I hear from Bukarest that Rumania is, at the moment, taking a very high line, and that prospects of peace are, for the time being, slight. The situation will change in our favour as soon as we have fixed up peace here.

March 7, 1918.

Nothing fresh here. We are waiting to see if Russia will duly ratify the Peace—they must do so within a fortnight. Otherwise we shall certainly march on Petersburg. In the meantime Lenin has summoned a great congress at Moscow for the 15th. Our operations in the Ukraine are going forward. We are, of course, moving more slowly than at first, as our Bolshevik friends are now beginning to destroy the railways.

March 8, 1918.

In the Ukraine we are still advancing—chiefly in the direction of Odessa, and then from Kiev to the East; in Esthonia and Livonia there is a sort of guerrilla war. Apart from this, for weeks past, everything that is not absolutely immovable has been put on the train for the West. I wish I could be there, but I haven't a chance. Even the greatest personages suffer from jealousy, so I don't think that Ludendorff is likely to let me have my finger in the pie.

Erzberger's story is, of course, pure imagination. It may be assumed that the Russians secretly hope that their Peace terms may be reconsidered at the general Peace. None of them said so.

March 12, 1918.

More serious trouble here. Mumm, who is to go as our diplomatic representative to Kiev, arrived yesterday, and also a Polish mission (General Musnicki). I have sent Brinckmann to Kiev to treat with the Ukrainian Government there. The difficulty in the Ukraine is simply that the Central Rada has only our rifles behind it. The moment we withdraw our troops their authority will collapse at once. The cause of this is the land problem. On the land question the more moderate Social Democrats, who compose the Rada, are just as idiotic as the Bolsheviks—*i.e.* they also have confiscated the landed estates and given them to the peasants. Consequently the agricultural industry in the Ukraine is ruined. The bulk of the land was represented by the large estates. The peasants have now divided and taken over these properties, but they will not risk cultivating them, because they do not know whether they will in fact be left in possession of the land. Everyone is rolling in money—roubles are printed and almost given away. A cigar costs six roubles at Kiev, and a cup of tea with sugar five roubles, dinner twenty-four roubles, and so on. The peasants have enough stocks of corn to live on for two or three years, but they will not sell it.

The Petersburg Government migrated to Moscow yesterday, so as to take a vote there on the ratification of peace. I think they will ratify, but I have got out of the habit of prophecy.

March 13, 1918.

Endless trouble with the Austrians in the Ukraine. They want to enter Odessa alone, and are behaving with their usual meanness when the knife is not at their throat.

March 14, 1918.

I don't yet know whether our worthy Comrades in Moscow have decided to recognize the Peace or not. It almost looks as if not, as otherwise they would have already wirelessed. In that case we must, of course, take Petersburg. Yesterday some more Russians suggested a visit. A representative of the Monarchistic parties has arrived in Vilna to ask our help for the restoration of the Monarchy. It costs nothing to give the man a hearing, so I have invited him here.

I am having the most frantic trouble with the Austrians in the Ukraine. It is a pity that the Italians do not attack. One can deal with the Austrians only when they are in difficulties.

As regards Eastern affairs the Reichstag—especially Erzberger—are making a mess of things. The Chancellor is shortly to receive a Lithuanian deputation, and I am afraid that they will then do something foolish in Berlin. It is possible to make something of Lithuania only if it is closely associated with Prussia: any sort of independent Lithuania would be hopeless. Whether Erzberger is too stupid to see this, or whether Roman interests would not allow such an increase in Prussia's influence, is more than I can say.

March 21, 1918.

I can't raise much excitement over Falkenhayn.[1]

1 After his recall from Turkey, General von Falkenhayn had received a command on the Eastern Front.

He will have no more important strategic problems to solve here, and personally I have nothing whatever to do with him—I deal with his Chief of Staff.

Much trouble with the Lithuanian Government. Comrade Erzberger has roused the National Assembly to fury against us, and the Chancellor seems to defer to Erzberger's most lunatic suggestions. These people want to go back on their resolution of December by which, in return for the recognition of their independence, they bound themselves to a close association with Germany, a military convention, etc. They now insist on independence first of all. I hope the Chancellor does not give way.

March 22, 1918.

The conquest of the Ukraine proceeds slowly but surely. I also believe that we shall get such supplies of corn as we absolutely need. At the same time it seems to me doubtful whether we shall succeed in helping the Austrians in time. We don't want ours till June : they want it in April, and we can't get it so quickly.

March 23, 1918.

There are serious riots among the dockers in the Black Sea ports, which are apparently giving trouble to our troops. I have no further information, as the troops in those parts are under Mackensen. Our movements in the Ukraine are proceeding according to plan.

Yesterday we had a visit from Lindequist, the ex-Secretary of State, with a German clergyman, representing the German colonists in South Russia and the Crimea. The clergyman talked a good deal about the right of self-determination, and, on this ground, suggested the union of the Tartars of the Crimea and the German colonists, thus combining the Crimea and the adjoining provinces into a German colony. I told him I had no objection.

There would be no object in my discussing the Lithuanian question with Erzberger, as our views are too far apart, and he has done too much harm already.

March 25, 1918.

I think it possible that the lately published Memorandum by Lichnowsky was disclosed by Witting: he let me see it too.

March 29, 1918.

G.H.Q. has produced a considerable upset here. As the establishment of transport facilities in the Ukraine is of the very first importance, it was decided that General Gröner, the former Director of Railways, should be sent there. As it was also felt that he would not get on with Linsingen (who is difficult), Linsingen was removed from his post and replaced by Eichhorn. Gröner becomes his Chief of Staff, so Keller also, the former Chief of Staff of that Army Group, is left high and dry. The Eichhorn Army Group (our Northern Army Group) is to cease to exist as a unit, and the three armies of which it consisted are to be under the immediate authority of Ober-Ost. This method of creating a sphere of authority for Gröner was simple, but a trifle high-handed. I have never regarded Linsingen as a great commander—still, for the last three years he has been one of our most distinguished Generals. I find it rather difficult simply to send him a telegram to the effect that " H.M. has no further use for your services."

April 3, 1918.

I had a great deal to do to-day, as Waldersee came in for a long talk. There was no particular

point in our discussion, as G.H.Q. and the Chancellor were not yet in agreement about Livonia,
and so many authorized and unauthorized persons
had got their fingers into the Lithuanian pie that
nobody knows what will be the end of it.

There is a further advance in the West, and they
all seem confident. We have not details of any
kind. Everything and everybody (even from the
Staff) that could be spared has been shifted to the
West. I often think that it is really a pity that
Hindenburg and Ludendorff did not get me a
Division. The command of a Division in the West
at present would, anyway, be much more interesting and offer much better prospects than my dead
post here. However, following the proverb, "Never
interfere with your military destiny," I shall do
nothing, but calmly await further developments.
I must just live on recollections.

April 4, 1918.

All proceeds according to plan in the Ukraine.
We have now occupied the whole of the Crimea,
and on the East we have nearly everywhere reached
the boundary of the Ukraine. All we need now
for the complete control of the Black Sea are the
ports of Taganrog and Novorossisk, and those we
must have.[1]

April 8, 1918.

I am expecting a number of visitors to-day.
The future Commander-in-Chief of the I. Polish
Corps, General Dowbor-Musnicki, is coming to

[1] Our operations in the Caucasus area were also conditioned by our
needs in regard to war material. We had accordingly to get control of
Baku and the Baku—Tiflis—Batoum railway in order to cover our shortage
of oil. By agreement with the Chancellor, Colonel von Kress was sent
to Tiflis to represent G.H.Q., together with an escort of two companies.
As the English tried, by crossing the Caspian Sea, to get possession of
Baku, Colonel von Kress was reinforced by one Cavalry Brigade and a
few battalions.

confer with representatives of the Governor-General
of Warsaw and a member of the Regency Council.
He would have preferred to go to Warsaw, but
Ludendorff would not allow it. I would have let
him go; it is useless to annoy people over such
trifles.

April 9, 1918.

We have taken Kharkov. I could never have
dreamt a while ago that German troops would
enter that little hole.

The discussions with the Poles were very interesting. They really have quite lost their heads. They
are visionaries, who spend their time dreaming, and
do not, or will not, understand realities.

April 24, 1918.

We are progressing slowly, but according to plan,
in the Crimea. We have taken Simferopol and we
shall shortly attack Sebastopol.

No news from the West, except that our great airman, Rittmeister von Richthofen, has been killed.

April 26, 1918.

In the Ukraine the situation is coming to a head.
The Government is making further difficulties, and
I am afraid that we shall have to look for another.
The storming of Mount Kemmel is the most important event in the West. From that point we
can control the whole stretch of country towards
the north, so that the English will certainly have to
give up Ypres.

April 29, 1918.

There is the devil to pay in the Ukraine. However, Eichhorn has the situation well in hand, so
that I think we shall emerge from it without serious
trouble. Part of the Government there has estab-

lished an anti-German League. Eichhorn has accordingly arrested these gentlemen. A wife of one of the Ministers (as might be expected) played a great part. She also is under arrest. It will, of course, cause alarm in certain quarters. If the Government retires we shall have to set up another; however, it will certainly be better than the existing one. Eichhorn is being most bitterly attacked in the Reichstag; but everything he does in the Ukraine is the result of most careful consultation between the Chancellor, the Foreign Office and G.H.Q.

I am in two minds at the moment. Shall I go to Kovno or shall I stay here? I think Kovno would be better for the future, but the situation in the Ukraine is so obscure at the moment that it is really more practical to be rather more on the spot.

April 30, 1918.

From the political point of view the chief event is that the Ukrainians have at last overthrown their Government. They have summoned a General to be Hetman of the Ukraine and Dictator.[1] As this gentleman stands by the Brest-Litovsk Peace and other agreements regarding the delivery of corn, etc., this is very likely to our advantage. On the other hand, as a result of the change of Government, Eichhorn's not very tactful treatment of the former Ukrainian Government may perhaps be forgotten —not that any blame attaches to Eichhorn personally, but certain minor personages behaved like the bull in the china shop.

May 1, 1918.

The difficulties of arranging for our prisoners of war to cross our lines at certain points take some

---

[1] Hetman Skoropadski had been a General Commanding in the Tsarist Army.

dealing with, and it is one of those tasks that must involve minor hardships. Everyone thinks he is the only one, and must be sent home at the earliest possible moment. There were about 1,500,000 Austrian prisoners and about 100,000 of ours. These are now all streaming back. In addition, there are about three to four million of the population of Poland, Lithuania and Kurland now wandering home again: part of them were carried off by the Russians, and part fled before our advance. The railways are hardly a practicable means of transport as we have too few locomotives. We must get rid of the Austrians as soon as possible, otherwise we shall have to feed them. So we can't provide a special train for everybody. I grant that it is trying and tedious to have to wait eight or ten days, but it can't be helped.

Nothing special from Kiev. The change of Government has been smoothly carried out and the city and the country are quiet. It is only the Foreign Office and the Chancellor who are anxious. God! It is really pitiable how afraid people are of the Reichstag! I have been only indirectly informed of the whole story, but of course I shall have to take up an attitude of opposition to the Foreign Office.

May 2, 1918.

The Don Cossacks have telegraphed to the German Emperor, asking him to help them against the Bolsheviks. . . . They are quite fond of us now. I am against mixing ourselves up in the affairs of the Don province—our Eastern movement must come to an end some time.[1]

[1] The Entente made a stand against Bolshevism. They organized formations of Czecho-Slovak troops in Russia on the Siberian border and gradually moved them forward to the line of the Middle Volga.

In the north, Entente troops moved up the Dvina from the White Sea,

May 6, 1915.

G.H.Q. is in direct touch with Kiev and believe they understand the position there better than we do. I am afraid that this will lead to the collapse of the Ukraine which cost us so much trouble to create. The efforts of G.H.Q. and Eichhorn are, though they do not know it, driving the Ukraine back into the arms of Great Russia. At the moment this does not greatly matter, but for future purposes I should have thought it useful to have preserved the Ukraine as an independent entity. I shall call attention to this again to-day, so as to clear my conscience, but it will not be much use—my political insight is no longer esteemed as it used to be. Well, I must try not to mind.

May 7th, 1918.

Dr Rohrbach, the well-known writer, came to see me yesterday on his way to Kiev. Interesting man, a Balt by birth, pan-German, and oddly enough well disposed to the Poles. I had a good talk for the first time for weeks, and learned a few things I did not know. He shares my anxieties about the Ukraine and promised to use his influence in the right direction at Kiev and later on at home.

May 21, 1918.

I have had long conversations with the famous Dr Rohrbach, who is just back from Kiev, and with

and southwards from the Murman coast along the Murman railway. On the Dvina the advance was very slow. The Murman railway was destroyed by the Bolsheviks. On the west of the Lower Volga the Don Cossacks under General Krasnoff were in conflict with the Soviet troops. German G.H.Q. entered into relations with General Krasnoff to prevent him joining the Entente.

In the Kuban province, between the Don Cossacks and the Caucasus, General Alexeieff was fighting Bolshevik troops with his volunteer army. Alexeieff was under English influence.

Olszewski. Rohrbach confirmed my fears that the Ukraine is steering straight towards a new Greater Russia. I hope that Brinckmann, whom I have instructed accordingly, may be able to use his weight against this. I have asked Rohrbach to let me have his full impressions in writing so that I may put the matter forward officially. Olszewski was very sensible. I had already agreed with Waldersee and Falkenhausen how far we could meet his wishes.

May 22, 1918.

Yesterday there were further negotiations with the I. Polish Corps of General Dowbor. As the Warsaw Regency Council has allowed itself to be involved in conspiracies with the Polish troops and the Ukraine, all still existing Polish formations must be disbanded and disarmed. I had not thought that Dowbor would have given way without a fight, and we had, accordingly, pretty strong forces ready for any emergency. He was, however, astute enough to accept all our conditions.

May 23, 1918.

The Ukraine still causes me anxiety. The men at present in control there are steering straight for union with Great Russia. However, that beautiful land is now fortunately in such a mess that the Hetman may perhaps think twice before he makes a move. For example, the partition of the land in Russia is by this time practically accomplished. The land has been taken away from the landlords and given to the peasants. Thus any future Government, whether the Monarchists or the Cadet Party get into power, is in a very difficult position. If they take the land away from the peasants the Revolution will start again, and they will find it hard to suppress it even if they can create a new army, for the soldier is a peasant. If, on the other hand, they leave the land to the peasants, they are founding their authority on the basis of a broad, illiterate democracy, without any higher stratum from which they can get officers and officials. So that the Russian problem is, I am thankful to say, by no means simple. We have information from all sides to the effect that the Bolsheviks will soon collapse from incompetence, but I don't think they will yet awhile. There is no one to take their place, as there is no army to support a new sovereign power.

May 25, 1918.

Nothing of any great importance has been happening here. The Peace negotiations between the Ukraine and Great Russia are slowly getting under way, the Don Cossacks have entered into an alliance with the Ukraine, with a view to getting their and our help against the Bolsheviks. I should have no objection to pushing farther and farther eastwards —I should like to get to India, except that the distances grow more immense, and our army does not.

I hear little or nothing from the West. I had thought that the lull would be over, and that they would be on the move again by now, but it seems that the preparations are not yet made. In any case, our troops there are ready for any developments.

May 26, 1918.

The Chief of Staff of the Dünaburg army has just rung up to say that they arrested sixty people there yesterday who had planned a large anti-German conspiracy—a peasant rising, murder of officers, etc. A good part of them were agitators released by the Bolshevik Government.

May 30, 1918.

I paid my call on the local Bishop yesterday. Like all important Catholic ecclesiastics, he is a clever, cultivated man. In contrast to his Vilna colleague, he is a thorough Lithuanian, and well disposed to the Germans.

The Entente is making colossal efforts to stir up trouble over here in the East. Their agents are trying to stir up the peasants—especially in the Ukraine.

June 4, 1918.

I have the impression that in the West our advance has gradually come to a stand on the Rheims—Soisson line. The French have apparently brought up all their available Reserves—as we hoped they would do. A continuation of the offensive here would thus mean very heavy losses—if I were in Ludendorff's place I would break it off at this point, and make a thrust at a place where the French have now no Reserves.

June 5, 1918.

The position here is unchanged. The I. Polish Corps (Dowbor-Musnicki) is being gradually disarmed and sent home, the negotiations at Novorossisk over the remains of the Russian Black Sea fleet are still in suspense, and the Peace negotiations in Kiev are proceeding very slowly. At home the Government, especially the Foreign Office, are in a state of terror over the possible antics of the next Reichstag. It is really pitiable.

The situation in the West is as I had thought—*i.e.* our offensive has gradually come to an end again. We must now wait patiently until another can be started elsewhere.

June 16, 1918.

It is not in our power to end the war, we are simply forced to go on fighting. Kühlmann is no fool. If he saw a means, or an opportunity, of getting America out of the business he would have long since seized it. The idea that America might make peace, if we took a step to the left in our domestic politics and transferred the sovereign power to the Reichstag, is in my opinion erroneous. On the contrary, we should go to the dogs, from a military point of view, if people like Erzberger and Richthofen were allowed to have a say in military matters. There is no help for it, we must set our teeth and hold on.

There has been all manner of fighting in the Ukraine in the last few days. Near Taganrog, 10,000 Bolsheviks from the Kuban province made a sudden landing and attacked our troops in Rostov. The Würtemberg Landwehr there were very much annoyed. South of Kiev there were a few Bolshevik peasant risings, but they were suppressed in a few days.

June 17, 1918.

The Austrians have actually attacked, and they report 10,000 prisoners. Anyway, the whole thing is a *succès d'estime*. I would never have thought that they could have induced their men to attack. They are so utterly sick of the whole thing.

The position in the West is good. The French are in a complete quandary. I hope we may have a few more long-range guns ready : I anticipate a strong moral effect from a more vigorous bombardment of Paris. The tone of the French newspapers is already different from what it has been in the last four years.

There is a great deal of work here as usual,

and not much satisfaction to be got from it. To-day I am expecting the Saxon Minister, von Seydwitz. The newspapers have been discussing the proposal for the union of Saxony and Lithuania under one crown, and now the Minister is coming to look into the position. I think the whole thing is lunacy. The Lithuanians themselves will make all manner of difficulties, and the Saxons have not enough officials to fill all the posts in the Administration. The King is, of course, extremely enthusiastic over it.

June 18, 1918.

A certain deputy, Michalkiewicz runs the administration of Lithuania in Vilna; he is a true blue Pole of the most besotted kind, and gives us a great deal of trouble. We have been trying for months to get rid of the man and to get in a Lithuanian in his place. The Poles, whose influence in Rome is greater than that of our Foreign Office, know how to put difficulties in our way. But when Michalkiewicz recently used the Corpus Christi procession for a large Polish demonstration Ludendorff's patience gave way, and we have orders to remove Herr Michalkiewicz. This will be done to-morrow, and will no doubt give rise to a great outcry. I should have thought that, if our Foreign Office had displayed a little more energy *vis-à-vis* the Curia, it would have been possible to secure his recall. But if nothing came of this, then I share the view that it is right to remove him by force. We must show these people that we mean business.

June 20, 1918.

Public feeling in France and Italy individually seems to be falling below zero, which is very encouraging. Their only hope now is America. Any considerable defeat before America's help makes itself felt will, I think, mean the fall of Clemenceau and Lloyd George. That would be an important step towards peace.

June 26, 1918.

Kühlmann has made an ill-advised speech. I assume that he will probably disappear. The difficulty is, who will be his successor? There are so few that are fitted for the post. And the regrettable thing is that Kühlmann probably meant something quite different, and does not deserve to be dismissed.

I laughed over Stresemann's flaming speech of protest. I often think of his and Bernstorff's demeanour at Witting's some while ago, and now he is a fanatical Pan-German, Militarist, and Annexationist.[1]

June 29, 1918.

As regards politics, it seems as though the Parties of the Left in the Reichstag want to keep Kühlmann : whether they will succeed seems to me doubtful. The Chancellor's visit to G.H.Q. has nothing to do with the Kühlmann crisis : he had been summoned there some time ago. It seems to me significant that our Ambassador in Christiania, Hintze, has arrived in Berlin. He has long been H.M.'s candidate for the Foreign Secretaryship. Hintze has been a naval officer, and a military attaché in Petersburg, and is regarded as a clever man. I do not know him personally, but judging from his dispatches he is rather unpractical.

[1] Secretary of State von Kühlmann, in his speech in the Reichstag on June 24th, had stated in general outline his views of a possible Peace, and in doing so had stated that the war could hardly be brought to an absolute end by a military decision alone, without diplomatic negotiations.
This observation finally led to his resignation and replacement by Admiral von Hintze.

July 3, 1918.

According to our representatives in Russia, the days of the Bolsheviks are numbered. I cannot be so confident of their fall, as I do not see who is to succeed them. Whether the Monarchists have the necessary courage and energy remains to be seen.

July 5, 1918.

The political and military situation is, generally speaking, unchanged. Every day we get several telegrams, "The fall of the Bolsheviks is imminent," but I do not feel so confident. It would be too stupid of the others to assume control before the beginning of the new harvest, as the essential condition of every new Government is to remedy a shortage of food. I do not yet entirely understand the speeches by the Social Democrats in the Reichstag against G.H.Q. I do not understand what Scheidemann's object is. Perhaps I shall find someone to explain it to me on my way through Berlin.

July 7, 1918.

In my opinion the Entente as well as the Cadet Party are behind this crime [the murder of Count Mirbach in Moscow]. Many hope that this may lead to a renewal of hostilities between Germany and Russia. I am sure the Bolsheviks had nothing whatever to do with it. They have promised to do everything they can to catch the murderer. We must wait and see whether they are successful.

July 20, 1918.

I had a tremendous rush in Berlin. Everything settled to my satisfaction at the Ministry of War. I could not agree with the Quartermaster-General about our situation in the East. In the afternoon

I met Kühlmann at the hotel, and had a very interesting talk with him. Towards the evening Your Friend, among others, came to see me.

The general feeling in the Foreign Office about the late resignation is not encouraging. They are all so uncertain. None of them dares to do or say anything until he knows the attitude of G.H.Q. on the matter. In many respects this is not without its advantages, but it leads to a good deal of uncertainty. The best thing would be for Ludendorff to become Chancellor; that would clear things up.

July 23, 1918.

The affair in the West is a nuisance, having regard to public feeling at home—though from the military point of view it is of small importance. Although the troops in the field were warned by G.H.Q., which foresaw the French attack, the troops allowed themselves to be surprised.[1]

July 27, 1918.

Our great administrative transformation is now in progress. Our Ober-Ost administration is coming to an end almost entirely, and will be divided between the administrations of Lithuania and the Baltic provinces. It is a good move, apart from the question of personnel, which has been badly handled. For example, in agreement with G.H.Q. and the Q.M.G., we had proposed Count Waldersee for the newly created Military Governorship of Lithuania. The Military Cabinet opposed this and appointed General von Harbou, who has never been in Lithuania before. By way of compensation,

[1] On July 18th the French counter-attack at Soissons began, which led to the evacuation of the Marne salient. The evacuation was carried out according to plan in the night of July 26th-27th.

he is to have a new Chief of the Administration who has never done any political work. We shall have to keep pretty wide awake to see that these fellows don't make fools of themselves. It is an excellent thing that the three Baltic provinces should at last come under a single administration. Gossler, however, is to be at the head of the combined administration, and I don't think he is fit for it. We seem to have an unlucky touch in personal matters. However, the whole reorganization is a step in the right direction.

Now we have got a new job too over the Russian propaganda. I had long been abusing the authorities for conducting our propaganda on the wrong lines. So G.H.Q. have skilfully got out of the difficulty by simply handing the work over to us. If only I had my old Intelligence Officer, Major Hey, it would be a very simple matter. But now I have got Prince George of Bavaria instead, so I must get on to the job myself.

July 28, 1918.

The position in the West is, as I have said, from the military aspect, extremely unimportant, but the effect of the retreat on public feeling at home is extremely unfortunate.

Lyncker, who has been ill several times lately, has left the Cabinet, and has become President of the Imperial Military Court. His successor is not yet known. Some time ago I should have been glad, as I was not on very good terms with Lyncker, but latterly he had been invariably open to reason, and agreeable to me, so that I am really very sorry he is going.

Waldersee gave up his post yesterday. I am very sorry. Besides, it was very stupid to take him away from here.

August 1, 1918.

All my enjoyment of the excursion, the lovely woods and the fresh air, was clouded by the news of Eichhorn's murder. It is the most damnable thing. The Social Revolutionaries are going back to their vilest Nihilistic times. From the purely personal point of view I was very upset. I was very fond of old Eichhorn and he of me. He often wrote to me, whenever he was seriously troubled over any matter. I also knew Captain von Dressler very well.

August 3, 1918.

I am overwhelmed with work. Now that Waldersee has gone, all the administrative officials want to see me. Until the major part of the administration is divided between Lithuania and the Baltic provinces this place will be full of people coming and going all day long. And trouble of all kinds.

August 6, 1918.

It is, of course, not impossible that the Russian Social Revolutionaries will try their hand at further murders, and it would be foolish not to take precautions. Those chiefly in danger are, of course, our people in Moscow, Kiev, Odessa, and such places in Russia itself (as compared with Ukraine) where there is much street traffic. Although we are not in much danger here, I have got a large number of Security Police about the place. Visitors are carefully watched and escorted, and the streets barricaded.

August 8, 1918.

If the English move farther south along the Murman railway we shall unquestionably have to go to Petersburg. We cannot let the English occupy Petersburg and Kronstadt. I do not imagine a march to Petersburg would be very difficult. However, we must be prepared for everything.

August 9, 1918.

In the West there seems to have been a further small mishap. Apparently we have again allowed ourselves to be surprised. Otherwise I can't understand what did happen, as we have plenty of troops, etc.[1]

The situation here is gradually coming to a head. The Entente has organized a vast propaganda in Russia. Whether we can still cope with it seems more than doubtful. However, we will try.

Our Embassy is to be shifted from Moscow, as it is too unsafe there. I should have proposed Kovno, but the Highest Authorities do not agree, so it is to come to Dünaburg or Pskov.

August 12, 1918.

Nothing new here. Yesterday I had a very interesting interview with a Russian Monarchist, a German Russian, on the situation in Russia and probable developments. He thinks (as I said months ago) that we were unfortunate in neglecting to make propaganda for ourselves and against the Entente, and that England is consequently ahead of us. He regards the English occupation of the Murman area as dangerous for us, and he considers that we must certainly deal with it in some way. Either the Russians must turn them out or we must. I hope that influential quarters may take this to heart: it rather looks as if they may.

---

[1] The 2nd Army was heavily defeated on August 8th between Albert and Moreuil.

August 14, 1918.

The position here is unchanged. The treaty with Russia is so far ready that Comrade Joffe has gone to Moscow to get it signed. I shall be curious to see what happens then. We cannot in any case tolerate any further English advances in Murmansk. Either the Russians must throw them out or we must. The affair in the West seems to be a wash-out. The only advantage is that the Reichstag was not sitting. The —— would, of course, have lost their nerve again, and talked the most appalling rubbish. That is clear from the fact that the *Berliner Tageblatt* demands that the Committee should meet.

Erzberger is behaving like an idiot again over the question of the Lithuanian crown. He has written to the —— that they need not be afraid—he, by the favour of God, Herr Erzberger, will see that they get their Urach[1] for King. The man is a public danger.

August 15, 1918.

Our Military Attaché from Moscow[2] was here to-day; he had come back with the Embassy. It is noteworthy that, to a man who has lived in all that beastliness, and been in the closest possible contact with the saner elements and heard their execration of Bolshevik rule, the political situation in Russia looks quite different from what it does to us here. In Moscow the entire Peace of Brest-Litovsk is regarded as a crime against humanity. How could the Germans have had anything to do with such brutes? It was unworthy of a great

---

[1] The Duke of Urach : a connection of the Royal House of Wurtemberg. —*Translator*.

[2] Major Schubert. He and the leader of the Delegation, Secretary of State Helfferich, were both agreed that Germany must break with the Soviets. Hoffmann took the same view. As to Hoffmann's attitude, see *The War of Lost Opportunities*, chapter xvii.

Empire, etc. These people forget that the Bolsheviks were the only party who made us an offer of peace, and that it was only as a result of the Armistice and the Peace Treaty that we succeeded in so dis-integrating the Russian Army that it collapsed, and we were able to transfer 1,000,000 men from the East to the West.

August 18, 1918.

Ludendorff seems to have got his way over the Polish business; with any luck, we shall get at least 1,500,000 more Polish subjects, and, therewith, the embittered enmity of the new Polish Kingdom. Well, it's all one to me.

August 19, 1918.

It is obvious that Ludendorff under-estimated the enemy, after the first great successes. However, the retreat seems to have been caused by gross care-lessness on the part of the troops. At one point where the French attacked they were actually get-ting in the harvest—so it is said.[1] It is the old, old story that the rank and file are always careless. At the moment I consider that our position in the West is secure.

I can only repeat that the blunder lay in the premature shouts of victory, the award of the Star with Rays to Hindenburg, etc. As a result of all this the nation was wrongly led to believe that all would be over in a few weeks: so that the disappointment was doubly severe.

My only hope now is that the English will try to bring off a coup from the Murmansk in the direction of Petersburg. Then we must attack. It is too boring here, and the whole thing is getting on our nerves.

[1] A myth. The cause was a surprise tank attack, under cover of mist.

August 22, 1918.

Yesterday I had a very interesting conversation on Russian affairs with one of the former Russian Generals who had retired to his estate in the area occupied by us, and I at once telegraphed the gist of it to G.H.Q. I repeated what I had been saying for weeks: we shall have to attack, otherwise the English from Murmansk will get us in the rear. If the Entente set up a Tsar in Russia, then Russia will be closed to us.

They have unlimited money and are working feverishly. But I hope we shall attack in time. G.H.Q. and the Foreign Office seem to me to be convinced of the importance of the affair.

August 23, 1918.

Solf's speech is very astute. I laughed over only one thing: he says roughly what Kühlmann had said; they shouted "crucify him" at Kühlmann, but nothing is too good for Solf. Hintze seems to me cleverer than Kühlmann and understands better how to deal with Ludendorff. I am curious to know the result of the Polish negotiations—I have heard nothing at present. But I am especially interested to know what will come of the point in dispute between Ludendorff and myself—*i.e.* whether we actually take that broad strip of buffer territory or not. I have always thought, and still think, it would be a political blunder, and a disaster, for us to annex one more Pole than was absolutely necessary.

August 26, 1918.

Yesterday I had a very interesting interview with one Herr von Maltzahn, Deputy and Provincial

Councillor. He was for a long time with the Crown
Prince, with whom he keeps up a constant exchange
of views. He gave me his impressions of the West,
where he was lately at Ludendorff's H.Q., of
Rumania and of conditions at home. He had had
an interview with Ludendorff at the request of the
Conservatives, who were considering how best to
encourage public opinion. I then explained my
views on the East, and asked him to make them
known and support them, which he gladly agreed
to do. I think it absolutely essential that we should
attack soon. If the Entente sets up a Tsar without
our co-operation we shall be eliminated from
Eastern Europe for the next half-century. As our
trade with the West will be negligible in the first
few years after the war it is doubly important to
keep the East open and an access by land to Asia.
I hope that our convincing appeals may get some
attention in the long run.

August 28, 1918.

I am waiting to see whether the Foreign Office
does not come over to my view—at present they
don't seem inclined to. I have suggested to G.H.Q.
that I might perhaps take a train to Berlin one day
and talk to the Secretary of State. I have not yet
had a reply.

August 29, 1918.

I am in an evil temper. Everyone is apparently
too blind or too stupid to see the growing danger
in the East. I don't mean in the military sense—
I don't think the Entente will succeed in ever getting a Russian army on its legs and inducing it to
fight us—but politically we shall be pushed out of
Eastern Europe—and for a long while too. I look

everywhere for some means of getting a finger into the pie later on, but I see no prospects.

September 3, 1918.

I talked to Hintze in Berlin, and, besides him, Radowitz, Winterfeldt, Richthofen, Erzberger. . . . I also had an evening at the Club, and met a crowd of princes, etc., there.

My general impression was not at all encouraging. Public feeling in Berlin is not good. For the most part people are saying what I do. We started the summer badly. All those laurels in advance, and all those jubilations, and then a retreat, make a bad impression.

The Secretary of State is definite and lucid, and I should say clever and well informed beyond the average. He has a certain self-confidence that is not displeasing—he knows everything. So long as he is right I don't care. To my astonishment I found that we were in agreement about the position in Russia and the necessity for an attack there in good time. We disagreed only on small matters, and the date. He thought we could wait a little longer. I consider waiting dangerous. G.H.Q. has also much emphasized the difficulties, apparently. It almost looks as if Ludendorff did not want to stick fast in the East. I also got the Prince to sign a long telegram, yesterday evening, in which I expressed my view. So that I have relieved my conscience. If, after all that, they do not do what I advise, I can help them no more, and must just wait and see what happens.

Anyhow I explained my view of the position in the East to everyone in Berlin. I see no military danger, but I see a gloomy commercial future for us in the East if we let the Entente get in with them and do nothing ourselves.

September 4, 1918.

Yesterday evening our plenipotentiaries to the Federal Council were here. I took the opportunity to explain to these gentlemen after dinner my views about the East. For the most part they had been hopelessly taken in—they all thought that the Bolsheviks were charming people and that all was in excellent order.

September 5, 1918.

Yesterday I had a visit from an important Russian banker, who made a deep impression on me. He was the sort of man who appears in modern novels —a superman: either the greatest genius, in the spheres of trade, industry and industrial policy, or a colossal swindler. He offered himself and his organization (as he would have me believe), Banks, Railways, Press, Priesthood, Senate, etc., in our support. I, of course, accepted, but I don't yet know what it will cost. It seems that he has a capital of 500 millions, against which there are, of course, gigantic debt charges. Probably he sees that a continuance of the Bolshevik regime will involve a gigantic smash, which he can avoid only if we invade Russia and he remains in power by supporting us.

September 7, 1918.

The position is unchanged here. Apparently G.H.Q. and the Foreign Office cannot yet decide to make a move here, so that I feel gravely anxious. As a result of the English plot there is a Red Terror in Moscow and Petersburg. The better classes are being arrested by thousands and shot by hundreds. I have no sympathy with these people—on the one hand all these sections of the population wanted war and must now reap what they have sown; on

the other, it was their own idiotic incompetence
that got them into this mess. The worst of it is that
we are made responsible for all this misery—" we
supported the Bolsheviks, we are their allies." This
idea, which is gaining ground in Russia, is arousing
an insane hatred against us. This is a matter of
indifference for the time being, but we shall suffer
for it industrially later on.

I had a letter from Helfferich to-day: he was
sorry he had not met me in Berlin. He had heard
my views of the Russian situation and was entirely
in agreement with them. Good!

September 10, 1918.

According to all the information from Russia we
are generally regarded there as allies of the Bolsheviks. Bolshevik and German is the same. That
means great danger to our whole future. All our
propaganda will not help us in this connection—
deeds are what is wanted; people will not be con-
soled with empty phrases. I hope the authorities
will still come to their senses in time.

September 11, 1918.

Nothing special here. Yesterday the first instal-
ment of the Russian indemnity—gold and paper
—reached Orska on our front line and was taken
over by the Reichsbank. The Bolsheviks are clever
and know how to touch us. Now, as they have
begun to pay, the Foreign Office and the Reichstag
are, of course, strongly for supporting the Bolsheviks,
without regard to what the future may bring.
The state of affairs in Petersburg and Moscow is
indescribable. I shall now say and do no more—
I shall forward all reports that come in; I have
made my views known everywhere.

September 13, 1918.

The situation in Russia has undergone a change, in so far as, since the Russian victory at Kazan, the danger from the English is not so acute as before. We need not now take action—speaking from the purely military point of view—at once. But the feeling against us grows more and more intense. The whole Intelligentsia hates us, because we look on and do nothing. The Rumanians appear to be coquetting with a renewal of hostilities, as indeed Burian has openly stated. Well, it is only the Rumanians that will regret it.

At G.H.Q. Ludendorff has reorganized his Staff. The former Chief of the Operations Section, Lieutenant-Colonel Wetzel, has been given the command of an army, and Heye is shifted to G.H.Q. I have not yet discovered the reason for the change, Personally I am much attached to Wetzel, and think a great deal of him. But if a change was necessary the choice of Heye is a good one. He is uncommonly able, and marvellously industrious and conscientious.

Until six months ago there was a chance for original ideas on the Western Front, now it is merely a question of defence. And for that purpose Heye seems to me the best choice. By the same token my friend Hell has again done well for himself. He fell into disfavour at the time of the Peace negotiations—he got on too well with Kühlmann. . . . He has commanded the 28th Division with distinction in the West and has now been appointed to Heye's former post—the command of an Army Group.

September 15, 1918.

A few days ago, in Odessa, two men and a woman called upon the Austrian authorities, as well as our

General Staff officer there, and asked for permits
to go to the Crimea for a few days to attend a
wedding. In the course of the interview one of
the men made himself known as the Crown Prince
of Rumania. He had only four days' leave from
his father, but he wanted to be present at a friend's
wedding, and he must be allowed to go through in-
cognito. He was told that it could not be managed,
apart from the fact that in the present state of
communications he could not get to the Crimea
and back in five days. He then gave up the idea
and stated that he wanted to go back home. On
the following day he appeared again, and stated
that as he was not allowed to go to the Crimea he
had achieved the object of his journey on the spot—
he and the lady accompanying him (Mademoiselle
Zizi So-and-so) had got married. What a family!

For some time past I have been taking a lively
interest in Rumania and the Rumanian situation.
These people think that we are in such a bad way in
the West that they can be impertinent. Well, they
—and their ladies, more especially the Queen—will
find they are wrong.

September 16, 1918.

To-day again I am feeling rather low after the
Austrian Emperor's feeble Peace offer. . . . It was
made at almost the worst moment for us. Of course
that dangerous creature the Empress Zita is behind
it—she hates us.[1]

I have only heard rumours about the origin of
the affair. It seems that the last time the Emperor
Karl was at G.H.Q. it was agreed that they should
wait until the present fighting in the West was over:

[1] Austria-Hungary, in spite of the German Government's objections,
issued a Peace offer to the Entente on September 14th. It was answered
with offensive contempt.

then, as Austria stated that she neither could nor would go on fighting, Peace negotiations would be opened through a Neutral Power; the Emperor Karl, however, did not abide by this arrangement, but took the initiative himself. On our side everyone is furious. I don't think anything will come of it, at least nothing tangible. If the other side condescend to answer they will make such absurd conditions that there is no sense in negotiating. The only advantage that may come of the whole business is an increased inclination towards peace in England and France. Well, we must just wait and see.

I must particularly emphasize the fact that what I have just written is not definitely known—it is merely a rumour. Very likely it all happened quite otherwise.

September 18, 1918.

I have for the time being given up hope of doing anything here—all my thoughts and efforts now are devoted to sending as much help as I can to the Western Front. The heavy attacks in the West continue, and in fact they seem to be preparing new ones. The Entente seems to be making every effort to force a decision this autumn. In such circumstances all our interests here are of secondary importance—all our strength must be concentrated in the West.

September 27, 1918.

The military position is far from good. In Palestine the Turks are retiring, without even fighting— perhaps there are not any more Turks. Down in Macedonia the Bulgarian Front is completely broken: and we hear rumours of separate negotiations, etc. We are, of course, sending troops at once,

Austrians, and German Divisions (the latter of course from here), and I hope a complete collapse may still be avoided. It's a bad business, anyhow. There is heavy fighting in the West. And the state of affairs in Berlin is not encouraging. Hintze seems to me to be a nonentity. The Chancellor's position has grown very shaky. Perhaps Solf will succeed him. Erzberger prophesied to me in Berlin last July that there would be a crisis over the Chancellorship: but I think it disgusting that it should come now, when the position is not favourable as it was then. It may perhaps be urged in excuse of our parliamentary friends that they were not in any way prepared for the Bulgarian collapse, as no one had foreseen it. Party intrigues there seem to have led to a shocking break-up of the army.

September 28, 1918.

The outlook is bad everywhere and sometimes I feel quite distracted. In Bulgaria the Tsar seems to mean well—it is to be hoped he may succeed in turning out the present Premier. Our Divisions are on the way, but in the present state of the railways it all takes time.

In the West the position is again very serious. I rack my brains trying how I can release some troops. We are gradually getting pretty thinned out here.

September 30, 1918.

There is heavy fighting in the West. I cannot understand how Ludendorff could have so underestimated the enemy Reserves. We are racking our brains here, of course, trying to think how we can help. But we are very near the bottom of the cask. I can't scrape much more out of it—only a few Divisions.

October 1, 1918.

The position is, of course, serious, but I have definite hopes that we may either put matters straight again — *i.e.* that King Ferdinand stays where he is and turns out Comrades Malinoff, Lukoff, etc. — or else that we may be able to construct a new Front with Austria. The most important point is the West. If we hold on there— and of that I have no doubt—we can quite well deal with the situation in the East.

Radical changes at home. . . . Hintze and Hertling go—and probably a few others, to make way for some of our parliamentary friends. Chancellor, probably Fehrenbach; Foreign Office, Stresemann; Under-Secretary for Home Affairs, or Labour, perhaps Ebert the Social Democrat.

If they had been sensible and given the franchise two years ago things would not have gone so far.

It seemed like a piece of historical *esprit d'escalier* when the Head of the Eastern Department, Geheimrat Madelung, came here yesterday, to get me to explain the position in Russia again and the reasons for my view that we ought to take definite action here, etc. He looked very astonished when I told him he had unfortunately come six weeks too late.

October 3, 1918.

The position—military and political—is serious. Of that there is no doubt. We have let slip too many opportunities and the Parties of the Right were too much in a rut. The main blunder was Ludendorff's, in still believing last spring that he could win a victory and thus using up too many troops, that we so sorely need now. But that is the story of spilt milk, on which there is no more to be said. How the situation at home is to be dealt with it is not yet possible to see. A Government based on the Social Democrats and the Centre would not be strong enough, and Social Democracy and National Liberalism are difficult to get under one hat.

Bulgaria is finally dropping out: it is merely a question of conditions. Are the Entente troops to be allowed into the country or not? And we must take our measures accordingly. We have at present enough troops in Serbia to hold up any advance in that part. It may be assumed that Rumania will again join the Entente. But if Austria holds fast we can deal with that too. We could, for example, retire from the Ukraine and use all the troops now stationed there against Rumania. Besides, I see other means of holding on in the East.

The decision lies, as it always has done, in the West. For a time the situation there looked very black, but the last two days it has improved. Generally speaking all the attacks have been repulsed, and the enemy has suffered very heavy losses. Moreover, his Reserves are not inexhaustible. If we can manage to hold on in the West for the time being—and I am confident we can—the others will listen to reason. So, as I have said, the position is serious, but there is no need to throw up the sponge.

October 6, 1918.

The development of the political situation at home is discouraging and disquieting. The humiliating Peace offer to Herr Wilson will not raise the spirits of the army in the West—on the contrary only the Entente will get a new impetus from it. Here in the East everything is to be reorganized —civil governments, self-determination and all the rest of it. I am very much on the stretch. I hope we shall not have to give up the control of the large estates, as in that case the provisioning of the country would be endangered.

I am not yet quite clear that Solf is the right man to represent us in our foreign relations. It is to be hoped I may be wrong. He is, of course, quite definitely better than Hintze. I am also curious about Excellenz Erzberger.

October 7, 1918.

I am waiting to see what answer the Almighty Wilson will make to our request—I imagine he will impose such conditions that it will amount to a refusal. I am also waiting to see what will happen in the occupied areas. As civil governments are now to be established here, I am more than curious to know how the new Imperial Chancellor will set about it. I don't like the look of things.

October 8, 1918.

I don't in the least know why I was wanted in Berlin. I was neatly side-tracked on every possible issue, even on those affecting the Eastern provinces —why, I really do not know. Since Ludendorff and I parted company (mentally, I mean), he has had no more luck, and perhaps that is why I am disliked. The abominable thing about this general collapse is that it need not have happened. Our troops are just as good as they ever were. We could hold on in the West—we only need to appeal to the men—and I will hold the East, if I must, without troops. But they have all lost their nerve.

October 10, 1918.

There was a Crown Council, yesterday evening, to discuss Wilson's reply. I am very glad I was not there. I should not have liked to have shared the responsibility. I think they have all lost their heads, and that the position is not so tragic as all that. Of course everything either stands or falls by the situation on the Western Front. What the outlook there is like, and how many Reserves we still have, I don't, of course, know. I have no fears for the West, even if Austria breaks down. In that case we should simply curl up like a hedgehog.

October 21, 1918.

I have still not been able to get any information about our Note. I don't think this is because it contains anything startling, but because it has to be first considered in all responsible quarters— Ministers, Federal Council, Reichstag — so that they may make suggestions. I hope it won't turn out too flabby a document in the end.

The military position in the West is developing as Ludendorff foresaw.

There was a certain amount of shooting yesterday here in Vilna. The Poles insisted on holding a political demonstration and the police had to interfere. The police were perfectly right, but of course there will be another outcry.

October 23, 1918.

I shall probably make a trip to Reval and Narva one of these days. I should like to have seen those parts once. Besides our policy up there is all on the wrong lines, and I should like to see for myself what ought to be done. We listened to the Baltic barons and to no one else, and the Esthonians and the Letts won't play. I warned our people of this foolishness years ago.

October 25, 1918.

Nothing new here. It was only to be expected that the Note would be reported to be offensive and uncompromising. But I have yet to learn that

Wilson has rejected our proposals. I really think that he attaches some importance to a continuance of the negotiations.

October 25, 1918.

Herr Wilson's answer has just come in. It is not agreeable—it is just about what was expected. My advice to our people would be: " Never mind the Armistice, let us go on negotiating without it."

October 26, 1918.

The situation, and the state of public opinion, is not cheerful. I do not know what we can reply to the American Note. Wilson says: " I will now consult my allies and they will then inform you of their conditions." So we must wait until we hear them. If the terms are unacceptable—and I imagine they will be so—we must just try to hold out. It is a bad time—I sometimes feel quite desperate—it could all have been avoided. We could not have lost the war and we might have won it.

October 27, 1918.

There was a telephone message yesterday to the effect that Ludendorff had resigned and left the Front.[1] I¦ am not quite clear why — apparently the dispute arose through a secret instruction of Hindenburg's to the Commander-in-Chief of the Western Armies, which in his absence was issued everywhere—even here—as an open telegram and thus became known. I suspect — though I can't

---

[1] After the publication of the Third Wilson Note, G.H.Q., believing themselves to be in agreement with the Government as to the interpretation of the Note, had issued a message to the troops, in which it was incidentally stated: " Wilson's reply demands military capitulation. This we, as soldiers, cannot accept."
This message was the ostensible cause of Ludendorff's dismissal which followed on October 26th.

prove it—that Nicolai and Bauer were behind all this. Whether it is simply stupidity, or whether they were trying to force a Military Dictatorship on the country at the last moment, I do not know. In any case they have done no service to Ludendorff or to the German people. Even though Ludendorff is undoubtedly responsible for the collapse—he should never have carried out his offensive—it will be difficult, indeed almost impossible, to replace him. Anyhow Lossberg—who, I expect, will succeed him—has no easy inheritance, he will have to bear the entire odium of a dishonourable Armistice and Peace.

I don't know whether Hindenburg will stay; I hope so; it would have a bad moral effect on the people and the army if he went.

October 29, 1918.

Well, Austria has capitulated unconditionally. I hope at least that we may thus get the German lands of Austria for Germany and so compensate ourselves for what we shall have to give up.

There is not a cheerful prospect anywhere. Gröner went to Berlin early and I suppose we shall hear of his appointment to-day. I am very glad that I have been passed over.

November 11, 1918.

I earnestly hope that, in general, it may be possible to prevent disorder. It must be made possible, otherwise the German Empire will go down. Nearly everyone realizes that. Consequently we must now all work to this one end. The Armistice conditions were such as might have been expected after a complete collapse. One of them was that we are to evacuate the Eastern Provinces. How soon this can be done I can't state even approximately. A Soldiers' Council has been formed here also, which has hitherto been functioning in a peaceable and sensible manner—and with which I am in touch. I had a long conversation with the head of it yesterday, and he gave me the distinct impression of a man trying to do his best in a quiet and orderly manner.

November 12, 1918.

The Revolution has been carried out here peaceably for the most part. Soldiers' Councils have been founded everywhere, whose main concern is, strangely enough, lest the senior officers should want to go home. How they have got this idea is a mystery to me — I have never dreamt of such a thing. On the contrary we must all do our utmost to get the Eastern army home in an orderly manner. We must, of course, begin with the evacuation. I am sorry for the people whose territory we are handing over to the Bolsheviks, but I cannot restrain our men — they want to get home. The forcible transfer of authority has, of course, made the troops rather unsteady. The majority think they are relieved of their military oath, and they want to go home. The Soldiers' Council here is trying its best to counteract this view — whether they will have any success in the long run remains to be seen. The Polish rising causes me further anxiety. The Poles have seized Warsaw and the railways, and are trying to invade our provinces. The general nervousness, of course, gives rise to the most incredible rumours everywhere about Polish attacks. I do what I can to keep my head.

November 13, 1918.

Of course the men all want to get home, and it is very hard to make people understand that to

carry out the evacuation in an orderly manner will
take many months.   Besides there are negotiations
pending with the Entente, who want to send troops
here, to keep order after our departure.   I should
welcome this, as such a proceeding would have a
calming effect on the situation in Germany.

November 14, 1918.

The worst of all is the dilatoriness of the Home
Authorities.   We cannot get decisions about a
quantity of important questions; so we have to
decide many matters for ourselves as best we can.
For instance, I am at present negotiating with the
Polish Government to try to get them to prevent,
or at any rate keep within limits, the formation of
Polish bands in the south of the occupied area.

November 18, 1918.

I heard yesterday that Ludendorff was abroad.
In spite of all his blunders he is a devoted patriot,
and it must be a dreadful thing for him to fall from
such a height and eat the bread of strangers.

November 19, 1918.

I am again very much annoyed at the behaviour
of G.H.Q.   Our troops here in the East belong to
the oldest classes: and we have got most of the
Alsace-Lorrainers.   Any serviceable troops were
taken away from us.   The older men, naturally,
want to get home. Discipline and order don't, for
the most part, exist, although the Soldiers' Councils
are, to their credit be it said, doing their utmost.
Now, of course, in spite of all this, G.H.Q. want
the Eastern army to be brought home as slowly as
possible. If they had so instructed us from the beginning we could have managed it easily, but first

they let things slide and then try to pull them back: it can't be done. Well, we must struggle along, I suppose.

November 21, 1918.

The main idea to get into people's heads is that we can get peace and public order only through a properly elected Government. Independent Social Democrats and Spartacus groups will produce a state of affairs like that in Russia, where everyone —and most of all the workman—is discontented, and every sort of industry is at a standstill. If Spartacus groups appear, then we shall inevitably come to a civil war, as in Russia. Besides, the Entente will send troops to keep order. We should then have to suffer the last horror which, among all our disasters, has hitherto been spared us: " War on German soil." So vote for a supporter of Ebert or a bourgeois Democrat!

November 23, 1918.

I still believe that the reasonable elements in Germany will conquer—if only because we can't take all our orders from Berlin, and because otherwise the Entente will refuse to make any kind of Peace with us. So far as is possible under present conditions I view the future calmly and confidently.

November 25, 1918.

At this juncture the essential question is whether the reasonable adherents of the Ebert-Scheidemann movement can keep themselves in power. If the Spartacus group gets hold of the Government, then the consequences are obvious.

Undated.

The troops are giving us rather more trouble just now. They are all wild to get home, and, in spite of the advice of the Soldiers' Councils, which have remained calm and sensible throughout, there is no holding them. The worst of it is that, if the men here behind the lines go off, our advance troops, especially those in the Ukraine, are left in the air. We are doing our best to shift the more reasonable elements among the troops back to the rear, so that they can take over the defence of the railway line against our other friends, the Poles: but we are in for a few trying days.

November 28, 1918.

There is pretty sure to be an inquiry into my conduct if the Spartacus movement wins. However, from all I hear, the more moderate element is likely to come out on top. Besides I am quite indifferent to any inquiry, since I had nothing to do with the outbreak of the war, nor with its prolongation: and I had no hand in the collapse in the West.

November 29, 1918.

I imagine that yesterday's inquiry from the Foreign Office arose out of the newspaper notice regarding my internment. I had in the meantime telephoned personally to say that the whole thing was a stupid and mischievous lie. I can explain how the rumour got about. On the first day of the Revolution there was great excitement here, as the rumour had spread among the rank and file that Ober-Ost was going home. It so happened that our train, with the saloon car, had been drawn up at the station platform, and the explanation given to me was that it was to be washed and cleaned out. The men still believe that we intended to clear out and leave them in the lurch, if they had not been on the look-out to stop us. This rumour naturally spread. After we had disbanded the Alsace-Lorrainers a few days ago one of them probably gave a somewhat embroidered version of the story to a correspondent, and that accounts for the telegram from Zurich. I only wonder at the stupidity of the newspapers for printing the news, though a simple telephone inquiry would have convinced them of its falseness.

December 2, 1918.

The newspaper paragraph about my being handed over to the Entente leaves me quite cheerful. I should like to see any court of law in the world—even the most venomous tribunal in England or France—that could bring any charge against me.

The situation in Germany would be unpleasant if the Liebnecht crowd came into power in Germany (not merely in Berlin). The people in Berlin are wrong if they think the decision rests with them alone.

December 3, 1918.

The position is difficult, but I hope that the return home of the Eastern army may be smoothly carried out. The Soldiers' Councils are reasonable for the most part and do their best: but the mass of the troops can think of nothing but getting home. They will be surprised to find, when they do get home, that they were mostly better off here than they will now be back in Germany.

December 4, 1918.

I feel confident that the population of East Prussia will remain sensible, even if the Spartacus crowd get to the top in Berlin. The returning troops from the West should produce a calming and sobering effect.

December 14, 1918.

Our quarters will probably not be shifted to Königsberg. G.H.Q. wants to hand over Ober-Ost to the entire defence of the Eastern frontier, making all the other commands subordinate to us. In that case we could not, of course, remain in Königsberg, but should presumably have to move to Frankfurt-on-the-Oder. The War Office have not yet decided. I had raised some objection to this, as it is not a grateful job; but orders are orders.

December 16, 1918.

The War Office have not yet decided whether we are to move to Königsberg or Frankfurt-on-the-Oder. The new regime does not function as quickly as the old. I had a long letter yesterday from Brinckmann, from Spa. I am glad I am not staying there, and I am even more glad to have no hand in the negotiations.

The situation here in Kovno is pretty well in order, but the outlook on the Baltic is not at all pleasant. Our men refuse to fight and are putting up no resistance at all to the Bolsheviks. As a result the evacuation is becoming very disorderly. There is also further trouble threatening to the south. The Poles in Warsaw have gone completely crazy; they have broken off negotiations there and shown our Ambassador the door.

December 17, 1918.

So we are to move to Königsberg. What is to happen then—whether we are to demobilize after we have got the greater part of the Eastern army home, or whether we are then to take over the defence of the frontier—is still left open.

December 18, 1918.

On the Baltic and in the Ukraine the situation is becoming more and more serious, but the Poles, on the other hand, are quite quiet.

December 20, 1918.

Hindenburg has solemnly protested against the military resolutions of the Berlin Congress of the Representatives of Workmen's and Soldiers' Councils; whether this will produce any effect remains to be seen.

December 21, 1918.

Yesterday I had two long interviews with one Biedermann, deputy for Nordhausen, and, at the moment, an Under-Secretary of State. He alleged he was an old friend of Lenin, Joffe and Radek. According to a telegram published in yesterday's papers he has also received money from Joffe, to bring about a revolution in Berlin. He came here with a representative of the Foreign Office to do what he can to help the Russian prisoners of war on their way home. I quite think this is his desire, but I suspect that the main object of his journey is quite different—namely, to get more Russian money. There are still 22 millions of Joffe's deposited with Mendelssohn's, in Berlin. But they are sequestrated, and consequently the Spartacus people can't touch them.

December 22, 1918.

Opposite the 8th Army on the Baltic, the Bolsheviks, and opposite the Kiev Army Group, Petlura's Republicans are giving us trouble. Still, I hope we shall succeed in getting the Eastern army (or the horde that now passes as such) back home in reasonable order, but it is growing more and more difficult. These fellows are too stupid and won't listen to reason.

December 25, 1918.

We are conducting, at this moment, very interesting negotiations with the Poles. They have offered to hold Vilna against the Bolsheviks, if we let them send their troops through from Warsaw to Vilna. I am in favour of it, as our troops will fight no longer. I don't yet know what the Government's decision will be.

December 26, 1918.

On the political side, the Spartacus people in Berlin, and the Bolsheviks in Russia, are making the greatest efforts to get together. The Bolsheviks are afraid that, without German help, they cannot maintain themselves against the Entente, and against the classes that detest them at home, especially the peasants. Hence this outcry. At the moment I don't think the Spartacus movement dangerous. But if, in spite of everything, the people in Berlin get the upper hand the Entente will occupy Berlin —which is not a pleasant prospect; but it does offer some sort of guarantee.

December 27, 1918.

The political outlook is not at present very encouraging. I don't think the Berlin Government can maintain itself, if they continue so vacillating and timid. The weaker we are at home the harder will the Peace terms be. For the time being I don't think the Entente has the slightest inkling as to the outlook in Germany, or they would have soon put an end to this nonsense. The Entente still has the idea that we have a properly organized army, and that the disorders in Berlin were a put-up performance.

December 28, 1918.

The events in Berlin are, of course, very depressing, but we must calmly await developments. For the time being the reasonable elements still seem to have the upper hand. It was, of course, inevitable that the Liebnecht people would do all they could to prevent the meeting of the National Assembly.

December 29, 1918.

In Berlin the Majority Socialists seem to have pulled themselves together a little. They have organized for to-day a great demonstration against the Liebnecht people.

December 31, 1918.

Everything seems quiet in Berlin for the time being. We are rather in a mess here unfortunately. We shall not be able to hold Riga.

The troops will fight no more.

THOUGHTS ON 1914

THOUGHTS ON 1914

In approaching the problem of the Great War the first question that forces itself on everyone is: Who was responsible?

Who was responsible for the fact that all the peoples of the earth fought for years with modern weapons and killed millions of men, and that the old order of things in Europe so collapsed that its peoples have not yet, eight years later, been able to recover?

The clause in the shameful Treaty imposed on us at Versailles, burdening Germany with the entire responsibility, a statement which the conquered were compelled to confirm in writing, is of no assistance to an historical inquiry. The revelations made subsequent to the war by all the Cabinets concerned, the *Memoirs* of a large number of statesmen have, indeed, meanwhile proved that the statement that Germany alone was responsible for the war is not in accordance with the facts.

Neither the German people nor the German Emperor willed the war, and did not need it. Were there, then, any peoples in Europe who could have desired a war or considered such a war necessary?

This question must be answered in the affirmative: France and Russia. France's vanity could not get over the defeat of 1870-1871 and the loss of Alsace-Lorraine, and from the Peace of 1871 the people were educated in the idea of revenge. Read the books used in the French schools on this subject: not merely the history-books but the reading-books for the smallest children are full of stories of the chivalrous, generous people of France, invaded by Eastern barbarians and robbed of two of their fairest provinces. For decades France was on the look-out for allies to help her to achieve an aim that, since 1871, she had never for an instant forgotten: the reconquest of Alsace-Lorraine and the recovery of "la Gloire" that had been lost in the campaign of 1870. France wanted the war, and worked for it with the fanaticism of a people brought up in a fixed idea.

Russia needed the war. The general situation in that gigantic Empire, the corruption of the official classes, the want of an educated middle class, the unsatisfactory agrarian position—in a word, a state of affairs from which only a genius could perhaps have extricated Russia—was driving the country steadily towards revolution. Only a victorious war could revitalize Tsarism and, in conjunction with fundamental agrarian reforms, save the Empire. It must of course be a victorious war. For the consequences of the 1905 defeat by the despised Japanese had shown that the inevitable and immediate result of defeat was revolution.

The situation, therefore, in the two countries threw France and Russia into each other's arms. But the Dual Alliance was confronted by the Triple Alliance of the Central Powers — it needed reinforcement. The wooing of England began; and German responsibility may undoubtedly be said to date from this time.

Those in charge of German policy should never have allowed the two great antagonists, England and Russia, to come to an agreement in spite of the many points on which they were at issue. It could easily have been prevented, for England herself much preferred an agreement with Germany to the Russo-French Alliance. Time and time again during Bülow's Chancellorship, feelers were put out by England to see whether an agreement could not be reached on all questions that interested England and Germany, for Germany's increasing trade and the building of her fleet were causing anxiety in England. Where the responsibility lay for not concluding an understanding between the two countries it is, of course, hard to say. Whether Bülow shared the unhappy Herr von Holstein's conviction, that an agreement between England and Russia was, and would remain, out of the question, and influenced the Imperial Master in this sense, or whether he could not force himself to give a definite direction to German policy for the next decade, only the Imperial Chancellor, Prince Bülow himself, could say, presupposing he is still quite clear in his own mind why he cold-shouldered the English suggestions. But, quite apart from the English efforts to reach an agreement with Germany, Prince Bülow had two opportunities of securing Germany's political future for a considerable period. He saw both countries hard pressed, one over the Boer War and the other over the Japanese War. No use was made of either of these opportunities in the interests of Germany. We got no thanks from either of them; on the contrary, in certain circumstances at least, doubt was cast on Germany's honour and good will. Whereupon H.M. the German Emperor gave Colonel von Lauenstein, Chief of the Military Commission with the Russian Army, an autograph letter to the Tsar Nicholas, in which he assured the latter of his friendship, and added that, in case of need, he might have no hesitation in withdrawing his troops from the German frontier and sending them to the East. In that event Germany would maintain peace in all circumstances. The thanks we received for this document may be read in the Official History of the War by the Russian General Staff. The letter is mentioned with the comment that no reliance could, of course, be placed on such an assurance—viz. the word of the German Emperor.

What our Foreign Office had regarded as impossible did, in fact, befall: England and Russia entered into an alliance against us. Then came a period of feverish preparation; France in particular put forth all her strength and actually reintroduced three years' compulsory service. This could not be a permanent measure. It pointed inevitably to the fact that Germany's enemies reckoned with an imminent, definite date for the war against Germany. What did we—" who were guilty of the war "—do in reply to this? We did not even arrange to enrol all our available men in the army. The Army Bill, brought in after a considerable delay, was so modest that even members of the Left Party in the Reichstag proposed that its scope should be enlarged.

If we had had two more Army Corps in peace time probably not a single Russian soldier would have set foot on German soil. Of course I would not absolutely maintain that the Marne disaster could have been avoided, as bad leadership, rather than shortage of men, was responsible for that.

Equally it should have been our duty to use strong pressure on Austria - Hungary to improve the Imperial Army.

That Italy would not fulfil her undertakings in the event of a European War, and place herself at the side of her allies, was not generally believed in Germany, and not at all in Austria. If General Pollio had been living at the outbreak of the war, and if, too, our diplomacy had not made Italy's breakaway so easy for her, it would have perhaps been possible to hold her down.

The Entente, called into existence as it was for an attack on the Central Powers, was of course a structure that, in view of the different interests of the parties, was intended to hold together for only a short time. The only question was whether there should be a further year's delay, so that certain deficiencies in equipment—*i.e.* the heavy artillery for the Field Army, in which Germany certainly had the advantage—could be made good. Then, on one ground or another, a pretext would have been found for war. Germany would never have begun it. There has never been a greater lie in history than Germany's war guilt. Our guilt—I say it once again—consists only in our geographical position, the ability of our manufacturers and merchants, and the incompetence of our diplomatists.

When, on June 28th, 1914, the Austro-Hungarian Crown Prince and his wife fell under the bullets of the Serbian assassins only a few suspected the risk of war it would involve. Unfortunately, the story of the murder and its originators is not yet fully cleared up, and it is not possible to judge whether the forces at work behind the scenes sent the assassins out in the hope that, in the thunderous political atmosphere of Europe, the deed would produce the desired war. The forces behind the murder perhaps felt nervous lest the negotiations carried on in 1914 by Kühlmann, then a Counsellor of Embassy, whose result was to be agreed by the end of July and signed on 4th August, might lead to a German-English understanding, which would make their intended war of aggression on Germany for ever impossible. If that be so, diplomacy certainly did everything to further the scheme. The brusque style of the Austro-Hungarian ultimatum to the Serbian Government, whether or not they were guilty of the Serajevo crime, lit up the political situation as though with a lightning flash, and Europe slid into the World War.

How far this war would spread and how long it would last no living man suspected in those first August days of 1914. The late Field-Marshal Count Moltke had in fact constantly pointed out that the power and resources of modern States was so great that they would not be content to give in after a first defeat, and that a modern war might consequently last seven, nay even thirty, years; but nobody believed the old soldier: they preferred to believe the modern bankers and industrialists, all of whom said that in these days a war could not last longer than from three to four months. Lord Kitchener expressed the view that the war would last three weeks, or three years. By that he meant that either the German Army would overrun France in a few weeks and force her to make peace, or the French would succeed in holding up the first onrush of the Germans, and then the war would last a long while. As Japan joined in, and as England and France saw themselves forced to bring in their coloured auxiliary troops, the war became something more than a European war, and the longer it lasted the more nations were forced to join in.

Whether it was wise on the part of the Entente to engage in military enterprises in the Colonies as well, and, for example, to teach the black man to shoot the white man, and maltreat and imprison his wife and child, was at the time very seriously doubted in England itself. The prestige of the white races received an inevitable blow; and England and France will, at no very distant date, have to suffer the consequences. The fighting in China, the attempts at independence and the insurrectionary movement of the yellow peoples of Asia are before our eyes to-day. It will be only a few years before the black peoples will follow with a demand for equal rights and the abolition of white supremacy.

If the population figure of the Central Powers is compared with the enormous numbers on the side of the Entente, the superiority of the latter is seen to be overwhelming. At the beginning of the war a rough estimate would be 130,000,000 on the one side, and 730,000,000 on the other. At the close of the war twenty-five States, with a round 1,350,000,000 inhabitants, were at war with the Central Powers. The comparison of the number of troops under arms at the beginning of the war was of course rather more favourable to the Central Powers. Against the 3,000,000 soldiers of Germany and Austria-Hungary, France, Russia, Belgium, Serbia and England could put, roughly, 5,500,000 into the field. I have, however, intentionally laid stress on the gigantic numerical superiority of the populations, to show what a reservoir of man-power the enemies possessed for the enlargement of their armies and the creation of new ones. The Central Powers had the advantage that, their troops being confined in a narrower space, they could be more quickly concentrated against a given point, and could strike before the Entente was in a position to make use of their numerical superiority.

The plan of campaign of the Central Powers had, therefore, to aim at securing a decisive success by a concentration of forces; any loss of time in the process was damaging and must be avoided. The plan of our great Chief of the General Staff, Count von Schlieffen, made proper provision for this fact. His proposal was to divert the bulk of the German Army against France, and drive through Belgium with a powerful, deeply echeloned, right wing. We should have to allow for the fact that this would add Belgium to the number of our enemies, but the

French eastern frontier was so strongly protected by fortresses that the process of forcing it would, in all probability, have taken too long.

The left wing of the German Army was to be based on Metz, and in the course of the German advance this fortress was to form for us the pivot of the turning movement. On the extreme left wing only weak forces were to be posted to protect Alsace against a French attack, and in case of necessity Southern Alsace was to be evacuated. The thrust of the powerful German right wing must cause any French troops pushed forward into Baden or Alsace to be hastily recalled to France. The considerations put forward by Count Schlieffen in support of his scheme are elaborated in the Imperial Archives (vol. i., p. 55), and their effect is entirely convincing. Why his successor, Colonel General von Moltke, departed, at first slightly, and then to an increasing extent, from the Schlieffen plan is incomprehensible. The Imperial Archives offer no explanation, and such of Count Schlieffen's colleagues as are still alive throw no real light on the point. It is, of course, true that Schlieffen's 1905 Memorandum deals only with war against France and England. Russia was at that time weakened by the Japanese War and the Revolution, and was not worth consideration as a serious army. But when Russia regained her military strength after the war, and when, by the help of French loans, she constructed her strategic railways and improved the armament and equipment of her forces, the General Staff was, naturally enough, faced with the question: " Is the Schlieffen plan still correct, as we now have to deal not only with France and England, but with the Russian millions?" Some supported the proposal that we should remain on the defensive in the West and send the bulk of the German Army against Russia, and thus free and secure our rear. I have never been able to understand this notion. Of course, if we moved strong forces to the East, it would have been quite a simple matter to attack in a southerly direction from East Prussia, join hands with an Austrian offensive moving up from the south, and separate Poland from Russia. But, in the issue of the war, this would have helped us little, or not at all, for when the time came for attack, at the conclusion of our advance, we should only have come into contact with the garrison troops of the Western Governments of Russia. The bulk of the Russian Army could not possibly have been in position by that time. We should have been beating the air— in the first few weeks of the war the massing of the German Army in the East could have served no useful purpose. On the other hand, when the Russian deployment was over, we should have had to reckon with the advance of the Russian steam-roller. These considerations point inevitably to the Schlieffen plan. Only by carrying out that plan, as exactly and quickly as possible, had the German Army any chance of winning a victory. If we had stripped our left wing and supported our right wing with every man we could spare, broken through the enemy Front by the capture of Liège, lengthened our right wing in the course of our advance until it reached the sea, interrupted—or, at any rate, delayed—the junction between the English and the French armies, and then continued the advance of our right wing to the west of Paris, we might have looked for a speedy and decisive victory against the French Army, if we could have forced the French to a decisive battle.

END OF FIRST VOLUME

MAP OF THE
EASTERN FRONTIER
Statute Miles

0   50   100

Railways   Canals

INDEX TO VOLUME I

267

Metternich, Count Paul von Wolff, M., Ambassador in Constantinople, 52

Michaelis, Dr, Imperial Chancellor, 199

Michalkiewicz, Polish Commissioner in Vilna, 222

Mirbach, Count, German Ambassador to Russia, murdered in Moscow, 1918, 224

Mirko, Crown Prince of Montenegro, 105

Moltke, Count Helmuth von, M., Colonel-General C.G.S., 7, 264

Morgen von, G.O.C. I. Reserve Corps, 51, 94

Mühlmann, von, General, 40

Müller, von, Admiral, Chief of Naval Cabinet, 83

Mumm von Schwartzenstein, Freiherr, of the Diplomatic Service, 52, 209

NAPOLEON I., Emperor of the French, 53

Nicolai Nicolaievich, Grand Duke, C.-in-C. Russian Army, 49, 58, 80, 91, 175

Nicolai, Lt.-Colonel, head of Section on the Great General Staff, 173, 177, 198, 245

Nicolaus (Nikita), King of Montenegro, 1894-1917, 97, 100, 105

Nicholas II., Emperor of Russia, 1894-1917, 58, 70, 80, 84, 145, 173, 259

OSKAR, Prince of Prussia, 108

PÉTAIN, Marshal of France, 180

Peter I. of Serbia, etc., 96, 97

Petlura, Republican leader in the Ukraine, 252

Pflanzer-Baltin, Austrian General, 138

Plessen, von, Colonel-General, Adj.-General to the Kaiser and Commandant of Imperial Headquarters, 121, 155

Poincaré, 58

Pollio, Chief of Italian General Staff before the war, 260

Prittwitz und Gaffron, von, G.O.C. 8th Army at commencement of war, 7, 16, 17, 37, 39, 40

RADEK (Sobelsohn), member of the Third International, and of the Peace Delegation of Brest-Litovsk, 252

Radowitz, von, Under-Secretary of State in the Imperial Chancery, 233

Reischach, Hugo, Freiherr von, Marshal of the Court, 88

Rennenkampf, G.O.C. Russian Army of the Niemen, 18, 42

Richthofen, member of Reichstag, 172, 174, 177, 233

Richthofen, Freiherr von, Rittmeister, airman, 214

Riemann, G.O.C. VI. A.C., 174

Rohrbach, Dr, author, 217

Rosenberg, Representative of the German Foreign Office at Brest-Litovsk, 204

SAMSONOFF, G.O.C. Russian Army of the Niemen, 18, 19

Scheidemann, Philipp, Secretary of State; People's Commissioner; Chancellor of the Empire, 224, 248

Schlieffen, Count, Field-Marshal, Chief of Great General Staff, 12, 263, 264, 265

Scholtz, von, G.O.C. XX. A.C., 68

Schubert, von, G.O.C. 8th Army, 42

Schubert, Major, Military Attaché in Moscow, 229

Seekt, von, Colonel, Chief of Staff to the 11th Army; later Commander of the Archduke Karl's Army Group, 108, 138, 140, 147, 148, 151, 156, 167, 193

Seydewitz, Saxon Minister, 222

Skoropadski, Hetman of the Ukraine, 215, 218

Solf, Secretary for the Colonies; Secretary of State for Foreign Affairs, 1918, 52, 130, 132, 231, 242

Stein, von, General, War Minister, 180

Stresemann, Dr Gustav, 223, 240

Stumm, W., von, Under-Secretary in the Foreign Office, 185

Suchomlinoff, General, Russian Minister, 91